# SOCIAL ORGANIZATION

*Books by*

R O B E R T  H .  L O W I E

AN INTRODUCTION TO CULTURAL ANTHROPOLOGY
THE  GERMAN  PEOPLE
THE  HISTORY  OF  ETHNOLOGICAL  THEORY
SOCIAL ORGANIZATION

# SOCIAL ORGANIZATION

---

ROBERT H. LOWIE

PROFESSOR OF ANTHROPOLOGY
UNIVERSITY OF CALIFORNIA

---

RINEHART & COMPANY
PUBLISHERS    *Incorporated*    NEW YORK

# PREFACE

DURING the last twenty years the several social sciences have been drawing together. Anthropologists, according to their individual interests, have tried to assimilate what history, economics, sociology, and psychology have to offer. In accordance with this trend the present book is, in principle, not a treatise on *primitive* society, but on the social organization of all peoples and of all times. An ethnographer naturally uses many illustrations from aboriginal tribes, but their purpose here is merely to indicate the great range of possible social arrangements and to help disengage what is indispensable from what is not. Authentic historical material bearing on the development of social forms I have freely used, whether it relates to English coffeehouse clubs, the European class system, the rise of Plains Indian military societies, or the changes of Chinese kinship terminology.

Second, I have pointed out the potency of economic forces, not in the abstract, which is hardly necessary nowadays, but by suggesting that certain specific changes in the economic life have led to specific modifications in the social life, even affecting sentimental attitudes.

Third, there is some emphasis on the problems, equally important for theory and daily life, of ethnic interrelations.

Fourth, cognizance is taken of the psychological aspects of social custom, which are at present being eagerly explored by a number of active young anthropologists. They have directed attention to important phenomena and their joint labors may be expected to produce significant results. At the present time a responsible textbook writer is, however, bound to practice reserve. Where so much is still hotly disputed it is difficult to say what can be regarded as a permanent contribution to knowledge. It seems more important to indicate lines of interest than to expound dogmas that may turn out to be merely crotchets of particular schools of thought.

Finally, in the same spirit I have mentioned recent applications of statistics to the study of correlation. My personal sympathy with such efforts notwithstanding, I felt obliged not to promulgate the specific findings of this school until they have been widely checked by other investigators. At the same time the student certainly ought to be familiarized with the general nature of this approach.

To my wife, Luella Cole, and to my sister, Risa Lowie, I am indebted for many suggestions and criticisms; my sister has also greatly aided in the preparation of the bibliography and the chapter references.

ROBERT H. LOWIE

*Berkeley, California*
*April, 1948*

# TABLE OF CONTENTS

vii

## III.  *SOCIAL UNITS*

## IV.  *SOCIAL ORGANIZATION IN ACTION*

## *APPENDIXES*

# I.  INTRODUCTION

# Chapter 1

# PRINCIPLES OF GROUPING

THE study of social organization deals primarily with the significant grouping of individuals. However, it must take cognizance of transient and inchoate assemblages of persons, because these often tend to merge into lasting and full-blown ones. To illustrate, the passengers on a bus form an artificial concourse of human beings, yet they offer raw material for a meaningful grouping. Thus, in our Deep South they *would* be sorted out by color, whites and Negroes being spatially segregated and emotionally divided. Similarly, Zulu children of the same age flock together in a loose company, but this becomes fixed when their elders gather together the eight- or nine-year-old youngsters of a district to pierce their ears, thus marking off as a definite set all who have jointly undergone the rite.

Though concentrating on the clearly bounded parts of social structure, we cannot, then, ignore the more shadowy, yet no less real, phenomena that precede and accompany them. G. D. H. Cole has distinguished between the two types of assemblage. "Association" is his label for any comparatively durable group pursuing a common purpose and following rules for common action; and the sum total of the social life thus organized he calls "society." On the other hand, he puts the uncrystallized social life under the heading of "community." The community is a subjective but self-sufficient group united by a consciousness of kind; it is "essentially a center of feeling." Sociologists generally agree in recognizing this distinction.

Our theme, then, will be society in Cole's sense, though community will inevitably enter the discussion.

The concept of "institutions," variously applied by different authors, also requires elucidation. Cole declares that the word is "difficult to define at all, and impossible to define in any but a largely negative manner"; yet it seems indispensable in the discussion of society. MacIver's treatment is most useful for our purposes. Whereas associations are bodies of human beings, "the established forms or conditions of procedure" linked with group action constitute an institution. It is more massive and basic than a mere custom. Cole speaks of it as "part of the underlying assumptions of communal life." Obviously, a person cannot *belong* to an institution, as he does to an association, but his conduct will be determined by it. The family, the church, and the state are associations; marriage, com-

3

munion, and law are institutions. The most important institutions socio-logically are probably kinship, marriage, law, property, religion, and education.

Various attempts have been made to classify all types of social units into a few comprehensive categories. Some of these systems are sugges-tive, but not one that I am familiar with is thoroughly satisfactory. This is due to the refractoriness of the data: social units are fluid and their underlying conditions are complex. Schurtz, for example, offers a two-fold scheme. Units, he explains, rest either on blood-kinship, with mem-bership independent of individual choice, or on voluntary attachment. The former are natural, the latter artificial (though this term is admit-tedly infelicitous); the former derive from sex relations, the latter from an urge toward sociability, which he virtually restricts to males. But hardly has Schurtz stated the dichotomy than he prudently shows that it cannot be rigorously applied: the family occupies an intermediate position, and, indeed, in most types of unit the lines of demarcation are constantly blurred.[1]

Accordingly, it is more profitable merely to consider the most impor-tant principles of alignment and to see to what extent, severally or jointly, they produce familiar types of unit. We shall discuss sex, age, kinship, coresidence, and voluntary association.

## Sex

Since every individual is inescapably male or female, it may seem that this simple fact automatically bisects society. However, this does not necessarily follow. For social purposes every people defines and trans-mutes the biological groupings of nature. The fact that women are the child-bearing and nursing half of humanity must, of course, have an effect on their place in society, but it is far from fully determining it. Sex is, indeed, in many societies a divisive factor of first-rate importance, but by itself it rarely, if ever, splits a society into two antithetical halves. In theory, to be sure, such opposition is common enough. Women are identified with the evil principle of the universe; they are excluded from public and ceremonial life; they do not eat with their husbands; the birth of a female infant makes the father a butt of mockery. But in practice the rigor of the rules is relaxed, if for no other reason because of two other factors not less natural than sex itself—individual variability and age differences.

[1] References are grouped by chapters and appear in Appendix II.

Individual variability is conspicuous when it brings women into categories from which their society normally excludes them,—if they are able to compete with men as poets, prophets, warriors, or in some other way to achieve masculine status. In Albania the female sex is unqualifiedly inferior and girls are married off with no attention to their feelings. Nevertheless a young woman can escape a repulsive match if she takes an oath of virginity, and she is thereafter entitled to wear masculine dress. Melanesians as a rule strictly separate the spheres of the sexes, but a rare woman can overcome the barriers, enter the men's clubhouse that is otherwise taboo to females, and even rank highest among native doctors. Conversely, those men to whom a warrior's career was congenitally repulsive were permitted by the Comanche and other warlike Plains tribes to put on feminine clothes and to become accomplished at women's tasks.

Extreme deviations of this sort would not, of course, be frequent enough to alter the usual social groupings to any marked extent. Contrariwise, differences in age affect the social meaning of sex itself. A Montenegrin father, who looks askance at a newborn daughter, grows hilarious over a boy as a potential hero, but actually there is nothing heroic about the puling infant. Accordingly, most societies that stress sex cleavage nevertheless treat young children as socially neutral, from which status the favored sex is raised only by a conventional rite. A Murngin lad (northern Australia) is circumcised when about six or eight years old, whereupon he joins the bachelors' camp; until then he ranks as a female. In the Banks Islands (Melanesia) adult men sleep and eat in the village club, which is entered by an expensive initiation and remains taboo to women. There are various grades, each owning a compartment of its own, and formerly any one who intruded into that of a higher rank "would have been trampled to death." Here wealth as well as age is significant, for a boy with rich kindred may enter very early, whereas a poor youth has to feed with the women until some friend rescues him from this ignominious situation.

But if young males are not rated as males at all, old women in a large number of instances lose the stigma of femininity. After her menopause a Comanche woman could wield supernatural power on a par with men, hence might take precedence of individual medicinemen. In a Wisconsin tribe younger women were barred from feasts because of their periodic impurity, "but the old women, who have passed their climacteric, sit right next to the men, because they are considered the same as men as they have no menstrual flow any more." Even the Australians tend to relent somewhat toward a very aged woman.

It is true that the division of labor can lead to a cleavage between brother and sister, husband and wife, among normal adults. Women go berrying, men unite for the chase; women cultivate their plots while the men go off on a raid. However, occupational differences of this sort need not lead to even an informal grouping; a native potter can ply her craft without companions. Further, if an association does evolve, it is not by any means necessarily an all-inclusive one, arraying one sex against the other. Among the Dakota Indians expert quill embroiderers and expert tentmakers had their respective guilds; only women could qualify, but the membership excluded the majority of the sex.

Sex, then, is an effective social assorter, but as the following paragraphs will show, it fully determines definite associations only, or mostly, when coupled with age or some other factor.[2]

## Age

All peoples distinguished the main stages in individual development, as is proved by their vocabularies. The Maricopa Indians (Arizona) have special words for infant, for a boy or girl above four, for an adult male, an adult female, an old man, and an old woman. On closer scrutiny, however, such terms often prove to be more than designations of age, whether physiological or chronological. They often indicate primarily a certain domestic status, what the French call *l'état civil*. Thus, a Maricopa is "old" if he has a grandchild, and the epithet may accordingly be applied to a man in his forties. The Western Apache go on calling single persons "youths" or "maidens"; only marriage makes "men" or "women" of them. In the rural Irish vernacular any man remains a "boy" until his father settles the family estate on him; as late as 1933 a deputy in the parliament of Eire pleaded on behalf of the poor "boys of forty-five and older." In other words, like sex—only more so—age is not merely a biological datum, but is conventionally defined in various cultures. The relevant groupings are, indeed, sometimes true classifications by seniority, as when the older countrymen of County Clare, Ireland, sit around the hearth, while the younger people seat themselves behind their elders and the children remain standing. But usually the classes that form are only indirectly connected with age while immediately expressing a stage in the social career.

Some aborigines develop a rather refined classification along these lines. On the Pau d'Arco, a tributary of the Araguaya (Brazil), a horde of the Northern Kayapo distinguishes eight masculine and six feminine classes. The young boys pass through two intermediate steps to the status of "youths," the fifth grade being that of men whose wives are pregnant for the first time, the sixth including husbands whose wives are nursing their first babies. Next come the heads of families, and finally the elders. Females comprise children, preadolescents, women between puberty and their first delivery, women before their second delivery, mothers of several children, and women beyond the menopause.

It is necessary to distinguish between a grade and a class (or set), concepts which may or may not coincide. The Canella, another Brazilian people, recognize essentially the three masculine grades of minors, vigorous adults, and councilors, but an indefinite number of age classes.

The Masai of East Africa likewise have three grades—uncircumcised boys, circumcised bachelors, and married men. But again the number of classes is indefinite. Here the minors are not organized at all. All the boys circumcised during the same four-year period form one set, whose solidarity continues for life. An initiate who subsequently travels to a strange camp at once seeks out a former fellow novice, who departs, leaving his home and wife for the guest. As soon as the bachelors settle down in wedlock, they attain the third grade, but this has no organization as such, solidarity obtaining only among fellow initiates or at most between two adjoining classes.

The Masai instance shows instructively that an elaborate classification correlated with age can spring up in the most natural way among people none of whom know just how old they are. The children who associate spontaneously and loosely are roughly coevals. All that is needed is to fix them into a definite body by a group name and some recognized procedure, such as the Zulu ear piercing or the Masai circumcision. The comradeship then tends to become permanent, so that subsequent experiences are also shared collectively.

To sum up, age may be accepted as a true creator of social units if it is understood (a) that "age" may be only indirectly involved; and (b) that generally the age grouping occurs among members of the same sex.[3]

## Kinship

Like age and sex, kinship in a sociological sense rests on its biological counterpart, but is not identical with it. Indeed, the natural blood relations are not only expanded and circumscribed by convention, but transmogrified. Thus, in various parts of Africa the legal father of a child is emphatically not its begetter, but the man who properly wedded the mother by providing the requisite property. A woman who has run off with her paramour may bear a boy three years later, yet the child will be regarded as the legal husband's son and heir. More familiar to us is the practice of adoption, by which unrelated persons are legally transformed into relatives.

Generally speaking, Western civilization recognizes kinship bilaterally, that is, on both sides of the family. In most countries, however, the surname is passed on unilaterally and patrilineally, children assuming only the father's family name. The same also holds for titles and certain forms of wealth, which pass from father to son and son's son.

In one sense all peoples the world over recognize kinship bilaterally, i.e., they all have terms of relationship for both the father's and the mother's kindred. Yet even in nomenclature one side may be heavily weighted as compared with the other. The North Albanians furnish an extreme case. They have words for mother, maternal uncle, and maternal aunt, but a cousin on the mother's side hardly rates as a relative at all and remains undesignated, while a patrilineal cousin is called *kushrin(a)*.

Though such exclusiveness in terminology is rare, simpler peoples commonly ignore one side of the family completely for particular—though not for all—purposes. The Australian horde illustrates the point. It is a landowning group whose permanent core is formed by an ancestor with his patrilineal male descendants, the wives being brought in from outside hordes, the daughters passing into others at marriage. So far as the economic exploitation of the territory is concerned, the descendants of these daughters have no rights, which they can acquire only from their fathers (the husbands of the women in question). Steward has pointed out that comparable arrangements exist in southern California, in Tierra del Fuego, and elsewhere.

Among the Hopi (Arizona) the reverse situation holds. Here women invariably own the houses, their husbands coming to live with them, a custom called "matrilocal residence" in contrast to the "patrilocal residence" of the Australians. As the Australian territory belongs to a permanent core of patrilineal males, so a Hopi house is the property of a matrilineal group of females,—an ancestress with her surviving sisters, if any, the daughters of these old women, and their daughters' daughters; the married men all come from strange houses and have no right to residence except as husbands of the permanent inmates. Here, however, an important point must be noted. A Hopi husband never severs his close connection with his natal home, which he constantly visits. Further, he retains as an unmistakable label of matrilineal kinship the group name, such as Corn or Rabbit, which all children inherit from their mother. All the unilateral descendants of a known common ancestor or ancestress are collectively called a "lineage." To adopt Lawrence's and Forde's terminology, the Hopi have matrilineages; the Zulu, patrilineages. Frequently a larger group of persons than can be actually traced back unilaterally to a particular ancestor nevertheless has a solidarity similar to that of lineage mates and usually assumes a hypothetical common ancestor. Such a composite of two or more lineages may be called a "kin." Most kins impose the rule of "exogamy" (Greek *exo,* outside; *gamos,* marriage); that is, fellow members are prohibited from intermarrying. An exogamous kin is called a "clan." Conceptually, kin and lineage are the same and may pass into each other; and some kins develop out of clans by dropping exogamy. Thus, the contemporary Zulu have patrilineal kins which were formerly clans and which have split up into lineages, the clan ancestor being "very often not known."

Rather rarely kins either definitely prescribe, or at least prefer, marriage among the members, a practice known as "endogamy" (Greek *endon,* inside). The Arabs and at least some Kurds favor union between the children of two brothers, who are necessarily of the same kin since descent in these cases is patrilineal. In still other cases the kins show no concern about whether their members intermarry or not; such indifference may be described as "agamy" (Greek *a-,* privative), a term already in use by biologists to denote absence of marriage and here made to designate absence of marriage regulations on the part of a social unit. Under modern influences native peoples have often abandoned earlier matrimonial restrictions so that their clans have turned into agamous kins.

The three terms—exogamous, endogamous, agamous—may, of course, be applied to other than unilateral descent groups. If a local group forbids marriage among its members irrespective of kinship, we speak of local exogamy; and our bilateral family is obviously exogamous since marriage between either parent and child, or between siblings (brothers and sisters) is taboo.

The family may or may not be wholly the result of kinship. In the ideal Arab family, husband and wife are first cousins, and since parents and children as well as any two siblings (i.e., brothers and sisters irrespective of sex) are manifestly related, all the possible interpersonal ties involve kinship. Among most Australian tribes a person must marry some sort of cousin, actual or putative, so that again kinship underlies the family ties. This no longer holds, however, to the same extent when the intermarriage of blood relatives is merely permissive or is positively forbidden. In other words, as Forde points out for a West African Negro people, the family is, indeed, the source of kinship, but is itself only partly a kinship group unless marriages between kindred are prescribed.

Kinship itself cannot create rank, but where rank exists kinship may extend and perpetuate it. In Tibet the ruler's office is not hereditary, but the family of the Dalai Lama-elect is automatically ennobled. The degree to which this principle is carried varies in different regions. In England and among the Polynesians of Tonga, for instance, primogeniture is in force, so that all but the eldest born children are degraded as compared with their fathers. Kinship enters into the creation of a caste system: if there is not merely a difference in status but also the rule of endogamy for equals, persons of the same degree are set off as a distinct caste. In other words, a caste is an hereditary endogamous class in a series of graded groups.

Even ostensibly voluntary associations are affected by kinship. As the son of a Harvard man is likely to go to Harvard and the daughter of a Vassar alumna to Vassar, so a similar tendency in other types of grouping becomes manifest. Freedom of worship is one of our shibboleths, but the infant who is baptized into the faith of his parents has no choice. In some countries and periods there simply are no alternatives. In medieval Europe, apart from Mohammedan centers and Jewish enclaves, people were either of the Roman Catholic or of the Greek Catholic Church, geographical residence deciding which it would be.

Like considerations apply to preliterate societies. Among the Crow Indians (Montana) any man could join a military organization, such as the Foxes, but if a member fell in battle the members tried to get a close kinsman to take his place. Similarly, in Yorubaland (West Africa) a cult group is not, indeed, a body of kindred, yet admission in part rests on kinship.[4]

## Coresidence

Coresidence, or local contiguity, underlies the modern state and all its subdivisions. In other words, political and legal arrangements are on a territorial basis. Our executive officials administer the United States, the individual states, counties, municipalities; and there are federal, state, district, and city courts. This type of arrangement is by no means a foregone conclusion. As Maine pointed out in 1861, kinship units in earlier and preliterate societies absorb political and legal functions. That is, a man fights for his kindred, not for his neighbors, and is responsible to the head of his kinship group. In case he is murdered, there is no neutral state (i.e., territorial) authority to see justice done, but his relatives avenge the death by killing the offender or a member of *his* kinship group.

Maine was wholly right in distinguishing the two principles of solidarity—kinship and coresidence. He was also right in stressing the predominance of the former in simpler cultures, though he overemphasized the point. Even the Ghegs of northern Albania persist in investing their clans with political functions to the detriment of the development of a modern state. They viewed King Zog as merely the head of his own clan, and if one of his judges punished the member of another clan the offender's relatives regarded the verdict as an affront to be wiped out in blood.

Nevertheless the absence of the local tie is not absolute. The Ifugao of Luzon, who stress kinship to an extreme degree, still do not treat unrelated neighbors as they would complete foreigners. Correspondingly, the Crow Indians rejoiced over the killing of an alien Cheyenne; but if a Crow of the Sore-lip clan killed a member of the Thick Lodge, the tribesmen not directly affected showed general concern and took steps to avert a feud. In other words, the local bond may be weak, but it is not therefore wholly wanting.

Further, Maine overlooked the fact that a kinship group may be at the same time a territorial one. In Australia the patrilineally related males also reside permanently within a definite tract of land. They are kinsmen *and* neighbors. Who can say categorically how far a man's behavior toward other men is due purely to kinship sentiment and how far to horde neighborliness as well?

Thus territorial contiguity may mingle with kinship in establishing solidarity. On the other hand, notions of kinship may invade arrangements purporting to be on a local basis. Since a race is nothing but a large descent group, discrimination against a racial body illustrates the kinship factor in social alignment. American citizens of Japanese ancestry who are forcibly evacuated are no longer treated as fellow citizens of the same territorial unit, but as a distinct kinship group; and Negro disabilities illustrate the same point. Ethnic minorities that are not so easily picked out by virtue of their physical appearance still fall under this head. For though the actual grounds for prejudicial treatment of them may be economic rivalry or cultural differences, the majority often alleges racial, i.e. kinship, idiosyncrasies to justify discrimination.[5]

## Voluntary Association

The first ethnologist to single out voluntary associations as a distinct and widespread cultural phenomenon was Schurtz. It was obvious, of course, that civilized countries have had innumerable religious fraternities, social clubs, guilds, and so forth; but prior to Schurtz no general treatise on earlier conditions had realized the frequency and importance of primitive parallels.

The voluntary factor, too, may be heavily interlarded with motives of another order. This does not seem to have been adequately recognized by Schurtz, who constantly stresses the common interests, sympathies, and tastes that unite males—in contrast to the allegedly unsociable female half of the species. Yet the Crow and Yoruba instances cited above show that kinship may partly determine membership in clubs and fraternities, and much equally striking evidence can be cited. The priests of the major Hopi fraternities succeed an elder brother or maternal uncle. Among the Canella a boy gets his personal name from a maternal uncle, which automatically fixes his membership in this or that association. In other cases the grounds for uniting with a particular organization are to be sought not in the inclinations of the persons concerned, but in the wishes of their elders. Until very recently a married couple was hardly anywhere a voluntary association, but one brought about by the parents' wishes. Again, in Australia a boy entered a company of other boys for initiation not because they were especially congenial, but because the elders of the horde so decreed. Similarly, a Sherente (Brazil) father determined which of four men's clubs his son should join, and though the lad's preferences counted for something, they were not decisive.

That associations of like-minded individuals are frequently of the same sex and age, as Schurtz contends, can be abundantly demonstrated. The minimum voluntary association—a pair of congenial spirits—corresponds to this pattern. To take a Biblical example, ". . . the soul of Jonathan was knit with the soul of David, and Jonathan loved him as his own soul . . . Then Jonathan and David made a covenant, because he loved him as his own soul. And Jonathan stripped himself of the robe that was upon him, and gave it to David, and his garments, even to his sword, and to his bow, and to his girdle." Damon and Pythias furnish a Greek parallel.

Larger groups readily evolve, both formally and informally, for a temporary or a lasting purpose; and as some earlier examples show, one type may develop into the other. Playmates thus turn into a loose or organized age set, comrades on a raid grow into a permanent military company.

The extent to which associations are wholly of one sex varies with the traditional conceptions of the peoples concerned. A Greek coffee house is an informal men's club that, even when transplanted to American soil, is altogether taboo to women. Australian male adults become through initiation a "men's tribal society," though it usually harbors distinct degrees that set off status groups within the sex. Other peoples display less exclusiveness. The Canella have men's organizations, but with girl associates playing a prominent part; and in the Tobacco society of the Crow Indians both sexes are admitted on equal terms. The contrast between the folkways of Southeastern Europe and of the United States in this respect appears in a comparison of the associations of first-generation immigrants and those of the native population. In an Indiana town with a population of 35,000, of whom 92 per cent were native white, the Lynds discovered 450 clubs, of which a considerable number were women's social and literary associations. In a town in Massachusetts with a population of 17,000 the investigators noted 357 societies; 40 per cent had an exclusively male, 31 per cent an exclusively female membership, and in the remainder both sexes were represented. But in the same town there was no Greek organization for women, and the Polish Girls' Club is the recent creation of an enterprising second-generation Pole who had been a crack athlete in high school.

Although elective affinity is a genuine and frequent motive for association, which is then properly styled "voluntary," we have seen that the adjective is often inaccurate. It seems at first blush to apply well enough to our modern clubs or fraternities, but even there various degrees of compulsion occur, even when there is no question of physical force. Main Street ostracizes a newcomer who has no church affiliation, and in the Indiana town investigated by the Lynds a businessman of standing "can hardly afford to stay out of the Masons at least." Better-class Negroes in the United States consider it "a sign of community spirit and social respectability to enroll in the National Association for the Advancement of Colored People." In several American Plains tribes a young man might or might not enter a particular military society, but that he should belong to none was hardly conceivable. In West Africa, by descending upon him in a body and playing havoc with his household possessions, a secret fraternity sometimes vividly brings home to an outsider the advantages of joining its ranks.

Yet associations wholly voluntary are often otherwise psychologically and genetically related to those which are not. For descriptive purposes we need a term that shall include both—associations not *primarily* connected with kinship or coresidence. It would include pairs of congenial comrades and groups of hobbledehoys, stock companies and trade unions, scientific societies and the Y.M.C.A., congregations of churches and bridge clubs. It is undesirable to coin new words; on the other hand, familiar ones—say, "corporation" or "society" —have other connotations and would in some contexts be ambiguous. The comparatively less common word "sodality" meets the requirements. In Latin *sodalis* designates a comrade, companion, bosom friend, associate, messmate, accomplice, the member of an organization (including priestly colleges). *Sodalitas,* the corresponding noun, is accordingly applied to the union of cronies as well as to a band of fellow conspirators. When in need of a generic term that avoids the irrelevant connotations of, say, "society," we shall then, use the word "sodality."[6]

It should now be clear why the principal types of social unit are not amenable to a simple classification. The principles underlying either formal or informal grouping rarely appear in isolation; hence a particular type rarely corresponds to a particular principle. Further, some of the most important units such as the family radically differ, as we have seen, in different societies. However, it is clear which are the outstanding social units.

## Consciousness of Kind

In the beginning of this chapter it was pointed out that over and above the clearly marked factors which make for unity there are "the more shadowy, yet no less real, phenomena" which Cole calls "community." This contrast had been earlier stressed in the German sociologist Tönnies's antithesis of "society" (*Gesellschaft*) and "community" (*Gemeinschaft*); and his American contemporary Giddings emphasized the "consciousness of kind" that binds men together.

Difficult as it is to define a subtle matter of feeling, it is easy enough to understand what is involved. "Community" in the fullest sense is connected with a narrow circle of kindred and neighbors; by way of contrast, nationalism, let alone cosmopolitanism, is invariably an artificial growth. History texts speak about the unification of Italian-speaking people in 1870. Sociologically and linguistically, this is sheer nonsense. There neither was then nor is there now a common speech in the peninsula except in so far as an artificial standard language is taught in school. Except when obliged to talk with outsiders, the peasant of Sicily or Calabria would never dream of using this Italian, which he learns in school as an American student may choose to do at college. There are not only various dialects in the country, but at least several mutually unintelligible languages. To be sure, they are all Romance and closely related, but that does not make the speakers able to exchange ideas or render them like-minded. Dutch and English are closely related Germanic tongues, but we cannot understand a Nether-lander, and his mental set is not the Anglo-Saxon one. It is a significant fact that even minor differences in pronunciation create sociological cleavage. This has been eminently true in Italy, where the term *cam-panilismo* (*campanile*, belfry) designates the parochial narrowness which excludes as an alien anyone beyond the range of one's own church bell. The phenomenon can be observed among immigrants in America. A "countryman" (*paesano*) does not mean a fellow Italian, but a fellow Neapolitan or Apulian. If two Italian women are seen walking together, they are almost certainly from the same district; in 1930 there was still some reluctance to marrying a person from another province; a Palerman in need of company walks five blocks to visit another from the same province rather than walk across the hall to a Sienese; an Italian foreman chooses laborers from his own district because it forestalls quarreling. In Greenwich Village, New York City, an Italian doctor served twenty-five lodges in a professional capacity, but since he was a Southerner not a single one with North Italian membership employed him.

*Campanilismo* is not specifically Italian; it is a generically human phenomenon. The Scandinavians are racially closer to one another than are a Piedmontese and a Sicilian, and their several languages are very closely akin. Nevertheless, their history shows little spiritual unification. The Norwegians insisted on becoming independent of Sweden in 1905; and they so deeply resented having ever had Danish rulers that in 1925 the capital, Christiania, was rebaptized Oslo in order to wipe out memories of rulers named Christian. In the United States it proved hopeless to unite Swedish and Norwegian Lutherans in church activities. As for Swedes and Danes, an authority declares: "It does not seem to lie in the plan of the universe for Danes and Swedes to work together."

But the Scandinavian immigrants were not merely narrowly nationalistic; they were victims of *campanilismo*. Norwegians did not merely seek out compatriots in the new country, but people from the very same parish. Sometimes whole boatloads of persons would sail together, all from one valley and planning to settle in the same locality across the ocean. When these folk wrote their friends about conditions in the New World, it was asserted that the stay-at-homes in Gudbrandsdal came to know more about Minnesota than they had ever known about the neighboring valleys in Norway. It was not that the variations in speech were so great as to prevent peasants of two localities from understanding one another, but the unfamiliar dialect "marked a person off as not, in an intimate sense, belonging to one's own people."

Germany presents still another parallel. Here there are at least three mutually unintelligible languages—Low German (nearer to Flemish than to the German taught in school), High German (on which the standard written and stage language is based), and Swiss,— each subdivided into numerous distinct dialects. In appreciable degree, though not wholly, these differences coincide with what historians call "particularism," which is merely a somewhat less narrow *campanilismo*. The inveterate opposition of Bavaria to Prussia is a notorious instance. The unification of discordant elements was indeed achieved in a political sense after the Franco-Prussian war, but only with the utmost difficulty and *without* overcoming the sociological conflicts of diverse linguistic and cultural groups. It is not generally known that under the German Empire Prussia maintained legations at the capitals of the other federated states as though they were foreign countries. Bavaria remained bitterly resentful of Prussian ascendancy. More than a decade after "unification," Prince Eulenburg, the Prussian minister at Munich, found that only men of science and art there had any sense of being Germans. On an excursion into the Bavarian Alps he would overhear people wailing over the stupidity of the Bavarians in having made a joint front against France in 1870 with the Prussians, who were their most dangerous enemy!

If Germans remained apart in spirit regardless of a partly common cultural and political tradition, and if Norwegians are suspicious of the farmers in the nearest valley, it is not surprising that differences of a major order have kept men apart.

*Campanilismo* would, of course, be fatal to any wider integration if there were not contradictory tendencies. When the rigid isolation typical of Norwegian valleys is lacking, when populations of different speech and folkways intermingle unhindered by legal barriers, there tends to be a linguistic and cultural osmosis. In the Caucasus Mountains, where a variety of languages exists within a circumscribed territory, many of the natives become polyglot; and even the Jews adopt their neighbors' practice of the blood feud. In Egypt the Christian Copts generally circumcise, abstain from pork, and remove their shoes before entering a church—all this in imitation of the Moslem majority. In this way the initial differences between two groups can be smoothed out. When assimilation is achieved in the fullest degree, the groups become indistinguishable; hence consciousness of kind embraces both.

Dr. Lindgren's analysis of her observations in northwestern Manchuria shows that under favorable conditions amicable relations are even possible when the coresident groups remain distinct. The Cossacks and the Tungus of the region practically never intermarry, but there is trading between them and neither community scruples to borrow the other's goods and customs. The natives obtain Russian pots and scissors, while the Russians adopt the reindeer-breeders' form of shelter and winter dress, sometimes even having recourse to a Tungus shaman (spirit-inspired wonderworker). The factors that make for friendliness are the following: The whites in this case are neither so preponderant numerically as wholly to swamp the natives nor do they overawe them by an immeasurably superior culture, the Cossacks being uneducated folk. What is perhaps most vital is that the two populations are not pitted against each other in their totality. Individuals meet as individuals, and there are no propagandists who exalt the superiority of their own people and vilify the strangers.

Like-mindedness, or even accommodation on the Tungus-Cossack pattern, is seriously hampered, however, if the groups brought into contact differ markedly in their outward appearance. This creates at once a sense of diversity. From this point of view the case reported by Dr. Lindgren has not universal applicability. Mongoloids differ less from Europeans than do Australians or Negroes; and Russians, whose country was for centuries dominated by Mongols and witnessed considerable interbreeding with the invaders, are not likely to be shocked by Mongoloid features. The case of the Negroids is evidently not identical. As Myrdal aptly remarks, the most assimilated colored man in the United States is still not accepted as a full-fledged American. Consciousness of kind does not automatically follow from cultural unity.

But how a society reacts to physical differences is itself a matter of social tradition. Exclusiveness is typical of an insecure group which regards even infinitesimal departures from its norms—whether in dress, gestures, speech, or what not—as danger signals. Racial difference is only one of a large series of potential tokens of this sort; *psychologically* it has no deeper significance than the others. It is unique only in not being changeable. *If* a conflict arises on other grounds, then the physical traits turn into convenient badges of the hostile group. White colonists who encroach on the territory of aborigines inevitably attach great importance to racial distinctions since survival may hinge on being aware of them; and sensitiveness on the subject may linger on among the invaders' descendants when the danger is long past. But there is no inborn hostility on the sole ground of racial differences. White Mexicans discriminate against Indians because they are poor, illiterate pagans, not because they are Indians; Brazilians correspondingly have no racial antipathy against Negroes; in the East Indies the Dutch segregate native Indonesian pupils on the sole criterion of language and socially accept half-breeds as equals. Germans are the foremost recent champions of racialism, but until a century or so ago they were largely ardent cosmopolitans. During our Civil War the ancestors of the Nazis generally sympathized with the slaves, and many of them flocked to Northern regiments on humanitarian principles. In the United States whites of the same Anglo-Saxon ancestry but in different sections of the country assume altogether different attitudes toward the Negro. The consciousness of kind thus proves a singularly malleable sentiment.[7]

# Chapter 2

# CONTEMPORARY WESTERN CIVILIZATION
## AND ECONOMIC DETERMINISM

### *Industrialism*

THE civilization of the United States or England today is as complex as any in the world, but living in it we know it immediately and intimately, whereas familiarity with the simplest alien culture must be painfully acquired. For that reason it is pedagogically sound to begin the study of social life at home. At the same time a phenomenon is understood only in relation to others: "He little knows of England who only England knows." Hence it is well to look at Western culture in perspective. Unless we do so, any alien institutions and attitudes linked with them are likely to be misinterpreted.

Contemporary Western civilization is unique in its economic system. As Lederer explains, its distinctive feature is industrialism—not a mere division of labor with mass production, which occurs elsewhere too, but production by modern machinery. This has ushered in changes in class structure and a radical alteration in the spiritual atmosphere even to the extent of affecting intimate interpersonal relations. As a result of this recent metamorphosis contemporary Westerners are in some of the most vital aspects of living less like their ancestors of, say, 1800 A.D. than these were like the modern Chinese or the majority of savage tribes. Lest the statement seem extreme, let us briefly survey modern China and some sections of Europe that retain traits which a century or two ago were universal.

Notwithstanding her vast population and many large cities, China remains agrarian. Even her ruling classes are rooted in the soil and tend to return to the countryside. The typical peasant himself has not become a businessman: he farms to support his household, not in order to reap profit. He knows little of modern technology and cares not at all for what we call "efficiency." Kinship and age play a part in social relations that is unparalleled in the Occident of today. The young, humble before elders, marry according to the wishes of their parents. The family is indifferent to outsiders, while "communistic cooperation" holds among kindred. A man who has a job to dispose of is not concerned with the candidates' fitness, but as a foregone conclusion gives it to a relative.

To turn to present-day rural Eire, the conditions of the small farmer there generically resemble those in China. These cultivators, too, consume most of what they produce; they, too, lack mechanical improvements, clinging to spades, flails, and scythes. Marriage serves the family interest, not the whims of romantic lovers. In labor of all sorts kinsfolk cooperate without expecting compensation. Even when making his purchases in town the Irish farmer is under the spell of kinship: he does not try to buy the best goods at the lowest possible price, but deals with a related shopkeeper. On the other hand, the tradesman freely extends credit to a patron-kinsman: he does not *want* him to pay off the whole debt, which would mean that the farmer is transferring his custom to another shop.

Every essential of this combination reappears in the picture drawn of the Polish peasant. Here again economy is for subsistence, not with an eye to world markets; marriage is arranged by the elders; and family solidarity is the supreme axiom of social life. What holds for the unindustrialized Europeans of today held for all Europeans until very recent times; and it holds for the illiterate peoples of the globe so far as their life remains more or less aboriginal. To repeat, in 1800 A.D. the average Western European was nearer, in the essential matters under discussion, to the savage of Australia than to his lineal descendants of today.

Conversely, the savage or the European peasant who has once come under the sway of industrialism turns into a new social being. It is not essential that he himself construct machines or turn into a factory worker. It is enough if his economy ceases to be for subsistence, if he begins to sell his goods or labor for money. The Croatian peasants had lived in large, self-sufficient households (p. 138), when sometime in the nineteenth century the ruling class decided on mimicking Western standards of living. This meant heavy taxation for the farmers, then forming 90 per cent of the population. The peasant was unable to meet his obligations to the state unless he abandoned economic autonomy and developed those specializations which fetched the best prices, the surplus being used to satisfy the government. Similarly, the Crow Indian ceased to hunt buffalo and is now raising alfalfa for the market. But in each case the shift brought a change of attitude: in Montana, in Celebes, in Tanganyika—wherever profit has become an important goal —the native system turned topsy-turvy.

How the capitalistic spirit saps the foundation of earlier conditions appears from the Thurnwalds' observations in the Solomons. Normally, in the tribe visited a woman goes to live with her husband's family, where her primary task is to raise crops and pigs. But one native had turned peddler for a white Australian trader and spent much of the year as a traveling salesman. In consequence, his wife went to live with her parents, where her husband likewise came on returning from his trips. Thus the normal mode of residence was reversed. But, still more significant, the wife no longer gardened and tended pigs, for with the money her husband earned it was easy to obtain the food required by the family. Thus, both spouses ceased to be employed in the traditional way. This departure from old custom had not yet become general in the district, but it illustrates the subtly undermining effect of the new economy. And it is not merely the division of labor or other objective aspects of economy that suffer a change, but also ethical principles. The Melanesian peddler no longer allows friends or relatives to appropriate his goods at will. The Crow who sells his alfalfa for the highest price he can get no longer ungrudgingly supports an idle or negligent fifth cousin.

Japanese history since the latter half of the nineteenth century is especially instructive. In order to keep the country abreast of the West as a military power, the ruling statesmen deliberately inaugurated a machine age. At the same time they insisted on preserving the ancient ideology of the country. Specifically, they deprecated individualism as "a selfish sin": as before, the nation and the family were to take precedence of individual happiness, women were to remain "dutiful, patient, and good-natured." But notwithstanding the systematic teaching of these principles with all the aids a powerful state commanded, the sifting of Western ideas by the ruling class was not nearly as successful as appeared on the surface. The elements of a culture are too closely interwoven to permit the selective borrowing which the Japanese statesmen desired. One cannot industrialize a country and at the same time shut out at will the aspects of industrialism which one dislikes. Accordingly, even here hitherto unheard-of tendencies came to the fore. The proletarians of the towns took kindly to democratic socialism; women began to talk of their rights, and there was even a nascent movement on behalf of birth control.[1]

It is profitable to recall some parallel developments in Western countries. There has been a similar reshuffling of classes. In Germany at the time of the Franco-Prussian War, about 75 per cent of the population was rural; within forty years the same proportion lived in the cities and social democracy grew by leaps and bounds. France did not undergo so extreme a change, but it was striking enough: in 1846 the percentage of farmers was 75.6; by 1886 it dropped to 64.1; by 1906, to 57.9. In Sweden until 1850 fully 80 per cent of the inhabitants lived on farms; in 1920 about 52 per cent were engaged in factories, trade, and transportation. England has notoriously gone further than any other nation, being unable to feed herself in recent periods, when less than 7 per cent of the citizens have been tilling the soil.

What is more, the cultivator himself has sometimes altered his mental set. A German in the Ruhr who no longer raises his own fodder, but buys it along with some livestock in order to sell it at a profit, is no longer a peasant in the old sense of the word but a businessman.

As to the effects outside of economics, our own country illustrates the influence of industrialism on marriage. In rural areas 660 out of every 1,000 females fifteen years of age were married twenty years ago; in urban areas the corresponding figure was only 564. Other implications of the machine age with regard to divorce and to interpersonal attitudes will be indicated later.[2]

Thus, an economic factor, machinery with its concomitants, has directly or indirectly affected the structure of society and various aspects of social life in Western Europe, the United States, Japan, and those primitive peoples who have been sufficiently exposed to contact with Western civilization. This naturally leads to the general problem of "economic determinism."

## Economic Determinism

What is meant by economics? An eminent economist defines it as the branch of knowledge which deals "with social phenomena centering around the provision for the material needs of the individual and of organized groups." In other words, it deals with the production, consumption, and distribution of "wealth"—a term of variable meaning corresponding to varying human needs. Though the term may be vague, for purposes of anthropology and culture history it is easy enough to give an intelligible meaning to the phrase "economic determinism." It implies that social phenomena directly connected with material needs mold other social phenomena which are not so connected; that specifically a change in the means of production ushers in changes in law, in social organization, even in intellectual activities and religion. In the preceding section the machine age was shown to have transformed social life, and the question now is how far other means of supplying material needs may have comparable correlates.

In a certain sense the basic character of economics is a truism. Unless a minimum of material supplies is available, every feature of social life must collapse. The Fuegians, being primitive hunters, could never hold their elaborate several weeks' festivals except through the lucky fluke of a beached whale, which provided food for a large camp while the ceremonies were going on. Wherever man lives so precariously, social standing is mainly determined by an individual's competence to gain a livelihood or to contribute to the needs of bare existence. The paragon of Ojibwa youths is an expert hunter; "this ability catches the attention of calculating parents who have daughters to marry off." On the other hand, a young man will consider whether his prospective mate is apt at dressing skins, fetching wood or water, and performing domestic chores. "Beauty is subordinate to all these qualifications."

Grim necessity may determine the size of human aggregations and their social organizations, even seasonally altering both among the same people, as Durkheim and Mauss have shown for the Australians and the Eskimo. Equivalent examples are known from the Plains of North America. The Cheyenne simply could not maintain a large camp in the dead of winter: in one historical case the attempt to defy nature very nearly caused general starvation, for the Indians could neither kill enough game for themselves nor procure fodder for their mounts. Parallel with this seasonal difference went a vital difference in regard to social control. During the summer the people were policed by club-like military societies, which were no longer either necessary or even possible when the tribe broke up into minor segments. The same seasonal change held for the Cree: by midwinter "the tribesmen scattered in small family units into the more densely wooded country," with similar social consequences. Here also "the societies did not function during the winter, except on those rare occasions when plentiful food and fuel made a large winter encampment possible." The rather more complex herders of the Old World likewise present seasonal phases. In the summer the Kazak break up into units of a few families so as to get adequate pasturage; in the winter even a moderate village comprises several hundred houses, and then blacksmiths and carpenters begin to ply their trades.

In the cases cited, nature circumscribes economic activities, which in turn permit or bar certain social arrangements.

The most systematic attempt to go beyond such truisms is due to the theorists of modern socialism, Karl Marx and Friedrich Engels.

Their contribution in giving proper weight to the material basis of society has been generally acknowledged. As Father Schmidt, the foremost Catholic ethnologist and certainly no Marxist, declares, "No reasonable man will deny to scientific socialism the merit of having most emphatically demanded the consideration of economic conditions." The principle enunciated by Marx and Engels is popularly labeled "historical materialism" or "the materialistic conception of history" —rather misleading phrases, for one can perfectly well try to explain institutions in terms of the production of wealth without being a materialist in a philosophical sense. Thus, Father Schmidt pronounces historical materialism "an excellent as well as indispensable heuristic principle."

In this connection some writers draw a sharp distinction between historical materialism and economic determinism. As Hook sets forth, the socialist theorists include under the former term not only the productive forces, such as agricultural methods, but the *social* relations developed in their use. From another starting point Thurnwald also sharply distinguishes between technology and economy. He correctly points out that identical techniques may go hand in hand with altogether different systems of distribution. In a democratic Melanesian community, he argues, the economic system is quite different from that of a typical Polynesian tribe, in which commoners yield the best part of their products to a superior class. However, if the subjection of the commoners is itself part of the economy, it is obviously not explained by the economy. On the other hand, economic determinism is at least conceivably in a position to offer an explanation. To revert to industrialism, no one could foresee that in the wake of the machine age would come instability in family relations, woman suffrage, and birth control. They were not logical corollaries, but empirical correlates or consequences. The point is to find such on various planes of social complexity. As the eminent French scholar Henri Sée has remarked, it is difficult "to unravel the tangle of causes and effects" in history; but "in the infinite sea of historical events economic determinism has helped to furnish us with a guiding thread which keeps us from being lost."

A profitable approach is to single out more or less datable innovations of the economic order and to observe the sequel. In so doing it is difficult to avoid a naïve use of terms suggesting a simple cause-and-effect relationship, a matter to be taken up later. The limits of an economic interpretation will likewise be discussed.

## Specific Innovations

When the mines of Potosi, Bolivia, were exploited soon after the discovery of America, the amount of silver in Europe was quintupled within a century. As the scarcity value of the metal dropped, prices soared proportionately. In France the landed gentry were hard put to it, borrowed heavily from wealthy burghers, finally even mortgaging and selling their estates. At that time ownership of an ancient fief *ipso facto* made a man a nobleman, so that many commoners were suddenly raised to a higher class. The entry of silver from Bolivia brought social mobility into France.

Another instance may be cited from British history. When textiles were being produced on a larger scale, it was more profitable to raise sheep for wool than to farm. Accordingly, about 1450 A.D. English landowners began to enclose vast areas by fences or hedges, thus dispossessing many peasants. The landless cottagers, hitherto employed on the lord's demesne, were also thrown out of work and obliged to leave. They turned vagabonds in large numbers, like the "Okies" of the United States; and the menace of these "sturdy beggars" altered the functions of government. An act passed in 1536 prohibited mendicancy and made the parishes support the needy; other laws followed in the same vein until in 1572 the goal was achieved by a direct assessment. Until then poor relief had been a matter for the Church and private agencies; henceforth it devolved on public authorities. Thus the rise of textile manufacturing made sheep raising more attractive to the landed proprietors, disorganized the agricultural class, and made the state take over altogether new functions.[3]

Let us now turn to primitive tribes.

The members of the Shoshonean linguistic family—Shoshone, Ute, Paiute, Paviotso—had their center in Nevada and adjoining Basin territory. They were among the simplest of American Indians; collecting wild roots, seeds, and berries, they hunted mainly rabbits and other small game, larger herd beasts being scarce because the arid country restricted grasslands. In exceptionally favorable districts there might be one native to every 2 square miles, but the average density was only one person to 15.6 square miles, and near the Great Salt Desert it dropped to one person to 30 or 40 square miles. The Western Shoshone, at best hard put to it to make a living, could do so only in minute family groups within which no true chiefs were required. Only a lucky accumulation of surplus food enabled these people to gather in larger numbers for a week's festivities. But as soon as the related Shoshoneans of Idaho had acquired horses, there came momentous changes. Greater mobility enabled the Bannock to invade Montana or Wyoming in search of buffalo; on these expeditions it was safer, and now quite possible, to go in large groups. In turn, sizable bands—and, of course, the example of Plains tribes of long standing—led to such novelties as true chiefs, tribal councils, and a police force.

What a new domesticated species may mean for a people is seen from a comparison of the two branches of the Chukchi in northeastern-most Siberia. Originally all of them were sedentary coast dwellers, getting their food, like the Eskimo, mainly by seal hunting. Later a part of the tribe got domestic reindeer and turned nomads, pasturing their stock, harnessing them to sledges, and slaughtering them for subsistence. Regular butchering is possible only if the herds are large enough, comprising, say, 300 to 400 head for the needs of two families. Near the mouth of the Anadyr many of the Chukchi are still obliged to rely mainly on sealing, for their herds are too small to permit butchering. In 1928 about 9,000 Reindeer Chukchi were scattered over 650 independent camps as against 3,000 Maritime Chukchi in 70 villages. The reindeer breeders, then, are an offshoot from an ancestral seal-hunting tribe. The change in means of subsistence was bound to modify the routine of life. Pastoralists must migrate, and nomads required a tent instead of a stationary house; sealers and herders naturally came to trade with each other, bartering blubber against reindeer skins. The question that concerns us here, however, is in how far the shift to a novel economy has affected *social* arrangements. This may be discussed with reference to property, the status of women, the prestige of old people, and the life of children.

Stock breeding implies a new form of property that tends to safeguard man against starvation, though at the expense of continuous trouble. Since the Reindeer Chukchi have more valuables to be stolen, theft is naturally more frequent with them than among their Maritime brethren; property marks develop to distinguish ownership of beasts; and there is more to-do about the inheritance of a herder's than about a sealer's estate. What is more, a rich Reindeer Chukchi takes a sentimental interest in his herds; not wanting them to remain ownerless after his death, he adopts an heir if he is without issue.

The status of woman is profoundly affected. Among the coast dwellers a woman is not normally expected to endanger her life by seal hunting, but among the stock breeders she learns to tend reindeer. The more animals there are, the more need is there for assistants; whence the principle of one wife for every herd, though brothers and cousins can also be drafted for service. Among the breeders, life without a mate is almost unbearable, so that there are definitely fewer bachelors than in the Maritime settlements. On the other hand, polygyny is commoner, and though poorer men also practice it, it is typical of wealthy herders. One man had four wives and over twenty children by them. A seal hunter cannot support more than one wife except in the rarest circumstances; the woman is an economic dependent. A Reindeer Chukchi woman earns her living by constant labor, but there are some compensations for her harder lot. Notwithstanding her still being considered inferior, she can not only acquire a few beasts for herself, but may sometimes become her father's main heir, enjoying the prestige that goes with control of a herd.

The position of children in the two groups differs in strictly parallel fashion. On the coast they grow up with less assurance of a food supply, but have a much longer period of play. A girl is of no use on a hunting trip, and even a boy under sixteen is reckoned more of a hindrance than a help in a sealing boat. But among the nomads a child no more than ten or twelve years old and of either sex may perform necessary chores about the herd.

Economic utility again affects the attitude toward old age. As a Maritime Chukchi grows weak and decrepit, he is no longer able to participate in the strenuous sealing life. He is, from the native point of view, merely an extra person to feed; hence he loses prestige. Not so among the pastoralists. Here the ownership of beasts ensures an old man consideration even in his dotage, and if necessary his younger relatives will carry him about.

Some other differences are worth noting. Hospitality is more developed among the Maritime people; otherwise travel would be impossible, since dog sleds cannot carry the amount of food feasible for reindeer transport. Again, in a coastal village the "master of the front house," i.e., the head of the household representing the earliest settlers, is likely to lord it over his poorer neighbors. Among the reindeer breeders an unrelated assistant is likely to be an active, vigorous young man who may play the bully and when angered attack his master himself.

Evidently the changes due to pastoralism among the majority of the Chukchi cannot be brought under a simple formula, but of the significance of the modifications there can be little doubt.

Whereas the influence of reindeer breeding on Chukchi life has to be studied by comparing the nomads with their more conservative fellows, corresponding changes among the Lapps of Northern Europe are in part a matter of recorded history. Originally hunters and fishermen, they probably adopted domesticated reindeer from the Samoyed in the eleventh or twelfth century. Here a herd of at least 200 to 250 head is required to support a household in comfort, so that the Lapps long depended on their earlier ways of making a living. The Swedish taxation statistics show that as late as 1609 the richest man in one district owned only 75 reindeer, the average being 22. Toward the middle of the eighteenth century the Lapps of Kautokeino were still moving "hither and thither in order to seek food in some fashion, for hardly any one was wealthy enough to sustain himself and his household solely by his reindeer." In 1753 a local census shows a single man owning 300 head; 16 having from 100 to 250; the rest, between 20 and 100. In other words, only the richest could afford to dispense with hunting and to rely on the flesh and dairy products of their herds.

How did the shift from hunting to stock breeding affect Lapp social life?

The prepastoral Lapps lived in units called *sit* or *sii'da,* made up of a few families that might or might not be related. A *sit* took its name not from an ancestor but from its fishing sites or winter quarters. It claimed a tract usually marked off by natural features, such as watersheds. A council of house fathers assumed such control as there was. It allotted and reallotted sites for fishing or other use and distributed the salmon catch. Property rights blended communism and individualism. Chattels were owned individually, and a man might hunt the less valuable game animals for the sole benefit of his family. But the more valuable species—reindeer, beavers, bears, and wolves—were originally claimed by the *sit.* In 1733 a council expressly reaffirmed the ancient rule that wild reindeer and beaver belonged to the *sit.* This was reasonable, for reindeer were most effectively hunted by a collective drive into a large corral, which could be constructed only by the whole group. On the other hand, the *sit* provided for the wants of every member, not as a matter of charity, but as a moral obligation.

However, during the eighteenth century the traditional rules tended to break down, probably under the influence of the reindeer breeders and of Scandinavian neighbors. Thus, the *sit* came to recognize individual claims to fishing sites and to certain kinds of peltry.

Let us now see what happened among the reindeer Lapps. In regions exceptionally poor in pasturage every family was obliged to shift for itself; normally, however, the *sit* remained, but in a characteristically modified form. Several families would find it profitable to merge their beasts in a single large herd. This union might hold for only a year or a season. The most competent breeder automatically became headman, deciding when the *sit* was to start on its wanderings and who should perform a particular task. Reindeer were treated as personal property and marked as such by characteristic incisions or bites into their ears.

The Lapps, originally without significant distinctions of property, even lacking words for "rich" and "poor," thus came to differ markedly in wealth, some owning as many as 5,000 reindeer, whereas others had as few as 20. With large herds came for the first time the need for hired help, a notion so novel that the Lapps still have to express it by means of the Scandinavian or Finnish words for "boy" and "girl." Nomadism made it difficult to take care of the decrepit; hence old people are worse off than in the hunting stage. Thus, the rise of reindeer breeding brought noteworthy changes—the fading out of communism, the employment of wage earners, the impaired status of old age.

An economic loss, too, can yield social consequences. The seafaring Polynesians who landed on Tongareva, northwest of Tahiti, without bringing any dogs, fowls or pigs, found themselves on an atoll where the paper mulberry, yams, taro, or sweet potatoes could not be grown, where even drinking water was scarce. Much of the time the fluid of the coconut at certain stages of growth provided the only possible beverage. The discoverers had "to climb for water," while the flesh of the coconut furnished the staple food. By spreading the tree it was possible to have a larger population, possibly 2,000, than could have been supported by a diet of fish and the native Pandanus fruit. However, typical Polynesian traits, such as the ceremonial distribution of pork and the ideas clustering about bark clothing dropped out automatically, and the impoverished culture did not favor the blossoming of chieftainship into an autocracy of Hawaiian pattern. On the other hand, the unique importance of the coconut gave a positive cast to Tongarevan life. The natives settled near the plantations of this tree, jealously guarding their property: "All fruit-bearing trees have owners, and the nuts on the trees and those that fall to the ground are private, not communal property." In order to preserve crops when coconuts were depleted, a Tongarevan community would have to declare a closed season, but since that shut off the people's mainstay it forced the members to raid other districts, with warfare as the consequence; indeed, "the main cause of war was the coconut." [4]

## General Considerations

If economy is everywhere potent, wherein lies the unique character of Western civilization? Certainly it cannot lie in the profit motive of industrialism; the sheep-raising English landowners of the fifteenth century and the Polynesian noblemen were as ruthless exploiters as the owners of modern sweatshops. What the machine age has done is to systematize and rationalize the urge for profits to an extent never previously approached. To be sure, even at a somewhat earlier period there were trends in that direction. The Portuguese and the British, for example, borrowed plants cultivated by American Indians and spread them in their colonial possessions in the Old World; and in the East Indies the Dutch introduced large-scale cultivation of the most marketable crops. But it was only when manufacturing took to expensive machinery that this tendency reached a climax. To install such equipment not only put the means of effective production beyond the reach of persons of moderate means, but also impelled the manufacturers to get the greatest possible profit out of their machinery; and this urge soon set the tone for the whole of industrial society. To sum up, the consistent rationalism that directs the profit motive, abhorring wastage and excluding sentimental scruples, is the differentia of contemporary Western civilization even when compared with the cultures immediately ancestral to it.

Concerning the simpler societies, some special features must be noted. For them, a consistently rationalized economy in our sense is precluded by the general structure of their culture and, specifically, by the lack of money *in our sense*. These consequences have been clearly expounded by Thurnwald, Du Bois, and others. They can be illustrated by an a fortiori case, the Northwest Californians, as avaricious a people as probably ever existed.

"The persistence," says Kroeber, "with which the Yurok desire wealth is extraordinary." It is reflected in the elaborate scheme by which every possible insult or injury must be paid for. These people and their neighbors had slaves, but they were worked to only a moderate degree, not from altruism, but because the economy did not stimulate full exploitation. With an exceptionally abundant food supply available, there was no point in overworking one's slaves at fishing or hunting, for there were no markets or investments for a surplus. No wonder a slave could be bought for one or two strings of dentalium shells—less than the cost of a good flint blade.

This shell currency itself had little to do with the practical aspects of life in this region. A Tolowa *bartered* one kind of useful goods against another instead of making a payment. He would not "translate the value of dried salmon or a basket into dentalia and then make exchanges whose dentalia equivalents are of equal value." Money was virtually reserved for luxury articles bearing a prestige value. But this is not a unique instance. Money, even where it occurs among simpler people, is rarely an abstract and generalized measure of value. Nineteenth-century Polish peasants still lacked that conception. The price of a cow was qualitatively different from the dowry brought by a wife; and land, a coveted commodity, was incommensurable with other values, so that a peasant was willing to pay ridiculous amounts for it.

Rational economy is further prevented by the terrific force of irrational standards of behavior. In East Africa pastoral invaders have repeatedly conquered Bantu peasants and degraded them to a subject status. They drive their cattle over the planted fields at will and compel the farmers to perform menial chores. But they do not exploit them to a maximum degree because the overlords taboo or despise the commoners' economic goods, such as vegetables, game, and fish. Still more extraordinary is Northwest Californian behavior in warfare. These people have made such a fetish of their schedule of fines for injury that the victors, instead of capturing loot, pay the customary indemnity, which actually exceeds the damages paid by the vanquished.

Outstanding among the irrational elements that affect economy is the urge for gaining a higher social standing. A Fijian may solicit a gift, which the person asked must surrender on pain of losing face. This craving for prestige sweeps aside considerations of material gain in many societies. The Melanesians of Lesu will pay *more* for an article than is necessary in order to make ostentatious display of their wealth; a British Columbian Indian will destroy a canoe to demonstrate his greatness. In such communities, wealth is largely ownership of luxury goods which have come to acquire a prestige value. On the other hand, pauperism is nonexistent, because the destitute or idle can always fall back on kinsmen or friends for the minimum of existence.[5]

Where such sentiments prevail a rationalized economy can hardly arise.

# Chapter 3

# LAWS OF EVOLUTION; CORRELATION; PARALLELISM

## *Social Evolution*

Industrial civilization has evidently developed out of an earlier and far more common type of society. But simpler peoples, too, are by no means static; as Chukchi and Lapp history demonstrates, a significant economic change may result in a social reorientation. In view of the universal occurrence of change, certain questions naturally arise. Do different societies go through similar stages? If so, is it always because of similar economic conditions, or must we take other factors also into account? Are the several features found in one society linked together from some inherent reason; and how? These are the problems of evolution, parallelism, and correlation.

The term "evolution," which originally comes from biology, is best defined in harmony with both its etymological and its biological meanings. Etymologically, "to evolve" is to unroll or unfold: the evolving thing manifests traits that have until then been latent. However, not any and every change falls into this category. Every individual differs in some measure from his parents, but these variations are not evolutionary changes; they are at best only starting points in that direction. Further, organisms put into a new environment sometimes exhibit new features, but promptly lose them when transplanted to their usual habitat. Such alterations, too, are not evolutionary. In other words, permanency is essential to the concept. Darwin and his contemporaries often use the phrase "descent with modification" as a synonym of evolution, conceiving modification as an hereditary change. When we transfer the concept to culture, it is proper to emphasize the element of permanence as being the closest parallel to be found. A language or a social organization evolves into a new one when the changes are not ephemeral, but lasting. If some member of a family begins to trill his r's as a personal idiosyncrasy, the change is not evolutionary; if he sets the pattern for his generation and succeeding ones, a new dialect may be on its way. Correspondingly, one henpecked husband in a village does not create a matriarchate.

Certain other characteristics of evolution have been suggested, but proved indefensible. This holds notably for the attribute of progress. There is now general agreement that, except in technological and purely intellectual phases of culture, "progress" cannot be objectively determined; hence it should not be tied up with a scientific principle, such as evolution is supposed to be. Better grounds can be urged on behalf of increasing complexity and differentiation,[1] but only with serious qualification. They are frequent but not indispensable accompaniments of the evolutionary process. "Descent with modification" can certainly occur without them. The English language unquestionably evolved out of Anglo-Saxon, but the eleven differentiations of any one adjective have dwindled down to a single form, and modern English grammar is notoriously simpler than its antecedent.

## Parallelism and Multilinear Evolution

That social phenomena have evolved, i.e., are derived from other social phenomena by a process of modification, is a generally accepted proposition. It could not be otherwise, for the matter is in part one of observation and written record. Our political institutions are the modified descendants of British antecedents. Islamic matrimonial law evolved out of pre-Mohammedan custom, partly preserved and partly modified by the Prophet.

However, scholars disagree concerning the course of evolution. Some believe that it is uniform, that peoples the world over have traversed the same stages of development. This is the theory of parallelism or unilinear evolution. Others insist that evolution has been multilinear, traveling by different routes in diverse areas.

Parallelism is typically represented in E. B. Tylor's famous statement: "The institutions of man are as distinctly stratified as the earth on which he lives. They succeed each other in series substantially uniform over the globe, independent of what seem the comparatively superficial differences of race and language, but shaped by similar human nature acting through successively changed conditions in savage, barbaric, and civilized life." A concrete application of the parallelist principle is the once widespread view that all peoples with patrilineal clans previously reckoned descent through women (p. 260). Probably the most ambitious scheme of social evolution is that propounded in Lewis H. Morgan's *Ancient Society* (1876) with reference to family life and marriage. According to him the several social and domestic institutions "are to be understood as originating in the several branches of the human family substantially in the order named, and as existing generally in these branches while in the corresponding status." His stages include promiscuity; the intermarriage of brothers and sisters in a group; the inter-marriage of several sisters with one another's husbands; the clan organization, barring sibling marriage; marriage of single pairs, but without exclusive cohabitation; monogamy. He declares that progress has been "substantially the same in kind in tribes and nations inhabiting different and even disconnected continents, while in the same status, with deviations from uniformity in particular instances produced by special causes." [2]

The believers in multilinear evolution do not form a single school. Some emphasize the uniqueness of historical events and would quote against parallelism an earlier statement of Tylor's: "Most of its [culture's] phenomena have grown into shape out of such a complication of events, that the laborious piecing together of their previous history is the only safe way of studying them." [3] Others, notably the Austrian school headed by Father Schmidt, explain social evolution essentially in terms of a threefold development. After a primeval period of hunting, they assume, man in one region perfected his hunting devices and created certain crafts; elsewhere he domesticated wild animal species, laying the foundation for pastoralism; in still another area he (or rather, she) invented farming. Each of these steps is supposed to have had repercussions in the social sphere. At subsequent periods the three primary cultures entered into various relations, yielding the range of observable phenomena.

It is important to note that Schmidt is not a whit less of an evolutionist than Tylor. This appears both from explicit avowals of a belief in evolution and from the way in which he outlines the course of his primary cultures. To illustrate, he explains by the following scheme how the clans of a tribe came to be linked each with a particular species of plant or animal (the "totem") which its affiliates, but not tribesmen of other clans, are forbidden to eat. At first, all tribesmen, Schmidt assumes, freely consume all their customary food products. Later, in some regions specialization sets in, a local subdivision of the tribe devoting itself, say, to gathering shellfish and hunting on the coast, while the rest exploit the interior. These two subdivisions will meet to exchange surplus supplies, as actually happens in the Andamans. But, so the hypothesis runs, each may come to barter away the entire amount of some special form of food, which means that the members have to do without it; and out of such a merely customary renunciation there will grow the definite taboo that characterizes totemism. Obviously, a later condition is here derived from an antecedent one through modification.

Still more clearly evolutionary is Schmidt's theory of matriliny. Woman, it is said, invented farming, hence claimed the crops she harvested and the land on which they grew. This gave her economic ascendancy; she remained by her plots, where her husband would have to pay her periodic visits. After a while he would reconcile himself to the new regime and permanently live at his wife's home or settlement, a custom called "matrilocal residence." Males thus sank to an inferior status, the whole culture turning matriarchal, with female deities and with initiation rites for girls only. However, a reaction set in. Feminism was tempered when a woman's brother appeared as her agent or protector, and tottered when he finally usurped full property rights over her land. The bridegroom, moreover, at times substituted a period of bride-service for permanent matrilocal residence, and later even paid for his wife, thus making her a chattel to be taken to his home ("patrilocal residence"). Finally, men revolted against their degradation, organized secret societies to terrorize womankind, and gained the upper hand, completely overthrowing feminine rule.[4]

At present the correctness of these views does not concern us; we are merely interested in their evolutionary character. Schmidt postulates a definite sequence of stages. In principle he differs from Tylor only in not assuming that institutions "succeed each other in series substantially uniform over the globe." The development outlined above is supposed to hold for only one culture sphere. Notwithstanding this limitation, logically there is nothing to prevent an indefinite repetition of Schmidt's processes. If the several causes used to explain the modifications are effective at all, then any tribe that borrowed the basic idea of farming should experience the same sequence of changes. There is no reason to suppose that diffusion would set in only when the entire matrilineal complex had crystallized. From what we know in historic times cultivated plants may spread with great rapidity; hence feminine agriculture might again and again usher in the same sociological consequences. Theories of multilinear evolution, in prescribing a fixed order, assume a *law* of sequence just as much as do the unilinear systems. In both theories specific *causes* bring about the alleged modifications.

## Causality in Social Evolution

In a recent symposium by historians on the theory and practice of historiography, "cause" is described as "an ambiguous and difficult term of varied and complex meaning." Some contributors would taboo it altogether; the majority recommend substituting the plural for the singular and suggest that even "causes" be used "only with great circumspection." The reasons for such caution are as obvious in sociology as in history. In both cases a phenomenon singled out for interpretation is normally interwoven with so many others that it is hazardous to pick out one antecedent as necessary for a particular result. Radcliffe-Brown and Eggan are certainly right in stressing the difficulty of determining *the* causal factor when historical data are lacking. This even holds when such information is available, because a scholar arbitrarily limits "the extent of past time in which antecedent interrelations will be sought" and arbitrarily assumes which factors shall be treated as constant.[5]

These qualifications by no means prevent our establishing significant connections, without which we should indeed be dealing with a meaningless hodgepodge of facts. But it is one thing to point out a connection, another to designate the reason for it. Tylor fully recognized this, as will be shown later.[6]

Most causes from which modifications of social institutions have been derived turn out to be highly speculative. For instance, why (as Schmidt has it) should woman's invention of farming make her dominant? The idea is plausible enough, but those economically most useful do not automatically gain control; otherwise the peasants of medieval Europe or the farmers of Japan would have lorded it over the military caste. On the other hand, Hopi women, who at least own all houses and all harvested crops, are emphatically not the main food producers. Again, the theory that males organized secret societies in order to dominate womankind can be easily bolstered up with a semblance of evidence, but it remains unconvincing for two reasons. First, equally plausible explanations can be given for the exclusion of women from sacred societies, e.g., the widespread savage fear of menstrual blood. Second, large areas exist in which woman is rated inferior, yet secret societies are wanting, as in Siberia. It is, of course, possible to pile one auxiliary hypothesis on top of another in order to save the basic assumption. For instance, it is said that where women fail to gain social control through their economic superiority it is superfluous for men to organize subversive societies in self-defense. But this is not a demonstration of the theory; it is merely an attempt to explain away discrepancies on the assumption that it is already established.

The great merit of the economic approach lies in its definiteness: we note a factor of this category and can then trace consequences that, in some measure at all events, can be connected with it. But many problems arise that defy an interpretation along economic lines. The majority of tropical South American aborigines gain their livelihood in basically similar ways and practice the same crafts, yet their matrimonial arrangements are far from uniform. Some tribes are only temporarily matrilocal, others are permanently so, and still others are patrilocal; some have no strict rule of descent, others are matrilineal, still others are patrilineal. Whence these differences? Again, neighboring Australian tribes often define incest in different ways without any observable differences in their "processes of production." An economic determinist may declare that he is not interested in such phenomena, but the natives are emphatically so; hence a comparative sociologist must be likewise. If, on the other hand, the contention is that the economic antecedents are merely latent in such cases, then it is our determinist's duty to render them manifest or at least to point the way toward an economic solution of these problems.

Even where *some* effect of economic modifications on social life seems certain, the specific nature of the effect is not easily defined. The aged Reindeer Chukchi are better off than their Maritime brethren because they retain control of their herds. But why are they allowed to retain it? The ethical standards of these people which permit retention are a necessary background for the continued social prominence of old men, whereas among the nomadic Lapps their condition is described as pitiable. The difference must lie in the prior norms of Lapps and Chukchi, and these norms thus codetermine the observed treatment of old people. A dosage of reindeer nomadism by itself is not a sufficient cause.

In short, it is necessary to keep before us the great complexity of the phenomena we are studying and to insist on the multiplicity of significant antecedent conditions. However, when the time element is not involved or is unknown, we can fruitfully substitute the mathematical concept of function and probability.

## Correlation

Two variable quantities are said to be functions of each other if a change in one brings about a change in the other. Thus, the area of a rectangle is a function of its base; it is not fully determined by the length of the base, but does vary with it. In our field, a change in the mode of residence from matrilocal to patrilocal might lead to corresponding changes in interpersonal relations—between husband and wife, between father and child. Considered from the point of view of probability, one of several related phenomena could be said to make the others more or less probable. In other words, matrilocal residence might be said to make abuse of the wife less likely and control of the children by the wife's relatives more likely. If the occurrence of an observed trait makes another more probable, the two are positively correlated; if the occurrence of one trait renders another less probable, the correlation is negative.

The literature of anthropology is full of alleged correlations which lack empirical support. So learned and judicious a writer as Thurnwald sometimes errs in this way. For example, he declares that the "levirate" (Latin *levir*, husband's brother), i.e., the inheritance of a deceased brother's widow, and the "sororate," i.e., marriage with a deceased wife's sister, occur "mainly where there are no clans." Levirate and sororate are, however, common in Australia, where clan organizations flourish; in North America the two forms of marriage frequently exist whether there are or are not clans; and the same holds for Africa. This very sketchy survey is enough to refute the high negative correlation asserted by our author.

Thurnwald is similarly at fault in positively correlating polyandry and matriliny. As a matter of fact, the most thoroughly established instances are reported from the bilinear Toda and Thurnwald's additional occurrences—Gilyak (Siberia), Tibetans, Arabians, Sakai (Malay Peninsula)—come from either a patrilineal or a neutral setting. The Eskimo, who locally practice polyandry, and the Shoshoneans of the Basin, who sporadically permit it, have no fixed rule of descent; the Bahima of East Africa are patrilineal. In short, the supposed correlation dissolves into nothing.[7]

Such defection from strict methods is all the stranger because over half a century ago Tylor took a step in the right direction, tabulating the customs of 350 peoples in order to determine both how every trait listed was distributed and what other traits "accompany it or lie apart from it." [8] Unfortunately he never published his full data, and (according to an oral statement of Tylor's successor at Oxford, the late Robert R. Marett) they are irretrievably lost. All we have is the preliminary paper he presented to a learned society in 1888, embodying valuable general reflections and new concepts, but only a few illustrations. It is thus not clear how he coped with certain technical difficulties nor precisely what his empirical evidence for the several conclusions may have been. Nevertheless, certain comments on the method are possible.

Of the 350 peoples examined, 45 turned out to prohibit any social relations between a son-in-law and his wife's parents; in statistical phraseology, the probability of the taboo is 45/350. The reverse rule forbidding social intercourse between a daughter-in-law and her husband's family was found 13 times; hence has a probability of 13/350. Tylor conjectured a correlation of these customs with matrilocal and patrilocal residence, respectively. The former had a probability of 65/350, the latter of 141/350. According to statistical principles, the probability of two or more events occurring jointly *by mere chance* is obtained by multiplying their several probabilities. Hence the likelihood of son-in-law avoidance along with matrilocalism would be 45/350 × 65/350 = 117/4900 (after cancellation) = not quite 0.024. Since the total number of tribes is 350, the number of cases in which mere chance would unite the two traits is 0.024 × 350 = 8.4. However, Tylor's tables showed that actually the combination had a frequency of 14, whence he inferred an organic rather than an accidental connection—in other words, a positive correlation. Again, the probability of the son-in-law taboo with *patrilocal* residence is 45/350 × 141/350 = 1269/24,500 (after cancellation) = 0.0518; and this fraction of the total 350 yields 18.13 cases to be expected on chance, whereas the tables exhibited only 9, thus indicating a negative correlation.

Daughter-in-law avoidance, on chance, should occur with matrilocal residence with a probability of 13/350 × 65/350 = 169/24,500 = .0069; the number of cases, then, should be 2.415, "but there are no such cases." Tylor infers a negative correlation. On the other hand, by chance this taboo may be expected to occur with patrilocalism 13/350 × 141/350 × 350 times, i.e., in 5.23+ cases. The observed number of associations, however, is eight, indicating (according to Tylor) a positive correlation. All these results seem to converge to the conclusion that "avoidance by the husband of the wife's family is in some way connected with his living with them; and vice versa as to the wife and the husband's family."

A statistician would feel uncomfortable about this inference because the disparity between the observed and the theoretical chance results is so small. For the frequency of chance occurrences is not absolutely fixed, but fluctuates within limits, and the differences noted by Tylor do not exclude the possibility that chance rather than an organic tie between the traits is at work.

Technicalities aside, in 1888 ethnographical knowledge was limited. Some of the features discussed by Tylor were probably not systematically inquired for until his paper had directed attention to them. His roster is thus unavoidably imperfect. Thus, he found teknonymy

(Greek *teknon,* child; *onuma,* name, the calling of a parent after his child, e.g., "Father of John"), in thirty-one tribes, but the custom does not readily obtrude itself on a traveler's notice. One can easily point out tribes sociologically little or not at all known when Tylor wrote, but since reported as teknonymous: the Gold of the Amur country, the Chenchu of Hyderabad, and the Semang of the Malay Peninsula; the Haida of British Columbia, the Crow and Hidatsa of the northern Plains, the Navaho, Hopi and Zuñi in our southwestern states; the Tupi, Botocudo, Yekuana in South America; the Kababish of the Anglo-Egyptian Sudan. It is not unlikely that careful scrutiny of the literature would reveal at least twice the frequency used in Tylor's computations. Similarly, matrilocalism and son-in-law avoidance are far more common than anyone could have inferred from the sources fifty years ago. From California alone about fifteen instances of the taboo have come to light, and in South America many tribes have recently turned out to be matrilocal.[9] Now, Tylor correlates teknonymy, matrilocal residence, and son-in-law avoidance, obtaining an expected frequency of 1.8 for the trio; and since it actually occurs eleven times, there is for once a rather impressive preponderance of observation over theory. Yet if each of the three single frequencies has to be corrected, the conclusion is no longer convincing. Possibly it would be borne out by data now accessible, but a rechecking is imperative. Such an examination naturally could not assume 350 as the total number of known peoples, but would have to revise the denominator, too, in the light of accessible data. Moreover, there is no way of guessing the frequency of the combination. In short, a painstaking inquiry is needed to bring the question up to date. Tylor deserves the highest praise for having attempted to define a problem and to attack it, not by sheer guessing, but in the light of then available evidence. But since his evidence was inadequate, the problem must be investigated with the aid of material now at hand.

Apart from this point, there are difficulties to be overcome in regard to classification. In order to obtain significant correlations we must accurately define the traits whose association is to be determined; and we must also properly define the units about which the traits are predicated.

At first blush it may seem easy to segregate a trait so definite as matrilocal residence. But as Tylor himself realized, the matter is not by any means so simple, for residence with the wife's family may be merely temporary, say, until the birth of a child, when it will be followed by patrilocalism. Further, it makes a difference whether a man comes from another settlement, as often happens, or whether he merely shifts from one dwelling in the village to another. On the former supposition he is a stranger in a strange land; on the latter he is never cut loose from his own kindred, on whom he may in a crisis fall back for support. Our sources do not always discriminate with nicety concerning such differentiations; but in planning an investigation it is essential to keep them in mind.

At least equally important is the second issue. What, for purposes of statistical inquiry, is a "people" or a "tribe"? The Arabs show great uniformity in some respects, but marked diversity in others. Thus, the Kababish of the Anglo-Egyptian Sudan seem alone among the Arabs in practicing son-in-law avoidance. Shall we, then, credit the "Arabs" with this taboo, which most of them lack? Or shall we refine our classification and list such traits as we can for each of a dozen Arab subgroups? And on the latter plan, is it proper to treat a minor unit of this order on a par with such a "people" as the Japanese, who number some 70 million, if they happen to be relatively uniform in custom? It would be illuminating to know how so balanced a mind as Tylor's grappled with this vexing problem.

The question must be viewed from another angle. Let us take the thirteen cases of daughter-in-law taboo. In an earlier work Tylor cited the Mongol, Kalmuk, and Yakut instances,[10] so that they were evidently included in his baker's dozen. But is it proper to list them as so many independent occurrences? The Kalmuk and the Mongols are offshoots of the same Mongolic stock; it is therefore wholly possible that they are merely perpetuating an ancestral feature. If so, they cannot be counted as two samples *in a correlation study,* but merely as one. For the whole point of the investigation is to determine which traits make the existence of other traits more likely. Every *independent* case of patrilocalism coupled with daughter-in-law avoidance strengthens the argument for a significant bond between them, but since the Mongol and the Kalmuk are primarily one people, the coupling in both instances should score only once.

But the argument may be extended. Not only the Mongols and their fellow Mongolic Kalmuk, not only the Yakut and their fellow Turkic Kazak, but utterly unrelated tribes adjoining them share this rule of avoidance. It is found among the Finno-Ugrian Ostyak, the linguistically isolated Ket,[11] the quite distinct Yukaghir of the extreme north. The details of the observances correspond so closely that independent development is out of the question: the whole of the Siberian area must presumably figure in a correlational count as a single sample of the association. The question then arises, how many independent instances are there in the world; and if it were demonstrable that there was a single center from which the two linked features were jointly diffused, the argument for an organic bond between them would collapse. Metaphysically, it remains possible that such a bond brought them together, but it would no longer be possible to demonstrate it. For it is one thing to have patrilocal residence and the taboo unite and spread in unison, and quite another to have one of them over and over again predispose the other to come into being. The significance of diffusion in this context was noted by Galton in his discussion of Tylor's lecture, but Tylor's treatment of the difficulty remains unknown.

Except when applied in the extreme fashion rejected by most scholars, diffusion does not eliminate the Tylorian approach. The repeated association of two or more traits in, say, six discrete areas would raise a presumption that one trait is favorable to the occurrence of the other. Actually some sociological features are distributed in such a way that a tolerably large number of independent origins is not improbable. This matter, however, would require a thorough reinvestigation of the field.

It is a noteworthy merit of Tylor's to have clearly distinguished between an empirical correlation, such as his statistics purported to establish, and the underlying cause. Thus, he suggests that a son-in-law is "cut" by his wife's relatives in order to mark him as an intruder into their midst. But Tylor at once concedes that "we pass on to less solid ground in assigning . . . a reason which may be only analogous to the real reason, or only indirectly corresponding with it, or only partly expressing it, as its correlation with other connections may eventually show."

Tylor further recognized that some traits that are descriptively separated are logical corollaries from the same basic condition so that "the relation is not one of derivation, but of identity." The example he furnishes is infelicitous, but it is easy to illustrate the principle by one that holds water. In South America, unions between a man and his sister's daughter are fairly common and orthodox. A moment's reflection shows that the tribes in question cannot possibly have matrilineal clans since niece and uncle, being of one such clan, would not be allowed to marry. In other words, there is a maximum negative correlation between a matrilineal clan system and avuncular marriage. Correspondingly, a man's marriage with his brother's daughter is conceivable among matrilineal peoples—it actually occurs among the Tlingit of Alaska—but is impossible in a patrilineal clan organization. Such a one hundred per cent correlation is, of course, to be expected only where traits are *logically* linked; otherwise too many coexisting factors contribute to the occurrence and absence of a trait to permit any one of them to be an invariable concomitant.

The most ambitious attempt since Tylor's day to study functional relationships of sociological phenomena by statistical techniques is connected with the "cross-cultural survey" organized at Yale by Professor G. P. Murdock. The participants compute correlations by Yule's association formula: $\dfrac{ad - bc}{ad + bc}$. If, for example, agriculture and matriliny are to be correlated, four numerical values have to be determined, representing, respectively, tribes exhibiting both traits (*a*); with no agriculture but with matriliny (*b*); with agriculture, but not matrilineal (*c*); and without either trait (*d*). Assuming 10 matrilineal agricultural groups; 5 that do not farm but reckon descent through the mother; 20 non-matrilineal farming peoples; and 18 that neither farm nor practice matriliny, we get from Yule's formula:

$$\frac{80}{280} = .28+$$

Since Murdock's major monograph summarizing these researches has been delayed by the war, judgment on the project must rest on two brief articles of his, a paper by Simmons, and a book by the same author. Without reservation we must hail this revival of Tylor's effort to replace mere impressions with precise knowledge. The vast amount of reading by both investigators likewise commands respect and, irrespective of their primary goal, yields useful data on the distribution of traits. However, any enterprise of this sort involves technical difficulties, which are in part explained by Murdock and Simmons themselves. Accordingly, it is necessary to approach the results announced to date with discrimination as well as with sympathy.

Murdock's earlier paper summarizes studies of well over 200 tribes with reference to patriliny and matriliny. Among other things he concludes, contradicting some earlier views, that "by and large simpler cultures tend to be matrilineal, more advanced ones patrilineal." The argument rests on the persistently high positive correlation of patriliny with generally accepted tokens of complexity, such as agriculture, large domestic animals, writing, metals. For instance, out of 166 tribes available for comparison, 88 were found to be both agricultural and patrilineal, 35 agricultural and matrilineal; 24 patrilineal tribes and 19 matrilineal tribes are recorded as nonfarming. The coefficient of correlation for patriliny and farming is computed at 33; for domestication and patriliny at 68; and this association of patrilineal descent with "traits indicative of higher civilization" is consistent, 145 out of a total of 189 coefficients being positive.

Unfortunately this preliminary publication, like Tylor's, publishes results with only an occasional indication of the raw data on which they rest. The reader is thus unable to judge whether the samples chosen are the best available; he even remains in doubt whether the moot point represents a real issue between Murdock and his supposed opponents or possibly rests on a misunderstanding of their position.

This, however, is a purely formal matter, which Murdock's forthcoming publication will unquestionably dispose of. More serious is the intrusion of a subjective element, for the value of the statistical procedure centers precisely in its objectivity. To take the first of Murdock's indices of "a higher level of cultural attainment," so long as other things are equal, agriculture—contrary to popular impressions—is not a trustworthy criterion, certainly not if so treated wherever it appears "as an adjunct, whether important or unimportant, to the food quest." As a matter of fact, farming in many cases—in North America, among the Ojibwa, Penobscot, Maricopa, for example—is of so subsidiary a character that these tribes are economically less well off than favorably situated hunters and fishermen, say, coastal British Columbians and Northwest Californians. By itself, agriculture ensures neither a greater density of population nor a greater stability of residence, as shown by various primitive farmers who are forever shifting their settlements either because their soil has been exhausted or for some sentimental or superstitious motive. It is only when the intensive stage of cultivation is reached that this form of economy becomes unequivocally superior. But who is to decide at what point that stage is reached? Interestingly enough, Murdock and Simmons disagree in the appraisal of Iroquois farming: the former describes it as "the primary source of subsistence," whereas to Simmons it appears only moderately elaborated, of "intermediate importance."

"Matripotestal" is another concept used by both authors; it denotes the superior domestic authority of the mother or *her* mother. This is regrettably a matter not easily determined by an observer, and accordingly the same people have been variously judged. Simmons chooses to tabulate the Creek as unequivocally matripotestal; actually the early writers on whose records we must largely rely in this case give diametrically opposite pictures of the situation.

At this juncture notice must be taken of Simmons's attempt to grade the importance of each trait in its culture. It is ranked as dominant; only moderately elaborated; incipient or unimportant. Quite properly, Simmons insists that it would be a distortion of reality not to distinguish between hunting as a people's mainstay and as an incidental pursuit. In any *genetic* study such differences would be vital; but in a statistical inquiry they merely augment the danger of subjective judgments. We have just seen that Iroquois agriculture can be differently assessed by members of the same school; a glance at Simmons's tables arouses many doubts. Why are the Ainu, whose farming is due to Japanese influence, credited with a moderate elaboration of the trait? Why is the same rank given to Ojibwa agriculture when part of the tribe are pure hunters? Why do the Yakut figure even as slightly agricultural, seeing that they learnt to sow from the Russians only as late as 1853? If such cases of recent loans from whites are reckoned, how many aboriginal tribes would remain nonfarming?

Grading is at least equally dangerous with respect to rules of descent. Again it is necessary to emphasize that a genetic investigation would have to consider degrees of bias in one or the other direction. But a statistician cannot afford recognizing the fluidity of social conditions. From this point of view, then, the procedure followed by Simmons is objectionable. A tribe is either matrilineal, i.e., reckons descent through the mother, or is not. If, like the Andamanese, it favors neither side, it should not be tabulated as moderately matrilineal *and* moderately patrilineal, which means that by the procedure followed it would actually be rated as bilinear; and the same applies to the Semang and the Yaghan. What may be meant by making the Omaha, with clear-cut patrilineal clans, both dominantly patrilineal *and* moderately matrilineal, remains an enigma.

From all points of view Murdock's later publication marks a great advance. It lists the tribes compared, so that the specialist can check factual statements. Naturally, other tribes could be substituted, but the principles of selection are fair, equal representation being given to the main areas of the globe so far as published material permits. It will be well to re-examine the problems with freshly chosen samples, especially as little-known regions become more familiar, but that qualification applies to all comparative work on a major scale.

Particularly commendable is the use of sharply defined concepts. In his second paper Murdock investigates the possible association of kinship classifications with the levirate, the sororate, exogamy, unilateral descent. For instance, does a single term for "mother" and "mother's sister" (instead of, say, calling the latter "aunt") go with exogamy? There is no arbitrariness in deciding whether a tribe merges the concepts of mother and maternal aunt or distinguishes them; and similarly, it must either forbid or not forbid marriage within a given group. A statistically sound procedure thus leads to acceptable conclusions.

On the other hand, the dangers inherent in the method when pitfalls are ignored appear in Simmons's argument against an association of matriliny with agriculture. Indeed, he gets a small negative correlation (0.08). By taking the same tribes, counting as "matrilineal" only those with matrilineal descent groups, eliminating bilinear cases, and correcting tabulations ethnographically vulnerable, I arrive at a different conclusion. To illustrate by specific examples, I do not class the Araucanians as matrilineal, for their rule of descent is in doubt; the Kutenai are bilateral and "weakly patrilinear"; the Pomo have indeed matrilineal succession to the chieftaincy, but lack kins; the Arunta, whom Simmons treats as unknown in this respect, are certainly not farmers.

This revised reckoning leaves 10 agricultural and matrilineal peoples; 6 with matriliny and without farming; 20 with farming and without matriliny; 16 with neither trait. The formula then yields $40/280 = 1/7 = .14+$. The figure is unimpressive, and no value is to be attached to it in an absolute sense. It does illustrate, however, the subjectivism that lurks in statistics: two investigators using the same data should not differ by so wide a margin. For a satisfactory inquiry into the problem itself I should recommend considering a much larger number of tribes; I should ignore tribes so imperfectly known as the Seri; and I should not overweight the Eskimo by using three of their subdivisions as separate units. Perhaps most important of all, truly bilinear peoples—all Australians, the Toda, and the Ashanti—must either be left aside or be given special treatment. How can one decide whether agriculture adheres to matriliny or to patriliny when a tribe (e.g., the Toda) has full-fledged patrilineal clans for certain purposes and equally definite matrilineal clans for others?

All this does not alter the fact that Murdock and Simmons have revived a potentially very valuable method and that some of their conclusions are doubtless acceptable, with such reservations as must attach to all empirical research. In the meantime it is worth noting another approach that, when applicable, has certain advantages.[12] It is the method of intensively comparing groups of common derivation, or with a basically identical culture, yet differing in some specific factor, the point being to ascertain what other elements likewise differ. This is illustrated by the comparison of the Reindeer and the Maritime Chukchi, of the Reindeer and the Hunting Lapps. The logic is obvious. Social phenomena are highly complex, i.e., result from a great number of determining conditions. If, however, we consider groups that share the same ancestral culture, or the culture typical of a definite area, most of the determinants may be assumed as constant. We thus approach the conditions of an ideal experiment for testing how effectively a particular trait renders certain other traits more probable.

We may not always be able to select such a feature as the horse or the reindeer, whose introduction is at least roughly datable, but so long as we are content to study correlation without necessarily establishing the sequence of events, such historical information is not indispensable.

To take our Pueblo Indians, they represent four linguistic stocks but all participate in much the same material and spiritual customs. One notable difference relates to the clan organization. In Taos, in the northeastern part of the region, clans are altogether absent, and men generally own the houses. Farther west, the Tewa have feeble matrilineal kins without exogamy, along with patrilineal moieties. As one proceeds westward, the matrilineal clan grows stronger, the moieties diminish in importance, and houses may be owned by either sex. In the westernmost tribes, the Hopi and the Zuñi, the matrilineal clans are highly developed and especially in Hopi villages exert a maximum influence on other phases of life, whereas the moieties dwindle away into at best ceremonial traces; here houses invariably belong to the women and there is matrilocal residence. It is hardly possible not to recognize a connection between house ownership, matrilocal residence, and matrilineal clan organization.

Here corroboratory evidence may be cited from a remote area. In northeastern Brazil the Canella, members of the great Ge family, have exogamous, matrilineal moieties, feminine house ownership, and matrilocal residence. Thus, the same usages are linked as among the Hopi. What clinches the matter is that another Ge tribe, the Sherente, has patrilocal residence (after the initial period of wedlock), patrilineal descent, and masculine ownership of the houses.[13]

It would not be justifiable to say that ownership of houses by women or that matrilocal residence is *the* cause of matrilineal clans. There are many South American tribes which are matrilocal, but not matrilineally organized. Likewise there are matrilineal peoples without matrilocal residence and feminine house ownership. Obviously other factors must cooperate and may operate to bring about or to sustain a matrilineal system. But matrilocalism and feminine house ownership narrow our expectations as to the rule of descent: matriliny is more likely in their company than with patrilocal residence plus masculine house ownership.

An intensive common-sense comparison of genetically related or culturally similar tribes within one culture area may, then, lead to sound correlations; and these can be tested in other areas among tribes related to one another genetically or culturally, but independent of the first set of tribes.

## Correlation and Laws of Evolution

Tylor's discussion of correlation merges in a defense of parallelism, i.e., of a natural trend in one direction rather than another, so that the same sequence holds generally. How is a correlation converted into a chronological scheme? Tylor, pursuing the geological analogy quoted above, plots three successive levels of development. His lowest stratum is that of matrilocal residence; his highest, that of patrilocal residence, with initial matrilocalism but subsequent removal to the husband's family intermediate. Combining the facts of residence with those of avoidance, Tylor finds that in the fully matrilocal condition there is only the son-in-law but no daughter-in-law taboo, since the woman and her husband's relatives have no chance of meeting. On the other hand, there are several cases of "survival" of the son-in-law taboo among patrilocal tribes. That is to say, the taboo, though incongruous with a rule by which the husband and his wife's family live apart, persists through sheer inertia. In the intermediate stage, it is argued, both taboos exist jointly since each spouse lives for a while with his or her in-laws. Hence, runs the conclusion, the sequence must have been matrilocal residence; initial matrilocalism, followed by removal to the husband's home; patrilocalism. For had the course of society been in the reverse direction, son-in-law avoidance would begin where the husband lived away from his wife's family; and daughter-in-law avoidance would be found as a sur-vival of the matrilocal stage, whereas no such cases occur.

The reasoning is, indeed, plausible *if* one assumes as a foregone con-clusion that either matrilocal or patrilocal residence must precede the other. Actually this is not an axiom, but a gratuitous assumption. It follows only if a fixed sequence is taken for granted. What the obser-vations at best prove is something quite different from a chronology: son-in-law avoidance is positively correlated with matrilocal residence, and negatively correlated with patrilocal residence; both taboos are mildly correlated with the "intermediate" conditions; and daughter-in-law avoidance is correlated with patrilocalism. These connections in themselves have no chronological import; *that* is injected only by Tylor's evolutionary bias. In other words, as the evidence goes, the mode of residence may spring up matrilocal in one region, patrilocal in another; and what is *logically* intermediate need not be chronologically so, but may be simply another of the rather limited possibilities in the case.

The same criticism applies to Tylor's alleged proof that a "mater-nal" system passed first into a "maternal-paternal" and ultimately into a "paternal" one. In the first of these, by Tylor's definition, descent is matrilineal; a woman's brother is the guardian of her children; rank, office, and property are inherited not by a man's son, but by his brother or his sister's son. In the "paternal" system these conditions are reversed: descent is from the father; the husband controls his wife and children; and his offspring succeed to his position and inherit his wealth. The "intermediate or transitional stage" variously combines these traits. Here again a logical grouping is invested with a chronological character that does not follow as a corollary. Tylor discovers that the levirate occurs in all three stages, but that in the maternal-paternal stage an addi-tional principle, viz. inheritance of widows by a son, likewise occurs; that, indeed, in polygynous Africa both principles may coexist, a chief's head-wife passing on to his brother, the other widows to the son who succeeds to the chieftaincy. "Looking at the distribution of these groups of customs, it is seen to be only compatible with the view that the pater-nal rule followed the maternal, bringing with it even while its preva-lence was but partial, the principle of paternal widow-inheritance."

But it is not at all necessary to assume that maternal and paternal systems bear a fixed chronological relation to each other. As Father Schmidt and I have contended, each may have arisen independently from diverse antecedents in distinct areas and need not pass into the other. The late Professors Marett and Boas were willing to concede that *if* a change occurred it was more likely from the maternal to the paternal; but that is very different from the view that they represent distinct strata, with paternal institutions uniformly later than the maternal.

The plain truth of the matter is that Tylor's empirical data suggest functional relations, but never sequences. The levirate is, as Tylor states and as later data corroborate, consistent with either of his two extreme logical categories and with the intermediate condition as well. Filial widow-inheritance is obviously probable only with a patrilineal bias, being merely one form of patrilineal inheritance; that is why we find it with other features of the paternal order.

To sum up, apart from other merits Tylor's paper remains epoch-making in introducing exact tabulation of sociological phenomena in the place of mere conjecture as a basis for a quest of correlations. But his attempt to convert correlations into an historical sequence must be regarded as abortive.

Of course, not even a score of failures can disprove the possibility of "historical laws." However, the use of the term "law" in any of the social sciences should be discountenanced as pretentiously boastful. Even physicists, so far as they have philosophical insight, no longer make the extravagant claims once advanced by natural scientists. For them a law is no more than a limitation of our expectation on the strength of past experience, a shorthand formula summarizing such experience.[14] However, given the comparatively simple phenomena of the external world, it is possible for the physicist or astronomer to make predictions with a degree of assurance not possible in the social sciences. This does not necessarily preclude generalization, but as the Committee already quoted puts it, "Historians may formulate generalizations of limited validity. . . ."

Unfortunately even reputable scholars are sometimes impelled to an undignified mimicry of physical science. Thus, an eminent anthropologist speaks of "a universal sociological law though it is not yet possible to formulate precisely its scope, namely that in certain specific conditions a society has need to provide itself with a segmentary organization" (such as the Australian clan and moiety system).[15] In the natural sciences a universal law whose scope cannot be precisely formulated would be an absurdity; and the conditions in which it operates must be specified, not vaguely hinted at. If we cannot meet these requirements, let us not prate grandiosely, lest we make a laughingstock of sociology.

Reverting to the question of matriliny and patriliny, we note that a proof of the priority of the former is not inconceivable. If it were possible to show from the sources that Egyptian, Babylonian, Greek, Chinese, and Arab civilization all independently passed through a matrilineal stage before shifting to patriliny, there would be at least some solid ground for assuming this to be a normal sequence at a certain stage of evolution. Now this has been vigorously asserted by various writers, but unfortunately in such cases they have started with a bias in favor of the traditional theory instead of simply accepting the testimony of their documents. In other words, they do not establish a sequence inductively, but postulate it first and then find illustrations congruous with their scheme. Morgan's treatment of the Greek case is typical. He admits that the sources fail to demonstrate a matrilineal period. Then he casts about and finds that various neighboring peoples, such as the Lycians, may be reasonably credited with matrilineal reckoning, which he takes as an argument that the Greeks, too, once practiced this rule of descent. But one could just as well contend on this basis that the neighbors had once been patrilineal like the historic Greeks. All that the proximity of the Lycians indicates is that the Greeks *may* once have reckoned descent through the mother, not that they actually did so. Morgan and his contemporaries assumed as a foregone conclusion that the licentiousness of early man made it impossible to distinguish the true procreator of a woman's offspring, who *therefore* could only be affiliated with their mother. We now know that primitive tribes in Asia and Africa are completely indifferent as to a child's begetter, and do not scruple to reckon it as belonging to the kin of a man who is known not to be its physiological parent, but who qualifies as the social father by virtue of a ceremony or of payment of the bride-price for the mother.[16] Thus, the a priori argument for the priority of matrilineal reckoning dissolves into nothing, and the historical evidence is admittedly wanting.

On the other hand, the critical use of documentary material—without an initial bias in favor of particular schemes—is decidedly promising. Chinese society has demonstrably undergone certain changes. Though patrilineal kins are ancient, exogamy was imperfectly followed in the Chou dynasty (1100–249 B.C.), becoming more stringent later, and being legally enforced from about 500 A.D. on. Can corresponding changes be traced elsewhere? They are certainly not universal, for nothing of the sort appears among the Arabs, whose patrilineal kins have remained consistently endogamous since pre-Islamic times. Teknonymy appears in China as early as 489 B.C.; at a certain period it seems to affect relationship nomenclature, a man calling his brother-in-law

"Uncle" in the spirit in which an American husband, similarly identifying himself with his children, addresses his wife as "Mother." Does teknonymy yield similar equations in other cultures? More particularly, is it possible to show that the teknonymous usage antedates the equation in question? Again, "cross-cousin marriage"—the union between offspring of a brother and of a sister—dates back in China before the third century B.C.; and in harmony with this custom a single word, *chiu,* is used for a man's maternal uncle and the father-in-law, relatives who would often be identical. Later this form of marriage dropped out, and *chiu* was thenceforth restricted to the maternal uncle. Are there comparable developments in other literate civilizations or in cultures described by literate chroniclers? [17] By such comparisons we may yet determine valid sequences, i.e., valid within limits.

Some sequences, indeed, are generally accepted as sound. Centralized authority over a large territory cannot come early in history, for such centralization implies means of communication to the margins of the area such as truly early man did not possess. The kinship bond is far stronger than the territorial bond among most primitive peoples; it persists where, as in some Negro kingdoms, a strong central government has been created; it remains potent in the less sophisticated strata of European countries and in the advanced civilization of China. The evidence for its priority is thus very strong.

Again, Boas and MacIver have stressed a noteworthy difference between our contemporary civilization and simpler cultures. The latter regularly fuse departments of social life that to us seem quite disparate. Farming and hunting, house building and warfare, are inextricably bound up with magical or religious rites; folk literature may also serve the purpose of philosophy; poetry is inseparable from song; history is involved with myth.[18] The evolution of our culture is marked by the gradual dissolution of this "primitive fusion." "This process," says MacIver, "inevitably arises in the evolution of society." In this form the conclusion goes beyond the evidence, but we may admit that since a rational ordering of society is a late development, the neat separation of logically incongruous elements naturally comes late and in association with a rationalistic trend. It has not been demonstrated that cultures uninfluenced by this tendency would follow a similar course.

Some interesting instances of parallelism can be adduced in the field of social psychology. Given a certain social atmosphere, the responses of individuals are often strikingly similar in remote areas. Among the matrilineal Lobi of the Volta region in West Africa, a man's livestock and his currency in the form of cowrie shells are inherited by his sister's son. But the deceased circumvents the law in favor of his eldest son, who alone knows where his father hid his money. The legal heir is thus obliged to bribe his cousin to divulge the hiding place—at the cost of one or more head of cattle. In this way, the son, who is legally deprived of the livestock, succeeds in acquiring some by a devious route. Now, from at least three other peoples there are data of strictly comparable character. A Guajiro Indian in northern Colombia theoretically leaves all his property to his eldest sister's eldest son. "However, in practice it seldom works, as the maternal uncle during his life continues to transfer his property in the form of gifts to his own male children, so that at the time of his death there is nothing, or very little, left of his property to be inherited by his nephew, unless the uncle is a very rich man." The Tsimshian of British Columbia and the Trobrianders east of New Guinea illustrate a similar conflict between the legal bond uniting uncle and nephew and the sentimental relations of father and son.[19]

In all four instances we find matriliny with a definite rule of nepotic inheritance, and in each case paternal love tries to thwart avuncular duty. Four cases are not sufficient to establish a "law," but they do suggest that the paternal sentiment tends to circumvent what seems an undue favoring of nephews as against sons. The question is, how frequently can the reaction be discovered in like circumstances?

To summarize, parallelism is not to be ruled out, but the extent to which it operates remains to be demonstrated by intensive study. Results to date suggest that "generalizations of limited validity" are wholly possible. They also indicate the extreme improbability of a uniform sequence over long periods. Morgan's scheme, for instance, implies an evolution extending over millennia. During such spans of time there are bound to be so many "deviations from uniformity . . . produced by special causes" that a law, if operative, could hardly be discovered by human reason.

# II. SOCIAL INSTITUTIONS

# Chapter 4

# KINSHIP

## *Biological and Sociological Kinship*

I<small>N THE</small> Introduction it was pointed out that kinship is differently conceived by different societies, that biological relationships merely serve as a starting point for the development of sociological conceptions of kinship. Society may ignore or restrict the natural blood tie, it may artificially create a bond of kinship, and again it may expand a natural bond to an indefinite extent. As Lévi-Strauss puts it, "A kinship system does not consist of the objective ties by descent or consanguinity that obtain among individuals; it exists only in human consciousness, it is an arbitrary system of ideas, not the spontaneous development of a factual situation." [1] The point is sufficiently important to warrant further illustrations.

In pre-Christian Germanic law, a newborn child did not automatically enter the family of its unquestioned begetter; the latter was obliged formally to recognize the child as his if such were his wish and was also at liberty to disown it. In a way this is the reverse of the African custom cited previously by which a man who cannot possibly be the procreator of a child rates as its parent provided he has fulfilled the traditional legal conditions of fatherhood.

Adoption, familiar enough to us, figures far more prominently among other peoples, such as the Oceanians. If a Mangarevan (Polynesia) lacked an heir, if he took a fancy to a particular youngster, possibly because it reminded him of a deceased son or daughter, or if he simply wanted to establish a friendly relationship with another family, he would ask them for one of their children. Indeed, he might do so if he had a brood of his own. The adoptive child acquired all the rights of ordinary progeny, so that a plebeian infant taken over by a patrician was thereby raised to higher rank. In Tonga it was generally an heirless person that adopted a closely related child. Thus, a woman without issue was permitted to adopt her own full brother as her son, which abrogated the otherwise strict Tongan taboo between siblings of opposite sex. Correspondingly, a Crow woman might do away with the foremost rule of avoidance in her tribe by addressing her son-in-law as "Son." In the Banks Islands (Melanesia) a man could pre-empt a newborn child by simply paying the midwife before its father had a chance to do so.[2]

Although with us the parent-child tie is uppermost in thinking of artificial relationship, elective siblings appear prominently in other cultures. In Yugoslavia the bond, sealed with blood, could embrace either two men, or two women, or a man and a woman. Medieval chronicles record these instances, which also appear in folk literature, and Emperor Basilius (died 886), a Bulgarian, is credited with such a brother. The rite consists in each party's pricking his arm or wrist, allowing the blood to mingle in a glass, and drinking the mixture. This establishes a covenant of mutual aid; the parents of one blood brother become adoptive parents of the other; and henceforth wedlock between the two families is forbidden. The custom is paralleled in Uganda, where it involves the comrades' clans as well, and in other parts of Africa.[3]

The kin and its exogamous variety, the clan, artificially exclude half one's blood relatives, but on the other hand extend the tie indefinitely on the side favored by the rule of descent, so that a tenth cousin or a clansman whose blood relationship is wholly imaginary is reckoned as related. Actually, it cannot be too strongly insisted, every people known recognize kinship on both sides, as is shown by their having special terms for maternal and paternal relatives. But, as in Albania, more relatives may be recognized on one side than on the other; also, it is in the nature of unilateral descent to ignore one side *for particular purposes*. Thus, in transmitting surnames we ourselves slight the matrilineal kindred, who nevertheless figure in sentimental and legal relations, e.g., in inheritance.

A number of peoples in India, Africa, Australia, Melanesia, and Polynesia are "bilinear," i.e., every individual belongs simultaneously to a matrilineal and to a patrilineal group. In Australia many tribes are divided into exogamous halves on both these principles, their combination producing the so-called four-section scheme. If we call the two matrilineal groups Smith and Jones, and the patrilineal groups Cole and Brown, then a particular individual must be either Smith or Jones through his mother, either Cole or Brown through his father. That is to say, he will be either Smith-Cole or Smith-Brown; either Jones-Cole or Jones-Brown. Taking one of the four possible combinations or "sections," Smith-Cole cannot marry a Smith-Brown because they are both Smiths; he cannot marry a Jones-Cole because they are both Coles; hence he can only wed a Jones-Brown, to whom he is not related through either parent.

Among the Toda of southern India every person belongs to a patrilineal clan within which property is inherited and to a matrilineal clan which exercises specific ritualistic privileges at funerals. The equivalent Yakö units of West Africa have a corresponding difference of function. Patrilineal obligations center in cultivated plots and cooperative farming, whereas livestock and currency are transmitted matrilineally. The paternal kin, moreover, is rigorously exogamous, while the maternal one is only approximately so, though unions within the kin are frowned upon.[4]

## Kinship as an Institution

In this connection "kinship" is conveniently applied to relationship by affinity as well as by consanguinity, a procedure all the more permissible because many societies require marriage with a blood relative.

Kinship is a veritable institution in most simple societies, for in Firth's apt phrase it is "the rod on which one leans throughout life," the regulator of behavior in innumerable situations. A kinsman renders services gratuitously for which an outsider receives compensation. He is a natural adviser and assistant in difficult circumstances, a companion in the chase and on the warpath. Similarly, related women cultivate their plots in company, join in domestic chores, nurse one another's infants. The relevant claims and duties are not, indeed, indiscriminately diffused among the body of kindred, who are divided into separate categories with distinctive functions. Even within each category the rights and obligations vary with the closeness of the relationship.

The importance of kinship is at once thrown into relief when the attitude toward kindred is set against that toward unrelated tribesmen. In Australia, as a matter of fact, social intercourse is possible only with a kinsman, real or fictitious; an outsider is brought into the universe of social relations by being arbitrarily adopted as, say, someone's son, which logically makes him a son of the adopter's wife, a sibling of the adopter's children, and so forth. A polite Dakota Indian always addresses a companion by a kinship term: "The surest way of gaining an entrée into a social group is to determine one's relationships promptly, and then not fail to use the proper term with each person. It helps you to 'belong' and it shows you to be a bona fide Dakota." Contrariwise, a storyteller at once labels a mythological witch as a sinister character for his audience by making her fail to respond with an appropriate kinship term when asked to enter a lodge.[5] An actual occurrence illustrates how the lines are drawn between kindred and nonkindred. A Crow family group owned a sacred arrow bundle believed to confer great benefits on the possessor. When Flat-head-woman, an outsider, sought a share in the holy objects, the chief custodian remonstrated: "Why do you want this so badly? You are not related to us, you are a different person altogether." Hillside, the objector's brother and the suppliant's friend, overcame the argument only by pleading that Flat-head-woman had been the special comrade of a deceased brother of the owners; hence he was not really a stranger.[6]

That the rural folk of Europe are similarly "clannish" has been illustrated previously. It is evident that contemporary Western civilization, however, has confined kinship within very narrow boundaries. It is only an exceedingly small circle of kindred that have claims upon us or owe us specific duties. Even our social relations with such close relatives as uncles, aunts, and first cousins hinge wholly on our *individual* feelings for them, not on their status; hence a congenial outsider may mean incomparably more to us and evoke acts of friendship denied to an unattractive kinsman. Kinship has ceased to be an institution with us—certainly in the sense in which it appears in unindustrialized societies. Accordingly, an account of our social organization dispenses with the descriptions lavished upon functions of maternal uncles and paternal aunts, wife's brothers and other in-laws which fill whole chapters in ethnographic treatises.

These functions form the principal theme of the present chapter. Since kinship itself is so differently conceived by different peoples, it is well to preface the treatment of kinship usages with a brief sketch of relationship terminologies. The object of this discussion is not to deal at all thoroughly with this technical subject, but to afford some notion of the range of ideas that have entered into the grouping of relatives by the peoples of the world.

## Relationship Terms

Relationship terms are philological, ethnographical, and sociological documents. A philologist compares our word "father" with its cognates, then traces them to a common Indo-European root; he notes shifts in meaning, as when French "cousin" denotes only a male relative while the English equivalent includes both sexes; he records special forms in address and in reference, as in "Papa" and "my father." The sociologist can utilize some but not all of such findings: a difference in vocative and nonvocative form, unless accompanied by a difference in classification of kinsfolk, leaves him cold, but he would be interested in the use of different terms for "father" by boys and girls since it suggests once more the social division of the sexes. The ethnographer, again, might profitably consider the distribution of specific aspects of kinship nomenclature in order to trace historical relations of tribes; and these in turn are sometimes of utility to a sociological study. The latter, however, has its distinctive aims.

The sociological approach presupposes that relationship terms reflect social phenomena. This does not mean that every social feature automatically has a repercussion on kinship nomenclature or that every variation in nomenclature must have a sociological "cause." Obviously, that one language formally expresses sex differences which another ignores is a linguistic phenomenon without sociological significance, witness French and English "cousin." But unless there were *some* correspondence of social traits and kinship terminology, the sociologist would leave the subject to the philologist. He would no more concern himself with it than he concerns himself with the fact that some Indians call light blue and green, dark blue and black, by a common word, respectively.

There is a strong a priori reason for assuming some correspondence of the kind mentioned. Languages do not group together wholly disparate things nor give an entirely unconnected sense to an older word. "Nacken" in German still means the back of the *neck,* not of the foot; aborigines may apply one word to light blue and green, but not to blue and red. Since kinship terms apply to social relations, a classification under one head thus presumably indicates some resemblance in social respects between the relatives designated by a joint word. It is accordingly worth while to inquire whether outstanding types of kinship nomenclature can be brought into correspondence with types of social unit or custom.

Unfortunately, a satisfactory classification of "systems of consanguinity and affinity" has not yet been achieved. The pioneer in this field, Lewis H. Morgan, recognized two main categories, "descriptive" and "classificatory." Neither term aptly describes what Morgan had in mind, but the purport of his dichotomy seems clear enough. In the "descriptive" terminologies the direct line of a person's descent and the immediate relatives of his own generation are set off from all other individuals. This holds for most European languages: the father, the mother, the children, the siblings are never confounded with more remote kinsfolk. In other words, the parent terms are never applied to uncles and aunts; nephews and nieces are not classed as one's offspring; siblings remain distinct from cousins. In the classificatory systems, of which Morgan noted two varieties, which for convenience' sake we may label the "Hawaiian" and the "Seneca," the line of cleavage between lineal and collateral, immediate and remoter kinsfolk, is partly or wholly blurred. The Hawaiian variety ignores the difference between uncles and father, aunts and mother; consistently with this, all members of one generation address those of the next lower generation as their children. But the Seneca only partly designate uncles as fathers, aunts as mothers: the father's brothers are indeed reckoned "fathers," the mother's sisters are "mothers"; the mother's brothers, however, and the father's sisters are conceived as less close relatives, the native word for them being psychologically the counterpart of our "uncle" and "aunt." Hence those members of the higher generation who are addressed as parents logically reciprocate by calling the speakers "son" or "daughter"; while the "uncles" and "aunts" respond by terms equivalent to our "nephew" and "niece."

That is to say, if A calls B (his mother's brother) "Uncle," B in turn calls A (his sister's child) his nephew; if A calls C (his father's sister) "Aunt," she addresses A (her brother's child) likewise as nephew. Inasmuch as the father's brother and the mother's sister figure as parents in the Seneca scheme, men and women thus use different terms for nephews (or nieces) as we conceive them. Evidently, this system pays attention to the sex through which an individual is connected with collateral relatives of the first ascending generation. Anthropologists have found it convenient to coin terms in accordance with these very common aboriginal discriminations. If the parent of A through whom he is related to an uncle (aunt) is of the uncle's (aunt's) sex, we speak of a "parallel uncle (aunt)"; if of opposite sex, we speak of a "cross-uncle (aunt)." The children of A's parallel uncles (or aunts) are his "parallel cousins"; they usually figure as siblings in native nomenclature. The children of "cross-uncles (aunts)" are "cross-cousins"; they commonly figure in native terminology as "cousins," i.e., under a term indicating a relationship less close than that of a sibling.

For the sake of clarity we may tabulate the cross-relationships as follows:

My mother's brother is my cross-uncle.
My father's sister is my cross-aunt.
My mother's brother's child is my cross-cousin.
My father's sister's child is my cross-cousin.

If A is my mother's brother's child, I am his (her) father's sister's child. If I am A's mother's brother's child, he (she) is my father's sister's child.

To return to Morgan's classification of kinship terminologies, he really distinguished three major types, for his two classificatory varieties are evidently very different from each other. Since Morgan's day additional data have come to light that call for revisions of his scheme. Among other things, we now know of terminologies that strictly segregate the immediate relatives, but also separate maternal from paternal uncles and aunts.

Kirchhoff and I have independently taken cognizance of this fact and propose a fourfold scheme, based primarily on the treatment of the parental generation. Following Kirchhoff's lettering for these several types we have

(A) Father, father's brother, mother's brother are distinguished from one another. Correspondingly, mother, mother's sister, father's sister are distinguished from one another.

(B) Father is distinguished from maternal and paternal uncles, who are put into one category. Mother is distinguished from maternal and paternal aunts, who are put into one category (usual European type).

(C) A single word designates father and all uncles. A single word designates mother and all aunts (Hawaiian type).

(D) There is a single word for father and father's brother, but a distinct word for mother's brother; a single word for mother and mother's sister, but a separate word for father's sister (Seneca type).

The above scheme ignores sporadic inconsistencies such as adherence to one type in a higher generation, and to another in a lower, as well as certain forms in which there is partial merging of generations. However, it serves for initial orientation.[7]

Let us now revert to our basic problem. What do our four types of nomenclature mean in sociological terms? Here we must draw a distinction. It is important to realize what social phenomenon is congruous with a type of terminology, but such congruity does not by itself prove a correlation, for it sometimes happens that some other phenomenon is equally consistent with the nomenclature. Where alternative interpretations are possible, either we must find empirical data to support one to the exclusion of the other, unless they turn out to be at bottom connected, or we must keep the matter in abeyance.

For example, Morgan interprets the Hawaiian system by the hypothesis that men at one time freely mated with their sisters as well as with other women. This alone, he argues, would explain a Hawaiian's calling his sister's children "sons" and "daughters." Unquestionably, the explanation harmonizes with the terminology: *if* sibling unions occurred, it would be natural to class a sister's children with one's own. But this congruity does not *prove* the form of marriage inferred by Morgan, for an equally consistent alternative suggests itself. Polynesia, we found, is an area in which adoption is carried to an extraordinary degree. In such circumstances a group of adults may well come to view the totality of a lower age stratum as "children." This word becomes a mere status term; hence a man may very well dub his sister's children "son" or "daughter" without any implication as to sexual congress. In a society of this sort, indeed, the terms applied may cease to bear any relation to known biological kinship. The childless Tongan woman who was permitted to become her own brother's "mother" (p. 57) is a case in point.

Again, Kirchhoff's type D, probably the most widespread among primitive peoples, is congruous with a clan organization, for with exogamy A's father could never be in the same clan as A's mother or maternal uncle, whereas the father and the paternal uncle would be clansmen; and correspondingly, the mother and the mother's sister would be of the same clan, set off from the father's sister. However, here also an alternative explanation appears. If a tribe practices both the levirate and the sororate, children would look upon their father's brother as their mother's potential husband and by anticipation might well call him "father." Correspondingly they would regard a maternal aunt as a prospective mother; indeed many peoples permit a man to marry one or more of his first wife's sisters during her lifetime, which makes them actually the children's mothers in the sense of the father's wives. Of course, levirate and sororate may coexist with a clan organization, in which case the true correlate of the nomenclature is not obvious. However that be, there are obviously more ways than one in which a grouping of kinsfolk can be interpreted in sociological terms. Additional evidence is thus required to establish that a particular classification is a function of a particular social phenomenon.

For our present purposes we shall consider only the correlation of types A and B with the family, and that of D with the clan organization. These two problems are conveniently treated together. The congruity of A and B with social organization dominated by the family unit is obvious: in both, the immediate kinsfolk are divided from all other relatives, whereas in D they are largely confounded. The question is, how far does the distribution of the logically congruous phenomena coincide in reality?

In America there are large areas with clans and likewise large areas without them, so that it is possible to make a satisfactory gross comparison. It is a striking fact that the latter—those in which the family does not enter into competition with unilateral groups—is also largely the region of types A and B. The Eskimo, the tribes of southern and interior British Columbia, the Plateau and Basin peoples, the natives of Washington, Oregon, Nevada, Utah, the northern half of California, are overwhelmingly of type A or B, and clans are conspicuously lacking throughout. South America is still imperfectly known from this point of view, but type A appears, at least sporadically, as among the clanless Yaghan (Tierra del Fuego). Type B is, of course, represented by our own and most other European systems, where it is a concomitant of the family, not of the clan.[8]

By way of contrast the major North American areas of clan systems —the United States east of the Missouri, the Southwest, and northern British Columbia—are pre-eminently associated with type D. In South America several tribes definitely known to have clans fall into the same category, e.g., the Canella and the Sherente. In the Old World the correlation roughly holds: numerous tribes in Africa, Asia, Australia, and Melanesia having clans share terminologies of type D.[9]

The force of the argument is somewhat weakened by the fact that D also occurs in clanless societies. This can be explained away on the ground that the tribes in question formerly had clans, but lost them, though retaining the old nomenclature linked with clans according to the theory. However, this is an auxiliary hypothesis that should be advanced only when there is specific evidence to support it. Hence it is better to fall back upon the joint action of the levirate and sororate, known to operate among clanless peoples, such as the Barama Carib (British Guiana). It might even be contended that when these forms of marriage accompany a clan system *they* are the significant factor for type D. However, this cannot be uniformly the case: Pueblo Indians have clans with the nomenclature, but do not permit the levirate or the sororate; and in California, where both marriage forms prevail, only 10 out of 72 tribes identify paternal uncle and father, and 57 fail to equate mother's sister and mother terms.[10]

Some weight attaches to the contention that, though there may be a fairly high empirical correlation with clans, type D primarily depends on unilateral reckoning rather than on *exogamous* kins. Since it is unilateral reckoning that assigns persons to one or another group, this argument at first seems overwhelming. Exogamy, however, is not a mere frill added to a kin, but a factor that vitally determines the alignment of individuals. This appears forthwith when we examine certain well-established cases of agamous or endogamous kins. The Arabs have endogamous patrilineal kins, and their kinship terminology emphatically does not conform to type D: the father's brother, who is at the same time the ideal father-in-law, is designated by a separate term, mother and mother's sister are discriminated. In Oceania the Polynesians commonly enough have patrilinear kins, but they are the perfect exemplars of type C, in which both matrilineal and patrilineal uncles merge into the paternal status class.[11]

Admitting, then, that unilateral reckoning by itself may influence the establishment of terminology D, we shall not lightly dismiss exogamy as negligible.

Far more satisfactory than gross attempts at correlation is the comparison of nomenclatures among linguistically or culturally related peoples that differ in some basic feature of social organization.

The clanless Tewa (New Mexico) are conspicuous among Southwestern Indians for the dearth of "classificatory" terms of relationship in their nomenclature, but the one Tewa tribe settled among the Hopi shares the Hopi clan organization and with it the Hopi variety of type D. The Hopi themselves may be compared from two different points of view—with their geographically nearest linguistic congeners of the Shoshonean (Uto-Aztecan) family, the Ute and Paiute, or with their cultural fellows of the Pueblo culture sphere. The clanless Ute and Paiute have a kinship system of type A. The Pueblo tribes are partly organized into clans, but among the Hopi the clan most powerfully affects social life generally, and it is there that terms are applied most consistently according to clan grouping. Thus, at Zuñi, too, the father's sister's son—a member of the father's clan—is classed as a father, but whereas the Hopi logically make a "son" of the kinsman who so addresses his cross-cousin, the Zuñi illogically include the mother's brother's son—not necessarily of the same clan as the father's sister's son—under the identical term. Finally may be cited a case from British Columbia. The Kwakiutl, though on the whole favoring the paternal side, have no clans, as demonstrated by their permitting marriage with a brother's daughter; their terminology is of type B. But the Northern Kwakiutl (Haisla), who do have clans, have a nomenclature of type D: the very stem which their congeners restrict to the father is extended in the north to the paternal uncle and to other paternal clansmen; the phonetic equivalent of the word for "mother" embraces the maternal sister and other clanswomen; the Southern Kwakiutl word for "aunt" is extended in the north from the father's sister to other clanswomen of his; for the generic "uncle" stem is substituted another to designate the maternal uncle and his clansmen.[12] Finally may be cited the facts from Albania and Montenegro, the only European countries that down to the present, or at least the immediate past, have preserved a clan organization. Their nomenclature, to be sure, corresponds in some respects to A rather than to D, since parents are distinguished from their siblings. But it is really of intermediate type; the Balkanese tend to combine collateral relatives of different degree and even merge cousins and brother, grandfather and great-uncle. It is surely no accident that these particular European terminologies should reveal classificatory features.

In the light of the foregoing facts we are warranted in defending a correspondence between social phenomena and the designation of relatives. It would certainly be rash to contend, as Rivers did in the first flush of enthusiasm over some of his discoveries in Oceania, that social conditions rigorously determine nomenclature, that "every detail of these systems has . . . been so determined."[13] But the reverse proposition is much farther from the truth and seems to be generally discarded nowadays. Certainly, in examining the usages associated with kinship, to which we turn next, we shall constantly discover an interrelation of terminology and structure or custom. *Nota bene* an interrelation, for the terminology undoubtedly can affect behavior as well as vice versa.

## Kinship Usages

Where kinship is an institution the observances pivoted on it are likely to be organically connected with one another. That is to say, a single usage is liable to serious misconstruction if wrested from its context. In an admirable paper Radcliffe-Brown pointed out that at least in several parts of Africa and Oceania peculiar attitudes and behavior toward the maternal uncle are balanced by equally specific attitudes and behavior toward the paternal aunt. Where care and indulgence is expected from the mother's brother and the maternal relatives generally, an individual "owes obedience and respect" to his father's sister. The maternal uncle is treated as a male mother, the paternal aunt as a female father. Pursuing similar lines of inquiry, Lévi-Strauss has recently advanced a novel idea: The relations between maternal uncle and sister's son, he argues, involve not merely two individuals, but four—

a brother and a sister, a husband and a wife, a father and a son, an uncle and nephew. Where the relationship between spouses is a tender one, Lévi-Strauss suggests, that between brother and sister is one of avoidance; where the tie between a son and his father is one of loving kindness, the maternal uncle represents stern authority; where antagonism divides father and son, the maternal uncle aids his nephew.[14]

Doubtless these particular generalizations require a broader inductive basis before they can be regarded as established, but the point of view underlying them is unquestionably sound. An isolated kinship observance can hardly be intelligible; it must be viewed in relation to others.

It is still clearer that the total cultural setting has to be taken into account. Why, for example, is it that contemporary civilization has such a dearth of relevant customs? Because treating a person according to his individuality and treating him according to relative status are antithetical, mutually exclusive ideas. In the pre-industrial era, status counted for something even in Western civilization, and accordingly there were patterns of behavior toward recognized kindred. In 1758 Samuel Johnson, then nearly fifty years old, addressed his ailing mother as "Honored Madam" and signed himself "Your dutiful son." A year later, when she was actually on her deathbed, he relaxed so far as to write "Dear Honored Mother" and to conclude with "I am, dear, dear, Mother, Your dutiful son." Contemporary Continental practice was equally formal: Lessing calls his father "Highly to be esteemed Sir Father" (*Hochzuehrender Herr Vater*), signs "Your most obedient son," and of course unwaveringly employs the formal *Sie* in place of the intimate *Du*. It is a far cry from this to the not altogether rare modern American custom of permitting children to address parents by their Christian names.

Because of space limitations it is impossible to present more than a single system of kinship usages. This will be followed by a discussion of certain specific relationships in order to indicate the range of variation as well as the rather considerable measure of parallelism in different parts of the globe. Inevitably there will be cross reference to topics more fully dealt with later; the systematic discussion of the sibling, the parent-child, and the husband-wife relationships is also reserved for a subsequent chapter. Altogether the immediate aim is to feature rather the sharply defined than the more elusive patterns of behavior.

Anthropologists have come to classify interpersonal relationships under a few psychological heads. At opposite poles are reverential avoidance and licensed familiarity, respect without avoidance being inter-mediate.[15] Although these attitudes sometimes shade into one another, they should be kept in mind as an aid in grasping the mass of pertinent detail.

THE CROW SYSTEM.—The Crow illustrate a number of widespread principles. For one thing, they exemplify the social significance of both sides of the family, irrespective of the rule of descent. Notwithstanding their matrilineal clan organization, the claims and duties of patrilineal relatives are as definite and important as those attached to the mother's kin. Broadly put, there is the sort of antithetical allotment of functions envisaged by Radcliffe-Brown and Lévi-Strauss. One's own clansfolk, i.e., one's matrilineal relatives, are expected in all circumstances to shield one, whereas discipline devolves pre-eminently on the paternal clan. This appears patently in the mutual prerogative of "joking-relatives"— persons of either sex whose *fathers* are of the same clan and who accord-ingly would be themselves clansmen *if* descent were patrilineal. The Hidatsa (North Dakota), the closest relatives of the Crow, share this custom.

To make the matter concrete, one joking-relative may play practical jokes on another or mock him in a manner that would be resented from anyone else. What is more important, he may and should publicly taunt a fellow for disgraceful behavior, thus making the culprit deeply ashamed. Against either the comical or the serious manifestations of these privileges the only redress is requital on some future occasion; any display of resentment is unthinkable. The Hidatsa tell a characteristic story. A woman was once aiding in the erection of a palisade, but proved rather slow at the job, when one of her "clan cousins" approached as a member of the police society and fired off his gun close by her legs. Looking around and identifying him as a privileged relative, she did not get angry. "Just the same she did not forget; and years after she had a good-humored revenge . . . ." Her onetime teaser, having suffered misfortune on the warpath, went out to seek a vision that should restore his good luck. As he happened to pass his former victim, she burst out in a song jeering at him. Recognizing her, he merely shouted at her to sing louder. "If she had been any one but his clan cousin [joking-relative], he would have been beside himself with anger. As it was, he kept his good humor . . . ."

Joking-relatives are patrilineal relatives, but not the father's clans-men. In contrast to the former, the latter—who are classified as "fathers" —are entitled to respect. The manner in which the Crow extend the term rests largely on two principles formulated by Radcliffe-Brown as (a) "the unity of siblings" and (b) "the unity of the lineage," the latter having a more restricted, though respectable, distribution in the world.

The levirate and the sororate may be considered projections into practice of the former principle: when a person dies, his conjugal status is assumed by a sibling of his or her sex, who is terminologically equated with the deceased. However, like many tribes, the Crow carry the extension further, to include the father's clansmen within his generation. It is merely a corollary from the foregoing to apply the term also to the husbands of the mother's sisters, as the following equations show:

> By (a)  mother's sister = mother
>   therefore: (mother's sister's) husband = mother's husband = father

In accordance with Radcliffe-Brown's principle (b), the Crow equate with the father even those of his clansmen who are in the generation above and below his. That is, the maternal lineage of males is grouped together: my father's maternal uncle becomes my "father," and so does one type of cross-cousin, viz., my father's sister's son. Correspondingly, the Crow have a single designation for the father's sister, the father's sister's daughter, the father's sister's daughter's daughter, and so on to infinity. To phrase it differently, a paternal aunt's female descendants *through females* are always "paternal aunts." On the other hand, as soon as the unilateral lineage bond is broken, the relationship changes: a father's sister's son's daughter is *not* a paternal aunt. For, to clarify once more by algebra,

> father's sister's son = father
>   therefore: (father's sister's son's) daughter = father's daughter = sister

The application of these terms, it should be noted, is not a mere matter of theory, but of daily usage. I have heard a man of sixty-five address a twenty-year-old interpreter as "father"; and was present when in reverse a boy of four called his mother's brother's daughter, two years younger, his "daughter." By way of checking I asked him in Crow, "Where is your daughter?" He at once protruded his lips in the direction of the little girl.

At this point a word of caution is indicated. Among the Crow, as in Australia and elsewhere, the principles of equivalence do not imply that no distinction whatsoever is drawn between near and more remote kinsfolk of the same category. On the contrary, such distinctions are significant. For instance, in consequence of a universal rule against incest, sex relations between a real father and his daughter are out of the question for a Crow. They are imputed only to a mythological flouter of all morality, Old Man Coyote. If the degree of kinship were irrelevant, a girl would regard all males in her father's clan as impossible mates for her. But the Indians discriminate in this matter, and there is some difference of opinion. The union of a woman with any "father" is certainly not desirable, but unless there is a close blood relationship the transgression is venial. The puritans of the community are scandalized, and joking-relatives have their fun at the expense of the culprits; but the people at large are not so fussy. In short, individual variability is permitted some leeway.

Further, equivalence does not mean that despite common sense a "father" four years of age is in all ways equated with a man of fifty. Nevertheless, in a variety of situations "fathers" do fall into the same category. They merit respect; they, as well as their sisters, are pre-eminently the persons whom a well-bred Crow periodically feasts and whom he would formerly present with some of the loot captured on the warpath. In return they pray on his behalf and act as his publicity agents if he has achieved some creditable deed, such as shooting his first deer or covering himself with glory on a raid.

The tie between a person and his patrilineal kindred appears also in the bestowal of names. An honorific appellation is often derived from a father's clansman, and the nickname an individual bears may reflect not his own but a "father's" or a "paternal aunt's" peculiarities.

Principle (a) makes all parallel cousins into siblings, since they are the offspring of men or women equated with the speaker's father or mother. Of the cross-cousins, the father's sister's children have been discussed; since they are raised one generation by principle (b), the mother's brother's children are automatically lowered one: addressing the paternal aunt's son as father, they are logically his "children."

Principle (b) once more operates in telescoping three generations of matrilineal males—the elder brother, the mother's brother, and the mother's mother's brother. Like most aborigines, the Crow distinguish between elder and younger siblings—a point never satisfactorily explained; and the males of higher generations than the speaker are naturally his seniors. The failure to have a special "uncle" term characteristically goes with a lack of avuncular function as such. The mother's brother is simply one of the "elder brothers," all of whom owe their juniors aid and protection. In general, siblings of either sex have a strong sense of solidarity, but this sentiment is coupled with a taboo between brother and sister. After puberty these two must not chat nor be together alone, so that a man visiting his brother-in-law would at once withdraw if he found his sister by herself. This restraint does not lessen mutual helpfulness. A sister makes moccasins for her brother and watches over his wife's moral behavior. Since a man had the right to marry two or more sisters, real or terminological, the wives of a polygynous household often stood to one another in this relationship and helped one another accordingly.

Here we once more meet with a correspondence of nomenclature and custom. A Crow calls his wife's sister, so long as she is not married to another man, by the several terms he applies to his wife; and a woman may apply the same word to her own and her sister's husband.

Affinal relatives are treated in part with extreme license, in part with the utmost restraint. A Crow has the right to romp freely with his brother's or clansman's wife and similarly teases his wife's unmarried sister, raising her dress to expose her nakedness, and so forth; she may retaliate in kind. But, oddly enough, two brothers-in-law are very circumspect in each other's presence. They are, indeed, friendly and exchange gifts, but no obscenity is allowable in each other's presence. A man immediately breaks off a ribald remark if he sees his brother-in-law approaching.

In harmony with the peculiarities of Crow nomenclature a wife's maternal uncle is treated as if he were her brother. On the other hand, here again the difference in degree is considered. It is the closest "brothers-in-law" that demand the maximum of respect; with a man who has merely married one's clanswoman, light jesting, say about his war record, is permissible.

A man is obliged to avoid the wife of his wife's brother.

A woman and her parents-in-law are under no restrictions whatsoever. She treats them and addresses them as if they were her own parents. On the other hand, the strictest taboo holds between a man and his wife's mother and grandmothers. They neither speak to each other nor look at each other. By principle (a) the rule extends to the young man's brothers, but apparently not to his remote clansmen. Further, he must never utter his mother-in-law's name, being obliged to paraphrase even any common word that forms part of it. A man's father-in-law is theoretically included among affinities to be avoided, but this rule has been much less strictly observed. On the other hand, the more conservative tribesmen maintained avoidance of their mothers-in-law at least as late as 1931. It is important to note that the in-law taboos are never an expression of hostility, but invariably betoken to the Crow the acme of reverence. Avoidance is here merely an extreme variant of a respect relationship.[16]

We shall now consider several of the crystallized behavior patterns between relatives by consanguinity and affinity.

AVUNCULAR RELATIONS.—In a large number of societies the mother's brother bears an altogether distinctive relation to his nephews and nieces. The word "avunculate" (Latin *avunculus,* mother's brother) has been used for relevant customs, but it is best restricted to those cases in which the maternal uncle is a person of authority, often arrogating (according to our standards) powers belonging to the father, where he disposes of his nieces in marriage and transmits property and office to his uterine nephew (sister's son) rather than to his own son. A typical example appears among the matrilineal peoples of British Columbia, such as the Haida and the Tsimshian. A Haida boy does chores for his uncle and when about ten years of age goes to live with him, being thereafter trained and disciplined by his host, who protects his charge, and indemnifies those who have suffered from the nephew's acts. After his death, the younger brothers of the uncle would inherit his possessions; but if there are none, the eldest sister's eldest son claims his deceased uncle's house, chattels, privileges, and widow. A maternal uncle and his niece are restrained in mutual intercourse during the period between her puberty and marriage; in exceptional circumstances she may succeed to his position.

Among the Hopi the mother's brother is vested with disciplinary functions, which parents rarely exercise, and in general he takes care of his sister's children. His advice is essential as regards the choice of a girl's future husband, and he helps prepare the wedding garments. From among his nephews he chooses one as his successor in ceremonial office and teaches him the requisite sacred knowledge.

Tropical South America provides various samples. Among the extinct coastal Tupi (Brazil) a man was entitled to marry his sister's daughter, an arrangement that absolved him from normal removal to the village of the parents-in-law since his wife and he were natives of the same village. Such unions are impossible among the Canella because of their exogamous matrilineal moieties, but here also the maternal uncle is of overshadowing importance. Though he cannot wed his niece, he has authority to forbid her to marry, a matter in which her father has absolutely nothing to say; the uncle may also keep a girl from joining a men's organization as an auxiliary. Constantly going in and out of his sister's house, he exerts a great deal of influence over the children there and enjoys more prestige than her husband. He formally transfers his names to his nephews, thereby entitling them to membership in certain organizations that play a dominant part in Canella life. It is the duty of the maternal uncle to demand an indemnity for the premarital defloration of a niece; and upon him devolve a variety of ceremonial functions, such as killing a deer when his nephew's ears are ritualistically perforated. Uncle and nephew, moreover, are obvious companions on a raid.

The foregoing exemplify the avunculate proper, characterized by exceptional authority on the maternal uncle's part. None of these instances, however, represents the facts in true perspective, for which supplementary data are indispensable.

To begin with the Haida, the distinctive position of the maternal uncle is in a measure balanced by the special functions of the paternal aunt. Wherever these are pronounced we are justified in speaking of an "amitate" (Latin *amita,* father's sister) as a counterpart to the avunculate. The paternal aunt of a Haida appears in every critical phase of life, fulfilling some obligation, but also receiving compensation therefor. Thus, when a girl comes of age, this aunt cares for her, and at a youth's wedding she conducts the bride to him. Her daughter, designated by the same term, as in Crow nomenclature, is a man's ideal mate. The nephew must protect his aunt, and she has the right to demand from him any possession that takes her fancy.

Among the Hopi, the father's sister also stands out prominently in her niece's ceremonial career, names a newborn child, and is especially affectionate toward her brother's son. Here, however, the relationship with the nephew involves licensed familiarity: both the aunt and the daughter terminologically identified with her are expected to bandy obscenities with the nephew.

Finally, the paternal aunt figures significantly, if less conspicuously than the maternal uncle, in Canella society. A little girl spends much time at her aunt's, and the sentimental tie between the two is likely to grow stronger than that between a nephew and uncle. The all-important transfer of names to the younger generation hinges on the aunt no less than on the uncle, for unless a man has a daughter on whom his sister can confer her own names the aunt will not permit her brother to pass on his names to her son.[17]

For a complete understanding of each of the preceding phenomena much fuller data would be required, but enough has been given to support Radcliffe-Brown's and Lévi-Strauss's contention that kinship usages are intelligible only in their context.

The avunculate is only a one-sidedly exaggerated form of avuncular usages. A rather different phenomenon presents itself where a matrilateral cross-cousin is preferred as a man's wife. Here the maternal uncle assumes the special role of a potential or actual father-in-law. Among the patrilineal Murngin this implies that elders point out even to a young boy his mother's brother and that he is expected on occasion to offer his uncle valuable presents. There is a strong bond between the two males; they freely use each other's property and help each other in a fight. The older man teaches what he knows of fighting, hunting, and magic to his nephew. In this tribe all the emphasis is on the uncle's tie with his nephew, whereas that with the niece is negligible. But even the former relationship is not exactly what we find among the matrilineal Haida: the uncle is not an autocrat nor the nephew a submissive heir-to-be. The younger man claims his uncle's daughter as his just due and, if necessary, fights for her possession.

Where cross-cousin marriage is not favored, these attitudes naturally drop out and a different pattern may evolve. In Tikopia, a Polynesian enclave in a Melanesian area, the matrilineal group, above all represented by the uncle, stands for protection and active aid, while the patrilineal kindred supply material provisions, with the father's sister figuring as a sacred person suggestive of an amitate.

The virtual reverse of the avunculate turns up in Tonga, where a sister ranks her brother in the family circle, and her children may freely appropriate his property. "The institution ... is a one-sided, non-reciprocal affair. The victims never have a chance to retaliate, but they exercise similar privilege towards their own mother's brother and his offspring." Radcliffe-Brown, followed by Gifford, plausibly suggests that here cross-cousin marriage may be an outgrowth of nepotic prerogatives: an uncle cannot well refuse a nephew's request for anything, hence must yield his daughter to him. Strikingly similar attitudes are reported from South Africa.

Two American Plains tribes, the Cheyenne (Montana) and the Arapaho (Wyoming), display customs reminiscent of some of the foregoing without quite paralleling them. Here the maternal uncle shows deep affection for his sister's children and has recognized duties toward them without disciplinary powers. There is also a mild reciprocal joking-relationship, and a nephew may take his uncle's property, but not without making an equivalent return.[18]

We should not forget that among a fair number of primitive peoples no peculiar functions attach to the maternal uncle.

The avunculate proper has played a notable part in anthropological theory. That a man should have greater authority over his nephews and nieces than their father or than he himself has over his own children was correctly taken as congruous with a matrilineal system that stresses kinship on the mother's side. However, it turned out that the same authority over nephews likewise occurred in tribes without matrilineal descent. In these cases, it was argued, we are confronted by a survival: the society observed might not be matrilineal now, but it must once have been so, because allegedly nothing else could account for the avuncular taking precedence over the paternal status.

This argument is unconvincing because alternative interpretations do suggest themselves. As indicated above, the usages revolving about the mother's brother are commonly offset by others connected with, say, the father's sister; and where the amitate (or any other authoritarian status) occurs, it is arbitrary to single out avuncular prestige as *the* significant phenomenon. We might just as well argue that a matrilineal people, like the Crow, among whom patrilineal kindred regularly receive gifts, must have passed through an earlier stage of patrilineal descent. Another alternative explanation is that the crucial connection of the avunculate may be not with matrilineal descent, but with matri-local residence, which often accompanies it. On this assumption the uncle's prestige would rest on his being at home in the household or community in which his nephews and nieces are raised, whereas their father is an outsider. In such tribes as the Hopi and the Canella, a man even when married keeps up constant contacts with his original home, so that he continues to associate with his sisters' children. Finally, there is the conventional ranking of family members according to sex. The Tongans, though organized into agamous patrilineal lineages, always regard a sister as superior to her brother, whence the supremacy of the paternal aunt, who "often controls the matrimonial destinies of her brother's children"—a typical example of the amitate. But the equally patrilineal Vandau (Portuguese Southeast Africa) have the reverse conception: as soon as a girl marries, her rank drops a step below her brother's. Since the position of spouses is equal, the married woman's husband is likewise inferior to his wife's brother, who thus becomes the head of the family. Thus "the avunculate may develop without any trace of maternal succession." [19]

GRANDPARENTS.—In addition to the expectable attitudes between grandparents and grandchildren, the literature sporadically reveals a marked joking-relationship. Two examples from different parts of the globe must suffice.

In the Upper Volta province of West Africa a grandfather will jestingly chide his grandson: "You don't work, you prefer to take a rest, you don't cultivate millet and give me some, I'm going to die of hunger." The child will reply, "You've been eating to glut yourself. Die! Long ago you were eating millet cake. Die, let us eat food, the rest of us." Either grandparent or any person falling into the classificatory category exchanges jests with his actual or terminological grandchildren about marriage. A man will say to a little girl: "You naughty one, I won't marry you." The granddaughter comes back with, "You are not buying clothes to offer me, I spurn you." An old woman has corresponding dialogues with her grandson.

Among the Hopi, insight into relevant usage is somewhat complicated by the fact that the native word *ikwa'á* means not only grandfather, but also father's sister's husband. In at least one village all the persons in the category are included in the practice; in two other villages, only the father's sisters' husbands. Restriction to the latter may represent the older custom, for it seems to follow from the peculiar relations between nephew and paternal aunt in this tribe, which might easily involve at least feigned hostility between the aunt's husband and her nephews. Local differentiation is intelligible: some Hopi may be supposed to adhere to the hypothetically ancient definition of the joking-relationship; others may have come to extend the custom from the father's sister's husband to the persons called by the same name. Why two such different relatives are grouped together is not hard to understand if we remember that in Hopiland

father's sister's son = father, whence
(father's sister's son's) father = father's father

As for the practices themselves, an *ikwa'á* will make a little boy cry by threatening to pour water on him or will make children roll in the snow "in order to make them strong." When the boys grow up, they get even for these indignities and retaliate in kind. A lad may taunt his aunt's husband by telling her that she is married to a worthless man while he, the nephew, could satisfy all her needs. The older man scoffs at the youth's laziness and cowardice, his wife invariably taking the boy's part. As in most joking-relationships, the partners are not expected to take umbrage.[20]

PARALLEL COUSINS.—As explained previously, parallel cousins are commonly equated with siblings, and in a sense the attitudes are similar in both cases. Thus, a female parallel cousin of the first wife is likely to be married by the husband where sororal polygyny is in vogue, and a deceased man's male parallel cousin may inherit the widow. However, as usual in classificatory extensions of kinship, the intensity of obligations and the rights lessens with the remoteness of the relationship. Further, as between the two kinds of parallel cousin—father's brother's child and mother's sister's child—everything hinges on the living conditions. That is, notwithstanding the theoretical equality of all parallel cousins, social arrangements may make some of them far closer than others. This is well illustrated by such exogamous matrilineal and matrilocal peoples as the Hopi and the Western Apache. Here the children of a mother's sister are fellow clansfolk, which the children of a father's brother need not be. Further, until the males grow up and go to their wives' families, the matrilateral cousins of both sexes will remain united, which would not hold for the sons and daughters of the paternal uncle, who are brought up in another home and possibly even in another village or camp. Hence the bond is closer in the former case. Again, in the Upper Volta province, parallel cousins are marriageable, though addressed by sibling terms. To be sure, cross-cousins seem to be preferred.

Such instances suggest that the principle of equivalence must not be mechanically applied.[21]

CROSS-COUSINS.—The fact that status by terminology is not the only factor that regulates behavior is further borne out by the data on cross-cousins from several areas. The Murngin, who prescribe cross-cousin marriage, definitely try to marry the actual maternal uncle's daughter and, if such is unavailable, substitute the nearest possible equivalent. Among various Shoshonean bands in Idaho, a man's physiological offspring and his stepchildren were called by the same terms, but a person was not allowed to wed his true cross-cousins, whereas marriage with the maternal uncle's stepdaughter, the stepmother's brother's daughter, or the paternal aunt's stepdaughter, was orthodox.

But it would be a grave mistake to suppose that the terminology fails to affect behavior, though it evidently does not do so with equal effectiveness everywhere. The Hidatsa class a man's maternal uncle's daughter with his own daughter. An old woman of this tribe was scandalized by the question whether her son might marry her brother's daughter. "The idea of a man's marrying his 'daughter'! It would be the same as though he were marrying his own child. She [the informant] had never heard of such a case. People would regard such a married couple as dogs." It is also worth noting that where parallel and cross-cousins are not distinguished in speech there is a tendency for differential behavior toward them to be absent. The Cheyenne and Arapaho, for instance, forbid all cousin marriage. Similarly in Tikopia cross-cousin marriage arouses as much disgust as that with parallel cousins.

The Navaho consider true cross-cousins as the persons whom one teases and bombards with obscene comments. In Lau (Fiji) the cross-cousins of opposite sex indulge in similar ribaldry. Among the Sho-shoneans of Idaho such freedom obtains between a person and the stepchildren of his cross-uncle and cross-aunt, irrespective of sex. A man may hide such a "pseudo cross-cousin's" clothes or accuse him of cowardice or jest about sexual matters. The Western Apache also dis-criminate between close and remote cross-cousins, for many feel that near blood relatives should not joke with one another, whereas distant cross-cousins are precisely the people to do so.[22]

TWO BROTHERS-IN-LAW.—Since marriage is generally conceived as an alliance between two families, a husband and his wife's brother as rep-resentatives of their respective groups are commonly close friends who aid each other in every way, as among the Murngin and the Hidatsa. However, this basic relationship is consistent with rather divergent behavior in detail. Crow brothers-in-law, we noted, must be circum-spect in each other's presence. On the other hand, among the Cheyenne these affinal kindred are definitely expected to play tricks on each other in public, to indulge in crude jests, and to employ mutually vituperative language. Again, an Hidatsa jestingly calls his wife's brother "Wife" and is called "Husband" in response; and on the battlefield the "hus-band" is supposed to rescue and, if need be, die in defense of his "wife." Wholly one-sided economic arrangements occur in the Trobriand Islands, where a man is expected to fill his sister's husband's storehouses with yams. In matrilocal tribes of coastal Brazil the husband was in the position of a servant toward his affinal kindred generally and might curry favor by capturing an enemy and turning him over to his brothers-in-law, who would thus gain glory by killing the captive.[23]

BROTHER-IN-LAW AND SISTER-IN-LAW.—The most curious phenomenon under this head is the extreme license, already noted for the Crow, granted to these connections by marriage. A Hidatsa man makes fun of his sister-in-law and vice versa. An Arapaho woman "may pour water on her brother-in-law while he is asleep, or tease him otherwise, and he retaliates in similar ways." Among the Blackfoot this type of conduct attains a maximum: here a man and his wife's sisters "are expected on meeting, to engage in bold and obscene jests concerning sexual matters. This is often carried to a degree beyond belief . . . . As practically all other relatives by marriage are forbidden the least reference to such subjects, the force of the exception is greatly magnified." In the Upper Volta country, the Lobi refrain from such practices, but their neighbors, the Dian, have brother-in-law and sister-in-law indulge in mutual insults and buffoonery. The man will say, "You're no good as a cook, if you keep on this way, I won't court you." The woman replies, "If I'd known that you were poor, I should not have married you. If you won't give me clothing, I'll leave you and marry a rich man."[24]

PARENTS-IN-LAW AND CHILDREN-IN-LAW.—There are four distinct relationships that fall under this head, but very rarely does any society consider all of them on a par. The conditions of living often render such lack of discrimination impossible. As Steward generalizes about all kinship behavior: "In order that obligations to a relative shall have significance, there must be assurance that one will see him sufficiently often and under sufficiently well-defined circumstances." To apply this to the present topic, wherever matrilocal residence implies a man's settling in a different village, not merely in a new household, his wife's chances of meeting his family are obviously greatly reduced and not to be compared with his own opportunities to rub elbows with *her* parents. This matter of residence is the one that forcibly impressed Tylor in his correlational study of the subject (p. 38 f.). Apart from this factor, the most important influence on the usages in question is probably difference in sex: affinities of adjacent generations and opposite sex seem to be more commonly limited in their social intercourse than persons of the same sex.

A good sample of pertinent behavior patterns is reported from Tierra del Fuego. It is improper for a Yaghan man or woman to speak to both his (her) parents-in-law, to look at them, or to take a seat by their side. If they are encountered outdoors, the child-in-law makes a detour to avoid the parent-in-law. In an assembly of men an otherwise loquacious native holds his tongue while his father-in-law is talking, and a daughter-in-law will show like deference and reserve toward her mother-in-law. Between the two women the austerity of the etiquette is slightly relaxed about a year after the marriage, though unconstrained speech remains impossible; for the men the taboo remains absolute as long as they live. If a man sees his wife's father approaching, he bids his wife go through the form of inviting him to their home, but the old man answers, "Many thanks, but I want to erect my own hut." This is done with the daughter's aid in order to preclude embarrassment. When the dwelling is finished, the daughter goes home and loudly announces, "I have invited your father-in-law, but he prefers to live in his own hut. He thanks you!" Now her husband shouts in reply so as to be heard by the old man: "I am very sorry that my father-in-law is not coming to my hut!" Thereafter the daughter repeatedly calls on her parent, while her husband appears there only once or twice and inquires of his wife concerning her father's needs. In order to tell his parents-in-law what they might wish to know the son-in-law loudly sets forth his recent experiences and other news, but without addressing anyone in particular. The parent-in-law acts likewise. If the two should be together without an intermediary, any requests must be voiced in the form of a soliloquy. Thus, the old man may say to himself, "Why, I've left my knife on the beach!" Or, "This morning I killed a sea-lion, it's a big animal. I'm an old man and was unable to drag it to the canoe; I let it lie on yonder rock." The son-in-law at once understands and executes the order, for he owes a parent-in-law even greater deference than to his own father and mother. The relevant attitudes are well reflected in two Yaghan traditions. One story tells of a man housing his widowed father-in-law and vainly trying to give his guest the food he craves. After many trials and when almost in despair he hits upon the bast fibres of an antarctic beech, which, oddly enough, satisfy the old man's palate. In another tale an irreverent son-in-law is magically punished by his father-in-law.

Here the striking fact, in view of the data from other regions, is that the avoidance seems most marked between son-in-law and father-in-law, while no concrete evidence is presented concerning the attitudes of in-laws of opposite sex. This is certainly less usual than the reverse phenomenon, which appears with various shadings. Sometimes, as in Australia, the only taboo stressed is that between a woman and her daughter's husband; sometimes, as in various parts of Siberia, prominence attaches to the reverse bashfulness of a woman toward her husband's father and elder brothers, though sometimes his female kindred are included. A Yakut daughter-in-law "must not show herself or uncover her body before the elder male relatives of her husband, particularly her father-in-law." A Kazak woman is even obliged to paraphrase such common words as "lamb" or "water" if they happen to form part of the name of these affinities. But there are other possibilities. Both forms of avoidance may be found together and in equal force. "No man was allowed to talk directly to his mother-in-law," Radin reports of the Winnebago (Wisconsin), "or to look at her, and the same rule held with regard to the attitude of a woman toward her father-in-law." Again, the Zulu have both forms, but the taboo is less strict for a man and his mother-in-law than for a woman and her husband's kindred, his mother and her fellow wives being included in the restrictions. Still another phenomenon is avoidance of both parents-in-law by the same person but in unequal degree. Thus, a Crow or a Hidatsa was not absolutely prohibited from intercourse with his father-in-law.

In order to illustrate the pertinent attitudes a few additional concrete examples from different regions seem desirable. During the first years of wedlock a Canella always uses his wife as an intermediary in communication with both her parents. After some time, particularly after the birth of a child, father-in-law and son-in-law begin to talk in fairly natural fashion, subsequently the mother-in-law also addresses the young man "though a certain reserve is maintained inasmuch as they avoid meeting or addressing each other when by themselves. In case of a chance encounter the son-in-law gives the woman a wide berth." To turn to Australia, the son-in-law and mother-in-law taboo appears to be universal. A Murngin and his wife's mother neither converse nor look at each other, any unwitting breach—a deliberate one is unthinkable—being supposedly punished by a sore or a swelling in the groin. The Lango (East Africa) carry the idea to such an extreme that a man wishing to pass through his mother-in-law's village sends a message ahead enabling her to keep hidden during his visit. If she has to approach his village, she is carried on a litter, whose bearers cover her with a hide on approaching, thus giving her son-in-law a chance to depart. A man who discovered that his wife had not informed him of an invitation to her mother soundly thrashed her and was upheld in this by her kindred even though no harm had been done, the two in-laws not having actually met. Equally extraordinary is the rigorous practice of the Semang (Malay Peninsula), who extend the rule against speech and contact to both parents-in-law and the children-in-law of opposite sex, believing that transgression would bring on a fatal affliction of the kidneys. In visiting Father Schebesta, one of his informants always went far out of his way so as not to approach the dwelling of his son's wife.

If the grandparents wished to see their grandchild, its father had to bring it over; under no circumstances would its mother dare enter a hut where she might meet her husband's father. Schebesta once asked a native, "What would you do if your mother-in-law fell into the water? Would you rescue her?" The reply was, "By no means, I'd have to let her drown, for I am not allowed to touch her." Similarly, in Ceylon the Seligmans knew a Vedda who would not assist an aged woman with an acutely inflamed knee to get up from the ground because any physical contact with a mother-in-law was out of the question. A man might eat food prepared by his wife's mother, but would accept it only if handed to him by a go-between. The same rules held for a man and his daughter-in-law.

The tenacity of these taboos is amazing. In 1907 I observed my Crow interpreter questioning his mother-in-law through his wife, who had to repeat every query and answer though her mother was seated in the same tent and able to hear every word. In 1931 a conservative middle-aged Crow still would not use the common Crow word for "mark" because it formed part of his mother-in-law's name. In 1925 Dr. Reichard had similar experiences among the Navaho: men absented themselves for meals and other gatherings in order to avoid meeting their mothers-in-law.

Tylor shrewdly noted that some matrilocal peoples abolished the taboo after the birth of a child since this fact established a common bond between the outsider and his hosts, giving him a new status. On the other hand, it is odd that elsewhere such deep-rooted customs can be abrogated by a purely conventional procedure. If an Hidatsa warrior went on a war party, returned with a scalp, and presented it to his mother-in-law, a parent-child relationship became optional between them. With other tribes, such as the Winnebago, no mitigation of the rule was possible; the Murngin allowed conversation with a very old mother-in-law, but only in a most formal manner.

All the available evidence converges toward one psychological conclusion: parent-in-law avoidance must not be interpreted in the spirit of our mother-in-law jokes; it is always and everywhere a token of respect, not of animosity. Among the Hidatsa, where presentation of a scalp made it possible to do away with the taboo, some would not avail themselves of the chance. Buffalo-bird-woman's husband had brought her mother two scalps, but "he honored her too much" to speak to her. One Hidatsa had married a woman from the Arikara tribe, which lacks the custom under discussion. "On one occasion her mother spoke to Joe in the presence of some of his Hidatsa friends, who were very much shocked and said, 'What's the matter with your mother-in-law, Joe? She does not seem to have any respect for you at all!' " [25]

## General Considerations

Kinship usages are among the most baffling as well as most fascinating social phenomena. For one thing, their distribution raises insoluble problems. Peoples utterly unrelated and separated by thousands of miles have customs that are not merely similar but identical in detail. For example, the Kazak of Turkestan and the Crow in Montana both have the notion that the name of a tabooed person must not be uttered and any words forming part of it must be paraphrased. On the other hand, tribes of the same stock or of the same area often differ fundamentally.

To take the avoidance customs, the son-in-law taboo flourishes among the Navaho, but is wholly lacking among the neighboring Hopi and Zuñi. The Lemhi Shoshone in central Idaho regard a man as crazy if he talks to his wife's mother; other Basin Shoshoneans have never heard of such a thing. The taboo is intense in the southeastern United States and the Plains, but lacking in various southwestern tribes, in most of the Great Basin, in Washington, Oregon, and British Columbia except in the extreme north. In California there is a virtually continuous block of tribes practicing the custom, while in the northwest and south it is absent.

The distribution of the phenomena suggests diffusion, but this cannot explain the ultimate origin of anything. For instance, the only Shoshonean group within California which practices the taboo is one directly adjoining the solid area of its occurrence. It is not difficult to understand how the custom could spread. This would be favored by two circumstances. For one thing, the minuteness of many primitive groups implies that a few resolute spirits can easily impose an innovation. Second, we have seen how intensely those accustomed to avoidance feel on the subject. A few intermarriages with a group in which free relations between in-laws is felt as the acme of indecency could thus bring about the adoption of a taboo hitherto unknown.

As to privileged license, the distribution is equally enigmatic. Why do the Lobi never chaff their sisters-in-law when their Dian neighbors constantly do so? Why, in general, are the joking-relatives so differently defined by tribes closely related in origin or culture? Among several Southern Siouan tribes a man might joke with his maternal uncles, but the Kansas forbade this. Further, in all this enormous linguistic family the Crow-Hidatsa alone vest in children of the father's clansmen the privilege of jesting and connect it with a serious censorship.

It follows that any *generic* psychological or psychoanalytic interpretation must be rejected as shoddy. As Reichard suggests, we must eschew "blanket explanations." This does not mean that all psychological interpretations are to be ruled out on principle, but that they can be taken seriously only if they take cognizance of the observed facts and account for negative as well as positive cases.

Concerning several theories that have been broached, it is clear that none of them covers the total range of phenomena. I once suggested that familiarity went with sexual license, i.e., one jests with persons with whom there is at least potentially sexual intercourse. This seems reasonable so long as one envisages the privileges of men with their sisters-in-law in various societies, but evidently this is not the whole story. The Winnebago, the Iowa, the Ponca include a man's uncles among the butts of jocularity; and the Navaho forbid mating of cross-cousins, who are pre-eminently those privileged to be familiar.

The descriptive accounts certainly leave an impression that avoidance is usually between persons of opposite sex, or at least is more intense with them. Yet there are such glaring exceptions as the Yaghan emphasis on the taboo between fathers- and sons-in-law. Again, there is plausibility to the closely related idea that rules of avoidance aim at barring congress with prohibited relations, and illustrations can be found without difficulty. But then the question arises, why do some societies that are not less eager to prevent incest fail to protect themselves in this fashion? Thus, the Sanpoil (northeastern Washington) frown on unions between any blood kindred, punishing even cousins "three generations removed" for transgression, but prophylactic taboos are wanting.

Finally, there is Tylor's hypothesis (p. 38) that the taboos obtain between a family and the newcomer who enters the fold by marriage. In other words, matrilocalism goes with son-in-law avoidance, patrilocalism with daughter-in-law avoidance. Favorable cases could be adduced beyond those cited by Tylor, but there are formidable contrary instances. The unequivocally matrilocal Hopi and Zuñi have no relevant rule; the patrilocal Australians have the son-in-law, not the daughter-in-law taboo. Then there is the coexistence of both rules. Tylor suggested that it occurred where matrimony was initially matrilocal and subsequently patrilocal, but it is not clear that this holds generally. Further, the hypothesis fails to explain the frequent emphasis on avoidance by individuals of opposite sex.

However, the entire problem of kinship usages calls not for sterile negativism, but merely for active skepticism. Nearly everything remains to be done in this field, but three lines of inquiry will prove profitable. With Boas, Radcliffe-Brown, and Lévi-Strauss we must study cultures as units. It can lead only to confusion if the avunculate is singled out without attention to a coexisting amitate, or if avoidance of the mother-in-law is stressed when the taboo is equally strong for a woman and her father-in-law, or for a man and his wife's father. But Tylor's "cross-cultural" approach remains valid. Whatever may be the explanation, the amazing parallels between the cultures of distant peoples cannot be ignored, and with proper caution we are right in seeking possible correlates. Finally, as in other departments of the subject, this quest should be supplemented by intensive comparison of peoples that are regionally close to each other or are known to be offshoots of the same stock. Doubtless even this triple attack will leave many questions unsolved, but it will just as surely yield a solution of some of the pertinent problems.[26]

# Chapter 5

# MARRIAGE

## *Definition*

**M**ARRIAGE and family are complementary concepts: marriage is an institution; family, the association that embodies the institution. Both are rooted in sex, but cannot be understood merely from the point of view of sexual relations. The latter are a matter of sheer biology; marriage and family are the cultural superstructure upon a biological foundation.

For this reason the admirable researches of Yerkes, Carpenter, and others about the sex life of the anthropoid apes do not directly help us. Invaluable for the student of primate behavior, they cannot, in the nature of the case, come to grips with *our* problems. The sociologist has to cope with the fact that every known society discriminates among forms of sexual intercourse. Biologically, rape, incestuous unions, fornication, concubinage, companionate, civil, and ecclesiastical marriage are not distinguishable; sociologically, the several forms of mating are outlawed, reprobated, condoned, accepted, or definitely approved. The forms enjoying the highest approbation constitute "marriage" in a given society. The sociologist's concern is to describe the types of marriage all over the world, to collate them with coexisting forms of less orthodox sex relations, and to offer such interpretations as he can of the observed phenomena.

A chasm, then, yawns between man's sex life and that of the gorilla or the chimpanzee. The question is not at all whether the gorilla may turn out to be monogamous or polygynous; the question is whether gorilla society countenances, punishes, or otherwise judges the sexual activities of its members. The term "promiscuity" is popularly applied to loose cohabitation. Such usage is not profitable, for there are various words of common parlance to cover the phenomenon. On the other hand, we require a word for a condition in which *all* restrictions are dispensed with, or rather, in which no restrictions are envisaged, and for this "promiscuous" seems the ideal designation. A gorilla might actually parallel the behavior of a Victorian gentlewoman, yet would be promiscuous in so far as his society had failed to evolve standards for assessing his conduct. Applying the term in this sense, we can state positively that, if evolution occurred, man must have begun as a promiscuous being, since norms could only develop with the rise of culture. How far back we should have to go to find a stage of promiscuity is a matter for conjecture; I should guess it to antedate fully human status. Certainly no recent group known has even approximated such a condition.

## Premarital Relations

Western civilization has generally permitted men to temper the theory of monogamous marriage with extramarital relationships. Brides were expected to be virgins; before the machine age they were married off at an early age, so that as a rule their sex life presented no serious problem. Men were for the most part economically unable to support a family long after they had reached physiological puberty. Accordingly, society condoned a variety of arrangements. European peasants might mate unwedded, their union being sometimes sanctified by the Church years after the birth of children. Southern gentlemen in the United States had access to Negro slaves; well-to-do town dwellers kept mistresses; men of moderate means carried on intrigues with married women or servants, established Bohemian households with their sweethearts, or patronized houses of prostitution.

This system of "the double standard" was accepted as a necessary sop to masculine depravity and defended by the most pious of men. In 1768 Dr. Samuel Johnson, a pillar of the Anglican Church, thus expressed himself to Boswell about adultery: "Confusion of progeny constitutes the essence of the crime; and therefore a woman who breaks her marriage vows is much more criminal than a man who does it. A man, to be sure, is criminal in the sight of God; but he does not do his wife a very material injury, if he does not insult her; if, for instance, from mere wantonness of appetite, he steals privately to her chambermaid. Sir, a wife ought not greatly to resent this. I would not receive home a daughter who had run away from her husband on that account. A wife should study to reclaim her husband by more attention to please him. Sir, a man will not, once in a hundred instances, leave his wife and go to a harlot, if his wife has not been negligent of pleasing." Boswell asked whether it was not hard that "one deviation from chastity should so absolutely ruin a young woman." Johnson replied: "Why, no, Sir, it is the great principle which she is taught  When she has given up that principle, she has given up every notion of female honor and virtue, which are all included in chastity."

In practice such rigor could not be uniformly applied. Exceptions were inevitably made in favor of the great. Even the immaculately pure-minded Austrian empress Maria Theresa, overcoming her scruples, would write polite letters to the French king's mistress in order to gain her consent to a matrimonial alliance of the two dynasties. A century or so later, even puritanical England extended broad-mindedness to lesser circles. George Eliot was living in sin with George Henry Lewes, who was prevented from divorcing his wife by the technicalities of contemporary British law; yet responsible opinion did not regard her as a strumpet—though Queen Victoria doubtless would not have received her.

Since then tolerance has extended its sway very far in the Western world, though with noteworthy national, class, and regional differences. Modern Greece, for one, clings to the traditional ideal of feminine purity, which even immigrants to our country try to preserve. A Greek-American soldier in an Army Specialized Training Programme class admitted that he had never been able to date a girl from a family of his own ethnic group. Undoubtedly certain circles of old American stock maintain earlier norms, but everyday experience and trustworthy inquiries published in recent years demonstrate a tremendous shift toward broad-mindedness in strata that half a century ago were uncompromisingly austere. The psychologist Terman compared the experiences of men and women born before 1890 with those born in or after 1910; the number of wives who admitted sex relations with others than their spouses had markedly risen in the interim, the percentages being 4.8 and 23.3, respectively. Premarital intercourse with fiancés and others was declared by 68.3 per cent of the younger group in contrast to 13.5 per cent by the older. But, irrespective of such figures as to behavior, which are difficult to check and may not be representative, common observation shows that in the United States, Great Britain, and the Scandinavian countries the attitude toward female chastity as expressed by Samuel Johnson is no longer dominant except in restricted circles.[1]

The double standard is by no means peculiar to sophisticated societies. It was conspicuous among our Plains Indians, as Wissler forcibly sets forth in his account of the Blackfoot (Montana, Alberta): ". . . virginity is held in very great esteem and extreme precaution is taken to guard the girls of the family. They are closely watched by their mothers and married off as soon as possible after puberty. For a girl to become pregnant is regarded as an extreme family disgrace." On the other hand, men were rather expected to be Don Juans: "The male lover enjoys unusual liberties. His efforts at debauchery are not only tolerated but encouraged by his family and should he lead a married woman astray [he] is heralded as a person of promise. Thus, while great pains are taken to safeguard young girls, boys are, if anything, encouraged to break through the barriers." This attitude was probably in essence common to all the natives of the culture area. There is, however, one marked difference from Victorian standards. Though a virtuous woman was highly esteemed and alone could qualify for certain sacred rites, an erring maiden did not become a "fallen woman" or outcast. Unless she constantly shifted lovers, there was not even likely to be much gossip about her; after all, not everyone was born a saint.

Several Brazilian tribes present parallels. The Canella recognize an unorganized class of "wantons"—girls who have lost their virginity, as well as divorcées and widows who fail to enter a fixed union at the earliest opportunity. Ten years ago these women numbered from twelve to fifteen in a population of three hundred. Anything but impudent in their demeanor, they discreetly choose their paramours, being under no obligation to gratify the lust of a man coveting them. Most of them, indeed, soon establish a permanent bond and get their lovers to sleep in their matrilineal home; after the birth of children the two are regarded as though they had been ceremonially wedded. "Privately and publicly the wantons are on a footing of equality in their relations with virgins and married women; they are simply not models and have certainly failed to live up to the ideal." [2]

In contrast to the Blackfoot and the Canella, numerous tribes set no value whatsoever on virginity, expecting the freest relations conceivable among the young people so far as they do not break the rules against incest. Thus, the Masai bachelors live in a corral separate from the married people, where they consort with the young girls of the camp. In the Gran Chaco a dance provides the occasion for indulgence: taking the initiative, a Choroti girl tempts the man of her heart into the brush; and in a neighboring tribe the sexes separate after a performance, the girls to lie in front of their huts, where they are serially visited by the young men. Yet after a period of premarital license the young women settle down to become good wives. Within this area the Toba have similar customs, but distinguish good from shameless girls, the former being less avid of change and of exhibitionism. The Polynesians are notoriously free in their sex life; the Tongarevans, being among the most prudish of their race, did not favor advances made by a girl. But after her puberty ceremony she "could have love affairs with whom she fancied with the exceptions imposed by consanguinity or marriage. Sexual appetites could be satisfied without social stigma that would affect her prospects of marriage." Here is a characteristic difference from Plains Indian practice, for a Crow would pay little if anything for a lewd young woman. But in Polynesia, too, license before marriage need not imply conjugal infidelity; the Tikopians, for example, have relatively few cases of adultery.[3]

## Extramarital Relations

Extramarital relations, which to us suggest adultery, may include acts that are approved by society and sanctioned by the spouse. To consider first adultery in the proper sense, we have already noted that Western civilization until quite recently recognized the double standard. The opening chapters of Tolstoi's *Anna Karenina* bring the attitude home even more vividly than the quotation from Dr. Johnson. Prince Oblonsky has carried on an intrigue with his children's former governess, his unattractive wife has discovered his unfaithfulness and threatens to leave; everyone in the house knows that the Prince is in the wrong, and everyone takes his side.

Notwithstanding the double standard, treatment of an adulterous wife varies with the social setting and the regnant ideology. In a strictly matrilocal group the mere presence of the wife's kindred may curb an irate husband's impulses; in any tribe they are swayed by the cultural pattern. A Hopi or a Zuñi does not resort to violence, but vents his spleen by magic on the whole community: "The cuckold does nothing to his wife or his successor, but seeks a way to hurt other people . . ." During one of Dr. Parsons' visits the Zuñi, worried over a landslide, were telling about one that had once been brought on by a Rain chief incensed at his wife's perfidy. Among the similarly matrilocal Canella, husbands also act with restraint: one man walked out of the house with his belongings, halted outdoors, and—loud enough for the neighbors to hear—announced why he was leaving. The repentant wife managed to patch up the rift, so that within a week the pair had been reunited.

In strong contrast to such complaisance is the reaction of a typical Plains Indian. An aggrieved Blackfoot would formerly kill his unfaithful wife, or cut off her nose, or turn her over to the fellow members of his military society to have their will of her.

Negro Africa displays similar divergence. In Uganda a suspicious husband was privileged to torture his wife in order to extract a confession; he might kill her with impunity if she were proved at fault, and if not would be only fined. The paramour usually suffered death; in any case he was disfigured and fined. Quite different is the procedure of the Jagga (East Africa). Though they recognize absolute grounds for divorce, such as urinary incontinence, adultery is not one of them. A man satisfied of his wife's faithlessness might try to reform her by a trouncing or by appealing to her relatives for aid. Another course of action was not to visit her and to withhold provisions, thus indirectly forcing her to return to her parents, who would induce her to beg the husband's pardon. Again, he might send the woman to her lover, who was then obliged to ask the aggrieved man to take back his wife, penitentially offering him a sheep and later two goats as an indemnity. If suit were brought before a chief, the penalty grew larger. Equally instructive are the reactions noted in the Upper Volta province. There the wife's transgression is deemed sinful rather than criminal: she errs against the Earth goddess and the tutelary deities of her husband's family, but conjugal jealousy lacks social support. By a confession and expiatory offerings to the supernatural powers, she is "wholly purified and pardoned. Her husband does not dream of sending her away, rather does he reclaim a fugitive provided she is a good cook and expert housekeeper; the children born of such extramarital relations are his children." The psychological import of these data can hardly be overestimated. In another part of West Africa, a Yakö husband is not legally restricted in his sex life, but may demand compensation from his wife's lover; he may also divorce her and recover the money paid for her, but "of itself adultery appears rarely to result in divorce." [4]

From adultery felt as such by the society in question we must sharply distinguish all extramarital relations socially permitted, approved, or even prescribed. The Eskimo furnish excellent illustrations: An Iglulik had been away from home for two years; "on the day after his return his wife gave birth to a daughter; he was delighted at the surprise." Men lend their wives for shorter or longer periods and cement friendships by exchanging wives. "If a man becomes angry over his wife's unfaithfulness it is because this is an encroachment upon his rights; the next day it may easily happen that he himself lends her out."

A different category comprises acts of extramarital cohabitation in a ritualistic setting. A major ceremony of the Murngin closes with an obligatory exchange of wives, refusal supposedly making a person ill. In America, the Hidatsa had a Dog society, at the end of whose dance the members cohabited with all the women present, none being permitted to refuse her favors. It is even said that on this occasion normal prohibitions were ignored. The same tribe and several of their neighbors formerly purchased ceremonial rights by temporarily surrendering their wives to the seller.[5]

## The Reasons for Marriage

The data on premarital and extramarital intercourse prove that marriage is not entered from motives of lust, which in many societies can be more than amply gratified without assuming any responsibilities. "The primary object of marriage, from the Tongarevan point of view, was the procreation of children to perpetuate the family." This statement has general validity: it is the wish to have legitimate offspring—legitimate in the native conception—that stimulates Polynesians, Masai, Bororo, and others to forgo the pleasures of sexual license and to settle down to matrimony. In the rarer prudish societies, say among the Sherente, where youths were expelled from the bachelors' lodge after a sex adventure and female kindred watched over a girl's virtue day and night, one would suppose a different outlook on the part of the young folks; yet the lads are extremely reluctant to leave the company of their fellows. The elders arrange engagements while their children are not yet of age, and when the time comes the younger generation seems to bow to an inevitable evil. The newlyweds are so shy that at first a wanton related to the bride lies beside the couple in order to minister to the husband's desires.

In a very large number of tribes economic life is so organized as to require the collaboration of the sexes. A Chukchi or Eskimo cannot indefinitely rely for feminine services on his mother or other kinswomen, for they have other duties to discharge: "a man needs a woman to dress the meat and skins of the game he kills, to cook his food and make his clothing." In Baffinland "the women have to do the rowing in the large boats while the man steers." At the southern tip of the New World a Yaghan wife is similarly indispensable. It is she that collects the mytilus shells which are the staff of life, she that paddles and moors the canoe on her husband's hunting trips.[6]

There are thus two principal motives for marriage: the universal object of founding a family and the constant need for cooperation in the daily routine of life.

## Finding a Mate

In Europe royal marriages have generally been arranged with some difficulty. The notion that a prince must wed one of equal rank, i.e., of a dynasty equivalent in power and traditional glory, limits the choice tremendously. When other considerations are added, such as a common faith, adjustments may become imperative: the last Czarina was an English princess who had given up the Anglican Church to embrace Russian Orthodoxy in preparation for the Russian throne. Corresponding difficulties face an endogamous nobility, who in modern times have often had to descend beneath their station.

The plight of these patricians is not a whit worse, however, than that of many savages, who often have to cope with demographic and traditional barriers. In one Semang camp visited by Schebesta there were fifty-four natives, including a large number of little children. Assuming a normal age distribution, there would be at best very few single girls for a young man to marry; but since he must not have any relative for a wife, local exogamy becomes necessary. In a Copper Eskimo settlement no youth was allowed to marry before being able to function as head of a household, i.e., able to build a snow hut unaided and to hunt caribou and seal. Similarly, in Nunivak a boy "could not seriously think of marriage until after he had caught at least one of each kind of seal . . . ." Such conditions make a man eager to get any female available, whether suitable in age or not. Girls tend to marry very early, whereas a man may not find a wife till he is in his prime; sometimes he will content himself with a woman old enough to be his mother, and again he may wed a girl of eleven.

Various conditions may make nubile females scarce for most men even when the absolute sex ratio is not unfavorable. In much of Negro Africa marriage demands considerable expense; hence polygyny is a token of prestige, the prerogative of chiefs and eminent men. In consequence the poor often have to wait till they inherit the widow of an older or richer kinsman, an abnormal situation that leads to intrigues with married women.

A dearth of women results likewise from a pronounced addiction to a particular kind of union, such as the Arab form of parallel cousin marriage. Accordingly, suitors lose no time, and in Palestine a newborn infant may get three proposals of marriage; a mature woman waits for a twelve-year-old cousin to come of age; and a man eagerly weds an eleven-year-old girl. In such situations the equivalence of siblings, especially when the concept takes in kinsmen, serves an essential purpose. It provides a makeshift for the orthodox rule through socially acceptable substitutions. Of course, nature does not provide Arabs with anything like the parallel cousins to make everyone happy; but when a father's kinsman is allowed to play the part of a paternal uncle the number of orthodox unions is greatly increased. Other societies have proved equally ingenious. A Murngin may not be able to marry a mother's brother's daughter because his mother has only sisters or because the uncle has only sons; but if the would-be groom may take the daughter of a mother's parallel cousin or of her clansman, all will be well, though not quite *so* well as in an ideal match.[7]

In considering widow inheritance, the disparity of spouses' age, and various other phenomena, we must view them largely as resultants of the two factors mentioned—the difficulty of finding a mate against heavy competition in small communities and the limitations, prohibitions as well as prescriptions, imposed by society.

We shall now consider several specific ways of obtaining a wife, such as exchange, service, purchase, and capture.

## Marriage by Exchange

If a man finds only a few nubile females, whether from natural or social causes, they acquire a scarcity value, which frequently implies the need for compensation. This difficulty can sometimes be obviated by exchange. Families desiring to establish an alliance exchange females: a youth from one marries a girl from the other, and vice versa. Individual attraction, we repeat, is not the basic factor; our own immediate ancestors and virtually every other society in human history would have rejected contemporary Western conceptions as absurd and vicious in principle. Since marriage is a group affair, demographic circumstances may yield grotesque results. It may come about that a Chukchi woman is allotted as the wife of a little boy, whom she then suckles at one breast while nursing at the other her own child, begotten by some mature male with whom she legitimately cohabits during her legal husband's minority.

In Australia and Melanesia a man's sister is commonly given to his wife's brother in return for the latter's sister. Thus neither family (horde) suffers a loss of women through marriage. However, such a system cannot work without modification since the requisite partners are not always available to satisfy the conditions of the bargain. The Banaro (New Guinea) tinker with nature by killing a newborn infant of the wrong sex: if a male birth follows another, the second son is done away with, and similarly with successive female births. They also admit clansfolk as substitutes for siblings. Nevertheless, difficulties occur. If the older of two sisters dies, a problem arises, which the natives solve by allotting the younger girl to the older brother of the second family. His junior, thus deprived of his chance, raises objections but is forced to yield, his consolation lying in the prospect of sometime inheriting his senior's widow. If one of the brothers should die, the survivor claims both sisters as wives. In spite of such adjustments, some men are bound to remain unprovided. These endeavor to obtain wives from foreign tribes, but that means having to offer compensation, which thirty years ago consisted in ten pottery vessels.

Exchange occurs among more sophisticated peoples. In the Arab village of Artas (Palestine) 26.5 per cent of all marriages fall under this head. "Take thou my sister and give me thy sister" is the current formula. However, it happens that a man gives his daughter in exchange for another man's sister, who becomes his second wife—to the first wife's chagrin since the daughter she has borne is the means of bringing a rival into the household.

Sometimes special rules of marriage bar exchange. Some Australians practice marriage with either cross-cousin, so that if A marries his mother's brother's daughter it is proper for the bride's brother to marry his father's sister's daughter, viz. A's sister. But the Murngin, while prescribing marriage with a maternal uncle's daughter, forbid it with the paternal aunt's, which automatically precludes an exchange of sisters.[8]

## Marriage by Capture

Given the difficulty of obtaining a wife, warlike peoples naturally get around it as opportunity offers, carrying off women from their enemies. Such captives lived until recently in most of our Plains Indian groups and normally were treated like other wives. The Yugoslavs, Orthodox as well as Roman Catholic, practiced capture well into the nineteenth century in order to avoid the expense of a wedding. The would-be groom's party organized, broke into the coveted girl's home, overcame the resistance of her kindred, and carried her off. "It is a disgrace for the whole village if a girl is captured . . . , but it is a still greater disgrace for the band of capturers if they come back without a girl." Much blood was likely to be shed in these enterprises.

These instances refer to abduction from an alien group. This is usually the form it takes, for within a community a regular practice of this sort would mean internecine strife leading to extermination. Very different is the extraordinary custom described for Tikopia. There kidnapping is customary within a comparatively small community, but associated usages mitigate the resentment of the despoiled family. Interestingly enough, the groom often takes a minor part in the affair, the brunt being borne by his family, who thus force a reluctant youth to wed or forestall a match they disapprove by snatching a bride they consider more suitable. So long as the kidnappers keep up traditional observances, little harm results, for the raiders willingly submit to a drubbing if only they manage to carry off the bride. On the other hand, if they flout convention—say by catching a girl while she is outdoors—there may be a serious brawl. Characteristically, the kidnappers reappear with propitiatory gifts and humiliate themselves before the captive's kindred, so that everything resolves itself in harmony. As Firth remarks, the case proves that capture and compensation need not exclude each other, but the phenomenon is exceptional.

Commoner is a ceremonial pretense of capture—once interpreted as a survival of real capture in the past. However, alternative explanations have been offered. The ceremony may accentuate maidenly coyness or be meant to dramatize the transition to a new mode of life. Often there is collusion between groom and bride, in other words, virtually an elopement.

A peculiar form of kidnapping flourished among the Crow. During a brief period early in the spring a member of either of two rival men's organizations was allowed to steal the wife of a man in the other society provided that she had at one time been the abductor's sweetheart. She might beg her former lover not to press his claim, but if he insisted there was no redress. As for the husband, he lost caste if he offered resistance; the decorous attitude was to feign indifference. Moreover, it was disgraceful for a man even to take back a woman thus taken from him or to visit her clandestinely. This was the very sort of thing that made one a target for the ribald mockery of joking-relatives.

In the village of Kambot along the Potters' River in New Guinea a surplus of females has led to groom capture. If a nubile girl cannot find a partner, her father visits a neighboring settlement that has a larger assortment of youths, lures a young man into the woods, overpowers him with the aid of accessories, and takes him to Kambot, where his intended starts to lay out a yam plot. In the meantime the lad's father arrives in great agitation, but is appeased with gifts and a banquet. However, as in bride abduction, so here also there is frequently a previous agreement with the groom; the kidnapping is a sham, resorted to because matrilocal residence is not customary in these parts, but can be excused on the plea of duress.[9]

## Marriage by Service

Gaining a wife by service is an ancient and a widespread custom. In Genesis 29: 18, Jacob says to his mother's brother, Laban, "I will serve thee seven years for Rachel thy younger daughter." After the lapse of the period he gets the older daughter instead, on Laban's plea that "it must not be so done in our country, to give the younger before the first-born." Accordingly, Jacob serves seven more years for the woman he loves.

The practice is intimately connected with temporary matrilocal residence. A young Winnebago was likely to spend the first biennium of wedlock with his parents-in-law. "During these two years he was practically the servant of his father-in-law, hunting, fishing, and performing minor services for him. Many Winnebago interpreted these enforced services of a son-in-law as part of his marriage obligations toward his father-in-law." The situation was strikingly similar among the Hidatsa, the husband acting as the servant of his parents-in-law and providing them with food. In tropical South America, as Kirchhoff has shown, the concepts of "serf," "captive," and "son-in-law" tend to merge. As an eighteenth-century missionary on the Orinoco puts it, "The treatment doled out to their slaves is extremely amiable; they order them to do no things but what they charge their sons-in-law with . . . . And if they turn out to be industrious and painstaking, their masters grow sufficiently attached to them to give them, without any misgivings, their own daughters for wives." In the Gran Chaco, too, a Chiriguano groom spends a year of labor with his prospective mother-in-law. Bogoras has indicated the wide occurrence of this usage in northeastern Siberia. A Maritime Chukchi suitor normally stays with his prospective wife's parents for two or three years, providing them with food, whalebone, tusks, and skins. Among the Reindeer branch of this people the prospective son-in-law is put through his paces for several months, doing the tougher jobs, mending utensils, and fetching heavy fuel. After this initial period of trial his tasks grow less severe and he will be granted conjugal rights, but it may be years before he returns to his home district. Such service is rarely rendered for a second wife.

Thus it is not necessary to connect bride service with any specific evolutionary stage in the history of marriage. The practice occurs among the patrilineal Winnebago, the matrilineal Hidatsa, the loosely organized tribes of the Chaco and northeastern Siberia. We are dealing with a simple, transparent economic arrangement. Consistently with this interpretation, the same people may well practice both service and bride purchase according to circumstances. A Yurok unable to offer the full bride price "paid what he could and worked out a reasonable balance in services to his father-in-law."[10]

## *Bride Wealth*

"Bride purchase" is admittedly a blanket term for various transactions. It literally fits some cases, but fails to cover the fairly numerous exchanges of valuables by both the contracting families, and becomes an utter misnomer when the bride's relatives offer property equal to what is presented by the groom's. Another objection has been raised, especially by students of African Negroes. They contend, correctly enough, that a "bought" woman is never or only very seldom literally regarded as a chattel. Whereas a buyer is privileged to sell goods he has acquired, a husband cannot sell his wife, irrespective of the payments he may have made for her. Hence, the argument runs, we ought not to speak of a bride price at all, but merely of a conveyance of "bride wealth."

The point is well taken as a qualification, but not as an elimination of the traditional ideas suggested by "bride purchase." The critique goes too far in ignoring the fact that human beings, being inconsistent, may alternately look at the rendering of payments as an economic purchase and again as a purely social transaction. Further, the same people may deprecate the notion of buying a wife in normal circumstances, yet accept it under anomalous conditions.

Virtually all the relevant issues are illuminated in Miss Granqvist's thorough and judicious analysis of Arab customs in Palestine. In times of extreme want a father may be driven to sell his daughter as he would cattle or slaves, but this is felt to be the greatest misfortune; and even in this situation the buyer's right is not absolute, since grave abuse will call forth remonstrances from his brothers-in-law. However, this does not militate against the husband's proprietorship; with us the Society for the Prevention of Cruelty to Animals interferes with a brutal horse driver without challenging his claims to the beast.

In typical Palestinian marriages economic factors are certainly significant. The bride's family receives compensation for loss of her labor power, and quite logically expects a higher price when she is removed from her kin and village. Family debts are sometimes paid with the money received, and—precisely as in Africa—the price serves to buy a wife for the girl's brother. On the other hand, a married woman never wholly belongs to her husband's house, but remains in some measure affiliated with her father's, even continuing to be called by his name as a surname to her own. It is also essential to note that she holds rights over the property she brings to the household and to anything she earns in the matrimonial state.

On one point there can be no doubt whatsoever: contrary to our conceptions, other peoples emphatically do not regard bride purchase as derogatory to the wife's status; quite the contrary. A sophisticated Arab will argue that paying for a wife is no worse than paying for a husband, as Europeans do when providing a dowry for their daughters. The Crow and the Hidatsa consider romantic elopement as disgraceful, while purchase is the most honorable for a woman—the higher the price, the more honorable: "It was usually a young, good-looking and virtuous woman who was purchased ...." A Cheyenne woman reports: "My paternal uncle started to talk to me saying how well my parents had brought me up, and stated that marriage by purchase was considered one of the greatest and happiest events in one's life." The Yurok exerted themselves to pay a big price, thus adding to their social stature and automatically securing status for their children, who were reckoned bastards at the bottom of the scale unless their mother had been properly paid for.

Innumerable facts show that, whatever may occur in particular instances, the economic aspect of the price paid is far from negligible. The amount required often greatly exceeds what a youth can afford to give unaided. Accordingly, his relatives assist him, which gives them an interest in the wife, whence the frequent refusal to release a widow and allow her to marry whom she wishes instead of a husband's kinsman. Another pertinent point is the return of part or all of the bride wealth in divorce. Lango law is fairly representative. The father or a paternal kinsman or, failing one, the maternal uncle will provide a young man with a wife, i.e., pay the required cattle, goats, or what not. The payment is divided among the bride's brother by the same mother, her maternal uncle, and the more distant male relatives who at some future time may have to be summoned to protect her against abuse. An adulterer must compensate the husband, usually with one cow, one heifer, and one bull; and any issue of the liaison belongs to the husband, i.e., the payer of the bride price. Divorce implies the return of the amount paid, including in strict theory even the offspring of the original cattle and goats, though this is usually waived. Widows are inherited by the husband's brothers, or for lack of such by his sister's son. In detail there is infinite variation, even within a single major area. The Yakö, for example, lack the levirate, so that a widow remarries according to her inclinations; but, suggestively enough, divorce is established only when an acceptable portion of the marriage payment has been restored. Again, a Lobi husband is entitled to recoup his bride wealth only if the wife is at fault; if on the contrary he has failed to support her or to render her the usual conjugal services, if he is a leper or a sorcerer, he gets nothing whatsoever.

In Northwestern America, parts of Africa, Indonesia, and Oceania, reciprocal offerings are made on an elaborate scale, often in installments. A Haida youth begins by serving for his bride; subsequently the contracting families exchange valuables; and a chief may go so far as to present his son-in-law with a slave or a canoe. A man avid of glory will deliberately set aside his financial interest in order to add to his standing. In Buin (Solomon Islands) there is similar rivalry between the spouses' fathers till either comes to the end of his means and throws in the sponge. Here there is, of course, no true purchase, but a competition for prestige.

Another type of transaction, though one-sided, gives the economic arrangements a religious, ritualistic flavor. The Jagga require a fixed sequence of prestations, beginning with the first negotiations by the two families and not ending until the first-born child of the union is at least seven years of age. Sixteen stages, each labeled with a technical native term or phrase, are recognized. One offering consists in four large vats of beer, another includes a goat, a later one seven vats, and the last two a heifer for the wife's father or brother and a heifer for her maternal uncle. But almost every scene of the long drama has a supernatural aspect. Thus, the seventh stage involves not only the transfer of two vats of beer and the cutting of a banana cluster, but also prayers to the ancestors while the intermediary between the two families fits sandal soles to the bride's feet. When the soles are done, the bride's father lifts them in front of his face, spits on them four times, and blesses his daughter.

Evidently this complex of usages is more than a series of payments for the wife. But it would be wrong to minimize the economic aspect of the proceedings. The bride's kindred are losing a valuable laborer; hence her mother wails, "Who will henceforth fetch water and kindle the fire, who will relieve me of my burden of grass?" On the other hand, the groom presents his fiancée with a shield in earnest of the cattle he hopes to loot for her. Finally, if the arrangement is nullified by the bride's side even on respectable grounds, half the property offered by the groom goes back to him; capricious rupture obliges the bride's family to restore the entire amount plus a goat.

Still other forms of procedure occur. In Alor both parties are expected to make series of payments socially balancing each other, but "theoretically, and almost always in practice, the bride-price exceeds the dowry," being typically three times as great.

European examples of complementary contributions from the two sides abound. Before World War I a typical arrangement of Polish peasants was to have the boy's family provide the land and the girl's the cash. Since it was customary for a farm to be left undivided to one son, his wife's money would serve to indemnify the other children for their interest in the estate. Parallel phenomena are reported from contemporary rural Ireland. These European instances are only formally like the elaborate reciprocal payments of Alor, for in Europe the purpose is not primarily social but economic.[11]

## Inheritance of Widows

Where women have a scarcity value the only easy means of acquiring one may be through inheritance. It is therefore not surprising that for many peoples disposal of widows is an important part of customary law. The fact that some societies definitely prescribe their allotment to the dead man's heirs refutes the notion that bride wealth never involves the conception of women as property.

Relevant rules vary in some measure with rules of descent. Patrilineal polygynous African tribes often follow the principle that a man inherits his father's widows except his own mother. However, within this general framework a good deal of variation is possible. Filial succession may be subordinated to other principles of law. Not every household is polygynous, and by universal incest rules, the son could not inherit his mother from a monogamous father. There is also the moral obligation to provide bachelors in the family with wives. Thus, the net result in a particular case will be a compromise. Junod surmises that of five widows, the principal wife is likely to be appropriated by that one of her husband's junior brothers who comes to control the estate, the second and third wives go to two other brothers, while a uterine nephew gets the fourth, and a son the fifth. Obviously, the lack of any of these relatives compels other arrangements. Common-sense adjustments are in vogue among the Yoruba, who distribute widows among sons, whether married or single, but also allow brothers to inherit wives.

"Thus a man may have the fortune to have an additional wife . . . thrust on him." In such a case he has the choice of either keeping her or of turning her over to a suitor who is willing to pay the standard price for widows—seven pounds, ten shillings.

Filial widow inheritance was reported from the medieval Mongol empire by both Rubruk and Marco Polo. It is not unknown in South America. The Araucanians (Chile) permitted the eldest son to inherit his father's wives; failing sons, a brother or the nearest kinsman fell heir. A similar combination of principles appears among tropical Cariban tribes: a man may inherit his brother's or his father's wives.

Filial inheritance, it appears, can coexist with the competing principles of the levirate and nepotic inheritance. The latter, though occasionally found among such patrilineal peoples as the Thonga, fits more logically into a matrilineal framework and is actually known to occur in such matrilineal societies as the Tlingit and the Haida of Northwestern America and the Guajiro (Colombia). But it is emphatically not universal among peoples with descent through women. Thus, the matrilineal, matrilocal Hopi and Canella, among whom women own the houses, have no inheritance of widows—neither by nephews nor by brothers. Presumably a conception of women as property in some sense must precede a fixed rule that she should marry the deceased's heir. Where a husband may be divorced any time by setting his possessions outdoors, there is obviously no such conception.

By way of contrast it is worth noting that the Sherente, relatives of the Canella, but with patrilineal descent, patrilocalism, and masculine house ownership, do have the levirate. "A widow with little children or, failing issue, of estimable qualities is married to a single or widowed elder or younger brother or parallel cousin of the deceased. Refusal on either side was reckoned as contrary to usage."

The levirate, as one of the most widespread customs and one intimately connected with other phenomena, has been repeatedly mentioned in other contexts. In probably an overwhelming number of instances only a younger brother inherits the widow. This is reasonable since the seniors are almost certain to be already married. Correspondingly, since girls married at puberty, the sororate—a custom hardly to be divorced in discussion from the levirate—applied to a younger sister.

It is important to distinguish between obligatory, preferential, and permissive levirate and sororate. Unfortunately our sources are rarely explicit on the point. In his survey of the Basin Shoshoneans, Steward is exceptionally careful to define the situation for each group. Some of these closely related tribelets prescribed the two practices, so that either could be escaped only by a payment to the parents-in-law. Other groups of this stock preferred such unions, but without insisting on them. The Chiricahua also consider it "an intolerable insult" for a man to seek a second wife outside the first wife's family and make a widower marry one of the deceased woman's sisters or cousins.

Characteristically, levirate and sororate generally require no additional payments or only negligible ones.

Some societies permit extension of the levirate-sororate principle not only to parallel cousins and other coeval clansfolk, but even to relatives of another generation. Thus, an Omaha or Miwok may marry his wife's brother's daughter, and an Omaha may also wed his wife's paternal aunt. Such extension is practically useful wherever the numerical weakness of a tribe, along with stringent prohibitions, produces vigorous competition for the available females. A widower may not readily find an unattached sister or cousin of his wife's, in which case the lineage of the deceased supplies another substitute.[12]

## Prohibited, Preferred, and Prescribed Marriages

This subject has already been repeatedly touched upon. Levirate and sororate, for example, were shown to be in some areas compulsory, in others at least preferred. Similarly, exogamy and endogamy prescribe marriage outside and inside some social unit.

Prohibition of matings between parent and child seems universal. Between siblings it is very nearly so, the only notable exceptions being the royal families of pre-Columbian Peru, of Hawaii, and of ancient Egypt, though in the latter the example set by the rulers may have been in some degree followed by others. Apart from restriction of intercourse between the closest blood relatives, peoples vary enormously; even linguistic cognates, neighbors, and sharers in the same general culture often assume totally different attitudes. Thus, in Australia the Murngin prescribe marriage with only one type of cross-cousin, whereas the Kariera permit it with either. Again, the Aranda taboo unions between any first cousins, regarding as orthodox only those between more remote kindred: a man marries his mother's mother's brother's daughter's daughter or his mother's father's sister's daughter's daughter.

Terminology influences peoples, and even individuals, in varying degree. Thus, a cousin's being called "daughter" is sometimes deemed a bar to marriage, but in other cases a sharp distinction is drawn between near and remote kindred falling under that head. It seems a safe guess, however, that parallel cousins are generally tabooed because they are so often classed as siblings.

It is possible to regard several different forms of marriage as equally orthodox. The Tamanak of the Orinoco River permitted the levirate, filial widow inheritance, the sororate, union with the daughter of the wife's sister, with the sister's daughter (avuncular marriage from the girl's point of view), and symmetrical cross-cousin marriage. In such cases figures about the actual occurrence of each form would be highly desirable, but the sources rarely give relevant statistics. It is therefore usually impossible to say which of the acceptable unions are actually favored, which—if any—are treated as mere makeshifts. That some allowable forms cannot, in the nature of the case, be frequent any-where is obvious. Thus, compared with other tribes, the Navaho have a high incidence of bigamy with a widow, or divorcée, and her daugh-ter by a previous marriage. One man is known to have married a woman and her two daughters as well as the woman's sister and *her* daughter, so that he was simultaneously practising sororal polygyny and triple step-daughter marriage. Obviously the majority of Navaho men do not wed widows, or divorcées by preference; and if they did, these wives would not always have unattached nubile daughters. Nevertheless, stepdaughter marriage can be an approved form of bigamy, as it is likewise among the Bororo.

How forms of marriage and kinship terminology are connected is an interesting and at times baffling subject—baffling because, as we have just seen, a tribe may simultaneously consider several different kinds of union equally proper. In such cases it is plausible to assume that the popular kind is reflected in nomenclature rather than one rarely followed; but it is also possible to infer that a current practice that has not impressed itself on terminology must be more recent than one that has. Gifford has developed a suggestive chronological argument on this basis. A Miwok, as we saw, may marry either a mother's brother's daughter or a wife's brother's daughter. Which form, Gifford asks, has been more potent terminologically? If the marriage with a wife's niece operates, there would be a number of logical inferences. For example, a girl would be a potential stepmother to her father's sister's children, viz. her patrilateral cross-cousins, whom, as a corollary, she would consider her stepchildren. Another corollary is that the girl's brother, i.e., these children's male cross-cousin, becomes their step-mother's brother, whence they are his "sister's children." There are less direct consequences: a man's sister and his father's sister are equated because both may marry the same person, becoming mothers to the children he designates as sister's children. Altogether Gifford discovers twelve equations that are congruous with the marriage form in question.

On the other hand, there are very few reflections of cross-cousin marriage. Where this flourishes it usually goes hand in hand with a series of terminological peculiarities. Notably, a man uses one word for father-in-law and mother's brother since the two relatives coincide in one person; there is no need for separate "wife" and "female cross-cousin" terms since one regularly weds a cross-cousin; and a word for brother-in-law becomes superfluous since he is merely a male cross-cousin. Now, the Miwok lack these otherwise frequent identifications. In one dialect, e.g., the maternal uncle is called *kaka,* while the father-in-law is referred to by the totally distinct stem *memu;* the mother's brother's daughter (as previously indicated) is raised to the mother's status instead of being identified with the wife; and so forth. One may reasonably infer that cross-cousin marriage is a relatively recent development; how Gifford supposes it to have evolved will be explained below.

Cross-cousin marriage has stimulated considerable discussion, and various explanations. When Tylor first formulated the concept in 1888, he assumed—legitimately on the available evidence—that where the practice occurred the paternal aunt's and maternal uncle's child were equivalent. This has turned out to be incorrect. To adopt Warner's and Radcliffe-Brown's phraseology, we may distinguish a symmetrical type (the one envisaged by Tylor) from an asymmetrical, in which marriage with only one of the two kinds of cross-cousin is allowable. We must further discriminate between a matrilateral and a patrilateral variety of the asymmetrical type: in the former, a man takes to wife his maternal uncle's daughter; in the latter, his paternal aunt's.

Working with the evidence he had, Tylor inferred that cross-cousin marriage was the direct result of an exogamous moiety system. He correctly showed that, no matter whether descent were matrilineal or patrilineal, a person would always be in the opposite moiety to any of his (her) cross-cousins, hence (he argued) would be a possible mate. If marriageableness depended solely on moiety exogamy, the second part of the statement would also hold true. To take one of the possible cases, if a man belongs to moiety A and descent is patrilineal, his mother and his mother's brother are B; hence the latter's daughter is also B and of the proper moiety for an A's wife. If descent is matrilineal, an A's mother and mother's brother are A, but the uncle must marry into B; and since the wife determines the children's group, the uncle's daughter is B, hence marriageable.

However, there are matrilateral tribes like the Murngin and patrilateral ones like the Sherente. In such societies only one type of cross-cousin is a possible mate; hence only symmetrical cross-cousin marriage is conceivably a direct effect of the moiety system. But there is still another objection. In such cases as the Murngin the point is not for a man to wed any female of the opposite moiety, but if at all possible his own mother's brother's daughter. Only when one is lacking will he cast about for a substitute. Cross-cousin marriage is not, then, a simple corollary from an exogamous dual organization.

Cross-cousin marriage is widely but discontinuously distributed in all continents except Europe. Some Australian groups prescribe, others prohibit it; Melanesia and Polynesia manifest similar diversity. The Hottentots and some Bantu have the custom, and Volta tribes show a predilection for it, while the Yakö consider the practice improper, though not punishable. The Vedda and Toda in Southern Asia regularly marry cross-cousins, which is opposed to Semang usage; in Siberia the Gilyak have the matrilateral, the Soyot the patrilateral variety. North America has three main centers—the northeastern and north-central Algonkian area, northern British Columbia, and central California. In South America the range is considerable, including the Cariban Tamanak of the Orinoco, the Arawakan Wapishana of central Guiana, the Jivaro of Ecuador, the Sherente in northern Brazil, the Nambicuara of the Matto Grosso, the Pilaga of the Gran Chaco. This world survey does not lay claim to completeness, but merely tries to indicate roughly the chief points of occurrence.

Evidently a feature that in one place applies only to one type of cross-cousin, in a second region only to the other type, and in still other tribes to both types, is not amenable to a single interpretation. Nevertheless, sporadic hints concerning associated motives make the usage less enigmatic. Where relations of a uterine nephew toward an uncle take the peculiar turn observed in Tonga and South Africa, Radcliffe-Brown's suggestion that the maternal uncle cannot refuse his sister's son the hand of a daughter is certainly plausible. Equally interesting is Rivers' observation in a Melanesian island that the man who marries his matrilateral cross-cousin escapes payment of a bride price. Again, in British Columbia it is the desire to preserve hereditary privileges and titles within a narrow family circle that looms as significant.

In short, economic factors seem to operate. Kirchhoff has compactly summarized several theories which derive cross-cousin marriage from an antecedent claim on women of a higher or a lower generation. These theories, however, do not militate against an interpretation in economic and demographic terms. To revert to Gifford's views, he infers from the nomenclature that a Miwok could once claim his wife's brother's daughter; this prerogative would be inherited by the man's son; and when he exercised it, he was marrying his matrilateral cross-cousin.

Gifford's interpretation is consonant both with a wider application of the lineage principle and with an economic explanation. As emphasized previously, primitive societies do not consider marriage from a strictly individual point of view, but are concerned with an alliance of *groups*. Now, when a Miwok marries his wife's brother's daughter, he is merely further cementing his group's bond with the same patrilineage; and in marrying this woman on whom his father has a prior claim, he is representing his father's lineage, whether the act be phrased in terms of inheritance or not. Among the Omaha, who are in some respects parallel, there seems to be no cross-cousin marriage, but a man may marry both his wife's brother's daughter *and* his wife's paternal aunt; in other words, having once established a tie with a lineage, he maintains it irrespective of the generation of his mates. Omaha and Miwok, it must be remembered, are both patrilineal. The Miwok have been more consistent in extending the lineage principle to both partners, the Omaha in extending it to a higher as well as to a lower generation.

But what does such extension mean? It means a short cut to the desired goal of matrimony. When the bond between two groups is once created, there is no need for fretting over a chance to get a mate, no need for heavy expenditure.

Such group alliances are among the most frequent phenomena. An exogamous moiety system may be conceived in these terms, but often the arrangement is less rigid: in a multiple clan organization, preferences develop so that two particular clans tend to intermarry more or less exclusively. This phenomenon is reported from the Ket and likewise from Albania. Among the Navaho "clans may become associated by having several individuals of one clan marry individuals of another . . . Thus it is most usual to find two siblings of one clan marrying two siblings of another." The Bororo have a dual organization, but a man will preferably marry only into one, two, or three particular clans of the complementary moiety.

We have seen that in some measure kinship terminology corresponds to social conditions. Some authors have used this postulate to deduce forms of marriage from a recorded terminology. So long as such deductions are merely a starting point for further inquiries in the field whether the inferred arrangements exist, there can be no objection to this procedure. But without such checking the method is hazardous, for a feature of kinship terminology can be due to several distinct social phenomena. Thus, in some matrilineal societies a uterine nephew inherits his maternal uncle's widow, which raises him to the level of "father" to the children of his uncle, who are his cross-cousins; and his sister becomes their paternal aunt. But identification of one's father's sister's son with the father may, we have seen, merely express the lineage principle since father and father's sister's son are obviously in the same matrilineal line of descent and clan. Thus, the identification is found in tribes not known to permit nepotic widow inheritance. Further, the equation is not even necessarily associated with matrilineal reckoning. In the Admiralty Islands the children of the paternal sister and her female descendants through females are classed together as paternal aunts because members of a matrilineal lineage share the same spiritual powers even though the inheritance of temporal goods and of clan affiliation is patrilineal. Still another possibility, pointed out by Aginsky, is that it may be customary for an individual to take over either parent's identifications, so that nomenclature would no longer reflect marriage forms. This would be the reverse of teknonymy, which makes adults view relatives from a child's point of view. If, on the contrary, the child customarily identifies himself with his father, the paternal aunt will become a sister; hence her children are sister's children, so that there would be no need for either a special type of marriage or a fixed rule of descent to bring about the observed terminology.

Accordingly, caution is imperative in drawing a conclusion from terminology to a particular form of marriage that has never been recorded in the region discussed. However congruous nomenclature and hypothetical matrimonial usage may be, it would have to be proved that no other social arrangement is equally capable of fitting in with the terminology. On the other hand, it would be hyperskepticism to renounce all correlations of this order. If a tribe using the equations that follow from cross-cousin marriage is surrounded by neighbors all of whom practice this marriage, it seems highly probable that the tribe in question also once practiced it, retaining the terminology as a survival.[13]

## Marriage and Divorce

Until several generations ago the majority of Western countries accepted the Christian conception of marriage as sacramental, hence as indissoluble except through special dispensation or for the gravest causes. The underlying principle was that of Matthew 5:32 and Mark 10:11:

> But I say unto you, That whosoever shall put away his wife, saving for the cause of fornication, causeth her to commit adultery: and whosoever shall marry her that is divorced committeth adultery.
>
> Whosoever shall put away his wife, and marry another, committeth adultery against her.

Although the several national codes differed in detail, all treated marriage as a veritable institution, not as a private contract between two persons that did not concern governmental authorities. Germany, France, and Switzerland introduced civil marriage, but this did not mean that the state was indifferent; on the contrary, it asserted its interest in the matter by insisting on legalization by one of its officials, whether or not there was to be an ecclesiastical ceremony also.

Even after secularism had gained ground, the mores of Western peoples accepted the seriousness, if not the sanctity, of the matrimonial tie. Divorce continued to be regarded as a calamity and a disgrace even by those who rejected the sacramental view. Moreover, until relatively recent years the traditional double standard favored men in a rupture of marital relations. The erring husband's philanderings were condoned before and after separation from his wife, while a woman who sought to lead a normal sex life apart from him put herself outside the pale. In a measure English law took cognizance of this disparity by allowing the wife to sue for restitution of conjugal rights.

As industrialization progressed, individual rights and individual happiness became primary considerations in the consciousness of many Western minds; also, the earlier conceptions of women altered. In consequence, divorce came to be treated in some quarters as a matter of routine that no longer implied ignominy for even the guilty party; accordingly, if legal impediments persisted, these circles extended tolerance to any adjustments the individuals concerned might find convenient. That industrialization was involved in this momentous change is clear when we compare urban and rural conditions, the divorce rate being almost everywhere appreciably larger in the cities. Thus, in 1925 Hamburg had 186.5 divorces for every 100,000 inhabitants against only 56.8 in the whole of Germany, and 39.7 in Bavaria. Here, as elsewhere, the denominational factor also enters, since Bavaria is predominantly Catholic. For our country Burgess and Locke give an illuminating table. Chicago harbors only 44.1 per cent of the total population of the state, but 50 per cent of the divorced population; for Baltimore the figures are 48.7 versus 58.6; for New York City, 56 versus 57.2. In Europe urban Sweden has a higher divorce rate than rural Norway. Yet obviously other factors figure, as the example of Bavaria indicates. Catholic Eire does not allow any divorce, and in England and Wales tradition was strong enough to keep the rate down. It had, indeed, gone up from .02 to .15 per thousand population from 1900 to 1938, but in the United States the corresponding figures are .73 and 1.88!

That industrialization is not the sole determinant appears from the data on Japan, where modern conditions have produced the reverse effect, viz. that of lowering the rate. This change was largely due to the fact that in the earlier era it was incredibly high, rising to 367 per thousand marriages in the eighties of the last century. Not being sacramental, marriage could be dissolved if a wife was reckoned unsuitable by her parents-in-law or if she disappointed the husband, who had had no voice in her selection. Here, then, individualism would give a young man greater freedom of choice to begin with, thus reducing the subsequent reasons for rejection of the wife. In addition, the government looked with disfavor on divorce and made it less easy.

Since primitive peoples as a rule lack both religious and governmental sanctions for wedlock, divorce may be achieved with little formality. One of Schebesta's male Semang informants had been married three times. In Greenland Holm found a young Eskimo woman who had just left her sixth husband; a contemporary Hopi woman is known to have had eight official husbands. In this latter, strictly monogamous tribe, Titiev discovered marked instability; 34 per cent of 826 men and women investigated had been divorced at least once, and the same tendency is substantiated by historical evidence for earlier periods. A Crow might divorce a wife for being "cranky." An exhibitionistic form of announcement, generally taking place after a quarrel with the woman or her parents, was to "throw her away" publicly at a

dance while at the same time giving away horses. Crow women sometimes eloped with lovers or deserted their husbands from jealousy or
on other grounds.

Facts of this sort are indisputable, but by themselves they convey
a distorted picture of savage institutions. For one thing, some peoples
do not practice divorce at all frequently; the Vedda investigated by the
Seligmans recalled a single instance that went back three generations.
But even tribes yielding a high incidence must be viewed with discrimination. For one thing, divorce is as a rule distinctly more common in
the opening period of matrimony. At a later stage Birket-Smith's
remark for the Central Eskimo holds very generally: "The children
are the bond which holds the parents most strongly together." Conversely, barrenness is a common ground for divorce.

Further, we must distinguish between different kinds of marriage
among a given people in relation to divorce. A Crow would soon get
rid of a woman he had kidnapped from a rival society—one who was
by the very possibility of such abduction stamped as not a paragon of
virtue. But he was extremely unlikely to abandon a woman he had
bought. Purchase was itself a tribute of respect for the girl; men would
not buy a wanton. Hence the Crow theory that a marriage based on
purchase was more durable is wholly credible, for the husband
esteemed his wife for her chastity, and this attribute eliminated the
temptations that might some time alienate a girl whom one had taken
to wife merely as a romantic love affair. The Canella of earlier times
stressed premarital purity in girls and regarded marriage with a virgin
as indissoluble.

Considering the difficulty of getting a mate in many societies and
the widespread notion of wedlock as a group covenant, there would
be powerful deterrents to hasty rupture of relations caused by individual disillusionment or caprice. Intimately linked with these factors are
the heavy economic obligations that attach to matrimonial arrangements. When an Alorese gets peevish toward his or her spouse, there
is a public reckoning of the payments and counterpayments made to
date. Sometimes a woman cannot free herself because her kindred are
unwilling or unable to give her the required financial support. From
such a plight she can be rescued only if some prospective second husband indemnifies her first. In Africa, severance of matrimony causes
serious embarrassment when the wife's family, as often happens, has
already used the bride wealth to purchase a wife for one of the sons.

Finally, the mutual economic dependence of husband and wife in

many societies would militate against lightly deserting a tried help-
mate.

In other words, notwithstanding the ease of divorce among savages, it is by no means the uniformly prevalent phenomenon one might
suppose.[14]

## Monogamy

The sex ratio, though not absolutely uniform, is approximately
1:1 all over the world; deviations nowhere approach 1:2, so that nature
militates even against bigamy, and even more against plural marriage
on a larger scale. Dr. Johnson accordingly expressed the common-
sense view of the matter when he said to Boswell, "No man can have
two wives, but by preventing somebody else from having one."
Actually, monogamy is the most prevalent form of marriage in fact,
but only, in a few societies is it obligatory. It has not always been so
even in Christendom. As late as 1540 Landgrave Philipp I of Hessen,
the patron of Protestantism, with the connivance of Luther, got his
wife's consent to a bigamous union with a lady of the Saxon court.
King Henry VIII may not have been technically polygynous, but the
free and easy way in which he divorced and beheaded wives to make
room for a more desirable successor made his monogamy decidedly
brittle.

The fact remains that for the generality of mankind a single mate
at a time is the indicated form of union irrespective of whether society,
as in most cases, interposes no objection to plural marriage. Thus,
the popular notion of Mohammedan marriage is fantastically wrong.
Theoretically a believer may espouse four wives, and Mohammedan
rulers have had harems, but the average follower of Islam everywhere
practices monogamy for the solid reason that he cannot afford anything else. Niebuhr, a famous eighteenth-century traveler to Yemen
and Hadramaut, reports that "an Arabian, in moderate circumstances,
seldom marries more than one wife"; and he adds that even wealthy
men are likely in the long run to be content with a single mate. Wherever a large bride price is customary, the poor would have difficulty
in amassing it once, let alone, a second time. This holds for the Moham-
medanized Kazak, and quite generally.

There are some primitive tribes that positively prescribe monogamy—among them the Hopi and the Canella. Why they developed
such intransigence is not clear. It has been suggested that matrilocal
residence interferes with plural marriage, but this would hold only for

marriage with girls from different families. As we have already seen, sororal polygyny is very common among savages and is wholly consistent with a husband's living among his affinal relatives. Why, then certain peoples object to this form of polygyny, which usually does not even require an extra payment, remains quite enigmatic.

Very few peoples in human history, then, practice monogamy on principle, but *de facto* the majority of persons in most societies live monogamously. This, we must remember, does not mean that an adult is necessarily restricted to cohabitation with a single woman. The uncompromisingly monogamous Canella form special comradeship alliances at the time of their final initiation ceremony, and "the handsomest proof of true . . . friendship consists in the occasional exchange of wives, but the women's consent is prerequisite . . . . Such exchanges are invariably temporary and in no way affect the permanence of the marital tie." In modern society the keeping of mistresses or the intrigues of married women have in no way broken down the dominance of monogamy. "Marriage," Cooper properly reminds us, "is more than socially approved or tolerated sex congress." It is the unequivocally approved institution corresponding to the ideal of the domestic association we call the family.[15]

## *Polyandry*

Polyandry is the marriage of one woman to two or more men. Remembering basic definitions, we must eliminate most of the reported instances. As Cooper points out in his exemplary discussion of the subject, the loan or sharing of a wife is not polyandry. The impressive list of allegedly polyandrous peoples includes the Marquesas Islanders; some Australians; the Namib Bushmen, Bergdama and Wahuma; the Chukchi, Gilyak, some simple tribes of the Malay Peninsula, the Sinhalese, Toda, and Tibetans; some Eskimo, northernmost Athabaskan Indian groups, Cree, and Basin Shoshoneans; the Yaruro (Venezuela), Aweikoma (Brazil), and Lengua (Chaco).

When most of these cases are scrutinized, they do not turn out to represent a prevalent form of marriage unequivocally approved by the people in question. Thus, in one of the Athabaskan tribes no instance of polyandry has been observed by investigators; there is merely a memory of such marriages, along with mythological references to them: "The Kutchin do not practice polyandry as an accepted pattern . . . ." What is actually known is that chiefs and other tone-setting men "have more than one wife, often three or four." Among the Aweikoma Kaingang, Henry reports a fair number of polyandrous unions, but infers that 60 per cent of all marriages are monogamous. Petrullo actually saw two Yaruro cases, but reports monogamy as the normal practice: "If no women are available, a man may share his young wife with his brother or parallel cousin . . . ."

Some excitement arose some years ago among anthropologists over instances of polyandry among Shoshonean groups. The typical situation was probably that described as follows: "One brother actually married the woman and was considered father of her children. The other brother lived in the same house and the woman cooked for both. But the second had sex privileges only when the first was away and with consent of the wife." In another Nevada group, "the younger brother looked forward to acquiring a wife of his own," preferably a sister of the mate hitherto shared with his senior; but thereafter wives would not be held in common. Throughout the area polyandry is nowhere the prescribed nor the most popular form of marriage; it is sometimes wholly absent, whereas permissive polygyny is universal.

The Eskimo data are somewhat comparable. The Nunivak practiced both polygyny and polyandry. Among the Caribou Eskimo no instances were found, whereas 25 per cent of the men were bigamous; the Netsilik are said to have many polyandrous unions. Jenness and Mathiassen observed a single case each among the Copper Eskimo and the Iglulik, respectively. According to both investigators, masculine jealousy rapidly put a stop to the arrangement.

The impression conveyed by both the Shoshonean and the Eskimo occurrences—and this seems to apply to other peoples, too—is that such polyandry as takes place is not institutional, but a rule-of-thumb adjustment to local and individual circumstances. Cooper is probably right in crediting such arrangements largely to marginal societies, i.e., on the whole the simplest, which have not so definitely crystallized their norms of behavior, hence are able to meet individual problems in pragmatic fashion. Steward was at one time inclined to stress the equality of the sexes as the significant factor, but is less confident in his later paper because of the wider distribution of polygyny within the same area. *Some* empirical correlation is plausible enough, for the marginal peoples generally lack an overwhelming bias in favor of either sex. In other words, their ideology would not automatically bar a polyandrous marriage where conditions rendered it convenient. Such sporadic, uninstitutionalized polyandry may well go back many thousands of years, as Cooper suggests.

All such occurrences, however, are rightly described by Schmidt and Koppers as "without fundamental significance in social life." By way of contrast they define Tibet and southern India as the center of institutional polyandry. They further point out indications of its occurrences in South Arabia and ancient Babylonia. Unfortunately, relatively full data are available only for the Toda. Here marriage of one woman to two or more men—generally brothers—is not only permitted, but dominant. We naturally ask how such a thing is possible. It would not have been except for artificial tampering with the sex ratio. For unascertainable reasons the Toda regularly practiced female infanticide; whence a scarcity of women and the possibility of polyandry. In the more conservative half of the tribe, Rivers found that the number of males for every 100 females had been 259, 202, and 171 in successive generations, the decrease being of course due to the influence of British administrators. The aboriginal custom was that if a man married, his brothers automatically shared in his conjugal rights, all living together. More rarely there was a gentlemen's agreement between unrelated men to become joint husbands of the same wife. The arrangements in regard to paternity have already been described; the effects of obsolescent infanticide will be discussed in a later section.

In the Marquesas Islands (Polynesia), men for some reason outnumbered women, so that polyandrous matings were general and polygyny very rare. From the evidence, however, it is doubtful whether *marriage* is the appropriate term for the arrangements in vogue. What happened was that the head of a household attached male helpers to his establishment who might cohabit with the wife "only when the husband himself was absent." The several mates were thus by no means on a par, and only one can be legitimately regarded as a husband. Monogamy with licensed cohabitation by the wife with other men seems a more appropriate description of the facts.[16]

## Polygyny

As polyandry is rendered probable by a surplus of marriageable males, so polygyny rests largely on a surplus of nubile females. This is apparently nowhere brought about by male infanticide, but usually by warfare or other hazardous masculine occupations.

Eskimo hunting is so dangerous that men frequently lose their lives, which would explain the ratio of 5 males to 16 females in one Greenland settlement. Such disparity, however, is exceptional. In 1922 the Iglulik totaled 504, of whom 146 were men, 161 women, the rest children. This would permit only a very moderate indulgence in plural marriage: Mathiassen found only six bigamists, though about a century earlier twice that number were reported. It was usually clever hunters that had two wives; in earlier times some were credited with having supported three. The Caribou Eskimo bands investigated uniformly show a preponderance of adult women, the ratios being 30:25; 28:22; 18:13; 31:25; 21:17. This is all the more interesting because just as regularly boys exceed the girls, the figures being 24:11; 31:26; 13:10; 28:20; 23:15. In these groups about 25 per cent of the men were bigamists. Among the Copper Eskimo the situation is different. One settlement had 67 males and only 60 females; another, 46 men against 42 women. This may be due to the relative frequency of female infanticide. Characteristically, Jenness found only a single native who had more than one wife for any length of time. Inevitably bigamy in this group not only involved arduous effort on the husband's part, but also exposed him to the resentment of "men who cannot find wives for themselves." Recalling that some of the Eskimo allow polyandry concomitantly with polygyny, we may say that the ideology of these people does not militate against plural marriage, but that local demographic and economic conditions determine its incidence, which never equals that of monogamy. Hans Egede, "the first ethnographer of Greenland," whose observations go back to 1721, summarizes them in accordance with all later inquiry as follows: "Usually each man has only one wife; several have two, three, even four, whereby they prove themselves as men stronger and more skillful than the rest, since they are able to support so many wives and children."

Utterly different are the conditions among the Murngin. There the numbers of males and females are about equal, yet a normal middle-aged man has at least three wives and covets as many as he can get without arousing too violent an antagonism from his fellow males. Here the explanation of polygyny lies in several directions. Girls are taken in marriage, though not yet for purposes of cohabitation, before puberty and henceforth rate socially as wives. Second, young men are often obliged to wait until they inherit a wife in this society run by the older generation. Third, and most important of all, the eternal feuds of the Murngin destroy a sufficient number of young men to permit general polygyny for the elders.

In Tikopia all men of rank had more than one wife before the coming of Christianity. Here infanticide, though practiced, played a minor role, since neither sex seems to have been markedly discriminated against in the practice. However, the fact that many young men perished on dangerous sea voyages accounts for the surplus of women. The elders sometimes ordered the young men to remain single in order to keep down the population, but without forbidding indulgence in sex relations.

The Yakö, again, made moderate polygyny possible for the majority by the wholesale purchase of young girls from foreign tribes.

Since Africa is the home of polygyny *par excellence,* data on the Negroes are of special relevance. There are trustworthy statistics for Tanganyika: the official census shows a 5 per cent excess of women, and the material from a Negro maternity hospital proves 596 female births per thousand over a ten-year period. In some districts the difference between adult men and women is proportionately still higher. In 1928 there were 37,929 Jagga women against 32,576 men; in 1929 the Rangi comprised 79,942 women and 34,941 men. The latter disproportion is, however, due to a special cause, viz. the emigration of men who hire themselves out as laborers for white employers.

Polygyny is the obvious mode of readjustment to a preponderance of women. The authenticated disproportion of births evidently does not begin to explain the extent of polygyny in the region. Here, as elsewhere, the cultural background must be taken into account, especially the accepted privileges of wealth and power. In 1931 Mrs. Thurnwald found that whereas poor men were monogamous, the more prosperous had two or three wives, rich men or chiefs from six to ten, paramount chiefs as many as twenty or thirty. In one tribe without marked differences in wealth there was a tolerably equitable distribution of women.

Inquiries in other parts of Africa support the upshot of the observations in Tanganyika. Uganda *peasants* are usually monogamous, rarely aspiring to more than two or three wives. In the chiefless Volta country, bigamy was the norm for a middle-aged man, and five wives with one husband were distinctly rare. The Yoruba rank and file are overwhelmingly monogamous, their chiefs never if pagan, very seldom even if Christianized. These people in 1921 numbered 996,320 males and 1,117,091 females—a ratio of 47:53. In Ondo, a town of 30,000 people, the king had 75 wives, one chief 205, several others from 25 to 43, about fifty men from 5 to 20.

This brings us back to the matter of the bride price. In Yorubaland a nubile virgin fetches 12 pounds, 10 shillings, the minimum figure for a young widow or an unmarried mother being 7 pounds, 10 shillings. It takes a commoner half a lifetime to accumulate that amount; hence he remains monogamous unless a lucky fluke, such as inheritance of a widow from his father's or elder brother's estate, throws an extra wife in his way.

In many American Indian societies, purchase of the eldest of several sisters gave a man a claim, without further expense, on the other girls as they came of age. Sororal polygyny was thus in some regions (Crow, Hidatsa, Chiricahua) a mode of getting several wives at the price of one. But widespread as this arrangement is, it is far from universal. The Yoruba tabooed marriage, before or after the first wife's death, with a full sister of hers; and though a half sister by the same father was not prohibited, she was rarely married by her brother-in-law. Again, the Kazak customarily practiced the sororate, remitting all or most of the usual bride price, but looked with horror on sororal polygyny. These cases again illustrate the enormous differences in attitude toward the same usage in different areas.

Because of the deep-rooted aversion to polygyny in contemporary civilization we must be particularly cautious in appraising the phenomenon where it is an institution. Three prejudices, above all, must be eliminated. The psychology of polygyny, contrary to popular ideas, has very little to do with exaggerated masculine lust. Second, the practice is not at all degrading to the wives. Third, co-wives do not generally tear one another's hair.

MOTIVES FOR POLYGYNY.—To my knowledge the best psychological explanation of primitive polygyny from the man's point of view is in Ward's account of the Yoruba. He does not deny the occasional concupiscence of these Negroes as a motive for seeking additional wives, but finds that this plays a minor part and lists seven other factors. Potent is the desire for children. A man supposedly incapable of procreation is an object of contempt; hence the husband of a barren woman will frequently take another in order to demonstrate his virility. Children in large numbers, then, add to a man's standing and of course provide an abundance of help. But purely sentimental considerations are also very strong. A Yoruba loves to have his progeny play around him and to show them off to a visitor.

A third factor is the stringent taboo against sex relations with a woman for three years after her delivery. Such prolonged continence is overcome by a second marriage if that can be achieved. As stated above, a fourth determinant is the lucky inheritance of a wife, married as well as single sons or brothers being rightful claimants. Still another factor working toward the same end in an earlier period would be warfare, which at times carried off thousands of active men.

A sixth motive is the direct economic utility of wives. Yoruba women are excellent traders, being adept at bargaining; they carry materials to and from the farm; and their auxiliary labor in the fields saves a farmer the cost of so many hired workers.

The craving for prestige and the desire to invest wealth are reckoned as separate factors by Ward, but are closely connected. Every native wants to achieve high social standing in his community, but the way to do so is to give evidence of wealth, and the ocular demonstration of that is an imposing array of wives. In a dispute one man downs another by flinging into his face that he has nine wives against his opponent's five. The chief with 205 wives loomed larger in the public eye than his king with a mere 75. A rich Yoruba cannot put his wealth into a bank, he does not need to buy land, his cultural tradition does not favor the building of fine houses or the purchase of exquisite furniture or of a picture gallery. "There is, however, one form of investment which stands out clearly in their minds, and which appeals to them. It is the investment in wives. And this is where all their surplus money finds its way."

Interestingly, it is this motive of investing wealth that Ward regards as the most important of all.

The validity of this interpretation appears from the complete corroboration it receives from other parts of the continent. For the East African Bantu of Tanganyika in aboriginal times Mrs. Thurnwald uses almost the same phraseology. Women formerly were an index of their husband's power, they were laborers in the fields, they represented "an investment of capital." Modern conditions have brought a change here. A paramount chief whose predecessor boasted of having 80 wives has only 10 at present, for his large revenue can now be converted into automobiles, stone houses, European clothes, and what not. Women grow less industrious and demand better clothing; hence a large harem has become burdensome rather than otherwise. As for the continence imposed after a delivery, that is likewise reported from other tribes, e.g., the Lango, and is an obviously strong incentive.

Of course, Ward's motives are not equally potent in all parts of Africa, let alone in the world; even among the Yoruba individual differences make themselves felt, and points stressed by them may drop out elsewhere. For instance, the Yakö do not associate prestige with the number of one's wives. But Ward's list does seem to include all the factors that operate anywhere, and his relegating carnal desire to a modest place among the determinants of polygyny must be heartily approved. It cannot be too often repeated that marriage is not identical with cohabitation. Among most primitive peoples the sexual instinct is easily gratified outside wedlock. A savage no more needed marriage for the purpose than did a lecherous French courtier at the time of Louis XV.

STATUS OF CO-WIVES.—Where polygyny is an institution, it degrades neither the first wife nor her fellow wives. As Driberg reports for the Lango, the women "would be the first to resent the institution of monogamy." This is a corollary of the demographic data cited: given 38,000 Jagga women and 32,500 men, monogamy implies 5,500 unmarried women. As for the Lango, each wife gets a house of her own, and the husband cultivates separate crops for each, providing her with a separate granary. Here, as in a series of other Negro tribes, it is the first wife that suggests the purchase of a second to assist her in her tasks. She would hardly do so if the step were derogatory to her dignity.

RELATION OF CO-WIVES.—The lurid picture of madly jealous co-wives is accordingly a popular fallacy. In the circumstances just described, such a situation is virtually precluded: the first wife usually is the recognized mistress who has acquired a maid or two in the persons of other wives, but each has her own establishment and a fair measure of independence. Details vary naturally; some Southern Bantu give precedence to that one of a chief's wives who has been bought with the aid of the whole tribe; whereas in Tikopia all co-wives are virtually on a par. Even in Africa there are peoples like the Yakö who ascribe no ascendancy to the senior wife.

Unquestionably disputes arise between co-wives as between any human beings thrust into proximity and in a sense put into the positions of rivals. Probably sexual jealousy, except when there is unusual neglect of a spouse, is rarer than resentment over a real or fancied injustice to one's children in favor of their half siblings. Individual temperaments also inevitably play their part. But, by and large, responsible observers best qualified to judge are of the opinion that Negro co-wives "get on very well together" (Ward). Yoruba women accept the axiom that a husband is primarily interested in his favorite—usually the senior—wife and in his latest acquisition, realizing "that such preferences are not innovations but part of the cultural pattern of the tribe."

According to natives in widely separated areas, quarrels are minimized when the wives are sisters, true or classificatory. In some American Indian tribes it is stated as a foregone conclusion that "sisters" as co-wives do not quarrel whereas unrelated wives do. In part this may be mere rationalization, but the great importance of kinship in these societies makes the assertion credible.

The Alorese have developed a curious purge of jealousy. The first wife is expected to kick up a terrific row when her husband buys a second one. The two rivals fall foul of each other, exchanging blows and embroiling their partisans in a free-for-all. These fights are at times sham affairs, but sometimes they spring from deep resentment. Then the senior wife will vindictively destroy the newcomer's crops and bully her into withdrawing, which means that she must plead with kinsmen to return the price paid for her.[17]

## *Evolutionary Schemes*

Speculative anthropology at one time attempted to bolster up evolutionary schemes by pointing to recent samples of the stages postulated. One of the earlier of these was "group marriage," i.e., "the intermarriage of several sisters, own and collateral, with each other's husbands in a group" and "the intermarriage of several brothers, own and collateral, with each other's wives, in a group." On the hypothesis this condition, a combination of polyandry and polygyny, preceded marriage between single pairs and followed a stage in which brothers and sisters were allowed to mate; it resulted by excluding blood siblings from sex relations.

As pointed out at the beginning of this chapter, promiscuity in the technical sense undoubtedly existed at that point of history when the ancestor of modern man had not yet developed a culture with norms for judging sexual behavior. In the absence of such standards *de facto* monogamy would be just as promiscuous, i.e., unbridled by customary law, as any other form of mating. The issue, then, is not whether at some remote period there was promiscuity, but whether there are solid grounds for assuming a course of development in agreement with the scheme.

Let us consider what supporters of the evolutionary system may reasonably be expected to prove. Group marriage ought to be found in the very simplest cultures extant, for though development is uneven, it can hardly be assumed that the unequivocally rudest peoples generally forged ahead to achieve the matrimonial conceptions of the most civilized. Further, the theorists should demonstrate that group marriage cannot come about otherwise than by the reformatory exclusion of siblings from sexual congress.

It is rather generally admitted nowadays that the evolutionary scheme remains unsubstantiated. To be sure, it is easy to find some instances in very simple societies suggestive of the hypothetical group marriage. Certain Australian tribes and the Chukchi have been conspicuous in this respect. However, the alleged proofs fall short of the mark; they establish within limits periodic sexual communism, not group marriage as the pre-eminently dominant social arrangement.

Thus, the Dieri (Australia) practice infant betrothal, each female becoming the promised wife of only one male who almost wholly controls her sex life. He may share her favors with a guest of the proper kinship status, but except at a period of special license no other man may abduct her. Correspondingly, the horde council may assign concubines standing in the proper relationship to a man, but the affianced wife always takes precedence of them when present. The Dieri are certainly far looser than *we* consider consistent with the marriage tie: brothers who have married sisters sometimes share wives, a widower may consort with his brother's spouse; eminent men have concubines allotted to them. But all these are in the main impermanent arrangements. The temporary mates do not assume equal obligations in *marriage,* which is not a matter of mere cohabitation, but of economic and parental duties. Malinowski and others have made it abundantly clear that the family, hence marriage, is as firmly rooted in Australia as anywhere. Radcliffe-Brown has pointed out that "wife" is a quite inappropriate term for the Dieri concubines, and that the relation of marriage to economic functions "is of greatly more importance than the fact that man and wife are sexual partners." Recent work in South Australia is wholly corroboratory: "Even with the many cases of unfaithfulness on the part of both wife and husband, and the cases of condoned extra-marital intercourse, family solidarity and morale are excellent. Its stability does not rest solely on the sex element, but on the economic aspect and on the desirability of parenthood."

The Chukchi instance is still more transparent. Kinsmen—never brothers, but rather second or third cousins—as well as unrelated friends unite for the purpose of sharing their wives, who, however, sometimes object to a particular mate. Five to six, or even ten couples make such arrangements, in which virtually the entire tribe is involved. This certainly simulates "group marriage." However, it turns out that "companions in wives" do not live together in a house community; on the contrary, they belong to different camps, so that the contractual rights are seldom exercised. The institution is a device for providing travelers with bedfellows; with marriage it has nothing to do.

Among other equally simple tribes, such as the Pygmies of the Andaman Islands, or the Malay Peninsula, nothing even suggestive of group marriage has been reported. On the other hand, there has been a recent evolution in that direction among the incomparably more complex Toda. Here the British administration forbade female infanticide, thereby restoring the natural sex ratio. A priori one might suppose that this would promote monogamy. But polyandry was so deeply rooted that development took a different course. The old institution was retained, but the surplus of women (as compared with earlier conditions) was used to combine polygyny with polyandry: a trio of brothers that formerly shared one wife, now share two wives. Thus, group marriage may evolve in very recent times and in a comparatively sophisticated society.

We may thus eliminate group marriage as either a necessary or necessarily ancient stage in the history of human marriage.[18]

## General Considerations

Although sociological phenomena cannot be reduced to psychological terms, psychological factors obviously enter them at every stage. They are never allowed free play, because every society imposes its limiting conditions; but there are also limits to social restrictions. At one time anthropologists wrote as though primitive folk "automatically" obeyed their traditional laws. Malinowski convincingly showed that this was nonsense. The simpler peoples are certainly very sensitive to public opinion, but there are points beyond which they cannot be restrained. Public opinion recognizes the fact and makes concessions.

In our own civilization prostitution has sometimes been treated as a necessary evil: the purity of womanhood as a whole could be salvaged only by throwing a sop to masculine concupiscence. The view implied that only males had an active interest in sexual satisfaction; it accepted as a foregone conclusion that they must defer marriage long after physiological maturity and that accordingly means must be found to appease their desires at the expense of an outcast minority of women for the protection of the remainder.

Among primitive peoples the rules for mating often strike us as extraordinarily rigid, but in practice they are considerably mitigated. The Australians are very strict about some of their regulations, but they make allowances as to others; in short, they realize that it is not possible to thwart the sexual drive. Hence develop all manner of makeshifts. In tribes that prescribe marriage with a mother's mother's brother's daughter's daughter it constantly happens that no such unclaimed individual can be found even by stretching extension of the kinship term to the utmost. The natives do not decree celibacy in such cases, but permit some alternative form of marriage. "If a man of a certain sub-section cannot find a wife in the proper sub-section he is allowed to marry into some other sub-section." Again, a Murngin calls the wives of his polygynous father "mother" and should abstain from sex relations with them. But if he yields to temptation, the act is venial provided the parent has become senile and is thus frustrating both his son's and a young wife's natural desires. An African ruler would put to death an intruder into his harem, but he might reward a trusted henchman with the gift of some superfluous wife. In Tikopia the elders enforce celibacy on young men, but make no pretense at prohibiting them from extramarital affairs.

In short, the sex urge is generally accepted as a datum. It is invariably channeled, but with a recognition of human frailty. At the same time the natives, like ourselves, take cognizance of individual variability. Only an impeccably virtuous Crow woman may perform a ceremonial act in the sacred Sun Dance and even a cook during that festival ought not to be man-crazy. Correspondingly, a man who looks on indifferently when his wife is kidnapped by the member of a rival society is lauded for his strong heart; one who grows violent under such strain is gibed at for the rest of his life. Such are the rewards and penalties under an aboriginal code of ethics.

Jealousy is far more malleable than sexual desire. Whether inborn or not, it can be so conditioned by society as to remain underground. Innumerable cases from American, African, and Australian aborigines disprove the notion, easily fostered in an Occidental atmosphere, that man everywhere sets value on the exclusive possession of a woman. "A Neobrazilian," says Nimuendajú, "is naturally struck by the Timbira's lack of that jealousy so excessively developed in his own society and practically the basis of sex life there." This is not to deny that ebullitions of temper occur. A Negro wife in a polygynous household may rebel against a neglectful husband. An impetuous Crow may defy decorum so far as to pull out a knife against a wife abductor. But, by and large, jealousy plays a significant social role only where society fosters it.

As has been pointed out, a differentia of marriage in contrast to socially inferior forms of cohabitation is the desire for offspring. Shall this be regarded as instinctive? Here we must draw a distinction. Love of children seems to be general on the part of adults. A touching Blackfoot story tells of a scout who discovers a tent occupied by a couple from a hostile tribe and their little child. The latter is playing with a horn spoon, dipping up soup from a kettle. While his parents are absorbed in talk, the child notices the stranger peeping in through a hole in the lodge and toddles over to feed him. The scout is so deeply touched that, contrary to his manifest duty, he warns the child's parents, making it possible for them to escape.

Truly an affecting tale; and at that the Blackfoot exhibited affection for a stranger's, indeed, an enemy's child. Many similar instances could be presented, notably the widespread adoption of children in Indonesia and elsewhere. It might be argued a priori that if human beings show love for other's progeny, they will be proportionately happier over their own, but this does not follow. Specifically, we must distinguish between the masculine and the feminine point of view. In contemporary Western society the novel conception of women runs counter to the demands made upon any mother's energy; individualism consistently developed bars maternity. A husband may crave children, but it is his wife that undergoes the travail and risks of childbirth, the inconveniences of nursing.

Attempted or actual elimination of offspring appears, as a matter of fact, sporadically in the simplest societies. A Murngin woman who has only recently given birth forestalls another child by abortion or clandestinely smothers the newborn infant in the bush to evade the father's wrath. In Alor, too, men are more eager for offspring than their wives. Obviously such attitudes cannot become general, but their existence at all sheds some doubt on the nature of the "parental instinct." It is not, however, always the mother that objects to the newcomer: in Tikopia the father renders the crucial decision, which hinges on the potential food supply. Elsewhere the masculine cast of a culture exerts an influence: the "paternal instinct" operates only on behalf of male progeny. "In Montenegro, the birth of a girl is regarded as an extreme misfortune, and for that reason the Montenegrin never supports his female children."

What follows from ethnographic observations is that the "parental instinct" is highly susceptible to cultural influences. African Negroes generally crave children; the Lango rate barrenness worse than the utmost profligacy and consider it a cause for divorce. Here a woman would naturally desire children as a patent of prestige, especially since delivery is easy. The Kikuyu, another East African people, also yearn for offspring, but they regard twins as a source of bad luck, hence kill one or both of the infants, superstition overriding philoprogenitiveness. Let us recall, however, that an African wants children, whether begotten by himself or not. He claims and treats as his own sons and daughters children not possibly his in a physiological sense, but belonging to him because he has paid the bride price for their mother. Combining this fact with the free and easy adoption of children in Eskimo and Oceanian societies, with the complete indifference of polyandrous Toda brothers concerning the fatherhood of their collective progeny, we must conclude that the deep-rooted love of children is a generic one, not limited to the product of one's own loins. From the continuance of the species we may infer that infanticide, abortion, and avoidance of parenthood in other ways loom less large in the total picture than some lurid accounts suggest; and that when Montenegrins commiserate or deride the father of a girl they are in some measure talking for effect. They may want to raise heroes, but they know perfectly well that without some baby girls there are not going to be any heroes.[19]

In upper-class Occidental circles the wife's function is often preponderantly to bear children; except by virtue of her dowry or private income she does not contribute to the maintenance of the household. It is otherwise among the European peasantry, where each sex has its allotted tasks. In Eire, men do the heavy work in the field and garden, women the auxiliary tasks of planting and picking up potatoes, kneading and piling up the peat which the men have cut in the trenches. The wife milks the cows, churns butter, and sells eggs. Primitive conditions naturally conform more closely to the rural Western type, i.e., masculine and feminine labors are complementary. We have seen that an unmarried Chukchi is hard put to it, and the same holds for innumerable societies. A Murngin man hunts and cooks the larger game; his wife gathers yams and shell fish, makes the fire, and prepares the food for which she is responsible. In East Africa the normal thing is for men to tend and milk the cattle, while women do the farming; in Uganda the wife provides food in the form of bananas, the husband clothes the family by planting fig trees, whose bark he beats into cloth. In some areas one sex may have a distinctly lighter job, but as a rule the division is a fair one. Such interlocking of services for the common good is what we mean in speaking of marriage as an economic arrangement: by it the daily routine is made possible in accordance with the accepted standard of living.

The preceding sections have made it sufficiently clear how economic factors constantly figure before and during wedlock, as well as in its dissolution. Since females are commonly economic producers and in any case enjoy a scarcity value, a wife is usually compensated for by exchange or purchase. This payment is sometimes understood to imply her ability to provide offspring, whence the right to divorce her if she proves sterile, or the claim to a second wife from her family. If the woman elopes from her husband or desires to leave him, he is usually entitled to restitution of his payments—a check on divorce. Certainly there are plenty of freakish specializations that elude our understanding but, as Henri Sée remarked, an economic interpretation does help us find our way through the chaotic welter of facts.[20]

# Chapter 6

# PROPERTY

## *Definition*

Property is an institution by virtue of its basic character in society. "As for the property law," writes Philbrick, "to say that social life creates it is a very great understatement of the intimacy of their relation. A biological mutualism, indeed, an intimacy greater than that term strictly connotes, exists between them. Each gives form and life to the other." And MacIver declares: "Every system of government sustains a corresponding system of property. To change the one is to change the other . . . . Property is not wealth or possessions, but the right to control, to exploit, to use, or to enjoy wealth or possessions."

If we adopt the lawyers' point of view expressed by Professor MacIver, a distinction often made in discussing property vanishes. It has been customary to distinguish "incorporeal" from corporeal property, the former comprising such rights as are involved in copyrights as opposed to tangible objects. As soon, however, as "property" is restricted to the *right* to control belongings, all property evidently becomes incorporeal, as Hohfeld indicates. To quote Hallowell, "rights may be exercised with respect to any valuable object of any conceivable kind."

Conceptions of property are constantly shifting with the development of technology and a change in moral ideals. Aviation, for example, limits the earlier notion that the owner of real estate had rights extending to the sky. Nowadays he can advance no claims against the flier of an airplane unless actual damage occurs. In times of crisis, such as wars, the fact is thrust home that no modern state tolerates absolute property rights on the part of individuals. Automobiles or other goods are requisitioned; soldiers are billeted on householders; in defiance of individual economic freedom, governments regulate prices for the common good. When wheat soared to $3.48 a bushel during World War I, "controls were instituted which kept the price at $2.20 a bushel during the rest of 1917, and $2.26 the year following." The more recent OPA rules need merely be mentioned in passing.

As a matter of fact, no crisis is required for a government to invoke the principle of "eminent domain" in order to expropriate property holders, with or without indemnifying them; or to limit individual rights to property on grounds of public necessity or enlightened moral-

ity. The emancipation of slaves abolishes property rights; any inheritance tax implies that the testator cannot dispose of his estate as its absolute master; in fact, any tax is popularly conceived as confiscation of
individual property.

As Philbrick puts it, "the concept of property never has been, is
not, and never can be of definite content." He points out the difficulties
that may result from transferring the principles of one country to
another: in England the landlord was usually responsible for improvements, in Ireland it was the tenant; thus the rule preventing tenants
from removing their fixtures proved a source of great hardship to the
Irish. Property concepts vary even in the several states of our country,
say, as regards inheritance; American ideas naturally differ even from
those of English law and still more from Continental ones. The German code, under the republic, e.g., did not include copyrights under
the head of property.

The changes as to property may, then, arise from technological,
economic, ideological conditions. They may also be due to political
expediency. When trying to curry favor with certain elements of the
population in 1920, the Nazis formulated a programme, allegedly
immutable, which demanded the "confiscation without compensation
of land for communal purposes." In 1928, Hitler, finding it opportune
to appease the big landowners, explained that the proposal envisaged
only Jews and proprietors who did not administer their estates "in
accordance with national welfare." On the other hand, ancient laws
may persist despite their unsuitableness to a modern setting. The great
English historian Maitland said of the modern English real-estate law
that it was "full of rules which no one would enact nowadays unless
he were in a lunatic asylum."

Evidently what the German jurist Bekker said about law applies
also to property: "it grows out of human life and grows back into life,
and any major mutation of it influences life." In other words, an exhaus-
tive discussion of property would be a complete account of human
society, past and present. No such account, of course, can be attempted
here. All we can do is to answer, in the light of present knowledge, a
series of relevant questions: Do all peoples recognize property rights?
To what kinds of valuables do such rights extend? How are they correlated with other aspects of social life? What are the rules of inheritance? These questions are themselves interrelated; they are also connected with matters that in part have already been treated under other
headings and in part will have to be dealt with later.[1]

## Privileges as Property

Some writers have denied that property exists among primitive peoples, whom they describe as either communistic or as recognizing only "possessions," i.e., mere physical control for use. As the preceding paragraphs indicate, *no* society grants unlimited rights of ownership. "Under no legal system," says Philbrick, "can it be doubted that possession is the normal manifestation of ownership." The alleged difference between savages and civilized peoples is thus one of degree.

One type of property commonly found among primitive peoples does approach the absolute form. It corresponds most closely to our patents and copyrights. There can be no invasion of the prerogative held, so that public or communal ownership is ruled out; and the holder's liberty to dispose of his title is limited only by the ideological preconceptions of the culture. The valuables in question include personal names, dances, songs, myths, and ceremonial regalia. They may be owned either by a single individual or by an exclusive group. Sometimes wholly secular, they are perhaps more frequently entangled with aboriginal religion and magic.

Typical of what has been called "incorporeal property" are the names, songs, dances, emblems, nay techniques owned by each of the Bororo clans: only the Bakoro people, e.g., may use a little lath covered with black thread and porcupine quills to decorate their bows. No cases of encroachment on this privilege are known, for the idea of anyone's wanting to invade it is inconceivable for the natives. Some branches of the Siouan family assign to their clans specific political functions: among the Winnebago only the Thunderbird people make peace, the Bears police the village, the Buffalo supply a herald. East of the Rocky Mountains sets of personal names are often the exclusive property of clans. In the Elk clan of the Omaha tribe a person will bear such a name as Soft Horn, Yellow Horn, Large Pronged Horn, Female Elk. In Australia, to mention an entirely different area, certain designs are owned only by particular Murngin clans.

It is sometimes contended that such prerogatives should not be regarded as property because the holder cannot sell them. This is a fallacious argument unless one would deny the term to innumerable inalienable estates of the European nobility and yeomanry. In Norwegian law no proprietor could alienate his farm at his own pleasure, for the right of inheritance—*odal*—was supreme. The constitution of 1814 explicitly declared that this principle was to be retained forever. Similarly, in

England entailed estates cannot pass out of the line of the original owner's direct descendants, and the German *fideikommiss* was an indivisible and inalienable family property.

Many intangible goods, however, are negotiable. The Northern Plains Indians commonly acquired songs and ceremonial privileges through visionary experiences. Crow informants told me of revelations that had qualified them to cure certain ailments, for which they received horses as fees, so that their sacred rights were directly transmutable into material benefits. Wissler has admirably illuminated the nature of Blackfoot "bundles"—collections of sacred objects dictated by a supernatural patron—from this point of view. The Indian "expects long life, health, and happiness to follow the ownership and proper care of bundles." Accordingly, the Blackfoot are eager to acquire one and willingly pay even more than it cost the present seller. By 1912 sacred pipes and their appurtenances, which at an earlier period could have been purchased for two or three horses, had risen in value so as to fetch up to thirty head. Destruction of the material objects in such a bundle was not an actual loss, for it was knowledge of the instructions originally conveyed by the spirit blessing the first owner that alone mattered, so that any one properly qualified could replace the lost feathers, tails, skins, and what not. No wonder that a Blackfoot regarded buying bundles as a safe investment—especially since in times of need most of them could be forced upon a wealthy tribesman in return for proper compensation. "While with us young men are exhorted to open a savings account, among the Blackfoot they are advised to become owners of medicine bundles." Even after a sale the former owner would be called in as a consultant when the bundle ritual was performed and would get compensation.

Quite comparable economically are the magical formulae of Northeast Siberians and Eskimo. A meaningless chain of words handed down from the past is firmly believed to make heavy loads light, to stop bleeding, to lure game, or even to change old clothes into a living being. Because of these miraculous qualities the owner of such a spell would not lightly part with it: some twenty years ago a gun with ample ammunition was a normal price among the Iglulik. One very old woman had taught a hunter her sacred formula, which had to be recited letter-perfect to be effective. "In return for this valuable information, Aua had provided Qiqertainaq with food and clothing for the rest of her life." The old lady had secured an annuity.

Whereas the Eskimo and the Blackfoot examples illustrate the economic value of privileges which the natives, however fantastically, assume to be of genuine utility, great importance sometimes attaches to rights that seem useless even from the native's point of view. Thus, a Crow was willing to pay a horse for the privilege of painting a certain design on his face, and he would have to pay the proper price even to his own mother.

The factitious value assigned to ceremonial rights is well illustrated by the Hidatsa military societies. These were arranged in a hierarchical series, every youth entering the lowest grade in the company of his age mates and then ascending the scale with them. However, entrance was not a matter of ordinary joining, but of replacement of the next older group; and this occurred not automatically, but only after heavy payments. The Indian conception was that membership in an organization was a socially valuable complex of rights which the owners would not give up uncoaxed and without compensation. Accordingly, if a group wanted to buy, say, the Kit-fox membership, its members would first of all make a joint conciliatory gift in order to put the prospective sellers into a favorable frame of mind. Fully conscious of holding the whip hand, the older company tried to extort the utmost payments possible without wholly discouraging the buyers. For a period stipulated, the Kit-foxes would then be feasted by their "sons," as the purchasers were called, and would give them the necessary instructions. Each buyer, so far as possible, selected from the Kit-foxes a father's clansman, from whom he bought individually the required regalia along with special knowledge and blessings. In these societies a man felt reasonably sure of recouping himself for any expenses whenever it came to be his group's turn to sell to the next company of bidders, but the benefits of membership itself were social rather than material. It was a foregone conclusion that every male of a certain age belonged to some society in the series, i.e., *owned* one of the complexes of songs, emblems, dances, and camp activities; and for the prestige value of such ownership the men were willing to pay through the nose.

The conspicuous absence of infringement noted for the Bororo in the beginning of this section seems to hold generally for comparable "patents." An Osage (Missouri) refused to tell about certain ceremonies "as they did not belong to the gens [clan] of the narrator." Even the secular songs of the Greenlanders enjoy immunity from pirating: "It is a characteristic feature that the author's poem (drum-song) is called his *pia,* i.e. his property. It would not be considered fair for any one else to sing or recite the author's poem as long as he himself may be alive. . . . When the natives had heard the first strains . . . they nearly always recognized the man or woman who 'owned' it. This shows that everyone stuck to his particular refrains and melodies."[2]

## Material Goods

The instances cited establish the existence of private property among primitive peoples. They tend to correct Morgan's statement, justifiable when made, that savages have little property, hence are devoid of "a passion for its possession." As just shown, simple hunting tribes may nevertheless crave immaterial privileges that supposedly secure safety and food or that enhance their reputation. These privileges, we noted, are sometimes individual, but may be held by an association or a kinship group of some sort distinguishable from the territorial group as a whole. We shall turn next to primitive conceptions concerning material belongings, which can be conveniently treated under the familiar heads of real and movable property.

Before discussing these it will be well to mention a few facts that bear on the issues involved. For one thing, ideas of property, as of every other social phenomenon, are to be viewed in their context. This means not only in the light of the associated technology and its practical implications, but also with reference to a people's ideology. Second, ownership of material goods, too, need not be individual in order to be private; it may be held by a social unit segregated from the totality of the territorial group. Finally, rules of property often vary according to the several forms of valuables, or according to practical exigencies even for the same type of valuables in a single society. Scarcity may precipitate an attitude utterly at variance with that assumed in less stringent circumstances.

## Real Property

Land has an entirely different significance for farmers, herders, and hunters. As a matter of fact, this truism is an understatement; for there are many ways of cultivating, and correspondingly it matters considerably what beasts are herded or killed as game. Hence relevant notions of property are also likely to vary.

FARMERS.—A primary point in regard to an agriculturist's rights is his relative stability. The Chinese and the typical old-fashioned European peasant are rooted in the soil of their fathers. The Austrian writer Rosegger could trace the estate of his peasant ancestors in Styria back to 1405, and it was not abandoned until 1868. In contrast to such continued association with one spot is the usually shifting cultivation of ruder farmers. A Canella can raise crops only in the narrow woods along the brooks of the Brazilian steppe. His annual clearings steadily increase the distance of the fields from the village until the transportation problem becomes prohibitively strenuous, when the settlement moves close to the latest clearings. After ten or twenty years of absence, natural afforestation usually permits returning to the old site; but though plots are said to belong to the women, ownership in such circumstances cannot have the same meaning as with us. It is rather a matter of "possession," giving the cultivators the prior claim merely to use.

The reason for migration often lies in other directions. The members of a Solomon Island group, finding their huts washed away by a high tide, retired to the cliff above. Subsequently, Miss Blackwood learned, they were tempted by a supply of coconuts to an islet, but later decided to settle on the mainland. They left once more because of a quarrel with neighbors. In the new village, however, three prominent persons died; hence from fear of sorcery the people migrated once more. In the interior of New Guinea, Thurnwald made similar observations, one tribe continually shifting its headquarters because of bickerings with other natives.

It is clear that where exhaustion of the soil, warfare, or superstitious fears make farmers move again and again they cannot evolve ideas of permanent ownership of the soil. In such cases real property in our sense, then, exists neither for an individual nor for a group.

But some primitive tribes do achieve stability. By virtue of intensive fertilization and an impressive irrigation system, the Jagga managed to remain for generations by the banana groves that supply their main sustenance. Here ownership rights were complex, but definite. Most typically, under aboriginal conditions, they were vested in the clan and validated by the presence of the skulls of the original planters. Second, there was land subjected in war by the chief, hence transferable by him at will. Finally, the chief might assign unoccupied land to alien immigrants, who were then entitled to transmit it to their heirs. Chief Rindi was accused of favoring foreigners; if he found a Jagga in possession of two groves one of which was neglected, he would assign it to an immigrant. On the other hand, such measures were not arbitrary; he would not interfere with the holder of even three groves who with the aid of his offspring was able to exploit them all. Effective use, then, was the basis of undisturbed possession. Within the ancient clan lands, plots were individually held; the occupant could lease them without the chief's consent, the lessee obligating himself and his heirs to pay a triennial rent in the form of a vat of beer. But sale of a grove is an innovation due to white contact and the introduction of individualistic notions. Land is inalienable among the Jagga, as it is nearly everywhere on their cultural level.

The need for irrigation developed clear-cut water rights. In recent times these have not been held by the Jagga clans, but by local associations, with the important qualification that the head must belong to the clan that first established the canal in question. All members participate in whatever repair work or other labor is necessary. Usufruct is regulated according to a definite plan: the slope is roughly divided into halves, the occupant of the lowest land on the right side of the canal starts to irrigate, being followed successively by those higher up until the approximate middle of the slope is reached, when there is a shift to the left side, with corresponding procedure. When the lower half is supplied, the holders of the upper follow according to the same principles. Special rights belong to the headman, who sometimes claims exclusive water rights on every third day.

The Jagga data are exceptionally complex, but for that very reason illustrate several points of great significance and wide applicability. In general, Jagga land is for the most part privately but not individually held; even in modern times a man may sell his grove only in the presence of a clansman, i.e., with clan consent; otherwise the chief invalidates the transaction. This notion of the sale of land, we noted, is recent, as with the overwhelming majority of primitive peoples. Further, the common sense that pervades the rules of exploitation is characteristic: cultivable land should not be allowed to go to pot; hence no abstract rights of ownership secure a neglectful Jagga from dispossession. Again, every Jagga has a right to exist; hence he must enjoy his share of the irrigation water. Finally, all rights to land are tied up with such basic features of the social system as the clan organization and the chieftaincy.

The way in which political institutions affect property appears when we compare the Jagga with another Bantu people. The Zulu, with a tradition of autocracy, recognize only the king or chief as a landowner; he, or his headman, allots the land, which the possessor naturally holds only for use.

Equally instructive are the data from Polynesia. In Mangareva about ten patricians owned the entire land area, commoners being nothing but tenants. In general, the relationship of proprietor to tenant was patriarchal, so that normally the cultivator was allowed to pass on his usufructuary rights to his eldest son, but legally he could be ousted at any time. The landlord, moreover, was entitled to the first fruits and the first two crops, leaving only the last and inferior one to the cultivator. In addition to this "rent," the nobleman also received a catch of fish.

The Hopi present still another type of phenomenon. Theoretically, the chief owns all the lands of the village; but since he has no coercive powers whatsoever, the clans are the virtual proprietors, though the chief has the right of allotting unassigned land. Because a flood may wash out the soil and blown sand continually spoils land, a clan property includes discrete sections, and the same applies to the family plots within the clan area. The matter of ownership is complicated by ideology: only women own real estate; hence though men do most of the agricultural work, the crops harvested as a result of their labors belong to their wives. "Since many clan members live in close proximity as an extended family group the precise title to land is often not clearly defined." Daughters continue to live with their mothers, their husbands living with them, so that the question of what female owns which part of the fields or the crops is without practical import. Apart from the quite theoretical claims of the chief, there is collective ownership by the clan and collective possession by the matrilineal lineages.

Among the neighboring Navaho, the first user of a tract or his heir held individual possessory rights, but if he failed to use it anyone might appropriate it. On the other hand, the crop—which everyone in the family had helped produce—belonged to the household as a whole. This may be regarded as the primitive agricultural norm.

Joint ownership of land occurs in Europe as well as among savages. At the turn of our century the Polish peasant still treated land as family property, not as that of one individual: the apparent owner was merely the manager on behalf of the family as a whole. This was precisely the result of the Norwegian odal system and represents the attitude often encountered among primitive peoples, both with reference to land and to other valuables. A generation ago the sale of a sacred bundle to an Eastern museum aroused great indignation among the Hidatsa on the ground that the seller had been merely the custodian and had ignored the interests of his fellow owners.

The familial interest in European farms likewise appears where it is customary, as in Styria or Eire, for the peasant to turn over the estate to a marrying son and to retire to a sort of reserve for the rest of his life. In such cases the other children's claims to the land are recognized, so that it is necessary to indemnify them. In western Eire the dowry brought by the bride is used to provide for her brothers- and sisters-in-law—just as the bride price among Palestinian Arabs and African Negroes serves to purchase a wife for the groom's brother.

The zadruga of the Yugoslavs furnishes still another example. As recently as 1932 Mr. Adamic encountered one of these house communities in South Serbia. Its inmates comprised the headman, his brothers, their sons, and grandsons, and adult females taken as wives from other villages. In other words, it was a residential unit composed of the males of a paternal lineage, their wives, and the unmarried females begotten by the members. Adamic's zadruga was composed of eleven single families living in one twenty-room house. They jointly owned a large tract of land and were a self-sufficient economic entity. Six women did the baking and cooking; eight others specialized in spinning, weaving, sewing; five men tended the livestock; one man made shoes. In Croatia the last house community, dissolved in 1900, comprised 24 individuals, who collectively owned 140 acres, 8 oxen, 6 cows, 2 horses, 55 pigs, and 100 fowls.

The Yugoslav house community was emphatically a joint corporation. Its head was merely the manager of the concern and the hereditary property was considered inalienable. Neither the house nor the stock could be sold without the consent of all the inmates, and originally any money earned by the members was pooled. In striking contrast to the hereditary estate, newly acquired belongings might be sold in case of need.

Thus, farmlands in most parts of the world are privately, but collectively owned, or owned by the dominant political authority. In modern English law the Crown is still the only absolute landowner, and we have pointed out that all modern states exercise the right of eminent domain. In general, then, both in civilization and among primitive peoples, individual holdings are possessory rather than proprietary.

Nevertheless, instances to the contrary occasionally turn up. The Mohave (Arizona, California) not only owned their farms, but sold them to tribesmen for war captives, beads, or other loot. In the peculiar circumstances of Tongareva (p. 29), the scarcity of land and the absolute dependence of life on the coconut has thrown individual claims into relief. The planter of a coconut had sole rights to its fruit and to the soil on which it grew. The nuts on and under trees "are private, not communal property. In former times, the trees were watched, and an alarm was immediately raised if anyone climbed a tree not his own.

Not only was there a natural desire to save inroads on private food supplies, but to allow strangers to take nuts was to admit that the tree was public property and so to diminish the rights of private ownership."

It hardly requires pointing out that, as in the last case, economic convenience, if not necessity, leads naturally to the kind of possession or property right recognized. In Yugoslavia, for instance, joint husbandry is often the only effective method and in a democratic society logically leads to collective rights.[3]

HERDERS.—For herders, land is significant as pasturage; hence the abundance or scarcity of fodder and water for their beasts determines notions of property. The Kazak case is especially instructive. Suitable winter quarters, with adequate shelter from the cold and with ample fuel and water, are scarce; hence they were eagerly fought over in earlier times and treated as individual property, set off by natural landmarks or by artificial signs. If a breeder lost a goodly part of his livestock, he no longer required a sizable winter territory and sold his surplus. In the summer the needs of the beasts are easily supplied; hence during this season grazing land was open to all according to their convenience, the question of property never arising.

The Lapps, an eminently peaceable people, lay no claim to definite areas, each *sit* (p. 28) respecting the customary rights of others, but not resenting trespass when due to necessity. Nor did the Nama Hottentot, of Southwest Africa, where rainfall locally drops to 4 inches a year, claim a clearly bounded area. For them permanent fountains or pools were the decisive factor for survival; hence *these* ranked as property of the several groups and newcomers into a region had to pay tribute for the use of water.[4]

HUNTERS, GATHERERS, FISHERMEN.—Peoples without domestic beasts and agriculture are generally organized in local groups which lay claim to a circumscribed area within which no outsider may use the natural resources without permission. The Australian and Ona hordes are typical illustrations. The association of a definite group with a definite tract goes so far that Australians and Buin Melanesians would never even dream of dispossessing a conquered enemy.

Some groups carry exclusiveness to extremes. In 1681 a Vedda gathering fruit from the territory of a neighboring band was reproved by one of its members, and the dispute led to a sanguinary fight involving other men of the two groups. In 1630 a traveler through Ceylon encountered a sentry at each group boundary. Similar guards are reported from the Maidu of central California. As Father Schmidt rightly emphasizes, the Caribou Eskimo are conspicuous for their total lack of any sense of communal sovereignty over any part of their habitat. The community "may decline to accept a stranger who settles on its territory; but it cannot forbid him to live there alone and make use of anything he chooses."

However, within the tribal or communal territory, hunters rarely claim land individually or by individual families. This is often a direct consequence of the mode of life: our buffalo-hunting Indians were obliged to follow the herds of their favorite game on its wanderings without restriction to a limited district. Nevertheless there are some clear exceptions along with some more dubious ones. Among the Yurok, up to a mile or so from the Klamath River "all land of any value for hunting was privately owned," and poachers were shot; prairies rich in edible seeds and streams valuable for fishing could be bought, a notable example of alienable land. The Washo (California) laid claim to individual or family patches of pine-nut trees, transmitting them to their sons; brothers would not quarrel over a clump and would let a married sister share in a plentiful harvest, but any trespass by strangers was resented. Why such ownership was not common in the Basin has been reasonably explained by Steward: a clump of pine-nuts yielded very capriciously there, failing possibly after one good season, then again affording far more nuts than a family could possibly pick, so that strangers were welcome to help themselves.

The Northeastern Algonkians of New England and eastern Canada present a vexed problem. Speck has forcibly argued that the tribal territory was split up into tracts, clearly demarcated, which belonged to individual families or at most to several closely related patrilineal families. Jenness, admitting that this held in recent times, regards the phenomenon as a consequence of contact with Caucasians. In his review of the earlier sources in conjunction with recent ethnographic inquiries, Cooper comes to the reasonable conclusion that the family hunting territories are ancient, but were strengthened by European influence. He and Schmidt properly raise, however, the important question how "family" is to be interpreted. Davidson's observations among the Tête de Boule of western Quebec indicate transmission of hunting rights from father to son either during the former's lifetime or by inheritance. If there are several sons, there is subdivision among the brothers. This procedure might soon lead to unconscionably small tracts in a single man's control, and it would be of interest to know whether, say, three sons still have at least a secondary title to the whole of the paternal territory. However this may be, some statements about other Algonkians suggest that the paternal lineage may be the true proprietor. If so, Cooper has aptly pointed out that it would sometimes be hard to distinguish the kinship group from the largest functioning "political" group. We may have the same sort of horde sovereignty based on patrilineal kinship that occurs in Australia rather than an actual "ownership in severalty." In other words, the Algonkian problem cannot be said to be definitively solved.

Drucker has vigorously argued that on the northwest coast of America, including northwestern California, it was really, despite appearances, the local group which held exclusive title to fishing sites and other economically valuable tracts. It is true, he admits, that an individual is *credited* with ownership, that his permission was essential to exploitation of the area, that the first seasonal yield belonged to him, and that these individual prerogatives were highly prized, going as they did with the headship of the extended family that formed the local group. "Nonetheless no instance was ever heard of an 'owner' refusing to give the necessary permission [for exploitation]. Such a thing is inconceivable to the natives." Hence the "owner" is a mere steward.

Significant as Drucker's point is, it does not quite invalidate the notion of individual ownership. It is a peculiarity of primitive societies, to be discussed presently, that ethical principles mingle inextricably with legal ones. In the case mentioned, two factors combine to temper the headman's legal privileges—the claims of kinship and the widespread willingness to share food even with an outsider. In practice, such considerations of "equity" might well override strictly legal claims without, however, nullifying them in theory. At all events, for the Yurok the possibility of a man's buying and selling land seems to establish individual property. Concrete evidence, moreover, proves that in the old days an individual could give away his interests in land. Sea lion flippers were a prized delicacy, and the right to all sea lions taken between two definite points was a highly valued privilege, whose infraction precipitated a feud unless the owners waived their claim. Most emphatically it was not the town, but a particular house in the town, and a particular person in the house that exercised ownership, so that a man could pass his right over to a favorite daughter.

In Asia there are at least two well-authenticated instances of such rights on the hunting-gathering plane. Not only did the local groups of Vedda "exercise a jealous supervision" of their boundaries, but individuals held hunting grounds within the general territory with the right to transmit them to their heirs. It is especially remarkable that a man was not free to hunt even on his brother's grounds without permission. Further, conveyance of land was possible, though normally it was transferred only to children and sons-in-law and required the consent of every adult male of the group. This, of course, is a limitation of ownership, but hardly more than in the case of an entailed estate in England. A stone and other small objects, such as a tooth or a lock of hair, were tokens of a transfer.

The second instance is from the Semang. Every adult male owns several durian fruit trees and one or more ipoh trees from which to derive the poison for his arrows. No one would dare cut into an ipoh trunk or climb up a durian tree unauthorized, though fruits lying on the ground are free to all.

Comparable to the last example is one from Queensland. Contrary to the general Australian rule, in one district patches of edible wild plants were assigned to particular women and inherited by their daughters.

To sum up, collective ownership of land is the usual thing on this level, but there are a number of noteworthy exceptions.[5]

## Multiple Possessory Rights

A striking fact in certain societies is the use of the same land for different purposes by two or more possessors. In New Zealand it might happen that one family would claim the right of digging up fern roots in a given locality, while another was simultaneously privileged to hunt rats there.

Under this head may be noted the regulations permitting a man to own trees on another's land, as commonly happens in Melanesia and West Africa. In Buin a man would pay shell money in order to buy the right to plant coconuts on alien property. Where this practice is in vogue, the European purchaser of a native farm has to compensate separately the landowner and any proprietors of trees on the estate. Interestingly enough, the Havasupai, who like all other American natives never knew of fruit trees in the old days, have evolved the notion that such trees "may be owned independently of the land on which they stand." This seems a convincing example of parallel development with no possibility of diffusion. The Navaho hold that a man who planted a tree and abandoned the land may assert his ownership to the tree years later, demanding compensation from a subsequent cultivator of the plot. Further, *wild* shrubs and trees on a man's land are not his, but may be utilized by anyone.[6]

## Movable Property

Movable property presents comparatively little difficulty. Except where an autocrat has power to divest any subject of his belongings, individual property rights are recognized on simple common-sense principles. The maker or the buyer of an object or the recipient of a gift figures as the undisputed owner even in societies that recognize only collective property in land.

This conception is, indeed, sometimes carried further than one would imagine. Irrespective of a woman's position in society, she alone as a rule disposes of her belongings, and American natives, at least, extend the idea to children. A Chaco Indian "would never give away what belongs to his wife or little child without asking them," Nordenskiöld reports; and Métraux tells us that a Toba woman in this area "disposes freely of her clothing and her household utensils." A Canella wife owns the utensils she has manufactured and the sleeping mats made for her by her husband. "Toys are the property of the child; to obtain them I had to get the child's consent," relates Nimuendajú; and I had the identical experience among the Paviotso of Nevada. On the other hand, Alorese parents callously disregard their children's property rights.

Slaves, though in a sense movable property, are not necessarily divested of all property rights. However, their status is best considered in connection with class systems.

The ownership of livestock strongly develops the sense of individual property, as indicated by the general use of brands or other property marks among pastoralists. The revolutionary effect of a herding economy imposed on a hunting culture has been previously illustrated by the example of the Lapps and the Chukchi. But stock-breeding is also likely to exert a social influence when combined with farming. A poor Jagga will ask a wealthy tribesman for the loan of a cow, contracting to tend it in return for her milk, which was so highly prized that the borrower gave the lender a thanksgiving present in the form of beer or grain. This made the rich man the poor one's patron: the borrower was likely to do odd agricultural jobs for the lender, who in turn would look out for his client's interests before the chief.

A significant development in East Africa merits notice. The cattle-breeding Wahuma locally recognize a sort of feudal tenure of live-stock; as elsewhere a chief or king holds all the land, so theoretically the Wahuma king is owner of all the cattle in the land and may dispossess the upper, herding caste of their stock.[7]

## Property and Ideology

Individual property rights, then, in some form are universal, but as various phenomena already cited show, ownership may be obscured by coexisting ideological principles. One of the most frequent of these is kinship. If two Murngin brothers cooperate in shaping a canoe—the most valuable of material possessions in this society—it belongs to both, with the senior of the pair naturally exercising more control as a rule. But by virtue of the kinship code, even brothers who did no work whatsoever share an interest in the boat. So long as primitive peoples remain unaffected by modern individualism, the Murngin conception usually holds. That is, the idler or the incompetent may lack esteem, but he does not lack food, shelter, and clothing; he may even borrow luxuries from his relatives. An earlier chapter lists specific kinship obligations, such as avuncular ones, that encroach intolerably, from our point of view, on individual rights. An additional example is a Canella's claim on his sister's husband's goods, so that a man living with his wife's kindred generally keeps some of his belongings at his mother's house, where they are safe from greedy brothers-in-law.

Whereas kinship usage often involves a markedly lopsided apportioning of benefits, many societies strongly emphasize reciprocity, whether among kindred or unrelated tribesmen. The attitude is reflected in our own phrase "Indian giver" and in our legal *do ut des* (I give in order that you may give). The underlying principle may force a transfer of property. In a Crow band the Horse Dance bundle, held by a small and exclusive clique, was reputed to bestow wealth on its owners. An impoverished Crow woman, known as a good skin-dresser, set out to obtain admission to the guild. Knowing that any direct appeal for initiation would be spurned, she insinuated herself into the good graces of the principal bundle owners by gratuitously tanning fifteen hides for them. The owners knew, of course, that some remuneration was due, and when the job was completed the proprietor's wife asked the skin-dresser whether she wanted a horse or some other valuable. "I said, 'No, I want to take your medicine' . . . The woman got angry. She said I should have told her that before. 'If you had told me before, I should never have let you finish the hides. Now I can hardly refuse you.' " She thus secured the coveted prize. "The other people were telling me I was very cunning because of the way I got the medicine." In other words, by performing necessary work for strangers the skin-dresser had set up so strong a moral claim that, reluctant though they were, the bundle holders found it impossible to deny her request, though legally they could have done so.

Simple as the Yaghan are, they have a well-established system of gift exchange. People gossip about a man who fails to make presents to his tribesmen. On the other hand, it is a foregone conclusion that he will be rewarded with a countergift, and "woe to him who acts stingily, returning trivial and useless things." Such a person is the butt of unfavorable comments. The system thus sometimes causes grave embarrassment: a person who has received some precious object may be hard put to it to find an equivalent within a reasonable space of time. Yet he cannot evade accepting the gift, for that would be regarded as a grievous affront; nor is it customary for a Yaghan to request something he really needs since he is expected to obtain that by ordinary barter.

In this respect Fijian practice differs. Anyone is free to solicit from a tribesman whatever untabooed property he craves, refusal causing a loss of face for the owner. But reciprocity operates here also, since the donor will some time later ask the recipient for something of greater value. Even pigs, canoes, and garden land thus change hands. The system "prevents accumulation and centralization of wealth by any individual and promotes continual redistribution. Property serves as the medium by which prestige may be acquired. A loss of property through gift exchange means a gain in prestige . . . ."

Again, a Crow war captain, having received sanction from a spirit to organize a raid, was strictly entitled to all of the loot. Yet probably never did a leader exercise this abstract privilege; had he done so, he would be considered a miser and would not have been able to recruit another war party. In other words, the rank and file, as a reward for their participation, had an "equity" in the spoils. Linton's data on the Comanche almost exactly parallel my own from the Crow.

To turn to another vital aspect of the subject, natives very commonly regard food as something to be freely shared. The Crow do not put it into the same category with other possessions; and the story goes that some American Indians were horrified on their first acquaintance with butchers—men so degraded as to charge money for meat!

The Copper Eskimo when seated at a meal offer every intruder some food, no matter how unwelcome he may be. Jenness, trying to conform to the folkways, would leave some of his rice for the natives present. "Often there would be twenty natives and only one plateful of rice among them all, but everyone, even the smallest child, had to receive a taste of it." At Nunivak anyone was free to help himself to the meat, blubber, and bone of a dead whale. In Tierra del Fuego a beached whale made people ignore the usual rules against trespass; all outsiders were welcome.

Experiences of this sort explain the belief in savage communism. Yet appearances are deceptive. The very same Eskimo who appear to be communists in matters of food meticulously regulate the distribution of the kill. The Nunivaker who scores the first hit on a specially prized species of seal gets the full credit for the animal, all the hide, intestine, forequarters, and bladder; the second gets the hindquarters. In Baffin Land the Eskimo allow special rights to the man who first strikes a walrus; he gets the head and the choice of the other parts.

In short, in ruder societies there is no abstract devotion to communism. The contrary impression arises because, though individual rights are recognized, they are constantly adjusted to ethical demands, to kinship obligations, to considerations of prestige, to a naïve and wholehearted admission that other human beings also have a right to exist.[8]

## Inheritance

Rules of inheritance, like the whole of property law, reflect the total ideology of a society. The Soviet law of 1927, limiting inheritance to 10,000 gold rubles and letting the state appropriate the remainder of a legacy, could not have arisen in a capitalistic country. The French Civil Code, aiming at protection of the family unit, limits the testator's power to will his property according to the number of offspring: he may dispose freely of half his property if there is a single child, one third if there are two children, and so forth, the denominator of the fraction he may assign at will exceeding by one unit the number of his progeny. By way of contrast, English law since 1715 has recognized the power of the property owner to disinherit his wife and children. In our country, Louisiana stands out from all the other states in recognizing the "legitim," i.e., rights of the widow and children irrespective of testamentary disposition. The growth of American out of English inheritance law is a good example of evolution—descent with modifi-

cation; colonial conditions were unfavorable to a rule of primogeniture, which had been abolished everywhere by 1798. The general adoption of inheritance taxes in Western civilization is another sign of the
influence of ethical conceptions on property rights. In short, complex
and simple societies alike have inheritance rules that mirror the social
ideology of the peoples.

Rivers distinguishes between transmission of property (= inheritance) and transmission of office (= succession). The distinction is
hardly justified. As this scholar admits, it is contrary to legal usage;
but what is more significant, if "property" denotes not wealth, but the
title to it, then office is simply one of the privileges potentially involved
in inheritance; hence it should be considered under the same head.
Among some peoples, indeed, offices form distinctly the most important
part of a man's legacy. Thus, in Australia artifacts are few and are
bound to remain such so long as the natives rove about without means
of transportation. On the other hand, a Murngin inherits from his
father the right to perform certain dances and in some localities his
magical power.

From our point of view, some primitive arrangements after the
death of a tribesman seem economically imbecile, others are thoroughly
practical, and still others blend unconcern for utility with sound common sense. Yaghan mourners "do all they can to blot out all remem-
brance of the departed." They burn his hut, inter or cremate all his
belongings, and for good measure throw in some of their own. A surviving husband who has other means of transportation will even
destroy his canoe because it would remind him of the woman who
used to paddle it. Other tribes proceed similarly from fear or because
the funeral deposits are believed to aid the departed while he is jour-
neying to the hereafter and on his arrival. The Arapaho burn a man's
belongings including his clothes and bedding "as it is thought that
the . . . spirit will revisit the locality if this is not done." Plains Indians, in general, buried the deceased in all his finery and killed his
favorite horse. The Shoshone of eastern California burnt or deserted
the dwelling and burnt the dead person's possessions, leaving no
material goods to be inherited.

Such wholesale destruction is probably peculiar to the simpler
hunters. The incipiently agricultural Maricopa already display another
feature. They, too, destroy the house with whatever it contains lest the
survivors sicken and die; then the mourners move to another locality.
Yet the mere fact that they *are* farmers introduces a new element: a

person might inherit not only the intangible possessions of his father—the chieftaincy or supernatural power—but also his land. The development of a herding economy likewise puts brakes on the urge to destroy; some beasts may be sacrificed, but hardly the whole herd.

Eskimo usage is not altogether uniform, but it often shows a compromise with economic necessities. A Baffinlander's property is largely destroyed at his death, but not entirely: a man's harpoon, sledge, dog, boat may be inherited, and this holds also for a woman's lamp and pots. The Cumberland Sound people believe that the late tribesman's hut and property must be destroyed, but only if he died inside the dwelling; accordingly, "a dying person is taken out of the tent . . . ." The Copper Eskimo always put part of the property on the owner's grave, but valuable implements are often recovered by the survivors in after years. In a similar spirit the Nunivakers show an admirable restraint. They deposit less lavishly at a burial for a person whose children have to be cared for; their idea is that of "providing for the deceased on his other-world journey so far as one could without seriously depriving the survivors."

Eminently practical is the frequent rule of having only females inherit from women and only males from men. This naturally disqualifies spouses, but is wholly fair from the aboriginal point of view since in many cases a person could not make use of the dress and implements essential for the opposite sex. We must remember that the ruder societies generally lack money, so that valuables cannot be converted into a standard of exchange.

The partly ideological division of labor and property between the sexes, of course, also affects inheritance. Over large areas the livestock are indissolubly linked with men. Among the typical pastoralists, such as the Kazak, "a daughter did not normally inherit," since property consisted so largely of domestic animals. Some Asiatics let all of a sonless man's stock go to a remote kinsman rather than to his daughter. Even the Lobi, who otherwise strictly adhere to the rule that daughters inherit from mothers and sons from fathers, let the cattle a woman may somehow have acquired go to her son or nephew because livestock is so definitely associated with masculine labor. On the other hand, a notion that certain forms of property are feminine will correspondingly disqualify men. No Canella ever takes over his wife's or mother's fields and house; if a daughter is lacking, they are taken by a sister or a sister's daughter.

We have seen that Western codes differ on the vital right of an individual to dispose of his property by will. Primitive law, too, is far from uniform on this point. In many cases no such thing as testamentary disposition is allowed, property descending automatically according to fixed rules, or according to group arrangements that could set aside the former owner's wishes. Thus, in Uganda the clansmen of a deceased person chose the heir, reserved about one tenth of the property to themselves, and assigned part of the cattle and part of the widows to the king, some of the women being appropriated by the members of the kin themselves. A remarkable instance of how kinship obligations bind a would-be testator is furnished by the Boloki (Belgian Congo). A sick man wished to bequeath some property to a friendly but unrelated medicine man, but there was no possible way of directly so doing. Accordingly, he resorted to a subterfuge. Inviting the doctor to his deathbed, he dealt him a light blow across the ankle. For this "assault and battery" the medicine man sued the heirs, demanding and receiving damages in the form of a slave, three pots of wine, two spears, and some brass rods—precisely the objects the deceased had wished to give him. Illiterate peoples, too, can circumvent the laws of inheritance. The case recalls the Lobi ruse to let a son get part of the legacy that should legally go to the nephew and the Guajiro way of thwarting the rule of nepotic inheritance by extensive gifts during the owner's lifetime (p. 49 f.).

Many of the simpler peoples lack fixed laws of succession, but even where such exist they may differ according to the kind of property that is transmitted. This feature, however, also appears in Western codes: Scottish law, for instance, prevents a testator from depriving his children of a share in his movable goods, but his power to dispose of real estate at will is not similarly limited. Natives often distinguish between hereditary property and that acquired by personal effort. This appears conspicuously in matrilineal parts of Melanesia, where the ground anciently cultivated continues to descend to the sister's son, i.e., remains within the clan or lineage, whereas the land a man has reclaimed from the bush and the trees he has planted are inherited by his children.

It is not surprising that sacred possessions are not necessarily transmitted on the same principle as secular property. When the Crow had land allotted to them, they at first naturally applied the familiar matrilineal rule, so that siblings inherited in preference to sons. But medicines and ceremonial privileges seem to have been always passed on in either line. A famous doll used in the Sun Dance had been revealed to a woman, who passed it on to her son, from whom another son inherited it. So far succession had been matrilineal. But on the second son's death *his* son took possession. Shields—also considered sacred objects—were willed either to a son *or* to a younger brother (a term covering a nephew as well).

Evidently there is no true inheritance wherever property is owned collectively by a fixed group, whether it be a Yugoslav house community or an African clan. The survivors simply remain in charge when one of the joint owners dies; that occurrence may make a considerable practical difference if the deceased happened to be an overshadowing personality, but in legal theory nothing is altered.

Seniority often plays a part in the succession to property, as in the widespread European dominance of primogeniture, and sometimes the eldest-born is surrounded with a halo of sanctity. This theme, however, is capable of variation according to the attention given to sex and rule of descent. The patrilineal Zulu recognize the eldest son as heir *par excellence;* among the bilinear Herero (Southwest Africa), who stress the mother's side for social, the father's for religious purposes, the eldest sister takes precedence of all other possible heirs to a man's stock; personal property is divided among the children; his sacred property, however, descends to the eldest sister's eldest son. The matrilineal Carrier (British Columbia) normally passed titles on to a sister's son or daughter; with the Haida all property went to a younger brother or, for lack of one, to the eldest sister's eldest son. A Hopi medicine bundle is similarly associated with the males of the matrilineage, but though theoretically a younger brother or the eldest sister's eldest son succeeds by preference, that sister's younger son or a younger sister's son may be chosen as the fitter incumbent. In other words, the Hopi are latitudinarians in practice, irrespective of theory. On the other hand, Tongans allowed titles to go only to the eldest-born. The Nootka (British Columbia) were equally fanatical about primogeniture, which implied superiority of rank and privilege. But they counted seniority not only by relative age, but by the relative ages of the parents. A grown man might call his ten-year-old girl cousin "elder sister" if her father was older than his own; and that meant conceding to her a higher rank.

Among agricultural peoples, including Europeans, the justification for primogeniture is that an estate which would be split into uneconomic parcels remains intact, hence an economically superior unit. However, the same result is achieved by settling the property on any one child, as is done in Ireland, where formerly all sons and daughters were provided for on the land. An arrangement diametrically opposed to primogeniture is to favor the youngest-born—a rule known as ultimogeniture or junior right. Frazer has given a useful summary of its distribution. It existed in various sections of England under the label of "borough-English," and in parts of Germany, Russia, and Hungary. In Asia it is typical of Turkic and Mongolic tribes, but also turns up in the south—in India, Indo-China, and Sumatra—as well as in the extreme north among the Yukaghir, and less definitely among the Chukchi and the Koryak. Passages in the Old Testament suggest the possibility of an early prevalence of junior right among the ancient Hebrews. In Africa the rule holds in a few tribes in the east and in some groups of southern Nigeria, but usually in a restricted form; for example, the Bogo (Ethiopia) assign the lion's share to the eldest son, but give the empty house to the youngest.

It is possible somewhat to extend the range of the custom as traced by Frazer. In Europe it is characteristic of some Lapp groups; in Asia, of the Ket (Yenisei area) and the Gajo (Sumatra).

Before taking up the conditions favoring ultimogeniture it will be well to examine a few concrete cases of its operation. When a young Kazak married, his father gave him livestock, thus enabling him to set up an independent household. Apparently the parent reserved enough cattle and horses to pay the bride price for each of the senior brothers, so that the junior as "residuary legatee" was likely to enjoy only a slight advantage. In Sumatra, the Gajo provide each marrying son with a section of a ricefield, one or more buffalo, and part of the communal house. The youngest son gets possibly twice as large a share as any one of his seniors, but is also expected to look out for them and to attend to their proper burial. Similarly, among the Skolte Lapps the youngest gets the best of his father's houses, but has to remain at home and take care of his parents. The Khasi of Assam, a strongly matrilineal people, recognize both primogeniture and junior right, but with reference to different forms of property. The youngest daughter inherits the house with its furnishings and the prerogative of performing the ritual of the ancestral cult; in case of her death without female issue, her sister's youngest daughter succeeds. But the chief's heirs are his eldest sister's sons in order of seniority; failing such sons, the next oldest sister's sons substitute.

It is clear that, by and large, the youngest child is not viewed with the special regard often bestowed upon the eldest. Frazer and after him Vinogradoff have correctly summed up the facts by saying that in junior right the youngest inherits the bulk of the property still held by his parents for the simple reason that he stays with them, whereas his seniors have departed. The cases in which junior right of a sort is coupled with primogeniture also militate against the notion that ultimogeniture is anything but a practical arrangement which naturally grows out of given economic circumstances.

Because the Turkic and Mongolic occurrences specially impressed themselves on Blackstone, he suggested a correlation with pastoralism. The facts of distribution at once refute the assumption. As Frazer and Vinogradoff point out, farmers as well as herders have practiced the custom—even such stabilized farmers as those of Western Europe. As a matter of fact, hunters are also involved. The Yukaghir are not properly herders, for with an average ownership of only eight to fifteen head of reindeer, a typical family cannot possibly maintain itself except by the chase and fishing. The Ket, too, are only in part reindeer breeders, much of the tribe subsisting on fish and game; and among the Lapps it is not exclusively the nomads that practice ultimogeniture. In short, fishing, hunting, herding, and farming are all consistent with this usage.

Possibly—in combination with other features—matrilocal residence may predispose a group to ultimogeniture. This form of residence certainly occurs to some extent in Lapland, but the data on the Yukaghir are particularly suggestive. Among these people matrilocalism predominates and is connected with bride service. But some of them, having adopted bride purchase from their Tungus neighbors, have turned patrilocal. We cannot say that their ancient form of residence is the *cause* of junior right, for any number of matrilocal peoples have no such rule of inheritance; but it is permissible to assume that in a particular setting matrilocalism renders ultimogeniture more probable.[9]

## General Considerations

To summarize briefly, individualism as to property of some sort is universal, but it may apply only to special types of valuables. Broadly speaking, individual property rights are clearest concerning patent-like privileges, especially if they rest on a supposedly supernatural basis. In such cases the owner is in theory limited in his rights solely by the conditions laid down by his spiritual mentor. If the visionary's patron had told him, for example, to initiate others in return for compensation, but never to transfer the essence of his revelation gratis, then the owner would make even his own child *buy* the privilege. Naturally,

in practice the visionary would be further restricted by the social setting, the sum total of the institutions peculiar to his culture—as when
a Crow feels morally obliged to share his privilege as payment for
unsolicited favors he has accepted. Significantly enough, privileges as
to songs, traditions, sacred objects, and the like already appear among
some of the sociologically simplest peoples, such as the Andaman
Islanders and the Eskimo. It is important to remember that for the
natives these "copyrights" are not useless in a practical way. Invested
with an aura of sanctity, they are believed to be the key to life, health,
and success; hence they are readily convertible into values of the most
tangible order (p. 132).

Chattels are also as a rule individually owned. When parents will
not dictate to a child what it shall do with its clothing or toys, when a
woman who has been "bought" remains undisputed mistress of her
earnings, when even a slave is allowed to accumulate wealth of his
own, individual proprietorship of movables can hardly be denied. That
altruistic principles or kinship considerations may restrain a person
from exercising his legal claims to the fullest extent does not militate
against the existence of property.

Land is, on the whole, rarely held in simpler societies according
to our conceptions of property, but we must never forget that Western
civilization, too, does not recognize absolute claims in this respect. It
would be preposterous to expect precisely the same notions of real-
estate property everywhere when real estate plays so different a part even
among agricultural peoples. Migratory and stabilized farming inevitably go with different attitudes toward the land; and in the absence
of a money economy there is no room for the modern speculator in
real estate. However, from the rude hunter's claims to individual hunting grounds to the modern farmer's title that normally remains unchallenged, but nevertheless cannot save him from dispossession whenever
the authorities decide that his land is needed for public utilities, there
is a mere series of gradations, not an absolute difference of kind. In
this department of social life, then, there seems to be no absolute break
between rude and advanced cultures.

Property may be viewed from two mutually complementary points
of view. How do other social phenomena affect property? How does
property affect other phenomena?

In answer to the former question various examples have already
been given, but it may be well to recall some and to introduce some
others. As we have seen, any notable invention or other accession to

the material culture may usher in changes that, even without an upheaval, are potentially revolutionary. It is no slight matter if a people of relatively communistic orientation like the early fishing Lapps acquire a keen sense of individual ownership along with their reindeer, and conceive social distinctions never dreamt of under the ancient economy (p. 28 f.). So the irrigation farming found among the Jagga implies a readjustment of property rights, for without it the system could not work. To take banal illustrations from our own past, the public interest has gradually achieved one curb after another on individual property rights in towns. The Danish historian Troels-Lund has given us a graphic picture of what urban life was like before the modern checks were introduced—when pigs still roamed the streets unmolested, when every citizen built his house as he pleased, and when only the public hangman ever tended to the latrines. Modern municipalities impose as a matter of course sanitary and building regulations that were once considered an intolerable encroachment on their rights by the householders.

Evidently political ideology can exert an enormous influence on property. In parts of Polynesia the chief of divine descent was regarded as so sacred that anything he touched was thereby hallowed, hence no longer to be used by men of lesser rank. A Tongan chief might seize whatever took his fancy, and regularly claimed his subjects' first fruits and a share of their catch of fish. Here, then, all property was vested in the ruler. As Professor MacIver points out in the article cited in the beginning of our chapter, the nature of Western governments, from feudalism to the Soviet system, determines the nature and limits of property.

On the other hand, it is equally true that property itself exerts a far-reaching influence. Our Lapp case illustrates both aspects of the problem. Domestic reindeer as a new form of wealth evoke novel ideas of property; but when these have ripened they react on the structure of society. Distinctions that have remained incipient in Lapland came to complete fruition elsewhere. In a remarkable treatise, Rudolf von Jhering, one of the greatest jurists of the nineteenth century, exposed the masked partiality of early Roman law on behalf of the rich. There was no explicit favor shown; but the inexorable demand of a heavy initial fee for any lawsuit made it virtually impossible for a poor plaintiff to proceed against a wealthy defendant. Similarly, in the middle of the fifth century B.C., Roman law leniently fined the perpetrator of bodily injuries, whereas a thief, even if he had snatched only a cluster of grapes, was chastised and enslaved by the person robbed, and he suffered the death penalty for stealing crops at night. Von Jhering plausibly points out that this differential treatment of maimers and thieves reflected class interest. Not the wealthy steal grapes, only the poor, against whom the law protected the propertied class. On the other hand, bodily injuries were likely to be inflicted by the rich on their poor servants and day laborers; the law imposed a fine for such acts—but so trivial a one as to be negligible for a person of means. The theme of "Rich and Poor in Relation to Fines in Contemporary Penal Law," is, Von Jhering concludes, still worthy of consideration. As a British judge quoted by Philbrick remarked in 1762, "necessitous men are not, truly speaking, free men . . . ."

Banal as the observation may be, it is worth noting explicitly that property affects not only social structure and law but also psychological attitudes sometimes naïvely supposed to be immutable. The bond between siblings, which among simpler peoples is one of the strongest conceivable, is often overshadowed by envy when property has advanced to a prominent place, hence the animosities to be observed in sophisticated societies among the closest relatives. The murder of brothers who compete for the throne is a common occurrence in African monarchies, our medieval history shows fratricide and filial rebellion in the highest circles, the impact of industrial civilization blots out the obligation to aid one's nearest kindred. Thus property affects even the sister institution of kinship.[10]

# Chapter 7

# LAW

## *Definition*

As MARRIAGE and the family, so law and the state are correlated concepts. "State and law," says Vinogradoff, "are two aspects of the same thing." In MacIver's terminology, which we have adopted, law is the institution corresponding to the association known as the state.

What, then, is the state? Max Weber defines it as "that human association which within a definite sphere . . . successfully claims the monopoly of legitimate physical force." It is the sole source of rightful force, which other associations possess only in so far as the state is willing to permit. Weber takes pains to emphasize that the use of force is not the normal or only means of the state, and that such use does not exhaust its activities. But what distinguishes the state from all other associations is not this or that task it performs, but only the monopoly of warranted force.

Authoritative definitions of law correspondingly stress the same criterion. "The decisive element of *organized* force," declares Thurnwald, "separates legal order from custom and usage." Radcliffe-Brown's conception virtually coincides; and the jurist Bekker defines law as "the rules created within the unit, i.e., by the labor of the membership, for enforceable things (*erzwingbare Dinge*)." The crucial issue is where "mere custom" ends and "law" begins. Following Llewellyn and Hoebel, we may place the point at wherever somebody with communal approval or sanction *does* something about the breach of a norm.

In civilized states that somebody is a policeman, district attorney, judge, or some other representative of the government. There are preliterate societies having such agents, and among them the African Negroes stand out, being in no sense primitive in their legal usages. Other natives, however, lack all semblance of official authority. Such are the Eskimo, the Chukchi, the Ona, and the Yaghan. The Yurok and the Ifugao also fall into this category, although they exact fairly definite penalties for a variety of transgressions. By a rigid definition we might have to deny "law" to all such societies, but from a broad historical and comparative point of view, it is certainly necessary, as

Seagle puts it, "to seek the embryonic forms and mechanisms which have developed into juridical institutions." Vinogradoff has aptly compared earlier attempts at smoothing out social difficulties with the more recent groping toward an international order. We shall, then, approach modes of control as a continuum in which the existence of permanently organized coercive agencies represents one extreme.

Accordingly, a series of specific questions arises. How does "law" originate? What means of control exist in the absence of official guardians? What kinds of disturbance call forth attempts at control? Who concerns himself with the maintenance of existing norms? What procedure does this "somebody" follow and what penalties does he inflict? Other questions will be treated, for convenience' sake, under the head of the State.[1]

## *Legislation*

The overwhelming mass of law among most peoples is not the result of deliberate planning, but of spontaneous growth. There are instances of designed innovations. For example, in the thirteenth century the Norwegians, having suffered from the internecine bickerings of pretenders to the throne, decreed that only the oldest legitimate son of a king—unless manifestly unfit—should succeed to royal status. A similar regulation, and for the same reason, is credited to the West Africans of Benin in the early eighteenth century. Unfortunately we do not learn details. One would like to know, for instance, who took the initiative and whether there was opposition to the novel scheme.

Conscious innovation probably occurs in simpler societies mainly in two ways. Where authority is strongly centralized, rulers can modify law by a fiat. Monarchical Africa provides the clearest cases. A Zulu king could create a lineage into a separate clan so as to permit his marrying a coveted girl without breach of incest rules; he could expel all the rain makers in order to concentrate their powers in his person; he could prohibit his soldiers from marrying. A Jagga chief converted torture from a judicial into a disciplinary measure; forbade men to carry daggers that had been freely used in brawls; and mitigated excessive fines. A second occasion for innovation arises even in some very rude societies whenever they have to choose between either curbing a powerful urge or modifying tradition. Thus, Australian hordes come to permit a substitute for the ideal mate rather than condemn a tribesman to celibacy.

However, it is important to note that even autocrats who receive blind obedience, so long as they conform to tradition no matter how cruel their exactions, are likely to meet opposition whenever they make wholly novel demands. Thus, the meek Chinese of the 1880's resisted new forms of taxation. Second, to borrow a phrase of Anton Menger's, the new legislation represents only arabesques or bow windows on the impressive edifice of customary law. Far more typical even in complex conditions is spontaneous development, which may ultimately receive overt recognition and codification. This is well brought out by the rise of medieval urban law. The nascent burgher class of the eleventh and twelfth century was in no sense consciously revolutionary, however seriously its very existence clashed with feudal conceptions. Its members claimed merely what was indispensable for their needs—free mobility and liberty to dispose of their goods. "Nothing was farther from the bourgeois mind than considering this as a natural right; in their eyes it was only a useful one." Many of them, immigrants from distant regions and of unknown origin, possessed *de facto* this liberty, which was soon translated into law. Indeed, it became a territorial rather than a personal privilege, which anyone acquired by living in a town for a year. Similarly, the code suited for the relations among a rural population obviously was no longer adapted to town life, whence arose the incipient *jus mercatorum,* or merchants' law, at first *without* any legal sanction, as a mere body of customary rules. But presently these wholly private arrangements and the courts of convenience that sprang from them were fully recognized by public authorities, receiving official approval long after they had come into existence and served their function.

The modern era, with its enormous development of new relations and rights, has naturally witnessed a corresponding number of new statutes, especially in the United States. However, the effectiveness of many of them has been reasonably doubted; and still more doubtful is it whether the changes and additions compare in vitality and permanence with laws of earlier date.[2]

## *Primitive and Modern Law*

Early law and modern law differ manifestly in a number of respects. Early law is conceived largely in kinship rather than in territorial terms; it coincides more closely with the ethical notions, hence the public opinion, of the peoples in question; it fails to discriminate public and private wrongs, the "crimes" and the "torts" of our jurisprudence. Though these differences can be illustrated by striking examples, they are far from absolute. We are once more confronted by a continuum of variations.

KINSHIP.—The recession of kinship as a factor in government and law is a criterion of industrial civilization. Not altogether of complex cultures, nor of European ones, for in modern China and Japan, in European peasant societies, among Albanian and Montenegrin herders, kinship has remained enormously important in social control, as will be seen presently in the discussion of law administration. Intermediate conditions are common in Africa, where the rise of kingdoms has often subordinated kinship patterns without eliminating them. In the Bushongo realm, "one finds no trace of the custom of blood-revenge" by the slain person's kindred, and a Xosa chief characteristically claims the fine for an injury to a subject's person which elsewhere would go to the injured party and his relatives. But even in so well integrated a state as Uganda the clans had significant political functions, and a district chief was expected to look out for the interests of dependent and sponging relatives.

In a sense even the most complex modern states take cognizance of kinship ties in legal relations. Any racial discrimination rests on the assumption that the group in question is a distinct group by descent. Logically enough, this attitude combines with the principle of collective responsibility. When a Jew in Paris killed a Nazi official, the Nazi government proceeded against Jews as a unit, precisely as one Albanian or Australian kin would against another. Similarly, the lynching of unoffending Negroes when one Negro has committed a crime is a reversion to common primitive usage.

PUBLIC OPINION.—In modern civilization, public opinion remains an important deterrent from antisocial behavior, but for obvious reasons it cannot rival the force of communal censure in an aboriginal group. In a homogeneous native settlement, traditional law coincides with accepted ethical principles: an Eskimo who has even by chance eaten venison along with the flesh of seal knows and feels that he has broken a taboo that involves his neighbors as well as himself in disaster. But except in the smaller centers of a Western country the several constituent subdivisions of the population have no such uniform standards. On such vital matters as birth control and divorce, Catholics differ from many Protestants and freethinkers. Other issues divide men according to their ethnic, educational, political affiliations. When in 1895 Theodore Roosevelt, as police commissioner, tried to enforce the New York law against saloons open on Sundays, a solid block of otherwise law-abiding citizens was arrayed against him and attempted to thwart his efforts. Similarly, in a "moonshiner" region, the people, not consider-ing the illicit distilling of liquor wrong, defy the law. Smuggling and evasion of tax payments fall under the same head. Immigrants from countries that license lotteries are not likely to disapprove of gambling in the United States, irrespective of legal restrictions. Again members of subversive parties, such as the Nazis in republican Germany, can-not be deterred by public opinion because that section of public opinion which counts for them approves their conduct in defiance of officially declared law.

By way of contrast, preliterate man is rarely confronted by multi-ple standards, so that enforcement of his customary law is furthered by his acceptance of its ethical basis. Add to this his sensitiveness to adverse group comment. Thus, chiefless and judgeless people like the Yaghan abide by traditional custom from fear of a bad reputation, cen-sure at times driving a man into voluntary exile. A method widely in vogue elsewhere is public ridicule, sometimes as among the Crow by persons standing to the malefactor in a defined relationship (p. 69). The Blackfoot also mercilessly grill a culprit in a semipublic conversa-tion exposing all the ludicrous aspects of his conduct. "The mortifica-tion of the victim is extreme and usually drives him into temporary exile, or, as formerly, upon the warpath to do desperate deeds."

Yet the difference is not nearly so absolute between native and civilized conditions if we compare what is properly comparable. In a small American town the sway of the Main Street code is proverbial; and even the most sophisticated circles kowtow to those standards which characterize their cultural subgroup. A scientist may laugh to scorn what the man in the street says about him, but he is extraordi-narily thin-skinned if his colleagues accuse him of unduly appeasing the taste for popular science, let alone of utilizing the results of others with-out proper acknowledgment. So in advanced as well as in backward societies it is the judgment of one's peers and neighbors that counts.

CRIMES AND TORTS.—Crime is, by definition, a wrong against the whole community or state, whereas tort is a merely private offense. In contemporary Western society only a properly qualified public agent proceeds against criminals; and even in civil law, where not the dis-trict attorney but the aggrieved party appears as plaintiff, it is still only official authorities that judge the case and execute the verdict. In most primitive societies the lack of officials is correlated with a large measure of self-help; it may even appear as though *all* wrongs were treated as private affairs, as though no outsider concerned himself with them. This would imply the lack of crime and the sole existence of torts.

It is, however, highly doubtful whether utter indifference to public, i.e., communal as opposed to individual or kinship, interest exists anywhere for the entire range of possible transgressions. What we do find is an approximation to this condition among such chiefless peoples as the Eskimo and, very generally, a rather different definition of crime from that we are accustomed to. Thus, murder may be conceived as not a crime; whereas witchcraft usually figures as unequivocally such. Examples will clarify the issue.

The Eskimo closely approach anarchy. In the Coronation Gulf region a man who coveted an object that a tribesman refused to sell "hacked him across the wrist and side with his knife" and no one took notice. Another, who had stabbed a neighbor in order to marry his wife, went scot-free. However, in this case the community interfered so far as to deprive him of his ill-gotten wife. Murder is avenged privately, but an abortive attempt to kill an enemy during Birket-Smith's visit to the Caribou Eskimo remained unpunished. The Iglulik have an infinitude of taboos, whose breach may cause calamity to the transgressor and to the whole settlement, yet no disciplinary measure is taken. However, a shaman is called to elicit a confession of the disease-smitten culprit, this act being believed to remove the misfortunes visited on the settlement. Yet the shaman is in no sense a judge: he painstakingly seeks assurance from the patient that it is not through the shaman's fault that the bad luck has come; otherwise he may be suspected of sorcery and be himself put out of the way. Here is the crucial qualification of Eskimo lawlessness: "People who have made themselves obnoxious are disposed of by common consent." This may be done to a common murderer, but is very likely to be the fate of the mischievous magical practitioner. One Hudson's Bay shaman convinced his people that another had caused many deaths among them; they talked the matter over and decided to dispose of him. Accordingly, while the supposed criminal was stooping down, an old man stabbed him in the back and "received the thanks of the others for his feat."

Evidently, despite the utter absence of official guardians of the established order, the Eskimo do at times rise to concerted action. This happens typically against evil sorcerers, who generally arouse aboriginal ire, and against individuals who have become a general nuisance.

Single murder, we note, often remains unavenged and is not regularly conceived as a crime. "It happens," says Egede of the eighteenth-century Greenlanders, "that a malefactor secretly and maliciously murders another man. Such an action is then regarded with the utmost indifference, without a thought of punishment. Only the relatives avenge the victim if they have the power and the courage." He adds that witches and others conceived as capable of fatal sorcery are at times pitilessly killed; the Eskimo considered them as not worthy of living since they clandestinely injured and destroyed their neighbors.

Even societies with chiefs and councilors may leave to private persons the redressing of wrongs that we consider pre-eminently criminal. The Crow furnish an illustration. In the first half of the nineteenth-century, Arrow-head, a member of the Piegan clan, was ambushed and killed by Whistling Water clansmen. The victim's elder brother, after a futile attempt at vengeance, was aided by his comrade and then succeeded in killing Honest, a Whistling Water. "Then the Piegan clan people were happy; they had their revenge." Honest's death was explicitly accepted as atonement for the murder of Arrow-head.

Yet in one respect this case is atypical. Though neither chief nor police society had coercive powers in such incidents, they emphatically were not unconcerned. The slaying of a tribesman and the ensuing feud were felt as weakening the Crow in their relations to alien tribes; hence the chief would exert himself as a peacemaker, inducing the injured clan to smoke the sacred pipe and to accept compensation for their loss from the kin of the murderer. Here, then, official cognizance of a wrong is taken, which thus becomes a public affair, even though no penalty is meted out by the representatives of the community.

Nevertheless, the Crow used coercive measures in particular situations. The police society annually appointed by the chief, and at least theoretically subordinate to him, forcibly restrained individuals who endangered the success of a buffalo hunt by prematurely attacking the game, or who refused to obey the rules of a war party or of a Sun Dance festival. At least for the first of these offenses they had the right to whip the culprit, break his weapons, and confiscate his kill. He was a criminal, and they represented law in the fullest sense of the word.

It is noteworthy, however, that witchcraft—which innumerable preliterate societies, such as the Eskimo, the Murngin, the Canella, treat as the crime par excellence—was not so conceived by the Crow. A person who supposedly suffered from the magical activities of a tribesman might use countermagic of his own or a friendly shaman's, but no public cognizance was taken of the fact. Similarly, whereas Australians were likely to put to death those who had infringed the laws of incest, the Crow did not penalize the offenders, though they strongly disapproved of the act and compared a perpetrator to a dog. Thus, primitives differ among themselves in their notion of crime.

INTENTION.—Notwithstanding our saying that ignorance of the law is no excuse, good intentions would commonly be taken as extenuating circumstances. On this point, too, preliterate peoples vary. Even so complicated a juridical system as that of the Jagga completely ignored the factor of accident in case of homicide. The spirit of the dead man was thirsting for revenge, they believed, hence a blood feud was indicated. This regard for the wrath of the deceased determined behavior—never the motives of the killer, say his being drunk at the time of the deed, or what not. As Vinogradoff points out, neglect of the subjective aspect of facts is equally typical of early Germanic law. But the Ifugao take the opposite view on this issue. If a man happens to put out another's eye or even to kill him in a scramble over a sacrificial buffalo, no damages are assessed. The Yurok, too, take cognizance of intent in so far as they demand additional compensation for malice aforethought.

By and large, primitive law probably pays less attention than ours to the element of motive, an attitude paralleling the primitive view of supernatural penalties. No matter how unintentional the breach of a religious or magical taboo may be, it is believed to react against the offender. A Crow who unwittingly ate of forbidden food might blame his illness thirty years later on this unintentional transgression.

This recalls the primitive fusion alluded to in an earlier chapter. Crime and sin are often indissolubly linked.[3]

## Administration of Law

In dispensing "justice" Western nationalities have exhibited all the principal types of action usually associated with aborigines. Kinship is a primary consideration in contemporary North Albania and adjacent Yugoslav districts. As an Ifugao in Luzon cannot proceed against a kinsman, so a North Albanian declares that "a family cannot owe itself blood"; hence wrongs perpetrated within the kindred go unpunished. On the contrary, an insult or injury by an outsider demands vengeance and accordingly precipitates a feud, for not to penalize the offending group means leaving a blot on the family and clan honor. The closest patrilineal relatives are pre-eminently those to seek retribution and do so on the principle of collective responsibility. Since the clan punished for a member's crime assumes the same attitude regardless of abstract right or wrong, many lives are lost. Less than a generation ago Nopcsa set the number of deaths due to feuds in certain districts as 30 per cent of all deaths. This is a staggering figure when we recall that women and aqueduct repairers are exempt from feuds.

Some aborigines combine disciplinary measures within the clan with the blood feud. That is, in order to forestall hostilities they do away with a notorious troublemaker in their midst. This is reported for the Chukchi and the Murngin.

Elsewhere self-help is coupled with a system of arbitration, as among the Crow. The umpire has no power to make the litigants submit to his verdict, but his function as adviser and go-between is recognized. This implies that other interests than those due solely to kinship are nascent, a point of crucial significance.

Yet even when jurisprudence is fairly advanced, self-help remains. Ancient Roman law allowed a man to visit direct penalties on a thief taken red-handed. The Western notion of a public agency that *permanently* upholds the law by coercion is very recent. In Charlemagne's day, official execution was possible only in special circumstances. Further, as Vinogradoff reminds us, the first step toward that goal was indirect: the criminal was put beyond the pale of human society, "outlawed," rather than directly compelled to conform.

Though modern jurisprudence theoretically eliminates self-help, the reality is more important than abstract ideals, and from this point of view there is nothing like the rigidity of theory in contemporary and recent practice. For purposes of their own, modern governments have sometimes connived at illegal justice by mobs and individuals. Jews are murdered for supposedly sacrificing Christian children, Negroes may be lynched without a pretense of defense by sheriffs, an American officer who kills a Hawaiian for an alleged attack on his wife goes scot-free in open court, women who shoot a faithless lover are acquitted. Our actual advance over primitive societies is thus far less than appears at first blush. No modern state consistently exerts its coercive powers. Our federal government, for example, doubtless could enforce constitutional amendments of clear import in Southern states that nullify them, but no president dreams of using the United States Army for that purpose. A Plains Indian police society that beat up and, if necessary, killed a recalcitrant buffalo hunter had, of course, the *power* to kill a murderer, but in many tribes he was not regarded as a criminal. What is more to the point, the organization did not even proceed invariably when entirely qualified to do so according to aboriginal norms. Once the Fox organization under Last Bull's leadership served as the Cheyenne police. A man named Grasshopper defied their injunction against hunting, and Last Bull shot the offender's horse. This incensed Grasshopper's mother to the point of cutting up the leader's tent. Last Bull issued an order to destroy the Grasshopper family's belongings against threatened resistance, but one of his subordinates counseled leniency in order to prevent bloodshed. Accordingly, the erring family was allowed to depart unmolested. In a similar spirit our federal government refrains from measures against flagrant defiance of federal law.

It is interesting to analyze typical cases of legal administration in preliterate societies. The Yurok and the Jagga provide instructive examples.

The Yurok are especially interesting because they combine an elaborate juridical scheme, which involves assessment of all manner of offenses, with a total absence of public officials to execute the provisions of the code. In short, by certain definitions they would have to be described as lawless. How, then, is the scheme put into operation? "Each side to an issue presses and resists vigorously, exacts all it can, yields when it has to, continues the controversy when continuance promises to be profitable or settlement is clearly suicidal, and usually ends in compromising more or less. Power, resolution, and wealth give great advantages; justice is not always done; but what people can say otherwise of its practices?" A concrete case dating back to about 1860 is illustrative.

A man named Minot, living in the village of Rekwoi, had acquired the right to all the sea-lion flippers taken within a certain tract. A man from the Layekw house in the settlement of Omen violated this privilege; Minot was indignant, but let the matter pass. When the offense was repeated, however, he felt as though "he had been trampled on." He lay in ambush, shot and wounded the offender, and fled. So far there is merely self-help. Now, however, a neutral somebody appears in the form of negotiators trying to bring about a settlement. Public sentiment was with the shooter: "One does not flagrantly defy established property rights among the Yurok without incurring disapproval, no matter how powerful one may be." The wounded man's partisans renounced any indemnity, and an intermediary declared that if Minot made any payment for his attack, its victim would have to pay more— this being in recognition of the prestige value of the flipper rights.

Minot's son was willing to make a token payment, which would have closed the case, but this was declined because the Layekw man did not wish to pay the heavier damages. The people from both towns went through a rite of reconciliation, from which the injured transgressor absented himself on the plea of being still ill. However, a few days later he emerged to curse Minot, whose grandson fell sick and died. This death was ascribed to the imprecation, and in revenge the curser was killed. His sister then cursed his enemies. A formal go-between was resorted to in order to settle the case peaceably. Functionaries of this type, chosen by the litigants from men not related to them, would hear witnesses and render a verdict, each receiving a large dentalium as a fee. In the present case Minot and his kindred offered valuables, but the bereaved woman insisted on getting the sea-lion rights, "because that is what he got killed over." Thus the privilege was transferred once more.

The Yurok had definite notions concerning compensation for injury and elaborate methods of checking general conflict, "but in the absence of any political power to direct the machinery one individual could upset the most careful planning." The go-between thus represents a vital stage in the development of effective social control, but his official powers are nil. There are innumerable parallels to this Yurok functionary, even in societies that have a partly or fully developed state machinery. North American Indian chiefs were perhaps in most situations peacemakers within the tribe, though in other circumstances they or others might control agencies for compelling obedience. We, too, have arbitration boards as well as judges and policemen.

Let us now turn to a Bantu tribe. In glaring contrast to the Yurok, the Jagga have a strong monarchical sense. For the present we are concerned only with the juridical powers of their rulers and the administration of law under them. As elsewhere in Africa, the tribal chief is at the same time a judge; correspondingly, the headman of a district acts as a justice of the peace and gives a preliminary hearing before a case is tried by the chief himself. Another dignitary represents the clan; chosen for his competence, political astuteness, eloquence, and standing with the chief, he acts as a sort of legal guardian for his clan, a member requiring his consent before bringing suit. Still another clan functionary, who works hand in hand with the guardian, is an aged ritualist who performs sacrifices on the eve of a lawsuit, and divines according to the appearances of the entrails. If the result is unfavorable, the clansmen drop their action as plaintiffs; if they are the defendants, they are likely to seek a settlement.

It is contrary to decorum to bring a private issue directly before the court. First of all, the plaintiff ought to summon his opponent to the district common, where the community, presided over by the headman, hears the case and delivers an umpire's judgment. This procedure also has the advantage of not involving a preliminary payment of fees, though voluntary gifts to the headman and a beer feast for the neighbors are in vogue. The decision, which rests on unanimity, is not physically enforced, but exerts an influence on all who have not yet been affected by foreign ways. Notwithstanding the informality of the proceedings, a chief almost always takes cognizance of them, being informed either by the headman or by his own warriors.

Far more elaborate is a genuine trial. The plaintiff proceeds to the assembly place in front of the chief's estate and is halted by the sentries, who accept the goat or cow brought as the initial fee without which no complaint is heard. The guardsman who takes the beast to the chief also explains the nature of the suit, and becomes the plaintiff's spokesman. A second sentry now summons the accused, who must offer an equivalent fee, and becomes *his* spokesman. When both parties with their sentry advocates have appeared in the assembly place, the headman of the district, or another speaker appointed by the chief, opens the trial in the presence of the men of the commune. It is this body that delivers a tentative verdict, for according to pre-European usage the chief awaits their recommendation at home. When those present have come to an agreement, the speaker and the two advocates, accompanied by decisive witnesses, report to the chief, who may either personally come to the assembly or permit the speaker to announce his decision—possibly a commutation of the first sentence. Normally it is only in special cases that the chief intervenes at once. This may be either at the assembly's request or on his own initiative if secret information suggests a miscarriage of justice or if he favors one of the parties.

In marked contrast to the Yurok, the Jagga officially execute an official verdict. If a man refuses to abide by the decision, the chief sends the loser's advocate and other men to confiscate the indicated number of cattle. However, this extreme measure is not lightly used against a wealthy defendant supported by a strong clan, which might threaten to emigrate. In such a case the chief resorts to persuasion, appeals to the refractory man's kin, or resorts to supernatural means. The latter, also used against unknown thieves, include curses pronounced in the open market as the officiating imprecator swings an unfired clay pot or effigy.

If a man condemned to pay alleges insolvency and is reasonably suspected of having hidden his stock, the chief's henchmen tie his arms and legs in squatting posture, letting him lie on the lawn all day so that he can only painfully roll about, and constrict his forehead with a rope exerting an unbearable pressure. As soon as he confesses the hiding place of his animals, he is released. Torture, however, is never employed in order to force a confession at the trial.[4]

## Evidence

Our courts establish the truth of the matter by examining witnesses under oath. The advanced jurisprudence of the African Negroes has close formal parallels. A Jagga chief summons witnesses, who have to be compensated by the winner of the suit. If the plaintiff receives a cow, he gives his witness a goat; if he is awarded five head of cattle, the fee is one calf. Each witness takes an oath, touching the chief's forehead and uttering the formula, "May the chief's forehead kill me (if I lie)!" If a defendant is cleared by the evidence presented, the plaintiff forfeits to him the goat he had to offer before the opening of the trial.

The ordeal is another typical technique for extracting the truth. It flourished in many forms in medieval Europe, trial by combat being probably the direct ancestor of the duel. Modern Negro Africa is another main center of occurrence, some tribes having several varieties. Very distinctive is the favorite Jagga method. Into rather less than a pint of water are put two handfuls of a Datura herb along with a banana blossom. The litigant solemnly addresses a magical formula to the herb while putting his right hand into the vessel, then the mixture is boiled and eight snailshellfuls are handed to the person to be tested. Requested by the boiler to say his say, the plaintiff describes the offense and urges the decoction to make the defendant fall down if he is guilty, but otherwise to spare him. The accused, with the container at his mouth, asserts his innocence and utters a corresponding wish. If any of the liquid drips, that is taken as a preliminary sign of guilt. After the potions are drained, the defendant is ceremoniously taken on a walk, which is followed by sundry minor rites. Finally, the decoction produces the desired effect of putting the drinker into a trancelike state in which he soliloquizes, confessing his guilt, denying it, or vehemently resenting the indignity of the test. Only if he makes a clean breast of his guilt is he convicted and condemned to pay all the requisite fees. On the following day he gets an emetic to purge him of the poison, but even so the effects probably will not wear off for over a month. The accuser of a defendant who is not driven to confess has to indemnify him with two goats, to which is added the pretrial offering.

In the West African kingdom of Benin, Nyendall witnessed four forms of ordeal practiced in 1702. In the first a priest greased a cock's feather, with which he pierced the defendant's tongue; if it passed through easily, the accused was held innocent and the wound would readily heal; otherwise he was guilty. One alternative was to have the accused pull out seven or nine quills from a clod of earth, and unless this was done without difficulty he stood convicted. Third, the operator might spurt the juice of certain herbs into the defendant's eyes, which were supposedly not injured if he was wrongly accused, but grew inflamed if he was guilty, in which case he paid a fine. Finally, the priest might stroke the prisoner's tongue with a red-hot copper arm-ring, pronouncing him guilty if the tongue was burned. A fifth variety, which Nyendall knew only by hearsay, is interesting because its general features occur elsewhere. The accused was thrown into a certain river, which inevitably drowned even an expert swimmer who was guilty, but spared the innocent.

Oaths and ordeals are both widespread in the Old World, though hardly in societies of the simplest type. The Alorese and the Ifugao practice them, but not the Semang or the Bushmen. In America, on the other hand, these traits are distinctly rare, though not wholly lacking. The comparatively amorphous character of Plains Indian law is brought out by a comparison of the Crow ordeal with its Jagga counterpart. If two Crow Indians disputed over which had first struck an enemy, each contestant took a knife, put it into his mouth, pointed it toward the Sun, called him to witness that the deponent was speaking the truth, and declared that the one who lied should die before winter. If some misfortune subsequently befell one of the contestants, he was adjudged to have lost, and his competitor gained the disputed honor. The extremely restricted field of application of this test is as noteworthy as its essentially unofficial character. The Cheyenne may have used the oath more frequently, mainly to establish adultery, but the practice was by no means a frequent one.[5]

## *Punishment*

In discussing other legal topics it has been necessary to mention forms of punishment. Of the penalties familiar in civilized countries—execution, imprisonment, fines—imprisonment hardly ever occurs in simpler societies. Means of effective incarceration are generally lacking, and even if available they would probably often run counter to aboriginal ideology. In Uganda, however, the king, a· chief, or a clan head could put a man in the stocks. The sentry, being open to bribery, sometimes permitted the prisoner to go home at night and engage the sympathies of his kinsmen, who would intercede with the authorities. In the severer form of this penalty both arms and one leg were inserted into the holes of heavy logs, a punishment that generally proved fatal within a few days.

On corporal punishment attitudes have differed notably at different periods and among different peoples. Captain Cook was praised for his humanity in never sanctioning more than two dozen lashes for even grossly refractory sailors, and in eighteenth-century armies flogging was an obvious disciplinary measure. Some African tribes approve of physical chastisement. A Herero thief, if unable to pay the fine imposed on him, is thrashed. The Pilaga chief, who leaves a murder case to private vengeance, gives a drubbing to a thief who refuses to make restitution. In the Plains of North America the police societies were authorized to whip offenders, but only for special transgressions. Naturally there was sporadic abuse of power; a famous Omaha warrior who violated the rules of the hunt at a time of famine was flogged so unmercifully by the police that he never fully recovered. The Hopi war chief likewise had the right of chastisement. Torture, which the Jagga rarely used at trials, was applied by Chief Rindi to discipline notorious idlers.

The presence of a class system or a monarchy exerts a great influence on the application of punishment. In some Southern states the slayer of a Negro goes scot-free, whereas killing a white man brings a death sentence. In Uganda the absolute ruler could have any of his chiefs bound, put into the stocks, or killed at will. If the king envied a chief for his wealth, he would simply trump up a charge against him and extort a heavy fine. Frequently in Africa adultery with a king's or a chief's wife is a capital crime, while the same offense against a commoner is a private grievance, sometimes not even a grave one. Again, Zulu law gave all fines for bodily injury not to the injured person, but to the chief or king; and the Shilluk monarchs permitted feuds so as to be able to collect cattle as fines.

To revert to the blood feud, its basic idea is retribution. The punishment is to fit the crime. This has often been carried out with meticulous precision on the Old Testament principle of

"Eye for eye, tooth for tooth, hand for hand, foot for foot,
Burning for burning, wound for wound, stripe for stripe."—
EXODUS 21 :24, 25

Obviously, then, a murder would be atoned for by a killing, and on the principle of collective responsibility any member of the murderer's group—or any member not expressly exempted by custom, such as women in Albania—sufficed. Sometimes, however, the idea was executed with an excess of pedantry. If a Jagga woman nursing a baby had been killed, then her clan tried to kill a nursing woman from the offender's clan so as to afflict them, too, with the sorrow of an orphaned child.

We have already seen that, in the interests of a wider group, neutrals tend to appease the aggrieved party by making them accept compensation known by its old Germanic name, *wergild,* in composition of the crime. These efforts are not always successful; the incensed kindred of the slain person may spurn all offers, regarding acceptance as weak and humiliating. Nevertheless, the persuasiveness of third parties combined with greed has often prevailed, and in some societies it has produced a fixed tariff.

The accepted wergild scheme reflects the basic social structure. The Ifugao may demand a lesser indemnity from a middle-class or a poor killer, though the difference is not so great as might be expected; in the absence of "a statute of limitations" the heirs would have to shoulder the debt. More clearly, old Germanic law set different values according to the slain man's status. At the time of Charlemagne a Frankish freeman's death was atoned for with 200 solidi, a free Roman's with only 100 solidi, while service with the king entitled the slain man's kindred to the triple amount. Again, some societies exact less for a woman than for a man, others more—not necessarily because women as such are more highly esteemed, but because of their economic value. Thus, the Jagga pay seven bulls and seven goats for a slain male, eight bulls and eight goats for a female.

It is also significant who pays and who receives the wergild. As already noted, an autocratic ruler may claim the whole indemnity on the ground that he owns the persons of his subjects. Anglo-Saxon law stressed patrilineal reckoning, so that the male patrilineal relatives claimed two thirds of the wergild and, as defendants, stood security for the same fraction thereof. The Chukchi, though loosely organized, also weight the paternal kindred, who accordingly are the avengers of a murder, the recipients of the wergild. Among the patrilineal Jagga, the victim's maternal clan received one head of cattle and one goat— in other words, one seventh or one eighth of the total according to the murdered person's sex. If the victim was a mother, her husband was allowed to retain two head of cattle and two goats, the remainder going to her clan. In general, the Jagga notion is to mulct the murderer's clan of an amount corresponding to the economic loss sustained through the victim's death.[6]

## General Considerations

Law has obvious connections with other institutions. Its relations with kinship have been sufficiently indicated, but property as defined, though treated separately for convenience' sake, forms only a segment of law. Marriage has strictly legal aspects when any breach of incest rules is treated as a capital crime, as in Australia, or when an adulterer is expected to pay damages to the wronged husband, as in Africa. The connection with religion appears clearly in the Eskimo treatment of taboo and will be further exemplified. Finally, education consists largely in familiarizing the child with legal and ethical principles.

Among the psychological problems of law, the question why people at large bow to it is of interest. It was once widely held that primitive man obeys his unwritten laws "spontaneously," and Malinowski deserves credit for explicitly rejecting the idea. Let us remember that social coercion has to cope with the most potent urges—sex, hunger, acquisitiveness. Why should a vigorous Negro male curb the natural impulse to carry on an affair with one of the innumerable wives of a chief whose harem imposes celibacy on many of his subjects? What makes a famished Omaha refrain from chasing buffalo no matter what the police society has decreed? As Devereux has argued, in situations of strain, proximate stimuli override those which are more remote.

If the native errs less frequently against group standards, it is presumably because they are actually those of *his* group, not those imposed from the outside, for we must agree with Devereux's statement that the most effective punishment is that "meted out by one's in-group and equals." However, individuals differ enormously in their capacity to resist temptation; accordingly, ethnographic literature records many transgressions of the social standard; of incest-breaking Australians who are promptly killed, of police-defying buffalo hunters who risk a savage whipping, of witches who vaunt rather than conceal their sinister practices. There can thus be no question of an *automatic* submission to law.

How the basic norms accepted by society originate lies beyond our ken, but we have considerable information on the "reception" of law systems through borrowing. Thus, in 1926 Turkey adopted the Swiss code; after 1867 Japan largely patterned her law on the German model; our own system is descended with modifications from English law. A private German codified the customary law of his native East-phalia under the title of the *Sachsenspiegel* (1220–1235), and this powerfully influenced Poland and Russia. In the fifteenth and sixteenth centuries, the Roman law was engrafted on the several particularistic German systems and, though ostensibly subsidiary to them, in large measure gained the upper hand in the empire. The earlier Roman law of imperial times naturally traveled with the expansion of Roman rule. Similarly, Napoleon's code extended to Naples and Poland.

Instances of diffusion are by no means psychologically equivalent. Napoleon, for example, prided himself on his code and imposed it by decree upon conquered peoples; Turkey and Japan voluntarily and deliberately adopted alien jurisprudence; in simpler societies, specific legal features were doubtless diffused without express planning. When two neighboring Plains Indian tribes, the Crow and the Cheyenne, employ the same type of ordeal, which in any form is a rarity in the New World, they must have borrowed the custom from each other or from a common source; and such diffusion, on general probability, may be assumed to have occurred without design.

Further, what holds for most of diffusion in any department of social life likewise holds for law. It is generally not taken over unmodified, but with an adjustment to the recipient scheme. This has been proved by jurists for the spread of imperial Roman law into the eastern provinces. In many cases modification is inevitable. The Church of England has a legal status which its nearest American counterpart could not have in a country without an established church. The same applies to the American equivalents of the Scandinavian forms of Lutheranism.

Economic factors influence law from various points of view. The sheer multiplication of material goods, the organization of industrial activity, the relations of capital and labor as well as of either to the state call for an ever-increasing body of official regulations. The development of automobile production alone has ushered in such features as parking rules, licensing of drivers, registration of ownership, new forms of insurance. Earlier periods are not without comparable phenomena. In 1703 Emperor Leopold I authorized his chamberlain, Heinrich Ernst von Rauchmüller, to introduce sedan chairs into Vienna, but their use was hedged about with curious qualifications: it was forbidden to carry any sick or liveried person or anyone of low quality, Jews being specifically excluded as fares, and no foreigners were to be employed as chair bearers. The new convenience, in other words, called for a new ordinance, and this was fashioned according to existing prejudice. Among preliterate folk, too, the acquisition of new possessions leaves an imprint on law. Quite generally, as Lapp and Chukchi history demonstrates, herding accentuates individualism; American and African tribes translate value judgments in terms of horses and cattle, respectively, which come to figure in payments of all kinds, including fines.

Most significant is the effect on law of economic interest. In the East African kingdom of Ankole, the Bairu peasants are the lower, the Bahima herders the upper caste. No peasant is allowed to own a productive cow; any herder could confiscate such an animal at will. In neighboring countries, the dominant herders drive their cattle over the peasants' fields irrespective of the damage caused. In early Rome (p. 154), the wealthy class safeguarded its members' property by the most stringent laws, but mayhem was punished with a trifling fine. In 1904, the German code still penalized larceny mercilessly, while an injury to the person received a disproportionately light sentence. What is more, the former figured as a public offense, the latter as a merely private wrong, of which the courts took notice only on the initiative of the injured person. In the United States we have had our "embattled farmers," the Farm Bloc, and lobbyists of every sort organized as pressure groups to promote their economic ends by legislative action.

But as Anton Menger forcefully suggests, in order to affect law it is necessary that an individual or group should hold the whip hand. Might makes right. In such tribes as the Chukchi or the Eskimo that is often true in the crudest sense—the physically stronger has his will. However, even in these cases the supposedly supernatural powers of a shaman may take precedence over sheer muscular superiority. Dominance is often gained by a well-knit minority that is capable of terrorizing the unorganized mass of its fellow citizens. This is equally true of the Ku Klux Klan in the United States and the secret societies of West Africa (p. 298 f.), which dispense justice according to their own notions. In one district of our "Deep South" the police beat colored men as they would not dare to beat fellow whites; courts convict a far greater percentage of colored defendants; and planters are encouraged to whip thieving Negroes rather than to bring them to court. All this is possible only because the superior white caste controls the means of coercion. The economic factor enters in so far as upper-class Negroes are likely to fare better, but it is secondary since the poor colored man is legally worse off than the poorest white trash.

The economic interpretation of law thus requires qualification. When a person or group has once gained control of the available coercive machinery, mere whims can exercise a greater influence than the material conditions. As Menger points out, the legislation created by Napoleon for the French could be imposed on the economically backward Poles and, what is more, it persisted there by inertia. On the contrary, when the Congress of Vienna rehabilitated the dethroned Elector of Hessen, a country far closer to France in cultural advancement, pre-Napoleonic law was promptly reinstated.

The history of Germany since 1918 strongly supports Menger's thesis. The rise of Nazism, the failure of all the republican governments to suppress subversive organizations, was an obvious consequence of the government's weakness. The government proceeded vigorously against Leftist rather than Rightist groups because the former were weaker, whereas the most brutal murders by Nazis went unpunished. The Nazis themselves, when weak, presented a party programme that in many respects was unexceptionable from a liberal point of view. As soon as they had secured supreme power, the most vital parts of the programme were abandoned; then not only the economic interests, but the fanciful prejudices of the party leadership could be translated into law. Law is on the side of the heaviest battalions.[7]

# Chapter 8

# RELIGION

$\mathrm{F}_{\text{OR}}$ convenience' sake, "religion" here is meant to include all forms of supernaturalism, including magic. On the other hand, these forms concern us only in their relations with social structure and custom, not with reference to beliefs and ceremonials as such. Logically, it would be better to treat supernaturalism as an institution separately from its correlated associations, say the church. In the life of peoples, however, the two are so interlocked that the separation seems impracticable.

Most societies attach enormous importance to their beliefs in the supernatural, which tend to pervade every phase of their culture. A Maori who chants a magical formula to prosper his crops and a Plains Indian who expects success in the chase from a rite that mimics the shooting of a buffalo typically illustrate the "primitive fusion" discussed in an earlier chapter. But the principle by no means applies only to savages. Thus, some of the most advanced countries in the world— Sweden, for example—have a State Department that supervises jointly public worship and the educational system. Such fusion, though sometimes imposed from above, often reflects the feelings of large segments of the population. Millions of Americans, though without a state church, let religious convictions determine their political and social attitudes. They recoil from the atheism of Soviet Russia; look into an office seeker's religious affiliations; or organize, on the pattern of the American Protective Association (1887), to keep Catholics out of public positions.

To survey, then, the interrelations of supernaturalism is an extremely ambitious undertaking. We shall limit ourselves to a few major topics—social grouping; marriage and the family; and government.

## *Social Grouping*

This theme may be attacked by taking either the groups or the religious element as a starting point. That is, we can inquire in how far a social unit is affected by supernaturalism; or how religion itself creates units.

SOCIAL GROUPS AS PRIMARY.—Sex, kinship, territorial, and national groups have all been significantly connected with magic and religion.

Sex dichotomy is, of course, partly dependent on biological differences, partly on the division of labor. One does not expect a female warrior society, but if women regularly embroider and dress skins they may come to form feminine craft guilds, as among the Dakota Indians. However, in many areas the sharp sex cleavage is to be connected with the belief in woman's periodic impurity, hence, in the malevolent influence she then irradiates. Orthodox Judaism not only insisted on her segregation at such times, but regarded any man who had had relations with her as unclean for seven days (Leviticus 15:24). To take a few random samples, the Lango believe that a man suffering from the measles would be blinded if he approached a menstruant female; a Creek woman had to retreat to a special hut for four days; and in Murngin myth one of the heroines precipitates a world catastrophe by defiling a sacred pool with her blood.

It is therefore natural for savages to exclude females from sacred performances; and wherever these occupy the center of the tribal stage such disqualification greatly restricts woman's sphere. The extent to which this happens, however, varies considerably. A Lapp woman was permitted neither to sacrifice nor to touch a shaman's drum; neither to step over her husband's feet nor to enter the rear door by which he brought in his kill, lest she spoil his hunting luck. Yet the position of women in Lapland is generally a favorable one. At the opposite extreme stand Australians and some Melanesians, who virtually debar women from their all-important solemnities. Intermediate are typical African and American aborigines. In Uganda, while ill, no woman was allowed to enter a house of worship or to render service to the gods, but in normal condition female mediums tended the temples. Similarly, in many American tribes a menstruant woman keeps away from holy objects, but otherwise the sex actively shares in ceremonialism.

It would be going beyond the evidence to ascribe all feminine disabilities to a single factor; but their elimination before and after the physiological phenomenon in question proves that the superstition of impurity is a real one. In Uganda certain religious duties may devolve on immature girls; in Australia and elsewhere restrictions vanish with the menopause.[1]

By virtue of membership in a family or kin an individual automatically enters a religious body that may be set apart from the rest of the population, a fact that cannot but add to the solidarity of the kindred. Though the differentiae seem minute to an outsider, they are vital to the believer. Relatives may intrude even into the domain of presumptively quite individual experiences. A Winnebago boy seeks a vision from a supernatural protector, but his vision is "censored"; the father listens to the report of his son's experience and insists on his trying again if the "wrong" spirit has offered a blessing. Correspondingly, the notion that certain holy objects can be purchased is not infrequently coupled with the principle that they are to be conveyed only to a kinsman. Hidatsa children bought bundles from their own father. Ancestor worship, as typically found among the Bantu and the Chinese, inevitably unites relatives as a cult group.

Under this head falls the phenomenon of "totemism"—the connection of a descent group with an animal species, more rarely a plant species, still more rarely a cosmic phenomenon or other object. The emotional significance of the totem varies enormously. Sometimes it shrinks into a heraldic emblem distinguishing one kin from the rest, but almost always the totemites are prohibited from eating, killing, or touching the totem; and in a few areas there is a truly religious aura investing it. A few examples must suffice.

According to his clan, an Omaha abstains, respectively, from the flesh of male elk or deer, of the black bear, of small birds, and so forth. Or some other restriction is substituted, as when the Deer-head people, though allowed to eat venison, may not touch the skin of any of the Cervidae. Among the bilinear Herero the patrilineal kindred (oruzo) submit to similar taboos: members of one oruzo will not kill the chameleon; those of another abstain from the flesh of the steinbock; another kin never taste the meat from a cow's thigh.

Such regulations hardly touch the essentials of aboriginal supernaturalism, but it is otherwise in Australia, where precisely the most sacred part of native belief and ritual revolves about the totems. The Murngin spend months performing the relevant ceremonies; and each male advances in the social scale as he learns more of the totemic lore. To treat an emblem improperly is to imperil the clan owning it, and within the last generation five men are known to have been killed for this misdeed. The ritual songs are full of references to the totems, the dancers mimic them, and even on his deathbed a man tries to imitate the animal's movements.

The Sherente, too, connect totemism with the core of religion. Sun and Moon are the outstanding deities, each being the totem of one moiety. Neither appears directly to his worshipers, but each sends astral deputies to commune with his half of the tribe.

Finally, the Yokuts patrilineal lineages have each a totem, which the kindred neither kill nor eat, but invoke in prayer and dream of, individual behavior toward it varying "from the perfunctory to the pietistic." So far the phenomenon is typical. But the Yokuts are peculiar in not regarding a common totem as itself a sign of relationship. Even within a single village two or more descent groups may share the identical totem without recognizing a social bond, so that unrelated Eagle or Dove people intermarry with the special approval of their fellow citizens.

This last instance instructively shows the range of possibilities. As a rule, however, common cults certainly do intensify otherwise existing kinship ties and may even lead to the fiction of a common ancestry.[2]

Territorial grouping no less than kinship directly affects religious affiliation, which retroactively creates or intensifies group solidarity. In the Holy Roman Empire, the rise of Lutheranism led to conflicts terminated by the Augsburg Treaty (1555), which set forth the territorial principle: "Cuius regio eius religio." That is to say, each ruler was to determine the Catholic or Lutheran faith of his subjects, dissenters having merely the right to emigrate. In 1648 the rule was extended to include Calvinist princes.

However, cleavage has developed from a quite different source. The Eastern Orthodox churches are "autocephalous," i.e., each nationality has its own ecclesiastical organization with an independent head, but without any departure in doctrine or ritual from the mother church at Constantinople. Thus, in 1870 the Bulgarians, while still under the Turkish yoke, asserted their nationalism, not against Turkey but against the Greek patriarchate. They prevailed on the sultan to grant them denominational autonomy and have since been under an exarch independent of Constantinople. Similarly, in 1922 the Orthodox Albanians acquired church autonomy.

The national principle is likewise exemplified in the several state churches of Sweden, Norway, Denmark, Finland, and Germany, all stemming from Lutheranism, alike in faith, yet forming so many separate associations. Essentially the situation is not unlike the Yokuts practice of a similar totemic cult extending over several independent social units.

In Germany not a few extremists sought to create a distinctively national faith after World War I. Spurning Christianity with its Judaic substructure, General Ludendorff advocated a return to ancient

Teutonic paganism. Following in his wake, many National Socialists, though at first professing "a positive Christianity," abandoned this principle; and their theorist, Alfred Rosenberg, heralded as a superior creed the Viking world view "with lavish expenditure of blood" and heroic carelessness. Prominent leaders fostered a German Faith move-ment (*Deutsche Glaubensbewegung*) to supplant Christianity. The example illustrates the tendency of groups to use religious symbols of their ethnic solidarity.

Subjugation of a territorial group that professes a different faith naturally throws into relief the difference between the conquerors and the conquered. The Turks made a pariah caste of Balkan Christians; the British have tended to look askance on Irish "papists." Whenever religion is a vital concern, it forms also an obvious social criterion.

But territorial separateness is not required to accentuate differ-ences if the dominated group is sufficiently marked off by languages, custom, and faith. Eastern Europeans generally reckon Jews a dis-tinct nationality irrespective of their place of birth. The Rumanians bitterly resented the demand of Western powers in 1878 that these aliens be treated as full-fledged citizens; in 1905 the historian Iorga still denied that any Jewish Rumanians existed, though there were hundreds of thousands of Jews born within the borders of his country.

PRIMARY RELIGIOUS DIFFERENTIATION.—Ethnically homogeneous pop-ulations also differentiate socially on a religious basis, but the signifi-cance of such fission hinges on the total ideology of the people con-cerned and on the nature of the creeds themselves. By and large it probably holds true that religious differences have proved more divi-sive among advanced peoples; witness the intense feelings between Sunnites and Shiites in Islam, and between Roman Catholics and Protestants in Christendom.

That a denomination spreads in accordance with the general prin-ciples of diffusion, hence comes to mark a specific area and then func-tions in harmony with the regional conditions, is obvious. Lutheran-ism came to be concentrated in the Scandinavian countries, Finland, and North Germany. There, accordingly, not to be a Lutheran remained until recently a distinct disadvantage: *Cuius regio, eius religio*. Norway excluded Jews until 1851 and persecuted Christian dis-senters; the pietist preacher Hauge was imprisoned for years; Quakers were driven into emigration by discriminatory treatment. A Swedish mob in 1842 attacked a Methodist revivalist, who barely escaped with his life; and even in the eighties, Lutheran pastors, escorted by police officers, were allowed forcibly to baptize the children of Baptist parents. Corresponding phenomena held in Great Britain; a century ago Edward B. Tylor, destined to become the foremost English anthropologist, could not enter Cambridge or Oxford because he was a Quaker.

It should be noted that denominational development may be intimately involved with social factors, so that it is difficult to say which aspect is primary. In the Roman Empire the all-embracing humanitarian gospel of Christianity naturally appealed to the poor and lowly, and this retroactively affected popular estimation: for a long period tonesetting Romans looked upon the new faith as the despicable creed of crude and simple-minded plebeians. As late as 250 A.D., it counted only occasional adherents among the upper classes. In more recent times pietism has blossomed among people of simple faith, reacting against what they resented as formal, spiritually unsatisfying theology. The religious schism thus betokens social or economic stratification. John Bunyan, the Baptist tinker, was not likely to appeal to the British cavaliers. In Norway, Hauge's preaching, which began in 1796, crystallized the farmers' opposition to aristocracy and the urban class. The social inferiority of the prophets here, too, reacted on the outsider's appraisal, which often lingers on as a survival. In the United States it is still more fashionable to be an Episcopalian than a Baptist or a Methodist.

Religious differentiation may, of course, develop without friction; the simpler peoples rarely quarrel over doctrinal issues, however insistent they may be on the maintenance of tribal ritual. Often a special religious organization, in fact, discharges a genuine or putative public function, as when a Nupe organization (Sudan) combats witchcraft. Among the same people, woodcutters, well-diggers, blacksmiths, and farmers all have their distinctive professional magic. The several Hidatsa sacred bundle cults coexist amicably, as do various Omaha fraternities recruited from persons blessed by the same spirits. Indeed, three of these societies were closely related, the Horse and the Wolf people being subordinate to the Buffalo visionaries.

Peaceable juxtaposition of this sort harmonizes with the comparative rarity of proselytizing on this plane. Aborigines are generally content to let their neighbors believe what they will so long as their *behavior* conforms to tribal standards. Nevertheless, propagandist cults do sporadically crop up, bringing dissension in their wake. Prophets, more particularly, arise in critical periods, promise delivery from present ills, and split their compatriots into followers and infidels. In the

Gran Chaco, a Chiriguano messiah appeared in 1778, claiming miraculous powers by which he could destroy unbelievers or transform them into stones. A similar cult ranging from British Columbia far southward involved the participation of all tribesmen, nonbelievers being marked for transformation into birds, beasts, rocks, or logs. The recent Peyote worship rent the Winnebago into two hostile factions—fervid propagandists and bitterly resisting conservatives. Earlier faiths of this order exhibit corresponding antagonism. A Shawnee leader, Tenskatawa, utilized his tribesmen's dread of sorcery to destroy enemies by a charge of witchcraft, but was at least temporarily checked by the brother of a woman he had condemned.

By and large, then, supernaturalism is less divisive in the simpler than in the more complex societies; yet it can produce genuine schisms, perhaps mostly in the case of messiahs' revelations.[3]

A religious association admits of subdivision, thus yielding additional groups. Frequently the priesthood is set off from the laity and is itself hierarchically graded. In the Orthodox Church the parish priests, who marry, are an altogether different class from the celibate bishops recruited from the monks.

As a rule, the social standing of a religious functionary is a favorable one, but with notable exceptions. The Orthodox pope (pappas) of Russia and the Balkans has not enjoyed the prestige of a Western priest or minister of the gospel. He is not a spiritual adviser, but often merely the mechanical performer of a ritual he has learned by rote. Indeed, outside his church he is regarded as a bringer of bad luck against whom protective magic is indicated. So low in repute was the office that in Russia the landed gentry offered their serfs as candidates for ordination and until 1796 these squirearchs were authorized to knout priests. Among not a few primitive peoples, as in California, the shaman enjoys a certain authority, yet is likely to be clubbed or shot to death if he has lost several patients in succession.

However, in the majority of instances the religious professional gains social advantages. A Tibetan often turns monk to escape the heavy poll tax; the English "benefit of clergy" exempted clerics from capital punishment by granting them the privilege of trial before an ecclesiastical court. From Britain to Hungary, the upper ranks of the hierarchy have formed the favored estate of lords spiritual in national parliaments. Before 1789 the Catholic Church of France held tax-free about one fifth of the land and derived a large income from tithes. In World War II American divinity students, including American-born

Japanese aspiring to Buddhist priesthood, were in a special deferred category.

In Liberia additional features appear. The Kpelle boys must enter the Poro when from seven to fifteen years of age and undergo several years of training in the bush. This many-sided organization is the masculine religious association and has a feminine parallel. It is of outstanding significance: "the focus and fountainhead of all secular and religious tribal values; it penetrates and dominates all social life as did the medieval Christian Church; it is the sanctum sanctorum of the people." The supposedly immortal grand master claims the power of killing and reviving human beings. Outsiders believe that he swallows the novices at initiation and rebears them at the close of their long retreat. The Poro, for one thing, segregates men from women and the younger boys; but, further, it is graded, the deeper mysteries being reserved for the upper ranks. Among the neighboring Mano, only very rich men were in a position to pay the heavy fees exacted for admission to the uppermost degrees. The oligarchy of elders in the highest status was thus able to reap considerable profit from the system.

Finally, religious bodies can give rise to essentially secular associations. The American Protective Association and the Ku Klux Klan are militant political societies stemming from Protestantism. In Germany the Center party was the champion of Catholic interests in the Reichstag. The Knights of Columbus form a Catholic men's fraternal order; the Y.M.C.A. and the Y.W.C.A. minister to the educational, recreational, and domiciliary requirements of Protestants.

## Marriage and the Family

The choice of a mate, though universally restricted by incest rules, is not necessarily regulated by supernatural sanctions. However, this has certainly been the case in the best-known forms of monotheism. The Hebrew scriptures (Leviticus 18:7–18) circumstantially specify lawful and unlawful unions; and Christian countries have generally framed their matrimonial codes to accord with religious doctrine. The Roman Catholic Church discourages the marriage of cross- and of parallel cousins; and until the passage of "the deceased wife's sister" bill in 1907 Anglican England tabooed the sororate as inconsistent with canon law. Mohammed transformed traditional Arab practice, forbidding, among other things, filial widow inheritance and sororal polygyny.

Some peoples arrange marriage by setting a horoscope for the prospective spouses. At the birth of a Burmese, careful note is taken of the exact hour, and henceforth an astrologer fixes the fortunate periods of his life. The child at first remains under the influence of one astral body, say the moon, later passes successively into the sphere of Mars, Mercury, and so on. It is essential that the days on which bride and groom were born should form an auspicious combination. Thus, if the days were Friday and Monday, or Saturday and Thursday, dire results would be inescapable.

Preliterate peoples usually dispense with such niceties, wedlock being entered without regard to religious or magical agencies, which, nevertheless, tend to assert themselves in other connections, notably in regulating marital relations. Not only during a wife's menses, but whenever a sacred ritual is to be performed, the celebrant must commonly remain continent. Among the Pueblos, priests stay away from their wives during a four or eight days' ceremonial retreat; curer and patient abstain from intercourse; indeed, any activity fraught with danger, such as a hunting trip, a communal hunt, a war expedition, imposed continence. Correspondingly, bad luck—a sick person's relapse or an accident—is ascribed on general principles to somebody's transgressing the rule.

Adultery, too, is significantly related with the supernatural. The Hopi may cite it as the cause of crop failure, and the Ganda impute to it the grave illness of an erring parent's offspring. Because a wife tends the man's fetishes, their anger over her perfidy also afflicts her husband. Some conjugal transgressions in the same area demand a ceremonial cleansing; others call for confession to a medicine man. The Lobi, though exhibiting little overt jealousy, believe that a wife's infidelity offends the Earth deity, this bringing disaster upon herself and all her family, which can be staved off only by her confession and by priestly offerings appeasing the outraged gods.

Religious and magical ideas can profoundly influence adult attitudes toward children. Chinese ideology insists on the parents' duty to procreate male offspring who can continue the paternal line, ensuring proper ancestor worship. In the Province of Quebec the Catholic stand against birth control explains the large families still to be found there. Contrariwise, superstitions about the bad luck due to multiple births lead to infanticide. A Jagga midwife will suffocate one of twins at birth; and the mother of triplets is despised as a moral outcast. In eighteenth-century Tahiti, the lower grades of the partly sacred

Arioi organization were in duty bound to kill their children on pain of ignominious expulsion from the order.

There is a widespread belief that a magical bond unites parents and children. Consequently, at the critical period after delivery, any hazards run by the elders would harm their infant, whence various restrictions on one parent or both. South American natives commonly emphasize the offspring's connection with the father, who is confined at home for a period while the mother may be already up and working her plantation—a phenomenon known as "couvade" or "men's child-bed." However, it is important to note that even in this continent the typical thing is the observance of taboos by *both* parents. Thus, a Canella husband and wife retire to a partitioned space in the house until the dropping of the navel string, and for another month or so they remain in less marked seclusion. They use neither paint nor other decoration, scratch themselves with special little sticks—never with their fingers—and abstain from all but vegetable food. The father must not do any hard work or otherwise exert himself. What is more, not only the mother's lawful husband, but any men with whom she may have consorted while pregnant are reckoned as co-fathers, and in the infant's interest willingly undergo retirement with all its restrictions.

A dominant faith is able to color interpersonal bonds. In West Africa, but also in Arizona and New Mexico, witchcraft is an obsession that destroys what are elsewhere reckoned the closest ties. The Navaho learner of the black art is expected to kill a brother or a sister by his magic; and in about 1880 one headman had his own brother executed as a sorcerer—an act that would be inconceivable in many other North American tribes. Kluckhohn offers the interesting fact that a Navaho sibling is often charged with the education of his junior, whence inescapable tensions: the elder sibling resents a task that keeps him from more congenial enterprises; the younger is balked by the senior in natural impulses. Given the atmosphere of witchcraft, members of the society use it, as occasion arises, against their flesh and blood. Among the neighboring Hopi, it was possible for a man who adored his mother and was inconsolable over her death to puzzle whether she had not, after all, been a witch, and whether her ghost was trying to compass his death. In similar spirit the West African Ekoi suspect their nearest relatives of bewitching them; a chief charges his daughter with magically blinding him; a husband thinks that his wife has practiced sorcery against her offspring; an old woman is driven to commit suicide by the abiding suspicion that she killed her grandchildren by her occult power.[4]

## Social Control and Government

Ethics and supernaturalism are variously related among different peoples and at different epochs. Where the connection is close, the question still remains in how far it is primary. That is to say, do people refrain from, say, incest because some god is supposed to have banned it; or because it precipitates automatically disastrous effects; or, by propounding religious and magical sanctions, are they merely rationalizing a social norm that has sprung up? For our purposes it is not necessary to answer this question. Suffice it that the association, whether basic or secondary, frequently occurs and that it influences conduct, if only by reinforcing a pre-existing norm. Thus, the Yaghan believe that Watauineiwa, their supreme deity, has laid down the moral code and punishes transgression. Fear of divine penalties, though not the sole motive, since public opinion in Fuegia powerfully checks antisocial behavior, remains a genuine deterrent. The belief in witchcraft, despite its sinister potentialities, is also capable of supporting moral standards. A Navaho will not lightly repudiate duties toward aged relatives or be a niggardly host or make trouble for the community, for the ready response of his neighbors would be an accusation of sorcery. Specifically, wealthy men are careful not to arouse too much resentment on the part of envious tribesmen. That such an atmosphere can be skillfully manipulated by chiefs, for both private and public purposes, will be illustrated presently.

Throughout a great part of history there have been several major variations on the theme of "State and Church." The monarch may rule because he is a god or a demigod; he may be recognized as spiritually supreme, yet be pushed into the background as an executive by generals or ministers; the spiritual leaders of his people may certify him as reigning by divine sanction; he may arrogate to himself supremacy in spiritual as well as in temporal matters; or there may be a complete divorce of the two departments, as (theoretically) in the United States.

The divine ruler loomed large in the ancient civilizations of the Near East, China, and Peru, and in parts of Polynesia and Africa. Innumerable fictions have grown up to bolster his position, but also to render him vulnerable. The Shilluk believe their king to be possessed throughout his reign by a mythical demigod, but as soon as he falls sick he is suffocated, weakness being inconsistent with his sacred character and assumed to bring disaster upon the country (p. 376). Polynesian chiefs rested their claims on descent from the gods, their own sanctity being transmitted as though by electrical conduction to whatever they owned and touched, which thereby became inviolable. In New Zealand this "taboo" was conveniently interpreted to protect the ruler automatically against witchcraft. Whereas a Hawaiian king required hereditary attendants to guard his wardrobe, his spittoon, and his excretions lest an enemy abstract something with which to bewitch him, his Maori colleague could forego such precautions, since his taboo power itself was considered sufficient to preclude evil magic.

A typical modification of the divine ruler concept evolved in Japan during the two centuries before the arrival of Commodore Perry in 1853. The Mikado, retaining social supremacy by virtue of his supposed descent from the sun-goddess, lost all governmental control to a military dictator. Close parallels turn up in remote areas. In the southern Congo, the Bushongo king of recent times, still considered the direct descendant of God, received reverential treatment even from his enemies, but actually his country was ruled by half a dozen ministers. In Tonga, the Tuitonga long exercised supremacy as the scion of a divine stock, but by about 1820 he had lost the temporal power to the representative of a collateral line.

The doctrine of divine right is familiar from European history. A sovereign, ruling by God's sanction, is entitled to the implicit obedience of his subjects. Hardly less than in the case of a literally divine ruler, then, does rebellion become impious heresy. In the classic example of the incipient Holy Roman Empire, church and state were in theory autonomous, yet mutually dependent associations, the sovereign being *ipso facto* the defender of the faith. As a matter of fact, the monarch in several countries was himself at one time credited with miraculous gifts. Scrofula was supposed to yield to the royal touch; as recently as 1711 two-year-old Samuel Johnson was brought to London to be stroked by Queen Anne and thus be delivered of "the king's evil."

In the simpler societies the counterpart to divine right is a revelation by some supernatural being that confers leadership on the person blessed. Even among the rude Botocudo of southeastern Brazil the tribal or band head was the man strongest in a spiritual sense—the one favored by a race of otherwise invisible sky beings. Inspiration of this type generally underlies the kudos of messianic prophets, though at times these have laid claim to literal divinity or at least to descent from an important deity.

A closer parallel to European history appears when the preliterate society, too, has specialists dealing with the supernatural—shamans, diviners, magicians, priests. The mutual relations on this level of "State and Church" are strikingly set forth in Gayton's report on a Californian people.

The Yokuts of the San Joaquin Valley are hunters and gatherers embracing many independent tribelets, each headed by a man of the Eagle lineage, whose eponym is believed to have functioned similarly in mythical times. Though far from despotic, the chief enjoys genuine privileges, such as being relieved of the food-quest by young hunters. On the other hand, he must entertain visitors and support needy tribesmen. Notwithstanding this obligation, he manages to clear an appreciable profit through sundry emoluments. As master of ceremonies deemed essential by the people, he pockets the surplus from "voluntary" payments, which in their totality greatly exceed his own sizable contribution.

Closely connected with each Yokuts chief is a shaman, whom the chief directs to smite with illness any recalcitrant "tax evader," i.e., a person who fails to contribute to the common weal by support of the established ceremonies. The culprit summons the shaman, who undertakes to cure him for an exorbitant fee or even lets him die. Aboriginal ethics on the whole will buttress the alliance of chief and shaman, for though they enrich themselves they are serving the public interest. A well-to-do tribesman who does not share in the expenses incident to a festival is viewed as a shirker who throws extra burdens on his fellows; hence he "received no sympathy if misfortune befell him."

Apart from this particular situation, the dread of sorcery exerts the same sort of social control previously noted for the Navaho. Men are restrained from cheating, adultery, and other antisocial behavior, "lest the offended person visit sickness or death upon him or some member of his family, either by his own power or that of a shaman hired for the purpose."

A rough parallel to the Yokuts arrangement occurs in the Trobriand Islands. The chief there is far more pretentious than his California colleague, yet he very rarely inflicts direct punishment. However, controlling the ablest sorcerers of the district, he openly orders them to kill the malefactor by their magic, knowledge of their machinations sufficing to terrify the criminal. Comparable use of magic is common in Africa, as is the accusation of witchcraft against the subjects whose wealth the chief craves—a charge that justifies him in destroying them and confiscating their property. Miss Richards shrewdly observes that the use of this device tends to be correlated with the extent of chiefly power. A genuine autocrat who can beat, maim, or dispossess his people at will need not resort to the circuitous means of bewitching them or charging them with sorcery.

This, however, does not exhaust the facts, for an avaricious ruler, no matter how despotic, may still desire to satisfy his greed in consonance with the dominant ideology. The data on the Nupe (Sudan) are revealing. An anti-witch society periodically petitions the king to sanction its proceeding against a reported country-wide epidemic of sorcery. Thus authorized, several members masquerading as spirits terrify the women of each village in turn, picking out some individual as a criminal, taking her into the bush, and making her scratch the ground with her fingers until they begin to bleed—a proof of her guilt. She has the choice then between paying a fine or being put to death. Thoroughly intimidated, the women may all run away and hide, disrupting the normal economic routine, until the village headman collects a large amount to turn over to the king with the plea that he recall the society. The total amount thus garnered from the entire realm used to come up to £300, of which the king would retain a third, the remainder going to the anti-witch society. Yet nowadays complaints are voiced that the people under European administration no longer have any means to combat witches! The case shows, then, not only how a ruler in collusion with a group of specialists on supernatural matters can extort money from the people, but how such exploitation is greatly facilitated by a firm popular belief in the reality of sorcery and the need of measures against it.

In West Africa the theoretical ruler is sometimes completely eclipsed by the oligarchy that controls the men's sacred and secret society. A handful of wealthy old men in the highest rank of the Poro, who periodically masqueraded as spirits, actually regulated civil life, stopping fights among villagers, exacting fines for breaches of the law, enforcing payment of debts, trying and condemning criminals, and even deposing the chief.

In Europe, as already indicated, religion has commonly been a prop of monarchy, which in turn has shielded an established church. Under Alexander III (1881–1894) a typical situation developed in Russia. The Czar staunchly supported Orthodoxy, whose official head was his one-time tutor, Pobyedonostsev, procurator of the Holy Synod. Between them they combated democracy and parliamentarism as cesspools of iniquity; deprecated popular education and freedom of the press; persecuted Orthodox dissenters and Jews in Russia proper, Catholics in Poland, Lutherans along the Baltic. Their joint aim was perpetuation of an absolute autocracy on a militantly nationalistic basis. This extreme, but not by any means unique, phenomenon in European history explains the fanatical anticlericalism of wide Continental circles, which tend to identify the Church and even religion with social and political reaction.

As Occidental history shows, however, the relationship may assume a totally different form. The Byzantine emperors rather consistently asserted their sway over the Church, maintaining the principle of "Caesaropapism." Justinian (527–565) did not scruple to imprison the Pope and to issue pronouncements on doctrinal issues. In a similar spirit Peter the Great (1700) abolished the patriarchate, putting a lay procurator at the head of the Holy Synod. The medieval Western emperors fought the Church with varying success over questions of authority. Characteristic was the monarch's claim to invest bishops with crosier and ring as emblems of their dignity—a prerogative waived by the Western emperor through the Concordat of Worms (1122). These conflicts involved no repudiation of Christianity, but an effort of the secular head to extend his control over ecclesiastical administration. Disputes on that score led to Louis XIV's Gallican movement, beginning in 1673, and to the parallel attempts of the Austrian emperor Joseph II to render the Catholic establishments of his realm independent of the papal see. The *kulturkampf* inaugurated by Bismarck in Germany soon after the Franco-Prussian War differed mainly in that the fight was waged by an essentially Lutheran state against the Catholic Church, to which a powerful minority of the population adhered.

Ruder societies have not been altogether lacking in attempts at Caesaropapism. Shaka once got rid of all Zulu rainmakers, himself assuming their functions. He was no schismatic, let alone heretic, on the subject that magic could produce a shower; but he decided to practice the art himself along with that of government.

We can easily understand why rulers try to control the ecclesiastical machinery where it exists or otherwise to exploit existing conceptions of the supernatural. It is an axiom of statecraft that the enthusiastic consent of the governed people smooths the ruler's path. An astute statesman accordingly does not flout deep-rooted attitudes but makes them support his aims. In 1884 the Navaho chief Manuelito had become convinced that salvation for his people lay in peace; hence he made up his mind to suppress the malcontents who preached rebellion against the federal government. But realizing that he would only lose standing if he arrested the troublemakers and turned them over to agents of the United States, he availed himself of the inveterate belief in sorcery, accused the insurgents of being witches, and thus had them executed without any difficulty. We have already discussed an African counterpart.[5]

## General Considerations

As the foregoing data demonstrate, the potential ramifications of supernaturalism are infinite: because of the tremendous hold of religious and magical beliefs on human beings they naturally tend to influence whatever phases of social life are important; on the other hand, those seeking to control their fellows will attempt to harness current forms of supernaturalism into their service. The multiplicity of developments in either direction hardly permits reducing them to a simple formula, but a few general remarks may be offered.

The significance of individual variability once more becomes manifest. A recluse, however ardent in his faith, can never found a vital social group; that demands the temperament of a proselytizer, humanitarian, "leader"; and again the nature of the new unit depends initially on the creator's personality and subsequently on his disciples'. An autocratically minded czar, such as Alexander III, naturally allies himself with a Pobyedonostsev, which a less dominant and more tolerant sovereign would hardly do. A Bunyan and a Hauge would explode if they did not preach as their spirits moved them; whereas others with like convictions dissent in silence and avoid martyrdom.

Economic factors repeatedly crop up in connection with the phenomena treated in this chapter. Tithes and exemption from taxes in Christendom, the taboo of Polynesian chiefs, the authority to levy contributions among the Yokuts, and the terrorizing of the common people by West African secret societies all exemplify the exploitation of religious and magical concepts for individual gain. However, the economic interpretation requires qualification. Frequently, there are specific obligations that are set off against the advantages enjoyed by shamans and divine chiefs. A South American shaman is paid by his pupils and patients, besides profiting from the work done by his many wives; but public opinion may demand that he annually share his good fortune with others on pain of losing his reputation. Again, the very prominence of the religious functionary or practitioner of magic is a source of danger. Primitive tribes, we have seen, kill unsuccessful doctors and treat sorcerers as beyond the pale. In complex societies a violent revolution may bring disaster on representatives of the established hierarchy.

Further, the religious professional may derive no material profit from his status. Some shamans go unrewarded for their pains, and neither a mendicant friar nor an Orthodox pope can be accused of wallowing in luxury. Finally, among aborigines as a rule "economic" gain has a meaning utterly different from that we ascribe to it in our civilization. It is in essence a largely ideological thing. The "wealthy" native is often one who owns articles that have a prestige value, not practically useful goods lacking among his neighbors.

But if it is impossible to reduce the data to a simple formula, it is highly profitable to examine wherever we can the evolutionary modifications of a religious institution in its social aspects and to determine the significant correlations. A single example must suffice. Chinese ancestor worship as a general family cult dates back barely 900 years. Before the twelfth century of our era it was neither general nor did it involve the widespread use of tablets. In early periods of Chinese history the clan took precedence as a social unit. Its members worshiped through stone or wooden images the heroic founder, real or putative, whom they considered their protector. Similar notions clung to the ancestor of a noble or royal family, his soul being supposed to dwell in his image. At the same time monarchs and officials of high rank held the prerogative of having an ancestor represented by a living substitute. With the collapse of feudalism and the growing emphasis on the Confucian principle of filial piety, ancestor worship became a general practice, and tablets inscribed with the ancestor's posthumous name took the place of the ancient images. The recession of the clan, as greater emphasis was put on the family, and the diffusion of writing are thus correlates of the modern custom. There has been descent with modifications.[6]

# Chapter 9

# EDUCATION

## *What Is Education?*

Tʜᴇʀᴇ is a temptation to think of education in terms of classrooms, teachers, and textbooks. From an anthropological point of view this is a narrow and purblind outlook on the subject. It is as though religion were inconceivable without houses of worship and ordained priests. As a matter of fact, hardly anyone consistently adheres to such a provincial position: the home and, in some circles, the church are recognized as important educational agencies; so are, potentially, the press, public lectures, the radio, and the motion picture—not to forget the extracurricular activities of young people of school age. What, then, is education?

An eminent German educationalist and philosopher, Friedrich Paulsen, has published reminiscences of his childhood, not quite a century ago, as a Frisian peasant boy on the west coast of Schleswig. In retrospect those years gave him unalloyed satisfaction, and he complacently contrasted his early opportunities with those of a modern city child. He and his mates, he declares, learnt about nature as no young town dweller ever does. They watched the sun and the stars, waded through ditches, snatched birds' eggs, caught fish, ploughed in the fields, and made hay in the meadows. "In short, the whole of Nature lay within the sphere not only of our eyes, but of our hands and feet, we lived with her as a part of herself."

Similarly, he got a firsthand acquaintance with the basic arts of life. The urban child sees only finished products; Paulsen saw them come into being. Through object lessons he learnt how people bake bread and brew beer. He watched the shoemaker handling awl and last, the carpenter his saw, the tailor his sewing outfit. A city boy grows up in a more complex world, but one he is unable to comprehend. As to social arrangements, a peasant lad did not have to cope with such difficult abstractions as the State; he could observe society operating at close range in the village, with its clear-cut strata of peasants, artisans, and a handful of professional men. And the basic facts of economics, of supply and demand, were daily themes of household conversation when parents discussed the effect of rising wool prices on the breeding of sheep.

In other words, Paulsen's upbringing prepared him for the totality of his people's way of living. That is the crux of the matter. As Counts and Mead independently phrase it, education is an induction into the learner's culture. Accordingly, it is as old as organized social life itself. Schooling in our sense is merely a highly specialized form of education. Once more industrialized civilization of today turns out to differ radically from its immediate ancestor. Compulsory schooling and the general literacy it has produced is a hothouse growth of recent times. For the overwhelming mass of Western Europeans, education until a century or two ago was of the pattern described by Paulsen, which means of the pattern typical of illiterate aborigines.

Defined as an induction into the culture of one's people, education turns out to be the most vital of all institutions since it embraces all others; and the corresponding association would be the totality of culture-bearers. Conceivably a people could dispense with religion, as the U.S.S.R. has tried to do; conceivably a state might refuse to distinguish fixed forms of sexual union as marriage. But education is indispensable to any society, for without it there would be lost all the accumulated knowledge of the ages and all standards of conduct. Education is the social economy that forestalls such wastage.[1]

## Earlier and Contemporary Education

Although neither preliterate nor industrialized civilization is any more uniform in its training programme than in other aspects of life, a gross comparison is helpful.

Contemporary civilization has accumulated an incomparably greater body of things to be handed down to posterity. Our technology alone dwarfs the sum total of what any preliterate or peasant group knows. However, as Paulsen points out, for the learner there are compensations. Precisely because our life has grown so complex, no one individual can control more than a tiny fraction of the entire store of knowledge. How many of us who drive automobiles, switch on electric lights, or travel on airplanes grasp the physical principles that underlie these activities? Young Paulsen did not himself bake bread or cobble shoes, but he observed and understood the necessary operations. The simpler societies may have specializations in skill, knowledge, and prerogative, so that by reason of inaptitude, age, sex, or class an individual is excluded from some facets of native culture, yet he is never so narrowly cribbed as the sweatshop worker in a metropolitan slum or the proverbial factory hand who manufactures nothing but pinheads.

In other respects the two systems differ less than might be supposed. To put it more precisely, the features that at first blush seem peculiar to advanced cultures have their counterparts in at least *some* preliterate societies.

SCHOOLS.—Schools—the unions of young fellow learners with socially sanctioned instructors—are specific educational associations over and above the all-embracing association that corresponds to education in its totality. Contrary to what might be assumed, such associations, though discontinuously distributed, are by no means lacking in the simpler societies. Indeed, the segregation of young people before or after puberty for the purpose of training them is so clearly analogous to our schools that the resemblance has not escaped the aborigines: African Negroes themselves speak of their "bush schools."

The curriculum embraces religion, ethics, etiquette and other folkways generally; physical discipline; and vocational drill. Some systems, however, stress certain aspects of culture to the neglect of others. As a rule, each sex is instructed separately, or only males receive collective schooling. The scheme of the Yaghan, except for its coeducational character, is typical enough to serve as an illustration.

Each Yaghan novice gets two sponsors, who supervise his conduct throughout the several months' seclusion. Physically, each boy or girl has to learn rigorous self-control, sitting still for hours in a cramped position, not stirring even when sparks from the fireplace touch his bare skin or when an elder deliberately tests his endurance by dropping a beetle on his back. The tyro must not laugh, no matter what jests are being bandied around him. For the initial days, moreover, he gets nothing to eat but a single Mytilus mussel a day and only a modicum of water to drink. Barely granted five hours of sleep, a boy may be roused in the middle of the night to be taken for a plunge into the cold water on the beach.

For moral instruction the neophytes jointly listen to some venerable tribesman's lectures. In addition to mass instruction, each boy or girl is tutored by some close relative who has noted defects in the pupil's character and now takes pains to correct them. Thus, a lazybones will be assigned some specially arduous task; a coward has to stay by himself on a lonely island. During the initiation festival any adult is at liberty to reprove and guide the novices of either sex, warning them not to steal or to maltreat dogs, admonishing them to treat old people with consideration and, when married, to avoid quarrels with their spouses. A girl is to be ever ready to fetch firewood.

Finally, there is true vocational preparation. The girls' training, to be sure, amounts to little more than rounding out previously acquired skills, for they have long been accustomed to help their mothers at berry picking, mussel gathering, and what not. The boys, however, are relatively backward at corresponding tasks of adult life, and hence require schooling. Accordingly, either a sponsor or an older kinsman tutors a youth in archery and harpooning. Only after a careful drill with his weapons is the pupil allowed to go on an actual hunt.

This multiple preparation—physical, moral, vocational—usually combined with religious rites and instruction, recurs in remote areas, sometimes with an amazing similarity of detail. In Nyasaland, East Africa, the elders annually select a batch of boys to be circumcised. They are secluded for a period ranging from four weeks to four months. For any breach of discipline they are beaten and otherwise punished, some having to sit for hours in cold water. Instructors teach the novices to make baskets and traps, to cultivate, drum, and dance; also the tribal myths and the social code. A corresponding girls' school emphasizes hygiene, household accomplishments, and ethics. Even young married women take a graduate course in how to act until after their first delivery, the instructions being partly fanciful and partly practical.

As hinted above, peoples vary in their comparative emphasis on this or that phase of culture. During a Murngin initiation, pedagogy seems to deal preponderantly with sacred and ethical matters. In Liberia, on the other hand, boys get a daily drill in archery, spear throwing, hunting, and sham battles; the older novices learn to skin animals and are taken on big-game drives. In their separate school the girls acquire skill at housekeeping, sewing, weaving, basketry; filial and conjugal duties are likewise impressed upon them.

Of course, all these subjects could be and sometimes are taught individually. Thus, in the interior of British Columbia, Shuswap Indian youngsters undergo much the same sort of training singly that is elsewhere given to a whole class. A girl who has come of age is secluded in a special hut, where a kinswoman attends her. She must fast for four days and for a whole year observe various taboos. She goes out only at night, gaining practice at running, climbing, digging, burden bearing, and each morning fetches firewood. Her fingers pluck needles from fir branches in order to grow nimble, and she learns to sew, embroider, make bags, and dress skins. Boys of the same age go off to obtain visions, fast, and get training at archery and gymnastics.

Evidently in the absence of schools, individual instruction *must* closely parallel that offered in group initiation elsewhere if the adolescent is to become a useful member of his community. However, it is significant that not infrequently one does find an approximation to the modern classroom.

In a stratified society the several strata tend to receive differential schooling. During the winter the Maori converted into a commoners' school a house that otherwise served as a recreational center or hotel. The pupils learned to hunt, to cultivate sweet potatoes, to manufacture weapons, and other useful arts. Women were admitted and were trained in their daily occupations. Though relatively secular, these institutions had a magico-religious side. The inmates ate only roasted fern root and had to sleep in particular spots. There was a recital of incantations, and a short staff was set up as a symbol of the deity presiding over each subject taught. This, however, was only one type of formal instruction. As in the aristocratic societies of Europe the upper class is trained in distinctive fashion—in the British "public" schools and the old universities, in the German secondary and cadet schools—so the Maori had "sacred colleges" open only to the nobility, especially to the eldest sons of chiefs. Batches of twenty to thirty boys would enter at the age of about twelve, staying for from four to five months over a three-to-five-year period. They underwent initiatory baptism and were pledged to secrecy on pain of expulsion. Priests lectured to them on Maori sacred history and taught the magical art and spells. A final examination supposedly tested the candidate's ability to perform magic—say, by supernaturally destroying a flying bird and ultimately by killing a man through the mere utterance of a spell.

ADULT EDUCATION.—Adults might advance to higher degrees of knowledge, as among the Murngin, where an initiated man continued to learn more of the totemic mysteries as he grew older. So a Winnebago entering the sacred Medicine society learnt esoteric interpretations of familiar tales and the ceremonial language connected therewith—"a special and difficult kind of education and training."[2]

DISCIPLINE.—Some accounts draw a sharp difference between preliterate discipline and that current in Western civilization until, say, half a century or so ago. As Dickens's descriptions in *Nicholas Nickleby* and *Oliver Twist* suggest—even allowing for exaggerations—our run-of-the-mill pedagogues were notoriously severe in inflicting corporal punishment on unruly and dull pupils. Indeed, there is plenty of evidence that harsh treatment of youngsters, far from being merely the practice of a few sadists, was prescribed by the considered judgment of the wise and august. Dr. Johnson praises one of his early teachers because he had flogged him well. Henry IV of France specifically ordered a governess to whip his son since nothing would benefit him more; and diary records prove how faithfully the royal command was obeyed. Thus, on October 9, 1603, the dauphin—born on September 27, 1601—"was stubborn and was flogged for the first time." Half a year later he is reported as "troublesome, severely whipped." Even after his coronation in 1610 he was not exempt from physical chastisement.

By way of contrast, primitive parents seem extraordinarily lenient. A naughty Vedda child hurled an ax at his father, who was annoyed, but did not scold, let alone strike, the child. Murngin society strongly condemns a "cruel and inhuman" mother who strikes her child. Of a South American tribe Nordenskiöld writes: "As among most Indians, children are never beaten. A little girl occasionally got into a tantrum and struck her father. He leapt aside. If the children get naughty, they are pushed outdoors."

As a matter of fact, such misbehavior is generally described as exceptional, many authors dwelling on the strange docility of aboriginal children, which enables elders to dispense with correction. Thus, East African youngsters impressed the Routledges as "singularly quiet and well-behaved." Once they observed twenty-two children under fourteen years of age, all of whom were quietly seated, though for the most part doing nothing whatsoever.

Such statements, however, are liable to misinterpretation. Aborigines do not beget superchildren, and where their deportment is conspicuously decorous there are probably specific reasons. North American infants, e.g., are commonly confined in cradleboards, which (as Pettitt argues) may well have a restraining influence that carries over into the subsequent period of development.

As for parental indulgence, Pettitt convincingly points out that many societies shift the function of correcting youngsters on the shoulders of such kinsfolk as maternal uncles, elder siblings, grandfathers. Indeed, where tribal initiations are in vogue, as in Tierra del Fuego, we have seen that almost any adult may become a harsh, if not brutal, taskmaster. Then, again, though primitive parents often fail to strike a child where almost any white would, instances of corporal punishment by them do occur. East African mothers beat excessively disobedient offspring, and an irate father will hurl a burning stick at the culprit. In Alor, parents are theoretically the only persons to administer bodily penalties and obviously do so with tolerable frequency. To be sure, they act on no consistent principle, alternately cajoling a child and beating it or tying its hands behind its back. It also happens there that the father will chide the mother for punishing a youngster and that on the next occasion she will take the child's part against her husband. In short, a young Alorese is not likely to develop a clear understanding of the nexus between his behavior and his elders' response. At all events, African, Indonesian, American natives somewhere and in some situations do strike their children.

Moreover, we must note disciplinary measures that for natives are just as severe as a thrashing. The Crow and Jicarilla joking-relatives, for example, uphold standards by caustic ridicule of one another whenever there is deviation from proper conduct. In both West and East Africa an incensed father may curse the offending child. Thus, a Pangwe publicly pillories the miscreant: "This son of mine is constantly disobedient, therefore may he never more enjoy good luck. . . . . He shall be cursed!" The object of this denunciation has to leave the village at once, and since the news of his misdemeanor travels he can find no place of refuge; hence he returns, humbly imploring forgiveness until the ban is lifted.

Finally, primitive parents freely resort to threats, using bugbears and supernatural conceptions of various sorts to cow their refractory children. A Zuñi mother calls the owl to kidnap a naughty boy and strikes terror into his soul by mimicking its hoot. She may also depend on the aid of mummers who regularly make the rounds of the village in pairs, entering the houses to lecture the young. "You must not mock your parents," they will say. "You must not soil the floor after it has been swept up." One of the masqueraders, disguised as a woman, drags a little girl to the quern and acts as if about to grind her up, while her companion threatens to lop off a boy's ears with a knife. To lend probability to the performance, the mother will complain of her children's behavior. The clowns who are of the mummers' party may seize an uncleanly boy and souse him in the river. At last, gifts are offered in appeasement, and the weird guests depart.

Notwithstanding qualifications, it remains true that by and large primitive parents are less strict than one would expect. But for a total perspective of aboriginal discipline we must take into account the penalties inflicted by other kin, the hazing during tribal initiations, and the liberal use of bogeys to frighten children. With all due appreciation of the lovable aspects of the parental-filial bond among savages, we cannot fully accept Knabenhans's dictum that the savage has anticipated the latest advances of progressive pedagogy.[3]

BAITS.—Our elementary school teachers goad pupils to maximum effort by the lure of golden stars or the prestige of being at the head of the class. Later there are prizes and scholarships. In imperial Germany a high school pupil was spurred to exertion by the prospect of only a one-year period of military service provided he could present proper credentials as to scholarship.

There seem to be some societies in which the hope of rewards is a negligible motive: specifically, the Alorese rarely promise to reward their children and even fail to fulfill such promises when made. However, theirs seems an exceptional case; the majority of known peoples dangle baits to stimulate desirable behavior; in other words, they offer some tangible or intangible remuneration—the latter in terms of kudos and praise. Crow practices are typical. When a boy returned from a raid with booty or otherwise distinguished himself, his father's clansmen—the proper kinsfolk in this tribe—came toward his lodge, performed a short dance, and sang laudatory songs. They acted similarly when a lad had killed his first deer. Pettitt, in assembling parallels from all over North America, shows that boys were often honored with new names in memory of valorous exploits. Contrariwise, the fear of ridicule, of losing face, is a powerful spur to socially approved actions. [4]

EDUCATIONAL AGENTS.—In our society the family, the school, and the church stand out as recognized educational agents. To these must be added the extremely important, though informal, influence of one's age mates, which often completely overshadows all others. If tribal cults are reckoned as the counterpart of the church, all of these agencies figure in preliterate societies, though with expectable modifications.

As for the family, we have already pointed out that discipline may devolve not on the parents, but on certain specified relatives outside the immediate circle of father, mother, and siblings. But these kinsfolk are often vested with much wider functions than mere correction. Thus, among the Jagga "it was above all the grandfather and grandmother who undertook to introduce the awakening human child into his environment"; and Gutmann has recorded for us the endless speeches they direct at their as yet uninitiated grandchildren. Similarly, the Jicarilla grandparent not only whips a naughty child, but trains him and regales him with didactic tales. Among the Hopi, the maternal uncle is the disciplinarian and ceremonial trainer, while the father teaches his son to farm and herd. Western civilization obviously lacks such specializations.

Another distinctive feature in some primitive societies is the removal of boys—more rarely, girls—from the parents' household. Thus, at about fourteen Sherente lads must permanently live in the bachelors' dormitory in the center of the village, where mothers or sisters bring them the required food. During the three or four years' residence there it is obviously the age mates who exert the most potent influence on a maturing youth. The place of the family in education is, of course, still further retrenched where, as in parts of Sumatra, boys from about eight years of age on sleep in the bachelors' hall with the unmarried men, widowers, and strangers. And this obviously holds true in still greater measure for South Australian children who, not long after weaning, leave the parents' hut to camp with older children. In Luzon very young boys and girls go off to the dormitories reserved for the unmarried of each sex.

We must insist on the effect of age mates' attitudes and norms, for psychoanalysis, in rightly stressing the force of early childhood impressions, has tended to obscure the potential effect of later associations. As Sir Richard Livingstone has said, "facts point another way." Education cannot be defined in terms solely of parental-filial relationship. In our own society the approval of one's fellows often nullifies that of elders. The "teacher's pet" is an object of mockery and contempt; it is the approval of coevals, not of elders, that a child craves. Neither prayers, entreaties, nor tears will make the offspring of immigrants to the United States spontaneously speak the language of their parents, for they are mortally afraid of being marked out as foreigners by their classmates. Except in totally isolated foreign communities, even language schools are pathetically unable to transmit a good knowledge of the mother tongue. Of my many Japanese students not one laid claim to a really adequate command of Japanese. Despite the enthusiasm of the older people, all efforts to keep alive Japanese culture, let alone nationalism, fail. When actors came to Hawaii from the homeland, their performances merely bored the nisei. The texts used in Hawaii, though printed in Japan, had to be adapted to the meager vocabularies of an American-born clientele. Similar experiences have been made with Norwegian-Americans and other ethnic groups. Friedrich Kapp, one of the German Forty-eighters who most incisively discussed the problem, wrote: "The second generation, however, is American and cannot be anything else. Whether they speak German or not, is immaterial; for they think and feel in the American way, and their views are specifically American."

It would be a mistake to suppose that the phenomenon is peculiar to societies with heterogeneous populations. The Jagga boys who are sent out to herd cattle have evolved a system of government, of "fagging," not unlike that of the British public schools, and they justify it on the score that it stamps out effeminacy. They evolve a "strong sense of solidarity, which overrides family loyalty"; and from a certain age on they increasingly resent punishment by anyone but their peers.[5]

PEDAGOGICAL METHODS.—Inevitably the methods used for instruction must vary with the subject taught: gymnastics, algebra, and the catechism require each a different approach. The attitude assumed toward a particular part of the curriculum is likewise significant. Sacred songs, prayers, and sometimes even myths must be learnt letter-perfect, since the slightest error in their recital is supposed to bring disaster. In such cases we must assume that the Jesuit principle, "*Repetitio mater studiorum*" (Repetition is the mother of study), holds sway among primitive peoples, too. The resulting feats of memory are at times astonishing. Two renderings of a Hawaiian chant of 527 lines differed only in the omission of a single word; another chant of 618 lines was absolutely identical in the versions independently recorded for Hawaii and on Oahu.

Spontaneous imitation of adults has been credited with a vital part in education; and there can be no doubt that juvenile play often parallels the elders' activities. As Tylor said of savage children, "their games are in fact their lessons." However, recent writers, though overshooting the mark, have independently shown that this point has been exaggerated. As Pettitt insists, imitation is at least often not spontaneous, but directed. To illustrate from a recent monograph, Jicarilla girls are *taught* to play with miniature tipis, *receive* dolls from older women, and learn to cook from *them*. A Jicarilla grandfather makes a good bow for a boy, tells him how it is manufactured and shows him how to feather the arrow. Mastery of a Jicarilla ritual also requires instruction. "I couldn't learn it by just watching," said an informant; "I would have to have someone show me." Among the Yaghan the father makes his little son accompany him, familiarizes him with native implements, makes him handle them, praises him for aptitude, and makes an awkward pupil do the task over and over again. At the initiation, we have noted, there is rigorous control in the use of weapons: the sponsor tests his ward with an old basket set up for a target, the bystanders compare the several novices' accomplishments, and the candidate must repeat his performance indefinitely before he may venture on a bona fide hunt.

As a matter of fact, many aboriginal techniques, such as pottery, are far too difficult for any amount of mere watching to yield competence.

Raum has made the point that what passes for imitation is an independent juvenile elaboration on the basis of mere suggestions derived from observing older folk. This holds to some extent—necessarily for any adult activity from which the youngsters are excluded and which they are thus compelled to construct imaginatively in "anticipation" (as Raum puts it) of the real thing.

Current thinking thus defines more sharply the nature of the learning process and the role of juvenile mimicry. It does not seem justified to eliminate spontaneous imitation, however, which necessarily operates with different degrees of effectiveness according to the nature of the model. Boys cannot unaided make a serviceable bow, but they can run races, have sham fights, and walk in parades without prompting from their seniors. Even in craftsmanship the *urge* to reproduce what is seen should not be minimized as a factor in learning. Yurok tots watched and tried to duplicate their mothers' baskets, naïvely assuming that good raw materials would yield results. The elders would ignore such play at first, but if a girl persisted her mother would start a basket for her. "After a round or two of the child's weaving the older woman took it from her to make a course, straightening the sticks where twining turns had been put in with uneven tension. The work alternated between them in this way until its abandonment as diversion or its completion as a rough little bowl." Here there is certainly direction and without it there would hardly be accomplishment. But the urge to reproduce what the girls have seen is equally clear.

Instruction in morals and folkways generically forms a chapter by itself. It is bound to differ from the teaching of a manual skill. Here it seems reasonable to allow a considerable influence to spontaneous imitation. Attitudes toward aliens or slaves may be explicitly inculcated, but observation of their treatment will start at an early age and affect the normal child's own behavior even without direction. Similarly he will absorb the differential attitudes shown toward men of prestige and try to mold his own activities accordingly. A Crow youth did not have to be advised to seek a vision; he noted that all highly esteemed tribesmen ascribed their success to a revelation by some supernatural protector and tried to emulate their example. Of course, it is not a question of "either . . . or," but of a union of spontaneous mimicry and express teaching, with rewards and punishments playing the role already described.

Storytelling forms a significant part of education. The Jicarilla explain a person's asocial behavior by his having had no grandparent to familiarize him with the traditional tales. Pettitt has shrewdly noted how many of the popular narratives of natives have boy or girl heroes, a fact suggesting that they were primarily meant for a juvenile audience. Several tribes, e.g., the Pawnee and the Thonga, are known to have special categories of stories avowedly for the instruction of the young, demonstrating, say, the dire effects of disobeying one's parents. But even when the moral is not obtruded on the listener, it may stand forth clearly enough. Innumerable are the aboriginal narratives that parallel our Horatio Alger series: a poor but worthy youngster surmounts early obstacles and becomes a great man, usually through supernatural protection. Then there is the motif of the haughty beauty who has spurned all suitors, but finally succumbs to the charms of a sinister character and nearly perishes in consequence. Apart from wholly fictitious tales there are also stories of actual or semihistorical events that point a moral—the brave who fights dauntlessly to aid his tribe, the faithful mistress who rescues a disabled sweetheart, the skillful hunter, the powerful doctor.

Quite apart from any initiatory training, young people of the most remote tribes—in Africa and America, at all events—are exposed to counsels of perfection that cannot be exceeded for prolixity. A Pangwe daily lectures his son on what to do and to leave undone. He ought not to divulge confidences, or his friend will take offense; he must listen to his father's words, for on his father he must depend for the bride-price; he must not devour food brought by his sweetheart in one gulp, or she will consider him a glutton and no longer love him; he must treat guests hospitably or gain a reputation for bad manners. "Treat your sister well. If she abuses you, do not reply in kind. Do not beat her, for the money she fetches when married off will purchase a wife for yourself. If you beat her, she may commit suicide and you'll have neither money nor wife, and people will not respect you." A Jagga warns his grandson not to strike another man's wife, no matter how provocative her conduct, lest he be involved in a lawsuit and be mulcted a goat. He tells his granddaughter to ingratiate herself with her parents-in-law; if her husband's mother picks out a fine yam for herself, the younger woman must not betray by the faintest sign that she begrudges her the fruit. Such advice occupies page after page in Gutmann's monographs. Similarly, an Aztec Polonius bids his son work, be moderate in food and dress, alike avoiding extravagance and squalor. A girl receives a double dose: her father urges her to become an industrious weaver, to pray, to be humble toward suitors; her mother explains how she is to walk, impresses the duty of chastity, and warns against the use of cosmetics. A Winnebago parent exhorts a son at great length to get supernatural blessings, and to go on raids, for "it is good to die on the warpath"; one should not abuse a wife; on the other hand, an uxorious husband will arouse nothing but contempt. Thus it goes on endlessly.

That such arid homilies should have much effect on the young seems highly improbable. They are of interest, however, in illustrating the prevalence of a rationalistic psychology in other societies, too. To be sure, the primitive preachers of virtue prop up their counsels with the familiar baits and deterrents, but unfortunately the rewards and punishments are remote, carrying little weight against emotional drives. An incensed husband will not be restrained from beating his wife by suddenly recalling what he heard as a hobbledehoy from his father's lips. For sheer effectiveness the bogeyman is a sounder pedagogical device than the sermon.[6]

INNOVATION.—In one important respect there is a vital difference between primitive and contemporary education. Since no society is wholly static, educational methods must reflect far-reaching cultural changes. If a hitherto hunting population acquires farming or stock-breeding techniques, these have to be added to the traditional curriculum; if men supersede women as cultivators, this implies that henceforth the education of both sexes must change. When Shaka forced young men into barracks, the work of herding and milking had to be learnt by girls.

However, in Western civilization change is not merely experienced but deliberately sought. This is part of modern individualism, which sets itself against authority and, for better or worse, launches into experimentation. To this there is no counterpart in other cultures. The aim of a Crow or Maori or Zulu sage is to maintain tradition, not to improve on it. If exceptions occur, they are extraordinarily rare: even messianic prophets alter details rather than basic features, continuing to operate within the established intellectual framework.

During the last century Western educational theory and practice have undergone many changes because individualism involves an ideology of its own. There have been kindergartens to adjust to the needs of early juvenile life; schools for the gifted and for the retarded; experiments in university extension and labor colleges. Thus, in 1927, as a result of reformatory zeal in the interest of the individual learner, there were no fewer than twenty-two types of boys' secondary schools in Berlin. Nothing like such conscious innovation is known from earlier cultures.[7]

## General Considerations

The goal of all education must include preparation of the normal individual for the economic role that falls to his lot in later life. In the simpler societies this means learning the skills required for getting food and whatever else seems indispensable. A Yaghan man must know how to hurl a harpoon; his wife must be able to paddle a canoe while her husband looks for his quarry in the sea. A Herero expects his son to become an efficient cattle herder, if nothing else. In such circumstances being educated after our fashion is superfluous and may even be a positive hindrance. The comments of an intelligent Reindeer Lapp on the schooling to which boys and girls of his people have had to submit in recent decades are highly instructive. The three R's are useful he admits, for a Lapp who knows them is less liable to be cheated by Scandinavian peasants and traders. But much of what is taught in the classroom proves useless. Above all, attendance in school during the most impressionable years of life keeps a child from gaining the all-important intimate knowledge of reindeer, the taming processes, and the art of lassoing. In this culture, then, school instruction is a boon of dubious value.

In speaking of economic training we must remember that not by any means is all that goes under that name, strictly speaking, essential. In Buin every woman ought to tend a vegetable garden and to raise pigs. The former task is truly indispensable for the support of the household; not so the latter. For pork in Melanesia is a luxury food, reserved for men and only for masculine banquets. A woman, then, has to take care of pigs not in order to maintain her or her husband's life, but to support her husband in the style which he considers his due. She is preserving a *standard* of living. Thus economic and ideological principles combine and crisscross.

Moreover, what is a mere luxury at one period frequently becomes later a veritable economic necessity. In Western civilization illiteracy is today a serious handicap, but it was by no means always so. In the early Middle Ages, reading and writing were "*clerical* arts"; even an emperor of the Holy Roman Empire now and then signed documents with a mark rather than with his name. In the fifteenth century Bavarian barons were still gibing at Duke Albrecht IV as "the scribe." For many Southeast Europeans, literacy has remained a superfluous accomplishment: until Ataturk's reforms, over 90 per cent of all Turks were unable to read or write; ten or fifteen years ago the percentage of Bulgarian, Rumanian, Yugoslav, and Greek illiterates was over 40, contrasting with that of 9.4 for Hungary, the nearest Central European country. The diffusion of literacy, however, was not solely due to contemporary needs of industrialized societies. Protestantism, by prescribing a knowledge of the Scriptures, greatly promoted that of reading. Since the introduction of confirmation in Norway in 1736, the art rapidly spread in that country; in Sweden, Finland, and Prussia illiteracy virtually does not exist today. Among the Raskolniks of Russia, who similarly stress familiarity with the Bible, reading was likewise widely diffused. By way of contrast, in 1920 the percentage of illiteracy for Spanish males and females was, respectively, 39.8 and 53.1.

Education, then, has not by any means been wholly determined by practical aims. Often it follows a given line for purely fanciful reasons; often it persists only because a practical motive once existed. When I went to public school in New York City, ten-year-old boys had to memorize such definitions as "A participle is a word participating in the properties of a verb, adjective, and noun." Only one bereft of his senses could imagine that knowledge of this phraseology would ever prove of benefit to the learner in his adjustment to adult obligations. In the eighth year of school we had to learn how to extract cube roots, a skill of subsequent utility to possibly one boy in a thousand.

Penmanship belongs in another category, for at one time a neat hand undoubtedly qualified for clerical and secretarial positions. However, by 1900 the typewriter had become so popular that no special emphasis on beautiful writing was needed. Yet when I began teaching in a grammar school, the principal made a fetish of the subject, drilling each of his subordinates in an impeccable Spencerian hand to be transmitted to the pupils. This was a plain anachronism, a good instance of what anthropologists call a survival of an old trait that is no longer congruous with its setting.

The prolonged persistence of classical studies—not as legitimate optional but as prescribed courses—forms a striking illustration. Once there was the strongest practical reason for making Latin obligatory:

it was the sole medium of scholars, hence the only means of acquiring book knowledge; as for Greek, it was associated with the revival of learning in Western Europe. By the nineteenth century these grounds had disappeared. Learned men were now writing in modern languages; it was no longer necessary to seek all inspiration in ancient Greek literature. Above all, the natural sciences were revolutionizing life, and adaptation to modern conditions implied a knowledge of science that was difficult to obtain so long as the classics remained the dominant subject in secondary schools. Yet in England Thomas H. Huxley had to fight hard for the recognition of science in the curriculum, and in Germany only graduates of the Gymnasia, schools with· compulsory training in Latin and Greek, were admitted to the university. That is to say, not only future theologians and philologists, but all lawyers, physicians, and scientists had to study both ancient languages, forgoing preparation that might be far more useful to them. A child can see that a grounding in biology is more important for a doctor than are the paradigms of a Greek verb, but it was only in 1900 that Greek ceased to be a prerequisite for medical study in Germany.

In this last case two motives besides sheer inertia are involved. There *was* an economic motive, only it was not the students', but that of the teachers at the classical schools, who were bent on defending their vested interests when competitors offered secondary courses in mathematics and the sciences. Second, tradition in this case also implied superior prestige. Historical accident had lent distinction to verbal facility, while manual dexterity and whatever savored of the utilitarian had long ranked low in the social scale. Thus it happened that the notoriously ill-equipped doctors of medicine of earlier centuries who speculated in Latin on the nature of disease were gentlemen and scholars, whereas the barber-surgeons, who had what real knowledge of medicine existed, ranked as mere mechanics. This attitude was not easily shaken; it took decades of a century conspicuous for scientific and technical progress to make educated men see the facts in true perspective.

Grotesque emphasis on a luxury accomplishment is illustrated by the place of calligraphy in Oriental education, the skilled penman ranking as an artist. In Lady Murasaki's *The Tale of Genji,* a Japanese novel of about 1,000 A.D., there are ever-recurring comments on the billets-doux the hero receives from an endless string of mistresses. One lady writes in a very aristocratic fashion, yet "quite without the graces of deliberate artistry." Another, alas! has a coarse, stiff, "very mediocre" style, the upward and downward strokes not being distinguished in point of thickness. A third arouses unstinted admiration: even in her lofty station she seems peerless for "the ineffable grace and elegance" of her calligraphy. In the Far East the ability to write aesthetically is obviously not a criterion of social usefulness, but of class. The accomplishment has come to be a symbol of status, like an Oxonian accent or a silk hat or the conscious hiding of one's light under a bushel that marks the Oriental and the British gentleman. As a matter of fact, *any* class system develops corresponding symbols. In coastal British Columbia, the nobility must be abstemious in eating, greed being the blemish of lesser men. Indeed, education is conditioned by status even when there is no caste cleavage. Sex dichotomy suffices to give the Australian woman an education quite different from her mate's, not only in the daily routine, but also with respect to the highly prized mythological and ceremonial lore, from most of which she is barred.

The demand that every individual, irrespective of sex or economic status, have an opportunity to develop according to the best of his ability is peculiar to modern democratic ideology. Typical is the New York law of 1921 whch forbade fourteen-year-old children to take jobs unless they had finished the eighth grade and further obliged them to attend school until sixteen if unemployed. In the same category belong our special classes or schools for exceptionally gifted, retarded, and defective children.

Democratization and indulgence of the individual have brought pedagogical problems of a new order. If everyone is given a chance to follow his bent, a situation can arise in which a desirable profession, say medicine, is glutted while equally necessary but intrinsically less attractive occupations are scorned. The results could easily be grave, if not disastrous, for society as a whole. Again, the policy of extending education to all runs up against the brutal fact of individual differences. Thus, in the United States the high school and college population has increased enormously between 1890 and 1938, the relative figures being, respectively, 300,000 against 6,736,939 high school pupils, and 150,000 against 1,350,000 college students. As a matter of sheer psychological equipment, there simply are not nearly so many persons fit for academic training as understood in the earlier period. The effect has been a lowering of standards and the admission of new subjects that *are* adapted to the average of the new "customers." The case illustrates the intimate correlations of social life. When an equalitarian ideology of education supersedes an older one based on the principle of rigid selection, the content and the methods of education cannot remain unaltered.

All ideological schemes are bound to adjust themselves to an economic framework. As part of a democratization programme, the Berlin authorities in 1927 opened the first evening Gymnasium for adult men and women who worked in the daytime. But whereas the American counterparts admit all applicants, "impoverished Germany could not afford such luxury for the time being." Accordingly, all would-be students were obliged to qualify by passing a rigorous examination. On the collegiate level Harvard some years ago tried to adapt the Oxford tutorial system, but its costliness proved prohibitive.

There is another limitation not less decisive than the economic. Those who dispense education or control its transmission enjoy a position of vantage: they can train the new generation to support not only the teachers' or masters' material benefits, but their prestige status and their world views as well. Among so simple a people as the Australians the old men not only reserve to themselves valued delicacies forbidden to the young, but also instill submission to the gerontocracy, social importance being nicely correlated with age. In more sophisticated societies, the masters restrict or devise education in a way that shall favor their continued dominance. The king's divine lineage is impressed on the people as a sanction for his rule; or they are taught to regard him as a wise and benevolent father to whom the subjects owe implicit obedience, whose decrees it is impious to question with a "subject's limited understanding," as a Prussian minister of the interior phrased it in 1838.

Two modern autocracies, Czarist Russia and Turkey under the Sultan, were conspicuous in their opposition to popular education as a menace to their regimes. This, however, involved them in a fatal contradiction: in order to survive in competition with Western nations, the governments were obliged to let some of their people absorb such knowledge as helped in developing a military system on modern lines. But, as happened notably with the Turkish emissaries, it proved impossible to restrict their training to fields useful to the sovereign, so that many returned full of enthusiasm for the French ideals of liberty, equality, and fraternity.

However, it would be a grave error to suppose that democratic and radical regimes fail to bolster themselves by control of education. As a work issued by the municipal school board of Berlin in 1928 puts it, the republican deputies of the Reichstag naturally tried to open the universities to those young men whose extraction guaranteed support of the new commonwealth. Notoriously, all governments foster an interpretation of national history that at the same time subtly flatters the vanity of the learners and ties them ever more strongly and uncritically to their own country's rulers. The results are at times ludicrous. "We Americans beat you British," an American-born boy once told his English father; and in 1914 the factotum of an anthropological department in the East told me that it was impossible for him to sympathize with the Allies, because "I can't forget the War of 1812." For the vast mass of public school graduates, there is no opportunity for gaining a saner view of history than that which they imbibe early in the classroom; here is laid the foundation for international misunderstandings. Forty years ago I had a chance to dip into a textbook used in Alberta and to my astonishment discovered that for Canadians the loyalist Tories of 1775 were the real heroes of the Revolution. It is comforting to learn that Scandinavian and Finnish historians are continuing "that mutual, detailed critique of controversial passages in school text-books in which the five northern countries have set an example to the world."

What kind of education is prescribed, fostered, permitted, or tabooed hinges on the dominant powers of a society, on their material interests, but also on their ideologies or even on pure whims. A Louis XIV, a Napoleon, a Hitler can set the tone in matters of culture and education where nothing is at stake but their individual tastes. In democracies, pressure groups exert themselves as a matter of course in issues that affect their income and status, but they are no less strenuous on behalf of ideological causes. In 1839 the German theologian David Fr. Strauss, who had created an epoch in the history of Biblical criticism, was appointed to the University of Zurich. Outraged in their religious convictions, a Swiss mob rebelled against the government and brought about Strauss's withdrawal. It is inconceivable that the insurgents could have gained anything but spiritual satisfaction from their enterprise.

In the United States, groups of citizens periodically protest against "unpatriotic" textbooks that do not sufficiently blacken the character of the British; elsewhere they object to the teaching of evolution. Yet they are hardly out of pocket if their children fail to idolatrize the Founding Fathers and come to question the account of creation in Genesis. Again, Americans tend to stress the puritanical ideal of family life, hence frown upon derelictions of teachers that in Europe would pass unnoticed as quite irrelevant. Only a few years ago the appointment of

Bertrand Russell to the College of the City of New York was bitterly and successfully contested by groups that disapproved of his private life and his theories of the family. Though he was to lecture on mathematics, the judge before whom suit had been brought decided that his moral turpitude would subtly affect the characters of his students. This verdict, like the protests of Russell's enemies, must be ascribed to a disinterested and passionate concern for traditional American values. That they are not values for the intellectuals of, say, France or Sweden is beside the point. In New York City the forces of conservatism held the whip hand; in other times and places the powers in control have maintained other interests, material and spiritual. But whether a society has an autocratic or a democratic form of government, the dominant forces will assert themselves triumphantly on all issues that are vital to it, and hence on whatever they regard as vital in education. [8]

# III.  SOCIAL UNITS

# Chapter 10

# THE FAMILY

## *Definition*

THE family is the association that corresponds to the institution of marriage, the socially approved form of sex relations. In what Radcliffe-Brown calls its "elementary" form it includes a single husband and wife with their child or children, this latter relationship to be understood in a sociological rather than a physiological sense. The definition thus includes adoptive children, but not even close kindred outside the conjugal, parental, and filial relationships. Even more definitely it excludes unrelated fellow inmates of the household, such as the slaves comprised in an ancient Roman *familia*, or the fellow lodgers of a hotel or labor camp sometimes grouped together as a "family" for census purposes.

Polygyny presents a complication. As Rivers notes, it makes a difference whether the several wives, with their children, reside together or occupy separate huts. In the former case the phrase "polygynous family" seems appropriate; in the latter, "it will be most convenient to hold that there are a number of families with a common factor, the father and husband." Corresponding considerations hold for polyandry.

An outstanding feature of the family is its instability, a trait that at once distinguishes it from lineages and kins. The death of husband or wife destroys the family; the marriage of a son or daughter alters its constitution, and so does any one of a series of institutional regulations or of individual occurrences. A young widow who rejoins her parents can hardly be excluded from membership in the family; on the other hand, if an American adolescent runs off to sea, settles in Australia, and is never more heard from, he is no longer in any effective way a member of the old family. Again, a Melanesian boy who takes up residence for good in the men's house, where he is separated even from his father because the two belong to distinct grades, hardly forms a social unit with his parents.

Occasionally there is something like simultaneous membership in two families. Since Canella matrilocalism applies not to the settlement but only to the household, a man is able to retain significant relations with his maternal home. Though he lays out a plantation for his wife and provides her with meat, he continues to give part of his kill to his mother; he keeps some of his possessions in her house, returns to it when ill, and makes every possible effort to meet his death there; in the daily routine he visits the old home of an evening, consumes the snack offered him, and freely discusses the affairs of his matrilineal relatives before going back to his wife.

With great freedom aggrieved Samoan and Alorese children leave the parental roof to be temporarily sheltered by other relatives. It may not be correct to reckon them of their provisional protectors' families, but neither do they and their parents form a full-fledged family of the usual pattern.

Social phenomena are fluid, making rigid definitions unserviceable because they tear asunder what obviously belongs together. Thus, if only the socially most sanctioned forms rank as "marriage" and only the correlated association is a "family," we should have to exclude units that functionally coincide with the family. In his comprehensive pioneer study of the European working class, Le Play describes the home of a Belgian tailor living in Paris in 1856 with his concubine and their two sons, accepted as such by their father. Le Play, though strongly disapproving of the illicit relationship, shows sound intuition in treating this household as a family, for a social unit can hardly be divorced from its functions. Now, according to Le Play's data, the tailor, his mistress, and the children were bound together by the typically familial bonds of sentimental and economic solidarity. The relations were at an infinite remove from animal rut; they were generically of the same order as those obtaining in religiously sanctioned unions dignified by the term "family."

It is thus appropriate to apply the concept with some latitude, to apply it to a continuum of conditions rather than to one type of rigidly circumscribed unit. The solidarity of mates with each other and between them and their offspring is indispensable, but beyond that we must make allowance for fluctuation. The solidarity may be of only a restricted duration; it may be limited by loyalty due to other units; the "parent" need not be the begetter or bearer; the "child" may be adoptive or classificatory. The distribution of the family in time and space can be profitably discussed only from this point of view.

Finally, as Lévi-Strauss has emphasized, no matter how important the family is, it cannot be self-sufficient for the simple reason that it is exogamous. A male can get his wife only by obtaining some other man's daughter or sister. The incest rule makes the offspring of any one elementary family dependent on some other elementary family. [1]

## Universality of the Family

Though biologically the species could not have survived without the initial bond between the two mates as well as between parents and children, it does not follow a priori that the family is an indispensable element of human society. For *sociologically* the biological trinity could very well be merged in larger units, as was at one time the popular doctrine. Unless there is a differential relationship between husband and wife, parent and child, as compared with relationships between an adult with other adults of opposite sex, and between an adult and *his* child as distinguished from those with other children, there is no family unit. It is therefore an empirical question whether, irrespective of coexisting groups, parents and children have always formed a distinct unit. Naturally, so far as primeval conditions are concerned, there is no direct evidence, and even for historic peoples our information is not uniformly adequate. However, on the basis of what we do know, virtually all recent scholars—Swanton, Malinowski, Radcliffe-Brown, Wilhelm Schmidt, to take a few examples—agree that the family occurs everywhere. And, going beyond contemporary indications, many infer that it antedated other units of larger extent, being found in clear-cut form precisely among tribes that represent materially and otherwise the simplest levels of culture. The clanless, stateless Yaghan form a good illustration. A couple and their offspring jointly own their hut, where even the closest kindred outside this narrow circle are only guests. Further, the members of this minimal group cooperate in producing the essentials for life and together consume them. The Vedda are of about an equal degree of cultural rudeness. They sometimes occupy a communal rock shelter, but each elementary family keeps strictly within its own section as though divided from its fellow inmates by tangible partitions.

The relations of the family to the clan will be discussed in a later chapter. For the present it is profitable to consider how it fits into a coexisting "joint family" ("extended family") unit.

THE EXTENDED (JOINT) FAMILY.—The extended family has been discussed as a property-owning corporation (p. 138). In the Yugoslav form, perhaps once typical of the Indo-European family, it was found to embrace the males of a patrilineage plus their wives and the unmarried females begotten by the members. It is thus emphatically not identical with such a lineage, for though it comprises the vital male core thereof, it excludes its females so far as they are married; and, on the other hand, it includes the wives, who come from other lineages and fulfill

important duties to the house community after their entrance. Notwithstanding the cultural gulf between Slavic peasants and Australians, the
zadruga in constitution corresponds to the Australian horde.

Of course, the specific features of the extended family were not altogether the same even in all branches of the Indo-European family. The
ancient Romans, for example, associated an ancestral cult with the male
half of the lineage that remained attached to the house; and a bride
automatically dropped linkage with the paternal ceremonial system and
was taken into her husband's cult group.

The reverse type of joint family appears among the Canella, where
the common dwelling is held by the females constituting the core of a
*matrilineage*. Here, by matrilocal residence, the males are lost to their
household through marriage, which brings them into the establishment
of an alien lineage. Economically, the Canella unit is much less potent
than its Indo-Germanic counterpart. The home represents the only
property held in common. Specifically, the land is not the property of
the extended family, each married woman owning her special plot,
which is cultivated for her elementary family. Unlike the Yugoslav
joint family, that of the Brazilians has no true head to assign tasks to the
inmates; and unlike the ancient Roman counterpart, there is no connection with any cult or even with the secular ceremonial that plays a
large part in Canella life. Solidarity appears mainly in shielding an
inmate from abuse. In this tribe the distinctness of the elementary
family emerges with exceptional clarity at childbirth. At that time both
the mother and father go into a partitioned retreat, observing food and
other restrictions. Where such taboos are imposed more conspicuously
on the man than on his wife, anthropologists speak of his undergoing
the "couvade," but actually in many tribes both parents usually submit
to natal regulations lest their infant take harm. These joint precautions
on behalf of the newborn set off father, mother, and child from the rest
of society, proving the distinctness of the family as a social unit in those
numerous tribes which impose natal taboos on parents.

A variation of the extended family is reported from the matrilineal
Bemba of Northern Rhodesia and the matrilocal natives in tropical
South America. In these cases the nucleus of a village or establishment
is not, as among the Canella, an ancestress with her female descendants
through females, but a headman with his wives, his daughters and
their husbands. In one Carib tribe the son-in-law initially works for his
father-in-law's elementary family, but the newlyweds cook on their
separate fireplace. They cultivate and harvest a distinct plot, and each

wife processes her vegetable food for her husband and children, though utilizing the communally owned implements. Minor utensils belong to individuals and elementary families. In short, though the elementary family exists along with the extended one, its integrity is clear. It is further demonstrated by the intensity of the couvade in this area.

EVIDENCE FROM KINSHIP AND MARRIAGE USAGES.—Data already cited in other contexts corroborate the argument. As pointed out, the behavior patterns laid down by various societies, notwithstanding classificatory extensions, do discriminate between nearer and more remote kindred of the same category: a Murngin wants to marry his real mother's own brother's daughter, regarding other cross-cousins as mere substitutes; a Crow may connive at a man's marriage with his classificatory daughter but never with his real daughter; and in Christendom the grimmest opponent of marriage with a deceased wife's sister—the sister "in law"—recoils far more violently from incest with a true sister.

CONCLUSION.—In short, the individual family seems to be a universal social phenomenon. That other units may compete with it, that any particular family is in the nature of things impermanent, that specific social customs greatly modify relationships within the family—all this may be freely admitted. Yet for at least the child's earliest years it and its parents form a close-knit social entity that is not confounded with any other.[2]

## Interpersonal Relations

The interpersonal relations within the family obviously involve those between spouses, between parent and child, and between siblings. Actually they are far more intricate. Even apart from the infinite variability of human beings, which affects any concrete case, the degree to which actual behavior conforms to the ideal, the age of the persons considered, the size of the family, and various other factors must be taken into account.

Theory and practice sharply diverge in the sphere of family relationships. As a glance at a daily newspaper proves, not all couples live in mutual adoration, parents may abuse their children, sons rebel against fathers, brothers are at times thoroughly uncongenial. Our ideals for these several relationships are certainly significant, but for the scientific student actual behavior is more important. Or perhaps it is fairer to say that what interests him most is to discover how far human beings, spurred on by selfish urges, renounce a maximum of egoistic satisfaction in obedience to the principles held up by their society. In Western civilization we can study the theme by means of biographies, the records of police courts, realistic literature, the tales and traditional sayings of the folk, not to forget observations among the circle of our acquaintances. Other literate cultures offer similar sources of information; and the personal documents recently gathered by ethnographers have given us corresponding insights into the realities of primitive family life.

The relative age of family members can have a crucial effect on their relations. Extreme disparity in the case of matrimonial partners notoriously tends to create conflict, infidelity, and divorce. Age combines with the number of children to flavor interpersonal ties. The enormous families of colonial days or of modern Quebec militate against the close intimacy that is possible among two or three brothers and sisters; of sixteen siblings, some are bound to be so much older than others that they figure as guardians rather than as fraternal peers. Benjamin Franklin, e.g., was apprenticed to his elder brother James, who abused him no less than he did any other of his apprentices until Benjamin ran away. This family is instructive from other points of view. The father, twice married, begot seventeen children. Among such a number of brothers and sisters individual relations were, of course, psychologically inconceivable. In his correspondence Franklin expresses polite concern over this or that sister's illness and refers casually to "my sister Lydia, who I hear is lately married." The sentiment is of that diffuse order which an Australian blackfellow feels, as a matter of duty, for a hundred clansfolk.

HUSBAND AND WIFE.—As shown in previous chapters, practical points of view are foremost in inaugurating and maintaining the conjugal state. They eclipse romance not only among aborigines, but virtually everywhere except in small circles of Western society. Romance need not be absent, but it is held inessential for that serious part of life which is marriage. For the Japan of the 1890's, Lafcadio Hearn, himself the husband of a Japanese woman, has made the matter very clear. His Nipponese pupils in a course on English literature were quite bewildered by Anglo-Saxon novelists' emphasis on love between the sexes as a prelude to wedlock. In their own stories heroines figured as devoted mothers, pious daughters, and loyal wives, and there were (as in *The Tale of Genji*) extramarital love affairs; but romance in relation to a chaste maiden and to the founding of a family seemed "very, very strange."

In the West, prior to the growth of industrialism, and of individualism in its wake, the average marriage conformed to the primitive pattern; there were *family* arrangements with an eye to utilitarian goals. Until approximately World War I French men and women under thirty required their parents' consent before marrying; and it is still customary to regulate the pecuniary relations of the prospective spouses by contract and a notary's certificate. Parents who could afford it supplied their daughter with a dowry (dot) or at least with the most sumptuous trousseau they could afford. In modern Greece a marriage portion for each girl in the family is deemed essential, so that impecunious fathers and brothers will emigrate to America in order to make the necessary money. Bavarian peasants, like the French, treat marriage as a family affair and unsentimentally engage a notary to draw up all economic obligations on both sides. Similarly in Ireland, a match is a matter of property disposal, of balancing the value of the groom's land against the girl's "fortune." Here, too, agreements have to be properly drawn by a solicitor. Polish arrangements are generically similar.

Naturally, physical attractiveness is not ignored, but it is secondary. Rosegger, descendant of a long line of peasants, has told us how a Styrian used to prospect for a bride. He and his godfather went to some homestead, engaged the stable maid in conversation, and found out whether she knew how to tend stock and to milk the cows. Homeward bound, the old man might say, "She's a good hand, she would do." The youth, if he liked her looks, would agree, and a few days later came an open proposal.

The emphasis on each spouse's competence within the sphere allotted to the sex in a particular culture is a matter of common sense. Marie Antoinette did not have to worry whether the dauphin could provide her with a meal nor did it matter whether she could scrub the palace floors. But among Irish farming folk it makes all the difference in the world whether a groom can tend the cattle and repair tools; whether his mate can bake bread, churn butter, and cook the meals. Similarly, a Yaghan wife must know how to paddle a canoe, a desirable husband is expert at harpooning seals, and so forth.

Most marriages, past and present, then, imply an economic partnership on behalf of the family, which by definition includes the progeny. This matter-of-fact basis, however, need not exclude deep affection and devotion, often fostered secondarily by common interest in the children. The argument that primitive people cannot feel love because they seldom choose their mates does not hold water in the face of empirical data. Apparently forbidding instances yield an a fortiori refutation.

The literature on aboriginal Australians suggests a very lurid picture of marital relationships. Customary law so rigidly defines who shall marry whom that little seems to be left to choice; elders monopolize young girls; wives are mercilessly beaten or speared. For all that, Dr. Kaberry noted cases of true devotion—an old man aiding his weazened wife at her chores, another native spending hours tending his sick wife. Looking back over their long past together gave great satisfaction to the first pair, and there was no thought of discarding the woman because she was no longer of service.

In South America, Sherente parents regularly arrange marriages without considering the young people's wishes, cowing refractory girls into docility; youths are extremely loath to leave their bachelors' club; and night after night a husband must count on having sexual advances repelled by his coy bride. Yet, such inauspicious settings to the contrary notwithstanding, three Sherente are known to have committed suicide because of a mate's death or desertion; a fourth never got over his bereavement, kept the wife's workbasket as a souvenir for years after her decease, and remained a widower because no woman seemed to be a fit successor to his spouse.

To take a Liberian example, the Kpelle regard women as property. A chief may either give one of his wives to a retainer as a reward or deliberately foment her extramarital intrigues in order to collect the customary fine for adultery from her paramours. Commoners betroth daughters in infancy or even before their birth and offer them to chiefs by way of currying favor. For all that, husbands do feel affection for their wives, rarely abuse them, and are proverbially prone to follow their wishes. To quote the close of a folk tale, "Woman's voice excels man's voice; man is strong, but it is woman's voice that man follows and yields to."

The money-mad Yurok buy wives and collect damages for any harm done to them. Yet a young man, even when unaided by avaricious kin, might for years work to give to the girl of his choice and her off-spring a suitable station in the community: "it is evident that affection and respect entered into the relationship both before and after marriage."

In Alor matchmaking is an intricate financial game. Nevertheless, young men who are left in the lurch by remiss kindred start out to win their beloved ones by their own efforts, persisting for years in spite of discouragement. In one case a romantic girl withstood pressure from her brothers, declaring that unless she married the man she loved she would remain unwed, thus depriving her relatives of the bride price.

Finally, the North American Indians, who have been vehemently denied any tender sentiment toward women, decisively demonstrated it in their tales, which among other relevant themes include the Orpheus motif of the ancient Greek myth. The Menomini version opens with the following words:

"A certain man was married to a woman; greatly they loved each other. 'If you die first, I shall go with you' he would say to that wife of his. And she, too, would say the same to her husband."

Thus a statement by Du Bois about the Alorese probably has general validity: "Such ties are within the range of possibility but do not appear to be modal." They are hardly modal with us either, except in theory.

Several of the usages previously described affect the mutual attitudes of men and women, hence of husbands and wives. Numerous societies, we have noted, sharply separate the sexes in their daily routine. Yugoslav peasants and Albanian herders, like many aborigines, lack joint family meals, females eating separately from males. In modern Greece and various Latin countries the conception of a woman as her husband's intellectual comrade is far less developed than in Anglo-Saxon and Scandinavian countries. This difference, which need not be interpreted in terms of moral appraisal, does make for a qualitative difference in the conjugal relationship: a wife who shares her husband's cultural and political interests is different from one who plays essentially the part of mother and housekeeper.

The mode of residence always tends to affect the conjugal situation. It is often correlated with economic factors. For when a husband lives with his in-laws, it is usually to render them services in return for the person of his bride; elsewhere his payments authorize him to take the girl to his parents' house or settlement; and in a normally patrilocal community the groom's poverty may force him to reside among his wife's kindred. Inevitably a wife feels at ease in the midst of her own relatives, whereas among her affinities she is in a position of inferiority. The young Chinese or Japanese wife is cowed by her husband's mother, as her Russian counterpart was in a joint family of a century ago. In *A Sportsman's Sketches* Turgenev still describes an old shrew bullying her daughters-in-law and cites the folk ballad in which a mother-in-law complains of her unfilial son who fails to beat his young wife. For the husband there is corresponding insecurity or freedom among affinities or blood relatives, respectively.

Finally, even apart from the effect of aging, there is the sheer lapse of time. Humanity being what it is, the mental set of husband and wife does not remain what it was at the beginning of wedlock. With uncanny realism Tolstoi's *Anna Karenina* describes the metamorphosis in Levin and Kitty, a young married couple. Before the wedding Levin is deliriously happy, feeling "that he and his happiness constituted the chief and sole aim of all existence." But the honeymoon brings unsuspected experiences; Levin is disappointed because not all his dreams come true, but on the other hand he has unexpected fits of bliss. Domestic life turns out to consist of endless petty detail. There are quarrels over trivialities, often because neither initially knows what is important to the other. Despite intense mutual devotion only the third month of the union assumes a more harmonious aspect. Levin chafes at his idleness and resents Kitty's apparent lack of interest in anything while she is looking forward to maternal responsibilities. After the baby has arrived, the marked difference in the parents' attitudes toward their child is reflected in their attitudes toward each other. Levin is inexpressibly happy over his wife's coming through the ordeal, but the infant in whom she glories appears to him at first merely a squalling, unattractive brat who at most arouses compassion.

Though Tolstoi's characters are of the Russian nobility in the nineteenth century, the phenomena he describes are of universal validity. [3]

PARENTS AND CHILDREN.—This phrase masks the fact, no sooner expressed than recognized as true, that it covers at least four qualitatively distinct relationships—that of father and son, father and daughter, mother and son, mother and daughter. Without bringing in psychoanalytic principles we note that by the traditional division of labor a boy will commonly accompany his father on the hunt while the girl picks up basketry and garden techniques from her mother where these are feminine skills. If bride wealth is important in a given society, a girl becomes an asset, adding to the family's resources and relieving the father of the strain of buying a wife for his son. Again, where male offspring are preferred on ideological grounds—as in Montenegro—both parents are conditioned to feel differently toward a son and a daughter.

In all of the four basic relationships the child's stage of development as well as the parent's age radically modify the nature of the tie. Here again Tolstoi has made profound observations. Though Levin strenuously strives for fatherly sentiments toward his newborn son, he feels nothing but disgust and pity instead of expected delight. But some time later, when the infant is caught outdoors in a thunderstorm, Levin is driven frantic with worry and discovers that he does love the child intensely after all. As Waller acutely remarks, the helpless babe that has no will of its own is the object of as pure a devotion as is possible to humanity. At the same time the care of the infant involves no mean measure of self-abnegation for a prolonged span of time. The parents cannot but remain conscious of their sacrifice; hence when the child later pits his wishes against his elders' they resent his willfulness as base ingratitude.

A vital factor in the estrangement of parents and their offspring is the overwhelming influence of the child's age mates, whose applause is dearer to him than parental approval and whose favor he courts no matter if that means riding roughshod over the feelings of father and mother. Even without prompting he may want to go his own way. As the parents remember what they have done to shield the infant, so the developing child revolts against such curbs as parents—or any other traditional initiators into the tribal norms—are bound to impose. He may grow countersuggestible, defying authority from mere impishness. In complex societies he may come into contact with a new idea system and with a convert's zeal mock what his parents regard as sacred values. Turgenev's *Fathers and Sons* classically illustrates this clash of "crabbed age and youth"; and in our country, with its many ethnic units, the youngster from the home of a minority group often comes to scorn the old-fogyism of his parents, whose very language he is frequently unable to speak.

But the clash appears in simple societies too. A Murngin welcomes a newborn son, the very fact of whose birth adds to the father's social stature. He protects him in childhood, tries to cure his illnesses, beats a neglectful or cruel mother, instructs the boy in essential practical skills. But time may turn father and son into rivals. A man of consequence tries to marry all the women he can, and with the dearth of available females not forbidden by incest rules a youth finds it very hard to satisfy his sexual urge. He comes to covet the younger of his stepmothers and even has intrigues with them—to the father's chagrin if an affair is discovered. The situation recalls the scene in Thackeray's *Vanity Fair* where Sir Pitt Crawley, "wild with hatred and insane with baffled desire," learns that Becky Sharp has become his son's wife.

Nor is competition limited to love. In Ireland, in Styria, and in other parts of Europe, a peasant is expected to make over his estate to a marrying son, reserving for himself and wife certain definite rights, say the use of a room and the kitchen with what food the old couple may need. Other children are fobbed off with a supposed equivalent of their interest in the land. Naturally, this arrangement may lead to restiveness and strife. An adult son is eager to settle down as a properly married father, while a vigorous and domineering father refuses to drop the reins craved by his heir, who is condemned to linger on as a menial. After the transfer has at last been made, adjustment hinges on the personalities of the old and the young couples. In ideal instances the son continues to consult his father and adapts himself to the old man's wishes, and the young woman comes to terms with her mother-in-law. However, not all temperaments stand the strain of the adjustment. The conflict between mother-in-law and son's wife is a favorite theme of gossip in the Irish countryside and, in accordance with the mores, in extreme cases the old woman would leave since a husband is expected to take his wife's side. Essentially similar occurrences are reported from Styria.

Corresponding phenomena are familiar in sophisticated societies. The lust for power and wealth drives princes into rebellion against their fathers; and aging monarchs remain on the throne to the sore disappointment of their successors. On this level, too, ideological differences separate the generations. The letters of the Empress Frederick to Queen Victoria reveal the intense animosity that developed between the relatively liberal dowager and her autocratic son, the German emperor William II.

The phenomena just dwelt upon require mention in the interests of the truth. Naturally they do not exhaust the range of pertinent facts; roseate mingle with gloomy tints in the total picture. In his realistic novel *Eskimo*, Peter Freuchen graphically depicts the agony of a native hunter who is forced to abandon his enfeebled mother—at her own urgent and repeated request. A mature woman in northwest Australia will visit her mother whenever she can, offer her gifts, and ask her advice. In an instance noted by Dr. Kaberry the daughter carried her blind mother toward her horde territory. She also tells of a girl of eight or nine who violently attacked a playmate for besmirching the assailant's mother's reputation. Filial devotion is proverbially intense in Oriental civilization, and parallels in Western societies hardly require emphasis. [4]

SIBLINGS.—In this relationship the differences in age and sex are especially obtrusive. Of extraordinary frequency is the verbal distinction between elder and younger siblings. It persists even in modern

Magyar, *batya* and *öcs* designating, respectively, the elder and the younger brother, while *nene* and *hug* are the corresponding sister terms. Fairly often we encounter an additional refinement: males and females use different words for what we consider the same relatives. A Crow man, for instance, calls his elder brother and younger sister by words distinct from those which a woman applies to those siblings.

Without doubt the primitive languages in question far more faithfully reflect the sociological realities than do European tongues. For the bond between a male and a female sibling is qualitatively quite different from that between siblings of like sex; and in any society that recognizes primogeniture or ultimogeniture, the levirate or the sororate, a senior sibling is socially a different being from a junior.

In this category, too, the contrast between theory and practice cannot be overlooked. The ideal held up in most societies is that of mutual affection and unlimited helpfulness. The elder brother is his junior siblings' protector par excellence; sisters make moccasins for a brother who starts on a raid; as co-wives, sisters do not quarrel as unrelated women would; brothers freely lend one another their most cherished possessions. The foregoing summarize the composite impressions derived from ethnographic literature. But some noteworthy exceptions have been brought to light. The Blackfoot preach sibling solidarity and give the usual excuse for sororal polygyny, but some elder sisters lord it over the juniors who share their husbands. Correspondingly, a senior brother grows jealous of a cadet's superior war deeds; either has been known to carry on an amour with the other's wife; brothers often fight and sometimes do not talk with each other for years. Even on this level the favoritism shown by parents causes envy and hatred in the other children. A social source of antagonism is the Blackfoot system of age societies, by which one brother may be arrayed against another.

All this is intensified in societies where wealth and power are supreme stakes. Not only in European history but also in Negro monarchies rival brothers become the bitterest enemies. The princes fight one another till the solitary survivor remains to ascend the throne; and should any of the defeated brothers escape, the victor tries to have him slain in order to forestall a rebellion. King Shaka of Zululand was murdered by his brother; and Southeastern Bantu tradition and history teem with tales of fraternal strife. Among the Xosa, at one time the infant Palo was the rightful heir, but his elder brother, Gwali, tried to usurp the chieftainship, failed, and seceded. Of Palo's sons, Rarabe rebelled against the successor, defeated him, but decided to move elsewhere. Thus it goes on and on among related tribes.

The mutual behavior of brother and sister falls into a distinct category. The overshadowing social fact in this connection is the frequent taboo against any, or at least against what to us seem naturally familiar, relations between these siblings. Relevant regulations loom large in America, Melanesia, and Australia; north of Mexico they are so common that Titiev cites their absence as proving the exceptional freedom of the Hopi from restrictions on social intercourse among kindred. A few examples must suffice.

Among the Sherente "a brother and sister avoid meeting alone outdoors, and if it should nevertheless happen, they walk past, giving each other a wide berth." Nevertheless there is intense solidarity. A Hidatsa never utters obscenity when a sibling of opposite sex is present. Until about ten years of age brother and sister may sleep together; thereafter they speak to each other only when it is necessary. "If I am married," Buffalo-bird-woman told me, "and Wolf-chief visits me with his wife, he talks with my husband and I talk with his wife. If he should come to my house when I am alone, we should settle any business or say anything special we may have to say to each other and then he would leave." However, they always tried to help each other: "I love Wolf-chief, and he loves me." The Yana (California) have the curious variant of forbidding brother and sister to use the singular pronoun to eath other.

The Hottentot prescribe complete mutual avoidance of grown-up siblings of opposite sex. For them a sister, especially the eldest one, is pre-eminently a person to be respected: she can stop a fight in which her brother is engaged; bad language in her presence spoken even by a merely classificatory brother would entitle her to a sheep as compensation; and swearing by a sister was one of the most solemn oaths possible.

Australians have the usual combination of solidarity and restriction. In the Kimberley area a girl of seventeen stopped working for a missionary who had inflicted corporal punishment on her younger brother; and though avoidance sets in after puberty, an abused wife can rely on her brother for assistance. The Murngin have evolved some distinctive features. Whereas some aborigines taboo any physical contact—an Apache hesitates to help his sister make a difficult crossing—a Murngin beats an adulterous sister and chaperons her in an alien horde soon after her marriage in order to keep away would-be lovers. Most remarkable of all is another custom. In a sister's presence a man must not hear anyone indulge in ribaldry; should this happen, he hurls a spear, not at the culprit but at his unoffending sibling and any other sisters, real or terminological, who happen to be about.

The restrictions in question usually begin to operate at puberty. Hence it is plausible to assume that the underlying motive is the desire to prevent incest by rendering it physically impossible. A Crow interpreter once twitted me with the indecency of whites, who prated of Indian immorality, yet freely talked with their sisters, a thing no self-respecting Crow would dream of. [5]

## General Considerations

EVOLUTIONARY STAGES.—The family has not evolved according to a single plan of development. So far as sex relations are concerned that has already been pointed out. If man was promiscuous in the sense defined so long as he lacked culture, he nevertheless did not approach the present ideal of monogamous marriage through identical stages by a slow progressive development. Extremely primitive tribes are monogamous, very advanced societies permit polygyny, polyandry is not restricted to any particular stage.

The same applies to interpersonal relations as a whole. It does not hold true that the status of the wife reflects cultural advancement. Tibetan women are noticeably more independent than their sisters in China and India, yet these countries rank incomparably above Tibet. The Manchu, who were until a few centuries ago a barbarian people, grant their women an exceptional status. A Chinese minister in Washington is credited with the remark that throughout the world only the Manchu girl enjoys a position in her family like the American girl's. Frenchmen, Spaniards, Germans, and other nationalities would certainly reject the plea that feminism puts American culture ahead of theirs. They contend that our appreciation of women is altogether unreasonable, surviving from the colonial era, when women were few and hence enjoyed an undeserved scarcity value. However that be, it would be manifest nonsense to rate the Hopi superior to the French simply because Hopi women enjoy property rights unknown to Frenchwomen.

Again, we cannot grade cultures according to the indulgence shown to children. As the section on education shows, the rudest peoples are not those who abuse and dominate their young—quite the contrary. It is typically the somewhat more advanced agricultural peoples who exploit the children. The Styrian peasant "does not zealously send his children to school, but prefers to keep them at onerous labors from an early age on"; and the same holds for European agriculturists generally. They are intermediate in technology, but not in the treatment of children, between the Paviotso of Nevada and the sophisticated town dwellers of the United States.

All this to the contrary notwithstanding, we must accept the fact of *partial* parallelism; in other words, of the independent development of similar stages on a limited scale. Thus, when industrialism once gains ground, remote peoples come to accept a similar outlook on life: the extended family, which had accompanied the elementary family, disappears; communal property interests wane; the profit motive comes to the fore; and individualism grows triumphant in every sphere.

FAMILY LIFE.—As Maine recognized decades ago, nothing is more difficult than an insight into the inwardness of an alien matrimonial system. Many people wrongly judge French family life from observations on the boulevards of Paris. As a matter of fact, we know too little about any Western family system. In his pioneer researches Le Play admirably investigated the setup of innumerable European workingmen's homes, meticulously registering whether the husband belonged to a glee club, at what hour the household sat down to dinner, whether the wife helped her mate in his business, how much she had paid for a mattress, how much annually for onions and lard and veal. All this has lasting value, but goes only a little way toward making us understand essential attitudes. Moreover, Le Play was not a wholly unbiased observer. Convinced that civilization was going to the dogs because heretics had made the cardinal error of believing that children were innately good, he blamed the French Revolution, Benjamin Franklin, and Thomas Jefferson for sapping the principle of authority, and with it the basis of family life. Recovery could come only, he argued, by restoring patriarchal sovereignty. This reformatory goal could not but warp the picture he presented.

Less than twenty years ago Misses Salomon and Baum's comparable study of German homes of the middle, working, and rural classes had the special aim of determining the stability of the family. They, too, secured valuable data. Thus, in a South German village of preponderantly Lutheran population, the parents were found still maintaining their authority and the family normally remained a unit for both production and consumption. To take a concrete instance, a man of fifty-three was living with his wife, aged forty-nine, and a daughter of nineteen. The husband competently cultivated his seven-and-a-half-acre farm; he tended to it alone because his wife was not strong enough to help and his daughter was working in a tobacco factory. Farming was for subsistence only. The household received a distinctive flavor from its dominant pietism. Not only was there regular church attendance, but even on weekday evenings during the winter from ten to twelve visitors would foregather at the house for hours of worship. The family avoided mundane amusements and restricted reading mainly to religious literature and a farmers' periodical. The daughter was brought up strictly and was still harshly reprimanded for any faults. She was permitted hardly any intercourse with other girls lest they corrupt her, and voluntarily handed over all her earnings to her parents, not even getting any pocket money.

Again, all this is very interesting, but obvious questions arise that are not answered. What, precisely, are the relations of the spouses? How does the girl really feel about the restrictive treatment meted out to her? Is the religious ardor of the parents an inherited tradition on either or both sides or are they sublimating some balked human drives? It is the indubitable merit of modern psychiatry to have directed attention to such questions. They are, of course, not solved for any society, but to envisage them is itself a great step in advance.

There are formidable difficulties to be overcome in a serious study of the family. Even small and homogeneous communities present kaleidoscopically changing situations, and in any complex society we constantly run the danger of mistaking for a typical sample what pertains only to a special class or to an individual case. For the sociologist the individual case is significant only in its relation to the social setting. This, indeed, likewise holds for the psychiatrist (or psychoanalyst), but with a difference in emphasis. The psychiatrist has to know the social background in order to understand his patient, who is his primary concern; the sociologist wants to define the range of variations possible within a given society. The most ambitious investigation to date along these lines is Du Bois' work on the Alorese through eight case studies of native men and women. Let us consider in what way they illuminate interpersonal relations.

Tilapada, one of Du Bois' informants, reports that she refused to have sex relations with her husband until he had bought her mother a strip of cloth as part of the bride price. Sociologically, this fact has no interest if it represents a unique or whimsical demand; a sociologist cannot take cognizance of all the idiosyncrasies of all the two billion living human beings. Dr. Kardiner, a psychiatrist commenting on the account, concludes that Tilapada, being sexually repressed, has presented her request merely to mask a "deep-seated unwillingness" to play the wifely role. To us the inference seems unfounded. For Lomani, another informant of entirely different personality, records the identical experience: she, too, did not grant favors to her husband until he had paid the bride price; and a third woman, Kolmani, likewise refused to sleep with her husband for the same reason. Wifely coyness until the economic aspects of marriage are settled is obviously a cultural matter, and this *social* fact is unquestionably significant for us. Wifely complaisance, not wifely bashfulness, would be a deviation from the norm, requiring an explanation in terms of psychophysiological idiosyncrasies.

The reminiscences of the several Alorese do amply illustrate a number of relevant points. Both spouses get jealous, and a husband angered by his wife's dancing with other men may beat her. A woman is expected to fight with a new co-wife; and though she ought to accept a newcomer acquired through the levirate, she is not always able to suppress jealousy. Both parents may inflict corporal punishment on a child, sometimes each in turn resenting the other's severity. Children constantly run away from home to be temporarily sheltered by other relatives. Elder siblings tend younger ones. Characteristic is the economic aspect of the relationship between siblings of opposite sex: even a small boy tells his sister that with her bride price he expects to buy a wife whose services will be useful to both of the siblings. This practical motive explicitly figures as the reason for sentimental attachment: part of Tilapada's bride price went to pay for her brother Mailani's wife, "so he liked me and my husband" and was generous with dowry payments.

The autobiographical approach used by Du Bois helps us determine what is cultural and what is purely individual; it demonstrates the individual's behavior within the limiting framework of his people's tradition. Regrettably the method does not reveal the innermost feelings of the subjects unless they happen to be spontaneously expressed. Thus, when Du Bois' Alorese cry over a bereavement, is it because they experience genuine grief or merely because that is the proper mourners' gesture?

For Western culture our intuitions are naturally safer guides. Here, moreover, we can draw on an enormous mass of documentary material which our acquaintance with the setting and with comparable personalities enables us to interpret by reading between the lines. For example, about ten years ago, Adelheid Mommsen, the daughter of the famous German historian Theodor Mommsen (died in 1903), described her father's home life. A superficial reading suggests a wholly roseate picture. As a matter of fact, the relations between husband and wife were ideal and altogether charming. At thirty-six the professor had married a girl fifteen years younger and had never ceased to love his far from brilliant, but tender and self-sacrificing wife. In a fashion unique in German circles of the period he gave her a wholly free hand with household affairs. She conducted the family correspondence and as the mother of sixteen children, twelve of whom survived her, she did much of the necessary sewing and mending. In relation to the youngsters Mommsen was affectionate, but undemonstrative and strict: they were allowed to eat at the parents' table, but were not to speak except when spoken to. In the evening the wife and children played at cards or other games, while the head of the house took to his work in the same sitting room, sometimes setting the girls some French or English translation to do, or having them guess the source of quotations. Except during vacation periods the boys were away at boarding schools and later at the university.

The mutual relationships of the many siblings are only imperfectly described, but enough is said to suggest typical conflict situations. Thus, the possibility of one sister's overtaking her senior in school was· a potential threat to harmony. A serious clash arose when Adelheid, who remained unmarried, grew restive in a household that left no room for individual development. However, untypically it was not the parents but her brothers who combated her notion of studying to become a teacher, a feminine career outside the home militating against the traditions of their class. Only the father's sympathetic understanding enabled Adelheid to realize her ambition. He even understood her subsequent urge to leave the parental roof in order to create an independent household, into which she adopted two foster children. That the old man would not let his daughters administer their inheritance from him was probably largely due to his own diffidence in financial matters.

Given our knowledge of nineteenth-century Germany, we readily grasp the outlines of the family picture, the nascent individualism of Adelheid, the fraternal conservatism overridden only with the aid of an exceptional father. The brothers evidently failed to understand the elementary phenomenon that their spinster sister, moping at home because the satisfactions of older norms were denied her, was naturally craving compensation outside the traditional sphere.

A detailed analysis of family situations, either as indicated in such biographical accounts or as provided by personal observations among our friends, is extremely rewarding. In each case the essential thing is to determine how the social traditions impinge on the several individualities and how these react to one another under the impress of the norms.

ECONOMIC FACTORS.—Kinship usages are often arbitrary and fanciful, hence rarely amenable to interpretation. On the other hand, marriage and the family commonly interlock with rational motivations. Certain biological and psychological drives, of course, must be taken for granted —notably the sex urge, the desire for children, the impulse to protect helpless infants. But the cultural superstructure on this basis is markedly intertwined with economic factors.

Ideology itself is commonly phrased in economic terms: the prestige that comes from polygyny in Africa is a function of wealth. It is true that deep-rooted attitudes can impede utilitarian developments: modern Greek folkways, for instance, still keep most women at home; and even in industrialized Germany Miss Mommsen had to struggle toward a common-sense solution of her personal problems. But economic forces themselves can and do shape new ideologies. Woman is sometimes favorably situated in other cultures, too, but unquestionably in our civilization her status has risen in proportion as spinsters, widows, divorcées, or wives have ceased to be mere dependents. Once firmly established, the individualistic orientation need no longer conform to a simple profit motive. Domestic servants are in many ways better off than factory workers and seem to average higher wages than unskilled labor, yet there has been a marked drop in their relative numbers: in 1880 they formed 19.7 per cent, in 1920 only 3 per cent of Americans gainfully employed. Doubtless there are other factors, but one of them is certainly the wish to enjoy a greater measure of individual freedom. Recent individualism, we have seen, makes modern lovers subordinate family convenience to personal inclination; it has taken the revolutionary position that wedlock should be preserved only if the mates are happy, thus threatening the stability of the family; it has decreased the number of children; partly because of the economic burden involved, partly because maternity is believed to encroach on the mother's individuality.

As indicated, family sentiments themselves are closely bound up with economics. An Alorese or African brother and sister are emotionally tied together by the fact that she is an economic asset, that her bride price will buy the boy a wife, that she is the indirect means of gratifying his biological and social desires. The custom of bride purchase also creates a special bond between the prospective groom and those relatives traditionally supposed to further his matrimonial prospects. Filial and fraternal attitudes may not be rooted in material interest, but they are strangely sensitive thereto. A Yurok son whose father is too greedy to buy the young man a wife resents such unpaternal conduct as a dereliction of duty. An Irish father who unduly delays transfer of his estate to a marrying son or who fails to compensate his other children out of his daughter-in-law's portion arouses very unfilial emotions; an heir who does not do the right thing economically by his siblings may become an object of hatred. In 1932 a young man killed his elder brother for not making the stipulated payment. Contrariwise, old-age pensions in Eire proved a wonderful balm in family relations. The small farmer—ineligible for a pension so long as he operates his estate—now makes the transfer earlier than before, and his ten shillings a week are a welcome addition to the household income.

In our own country the fantastic wages paid during World War II often enabled a young man to make more money than his father in employments where the rapidity of youth counted. In a civilization so saturated with the idea that wealth is the measure of status, the natural consequence was a still greater independence of the younger generation.[6]

# Chapter 11

# UNILATERAL DESCENT GROUPS

## *Lineage and Kin*

IN CONTRAST to the bilateral family, lineages and kins ignore one side of the family. This does not mean that the peoples organized into unilateral descent groups take no cognizance of the other side, but merely that for specific purposes—say the transmission of names—only the matrilineal or the patrilineal kindred are significant. Conceptually, lineages and kins are alike and usually so figure in the native mind. But objectively there is a difference: the lineage is made up exclusively of provable blood relatives, i.e., all members are demonstrably descended from a common ancestor or ancestress; members of a kin may *believe* in such community of descent, they may conceivably be right in their belief, but it is impossible to prove it. The kin, then, is made up of two or more lineages.

It may happen that a tribe is divided into unilateral divisions some of which are by definition lineages, others clans. In the Hopi village of Mishongnovi, the Lizard, Eagle, and Squash people proved to be each composed wholly of persons related by blood; other groups included two or even three bodies of true kindred. From the native point of view, however, all ranked as equivalent types of unit.

Either lineages or kins are, like those of the Hopi, settled in pairs or larger numbers which jointly form a political entity, or each unilateral descent group owns a distinct tract of land and is politically autonomous. Of the latter type is the core of an Australian horde or the Miwok *nena,* landowning patrilineal body of kindred who remembered their exact genealogical relationship to one another. As a consequence the territorial lineage cannot be *socially* independent of other groups, since incest taboos force its members to seek wives elsewhere. On the other hand, the Tongan *haa,* though *described* as lineages, are self-sufficient localized kins, for they embrace putative as well as true kindred and permit marriage except between close blood relatives.[1]

## *The Clan*

By convention most contemporary English-speaking scholars define the clan as a unilateral exogamous group; at one time totemism was added to its criteria, but being frequently absent in America, Africa, and Asia, this trait is best dropped as inessential. The definition adopted coincides with common French usage and is not unusual in Germany; in England, Tylor conformed to it in speaking of Chinese and Iroquois clans. On the other hand, the old Scotch clan corresponded more nearly to a tribe, though its core was doubtless composed of patrilineal kindred. In America, Major Powell restricted the term to what we call "matrilineal clans" and called patrilineal ones "gentes" (Latin *gens,* descendants of one ancestor; originally applied only to patricians). Powell's nomenclature did not gain converts beyond the United States, where it no longer predominates.

Because of the former conflict between British and American usage I suggested the Anglo-Saxon "sib" for unilateral groups irrespective of the rule of descent, but since the proposal was not generally adopted I have reverted to prevalent British and French terminology. Morgan originally spoke of Iroquois "tribes" in the sense of clans, later substituting "gens," not with Powell's restricted meaning, but to include any clan in modern parlance.

To turn to another terminological issue, is exogamy really important enough to distinguish one type of kin from another? It is tempting to answer negatively since genetically the two are often related. We know, for example, that under white influence ancient bars to marriage are often relaxed without the dissappearance of the unilateral tie. But functionally the difference is considerable. For, if a sufficient number of persons were to marry within the kin, how could one continue to speak of matriliny or patriliny at all? The children of such a union are no longer able to draw that sharp distinction between maternal and paternal relatives which is so conspicuous in many societies. A Crow in such circumstances loses his bearings and perplexes his tribesmen. For he owes specific obligations to his father's relatives and others to his mother's, who are now hopelessly confounded. The sons of his father's clansmen ought to be his censors, whereas his mother's are bound to shield him from criticism; but now the very same persons are his joking-relatives and his clansmen! The dilemma affects others as well as himself.

Thus a clan is truly a distinct form of kin. On the other hand, Kirchhoff goes too far in casting doubt on the very existence of patri-linear or matrilinear agamy, for too many African and Polynesian societies have been authentically described in these terms. To be sure, they cannot be regarded as uncompromisingly unilateral; yet the reported rule of descent is evidently prevalent, whether the facts betoken a nascent or a decadent clan organization or some special obstacle in the way of complete consistency.

At all events, in view of terminological differences in the past, we must carefully scrutinize any reported "clan" system until we are sure that the author's conception of one conforms to ours. It is equally important not to jump to the conclusion that some old source must refer to clans when it merely registers some phenomenon that might conceivably be so interpreted. Past construction of Spanish chronicles concerning American Indians is especially suspect and requires discriminating analysis. The Chibcha of Colombia, we learn, had a ruler or priest succeeded by his sister's eldest son. The fact evidently harmonizes with matriliny, it quite properly should make us alert to any further diagnostic criteria of matrilineal descent, but by itself it is not proof. As a matter of fact, the chronicles also tell us that sons inherited personal property, and nothing is said about the practices of the common herd. What is positively known thus admits of several interpretations. Conceivably the Chibcha were in a transitional stage toward patriliny, as older theorists would at once assume; conceivably the people were bilinear; conceivably the rulers had principles of descent and inheritance different from the commoners. In short, we do not know.

Again, the *ayllu* of early writers on Peru has often been conceived as a typical patrilineal clan. However, the unit at present so called by Aymara and Quechua Indians is definitely nothing of the sort, being an alliance of *unrelated* joint families, each claiming descent from a separate founder and with a strongly endogamous tendency. The old sources do, indeed, indicate a more or less patrilineal body, but one that also favored endogamy. There can thus be no question of clans. In Mexico the *calpulli* of the Aztecs remains an enigma, some specialists interpreting it as a clan, others as a military association. On the other hand, some of the western and southern Mexicans may really have had patrilineal clans; and the recent Lacandon of Yucatan are credited with preponderantly exogamous moieties, i.e., two major clans.[2]

## Phratries

In ancient Athens a *phratria* was one of three political subdivisions of the tribe (*phyle*), kinship originally determining membership. Morgan conveniently applied the English form "phratry" to a group of two or more clans united for certain common objects. Though most of the tribes he knew happened to group all their clans into two major units so that their phratries were moieties, he correctly spoke of the three phratries of the Mohegan. In the light of our present knowledge it is useful to retain the word for a union of kins, but to designate as "exogamous moieties" (French *moitié,* half) the two major kins, whether undivided or subdivided, that make up many tribes. This type of unit will presently receive separate discussion.

Phratries may or may not be exogamous. The thirteen Crow clans were grouped in six nameless major units, four of which certainly did not regulate marriage. On the other hand, in the Hopi village of Oraibi, the nine anonymous phratries, each embracing from two to six named clans that share ceremonial privileges, are the largest exogamous units known to these people.

Kin unions of different type may coexist in the same society. Of the sixteen Kansas clans, eight formed one exogamous moiety, the remainder the complementary moiety; and this dual division found spatial expression, the men of one half-tribe with their families camping on the left side, the men of the other half on the right side of the circle. But in addition "those who sang together" formed phratries, of which there were six.

When kins are localized within a settlement, the domiciliary arrangements may go with distinctive mutual relations between particular kins. Of the eight Sherente clans living each in a particular part of a semicircle, a clan on the north side is paired with its southern counterpart, so that four phratries result. Each member of a couple is charged with decorating and burying the deceased of the allied clan.

However, such obligations are not dependent on localization within a settlement. The four Lobi kins, too, are paired. At a funeral the mourners of one of the two linked kins are guarded by members of the other kin, who prevent suicidal attempts and comfort the bereaved, for which they receive a proper fee. Joking privileges obtain between the two groups, which also exercise the serious function of peacemakers in domestic quarrels and in armed brawls. In the latter emergency, a blacksmith, a xylophone player, or a diviner intervenes and, on pain of suspending his services, orders the fighters of the kin allied to his own to desist. These phenomena correspond to some often typical of moieties, but though the Lobi phratries are half-tribes, the mutual obligations in this tribe obtain not between the moieties, but between the halves of each moiety.

An extremely ineffective alliance of clans, based on putative linguistic affinity or a common totem, occurs among the Murngin, but is of interest mainly as a groping toward major social units.

"Phratry" is evidently nothing but a convenient term for a kin linkage. The features covered by it do not by any means correspond to a single sociological phenomenon.[3]

## Moieties

Etymologically, moieties are half-tribes. If exogamous, they are simply major clans, but this does not necessarily imply that the lesser clans comprised in a moiety bear a direct genetic relationship to it. Whether this holds in a given case is to be determined by special evidence.

The dual organization may be regarded from several points of view. We must consider the attributes of moieties; the relations of exogamous to agamous moieties; the unity or multiplicity of origin of moieties.

ATTRIBUTES OF MOIETIES.—Moieties may be exogamous, agamous, or (more rarely) endogamous. The Toda units, though subdivided into clans, are of the last category and one of the moieties ranks the other, so that they correspond to the castes found in other parts of India. Agamy may mean that a once exogamous dual organization has relaxed the rule preventing marriage within its fold; but it may also mean that for some reason the sense of kinship has never been extended, or not fully extended, to the moiety.

Exogamous moieties require special attention. They are widely distributed, occurring in most of Australia and parts of Melanesia; in India and neighboring parts of Asia; and in several parts of both Americas. Their complete or virtual absence in certain other vast regions is also noteworthy; except for a few dubious exceptions they are wanting in Africa and seem to be found only in the westernmost part of Siberia, among the Ostyak and Vogul.

An exogamous dual organization differs from a multiple clan system in significant respects. For one thing, if the rule of descent and an individual's moiety are known, the moiety affiliation of all his relations can be logically deduced. For, given two matrilineal tribal halves called Wolf and Eagle, a Wolf individual's siblings are also Wolves since, by hypothesis, all children follow their mother; by exogamy his father and the father's siblings are Eagles, and for the same reason the father's sister's husband must be a Wolf. Thus we can go on indefinitely. But if there should be three clans, the relatives' affiliations are only partly determined, for any individual can choose a mate from *either* of the two clans to which he himself does not belong.

*Any* dichotomy brings about distinctive mutual attitudes that do not appear when there are several or more groups. The political system of the United States with its two major parties is quite different from that of France and Germany with their numerous discordant factions. Similarly, the dual organization of primitive tribes exhibits distinctive features: complementary moieties owe each other specified services, compete in games, use contrasted decorative paint, occupy separate parts of the camp or village, and may be associated in native consciousness with antithetical aspects of nature. A few illustrations will make this clearer.

Among the Tlingit (Alaska) a man never gives property to one of his own half-tribe or employs him for any services. A Raven always gets a Wolf to put up a house for him, to pierce his children's ears, to initiate the youngsters into secret societies, and vice versa. Feasts are given exclusively for the other half. There is great rivalry between the two parties, "and their endeavors to outdo each other sometimes almost resulted in bloodshed."

In the eastern United States, the Choctaw moieties performed funeral obsequies for each other and were associated with war and peace, respectively. The comparable Winnebago divisions are called "those above" and "those on earth," the former comprising clans named after birds, the latter called after land and water animals. The moieties formerly occupied each a definite half of the village and, as in several other Eastern tribes, were pitted against each other in lacrosse.

Many Brazilian aborigines have corresponding features. The Bororo apportion the north side of a village to one half-tribe, the south side to the other; in one district there is an additional dichotomy, an axis perpendicular to the Vermelho River creating an Upstream and a Downstream moiety. The primary moieties have reciprocal duties: after a person's death members of the opposite half must kill a game animal, and the performers of a dance must be washed by their opposites. The Apinayé contrast their halves as "Lower" and "Upper," though they actually name them after two species of chestnut; they associate one with the sun and red paint, the other with the moon and black paint. The related Canella dichotomize the entire population according to two separate schemes, and males by two further principles of dual division. Moieties of one type are exogamous, matrilineal, and linked with the eastern and western half of the village. Membership in the second type of moiety hinges on a person's names. The resulting halves differ in decorative paint, use distinct battle cries, and run races against each other during the rainy season; they are further associated with complementary phenomena of nature—one moiety with the east, the sun, day, the dry season, fire, earth, and red; the other with the west, the moon, night, the wet season, firewood, water, and black. A third scheme sets off males according to their affiliation with one or the other of six groups, three of which are ranged as an eastern moiety, while the rest take up positions in the west. These half-tribes figure prominently at the boys' initiation ceremony and at another festival; in associated races the teams are recruited from the complementary moieties. Finally, the four athletically active age classes are localized in pairs, respectively, on the east and the west side of the village plaza, couples competing with each other in races held during the appropriate season.

To take still another example, Australian moieties, often nameless, in part bear such designations as Eaglehawk and Crow, in part names that cannot be translated. The Murngin system duplicates some of the conceptions found in America. At the end of one ceremony the members of the two groups exchange food; at another the men of one half-tribe are privileged and obliged to construct a sacred emblem, for which their opposites compensate them; for ceremonial decoration, one moiety uses red feathers, the other opossum fur. Most interestingly, the Murngin scheme, like one of the four Canella systems, divides the universe between the two halves.

Reciprocity, complementary functions, conceptual antithesis, and rivalry obviously occur in widely distant regions of the globe. It is worth noting that where these functions go with exogamy, they may be nothing more than extensions of the behavior patterns connected with relatives of the paternal and maternal side. For in such an organization every tribesman must belong to either the paternal or the maternal moiety. On the other hand, the implied extension does not occur everywhere, and may be greatly attenuated, so that moiety solidarity is eclipsed by that within the lesser clan or the family. [4]

EXOGAMOUS AND AGAMOUS MOIETIES.—Exogamy readily disappears and readily develops in connection with a dual organization. The Iroquois once regarded fellow members of a moiety as siblings and hence barred marriage among them; recently their restrictions held only within the clan. Nowadays, many Canella defy the traditional rule of moiety exogamy—to the chagrin of the older generation. According to the Angami of Assam, whose moieties will be reconsidered presently, the Pezoma and the Pepfüma were once intermarrying moieties, but for some time the taboo has been observed only within a lesser subdivision.

Agamy naturally develops as a sequel to exogamy in a dual organization. For one thing, a prosperous moiety grows so large that its members lose a sense of kinship or find it greatly weakened. Second, the usual difficulty of finding a mate would make a regulation very irksome that ruled out fully half the men or women of the tribe as sex partners.

But the undoubted loss of the exogamous feature in some instances does not prove that all agamous moieties observed must once have prohibited marriage. Whether such a hypothesis is at all probable depends on the total context. To take the agamous moieties of the Apinayé, this tribe is of the Ge stock, which includes its closest relatives, the Canella to the east, the Northern Kayapo to the west. With both these groups they share matriliny, localization of the moieties within the settlement, their association with ceremonial and with the same form of sport. As among the Kayapo, the half-tribes are referred to as "upper" and "lower"; as among the Canella, red and black paint are the contrasting decorations used, and each moiety owns a set of personal names. Given the established linguistic affinity of the three tribes, the facts are best interpreted by the assumption of descent with modification. Each of the tribes in course of time developed specific features, the Apinayé dropping the restriction concerning sex relations.

On the other hand, the Pueblo Indians of New Mexico present a rather different condition of affairs. In the eastern villages dichotomy is conspicuous, the halves being connected with summer and winter, turquoise and squash, respectively, but in no case have they anything but ceremonial significance. At Santa Ana, persons of certain clans belong by that fact to the Squash ceremonial chamber, those born into the remaining clans to the Turquoise chamber, but the moiety has not developed any feelings of kinship among the several clans of a half-tribe, remaining a purely ceremonial association. In this area, then, evolution has not occurred from an exogamous to an agamous moiety pattern.

But there is another logical possibility. Instead of losing or never having had the marriage-regulating feature, a dual organization may acquire it secondarily. Continued association may ultimately produce a sense of kinship among fellow members of a ceremonial, sportive, or political moiety, this sentiment being reflected in aversion to marriage within the group. This hypothesis may perhaps be plausibly applied to South America. Olson has stressed the wide occurrence there of half-tribes designated as "lower" and "upper," "east" and "west"; and since his paper additional instances have come to light. Some sort of diffusion is certainly indicated, but how is it to be conceived? The dual organizations now known are in part exogamous, in part—as in Bolivia—they are emphatically not so; yet the agamous Uro-Čipaya divisions, precisely like their Canella counterparts, have their quarters in the east and west, respectively, of a village.

Since the higher Andean civilizations are credited with a dual organization, it is tempting to derive its samples among such simpler peoples as the Ge and Bororo from that source. Lévi-Strauss has suggested that the system arose on an intermediate level of culture, persisting both among the Peruvians and Bolivians as they advanced in material equipment and among the simpler tribes, whom he conceives to have fallen from a formerly somewhat higher estate. This is certainly possible, but the hypothesis requires amplification in order to do justice to the facts. For, oddly enough, it is the simpler peoples who have a highly elaborated dual organization with exogamy and other features not paralleled in the Andes so far as we know. Hence what persisted on this assumption was the bare notion of dichotomy plus spatial segregation of the two halves. This colorless scheme must then have been enriched by the decadent tribes to the extent observed, specifically, by attaching exogamy to a hitherto agamous arrangement.[5]

MOIETIES AND CLANS.—Moieties, exogamous or otherwise, commonly comprise lesser clans. What is the historical relation between the two? There are obvious abstract possibilities: a moiety may have several offshoots that retain a sense of kinship; multiple clans may group themselves into two large phratries; of several clans, some may die out, leaving only two; moieties and lesser clans may arise separately, but subsequently be joined in one consistent scheme. For all we know, every one of these events may have been realized in the course of history.

Morgan favored the first hypothesis. A basic clan, he explained, would grow larger and be segmented into several lesser clans; given two original clans both of which split up, yet retain solidarity, the end result is a typical dual organization. That clans have subdivided is a fact, historical instances being known from the Hopi and the Southern Bantu, though in these particular cases moieties failed to develop. Segmentation is suggested by the very names of certain units, as when three independent Ojibwa clans are called, respectively, Mud Turtle, Snapping Turtle, Little Turtle. However, unless the primary clans number two, the resulting phratries cannot become moieties.

Sometimes the names of tribal halves suggest the contrary process. Such names as Four-clans and Three-clans among the Hidatsa indicate an alliance rather than segmentation. Hopi clans have repeatedly combined in phratries without achieving a dual organization, but illustrating the process which in some circumstances might yield that result. The same holds for South African tribes. That fusion of a different order, i.e., not involving lesser clans, may also result in a moiety system will be shown presently.

The third possibility is of great importance. In Europe, titles of nobility have constantly lapsed because they could be passed on only to sons. As Boas has pointed out, the unilateral groups of aboriginal societies present a parallel. Given a small number of persons in a clan, the time comes when one generation will comprise only males or only females, which means that in the former case the matrilineal, in the latter the patrilineal, group becomes extinct. If we start with only a few clans, they might thus easily be reduced to two. This actually happened in the Hopi village of Shipaulovi; in 1916 I found only two clans there, the Bears and the Suns, but informants recalled two others that had died out; in one case the male survivors had joined the Bears. Thus, a typical dual organization would have come about except for the fact that the Suns so greatly outnumbered the Bears that many had to seek mates outside the village.

Perhaps the virtual lack of a dual organization throughout Africa is in part due to the absence of the conditions just discussed. Negro tribes often have enormous populations compared to those of other natives, and their clans are likely to be numerous. Uganda had thirty-six clans in Roscoe's day and the number of inhabitants, even in a period of decline, was set at a million. Though some clans were absorbed by others, the chances of thirty-six being reduced to two were thus exceedingly slight. To take a less extreme case, the Lobi proper, with only four matrilineal kins, numbered 69,484 in French territory (1931); on British soil a census of the tribe ten years earlier gave the figure of 32,140, said to embrace ten matrilineal kins. Such figures contrast sharply with the barely 100 inhabitants of Shipaulovi in 1916.

The fourth possibility seems to have been also realized in the southwestern United States. As E. C. Parsons has shown, the western Pueblos are organized into matrilineal clans, whereas the easternmost tribes of the region lack them, but have well-developed agamous ceremonial moieties. Where the two schemes came into contact, some adaptation of one to the other would be expectable and actually took place at Santa Ana (p. 243).

Since in principle clan and lineage are the same, the data from southern California may be cited as relevant. The patrilineage is the fundamental unit in this area. To this some tribes added the moiety concept, probably modeled on the Pueblo pattern, without necessarily allowing it to alter the essence of their social life. Of the more than forty tribelets constituting the Yokuts stock, only a dozen or so had the dual organization with a tendency, but only a tendency, toward exogamy. The principal functions of the moieties were ceremonial and sportive. So many patrilineages were simply grouped together as one half, counterbalancing so many others.[6]

UNITY OR DIVERSITY OF ORIGIN.—The foregoing considerations support a multiple origin for the dual organizations of the world. Undoubtedly particular features of such systems have been borrowed and widely diffused, but this may happen without a diffusion of the structural basis of the system. The Pawnee (Nebraska) split up into a winter or northern moiety and a summer or southern one; and the dual arrangement pervades all their ceremonial. The association with antithetical seasons can hardly have sprung up independently of that found on the Rio Grande; but the most vital principle of all, filiation, did arise independently, for it is at least partly matrilineal among the Pawnee, patrilineal among the Pueblos. All other traits sit more or less loosely on a moiety scheme; hence it is not surprising that a tribe, observing some sort of dichotomy in a neighbor, should adopt it along with such elements as contrasting ideas or paint. But until the *structure* of the dual divisions is traced to an outside source we have not explained the presence of the system.

Now, the distribution of moiety systems does permit the inference that systems themselves have spread, though not so frequently as, say, the mere idea of teaming some permanent unit of a tribe against another or setting off rival groups of whatsoever constitution by contrasting names and badges. On the other hand, there is positive evidence that moieties are constantly evolving, disappearing, and reappearing. To the example of Shipaulovi we can add a Brazilian and an Assamese instance.

In 1938 two dialectic subgroups of the Nambikuara (Matto Grosso), which had been diminished by feuds and disease, joined forces, but retained their identity and their respective headmen. The Nambikuara regard cross-cousins as ideal mates. In uniting, the adult men of the two units decided to consider one another "brothers-in-law," which automatically made any adult woman of group A the "sister" of the men in group B, and vice versa. In the following generation, then, the offspring of A would intermarry with the offspring of B in precisely the fashion characteristic of moieties. Cross-cousin marriage and the union of our tribelets without loss of identity created a veritable dual organization, even though not labeled as such. Obviously a moiety scheme caught in its hour of birth cannot yet manifest all the characteristics of the full-blown systems of long standing.

Assam, an area full of established moiety systems, illustrates all the same how fluid such systems are. To revert to the Angami Naga (p. 242), their traditional moieties, Pezoma and Pepfüma, which are subdivided into clans, were once exogamous, but in recent times a village is sometimes made up wholly of either half-tribe and there is no objection to the marriage of fellow members. The inhabitants of Kohima, for instance, are all Pepfüma, but they freely intermarry unless of the same clan. According to the natives, there were only two clans here at one time, the Cherama and the Pferonoma. *In other words, this village had exogamous moieties.* But whereas Cherama remained undivided, Pferonoma split up into six segments, making altogether seven clans at the time of Professor Hutton's researches. In other words, recently a Kohima might marry into any one of the six clans outside his own.

A pertinent observation was made by Rivers among the Toda. One clan had grown to such proportions there that in order to marry at all its members had to take spouses from all the other clans, leaving very few people of the other clans to intermarry among themselves. Thus, there was a close approach to a typical dual organization, the hypertrophied clan assuming the part of one moiety and all the small clans jointly forming its complement.,

A moiety system, then, is not an abstruse intellectual creation, but a form of organization that naturally and, in some cases, inevitably arises from demographic conditions. In a multiple clan system the dying out of all but two clans establishes moieties; so does the extravagant growth of one clan at the expense of others. In the absence of clans, the union of two local units in Nambikuara fashion achieves the same end. Thus, even if we consider only exogamous moieties, a diverse origin seems clear. Dual organizations illustrate convergence.

## From Lineage to Kin

The evolution of a kin out of a lineage presents no serious difficulty. It implies nothing but the very common primitive tendency to extend the notion of kinship to others than blood relatives. It is true that this tendency is far less pronounced with some peoples than with others; and in such cases the development may be inhibited. The Yokuts (p. 246) are so chary of admitting putative relationship that common totems do not suggest an ultimate bond of blood, and the offshoot of an established lineage quickly loses all solidarity with the parental group. This fact also explains the modest role played by the dual organization even among those tribelets of the stock that have adopted it. A detail of importance in this connection is the anonymity of the lineage: without the convenient label of a name, relationships beyond the third degree are lost sight of.

Contrast with this the Western Apache parallel. Any fellow clansman is *ipso facto* a sibling, mother, maternal uncle, sister's son. The bond is weaker than with true blood relatives of the corresponding category, but it is real. "It is this which makes the clan function as it does." Here the name is an effective symbol of unity. There can be others: in the French Sudan the same taboos create solidarity, regardless of linguistic and religious differences. A pagan Mossi six hundred miles from home is aided and protected by a Moslem Wolof who learns that the stranger is under identical dietary restrictions.

It is not difficult to understand how a man feels toward a remotely or fictitiously related clansman. Except for special reasons the sentiments must resemble those in an extended or in a very large elementary family. The joint family of Polish peasants subordinates personal feeling to a diffuse sense of loyalty toward all. As soon as strictly personal emotions come to the fore, the fact indicates the decay of the larger solidarity. This latter, precisely because it implies little emotional attachment, demands overt expression: a Hopi woman learning of a clansman's death ostentatiously begins howling aloud to manifest a grief she does not experience, cannot possibly experience in a manner proportionate to her demonstration.

The extension of kinship terms, the inevitable dwindling away of numerically weak unilateral groups which join stronger units, conquest and deliberate absorption of alien groups lead from lineage to clans; similarly they may enlarge clans themselves, sometimes into phratries and even tribes. Some historical instances have already been cited, and others are available. Kazak kins repeatedly all but died out from warfare or natural causes, the survivors amalgamating with stronger kins. Hottentot tribes more than once entered a new district, crushed the occupants, and absorbed the remnants in the conquerors' clans. Similar events occurred frequently in Bantu history.

To repeat, the development of clans out of lineages is easily understood. The real problem lies in explaining the origin of the lineage, that is, of unilateral descent.[7]

## *The Evolution of Unilateral Descent*

THE NATURE OF THE PROBLEM.—Morgan regarded the conception of unilateral descent as "essentially abstruse," a view more recently entertained by Olson. What worries these writers is why primitive man should have gathered only part of his blood relatives into a unit, excluding the other half though it is biologically quite as close. For this reason Morgan assumed a single center for the origin of the idea; its artificiality, he argued, made "repeated reproduction in disconnected areas" very unlikely. If the unilateral alignment of kindred had been a deliberate and arbitrary affair, it would indeed be improbable that peoples in, say, India and North America should independently hit on the identical way of assigning certain relatives to a group and excluding others from it. But this intellectualistic approach is psychologically unjustifiable. The point is to lay bare conditions that would *spontaneously* yield the observed alignment of relatives.

Forty years ago Swanton clearly formulated the problem for America north of the Rio Grande. In this continent the simplest peoples have only the bilateral family and some local unit; the tribes somewhat more advanced in an economic way are patrilineal; those still more complex, by and large, tend toward matriliny. Swanton did not postulate a necessary sequence; he demanded, however, that we "show tendencies which might point towards an evolution into a social status like that of the Pueblo or Iroquois."

Following in his wake, but not restricting our survey to North America, we shall try to show tendencies toward (a) patriliny, (b) matriliny; and we shall further try to explain (c) the failure for the development of either. Before so doing, it is necessary to discuss the moot question of diffusion.

WHAT IS DIFFUSED IN DIFFUSION?—Several scholars have been greatly impressed by the fact that matrilineal and patrilineal systems adjoin each other. They infer that the unilateral principle which underlies both is the historically basic reality, which merely happens to develop in this or that direction. They support the position by citing many resemblances which usually characterize adjoining unilateral schemes of either order.

The view rests on an intellectualistic misconception. "Unilateral descent" is an abstraction, useful for the sociologist, but nonexistent for the native. *He* knows only that for certain purposes his matrilineal relatives function differently from his patrilineal relatives. For him the two kinds of system are not varying embodiments of one idea, but utterly diverse, antithetical realities. Assuredly either kind of organization may influence the other, but as in the case of moieties we must ask wherein that influence can at bottom lie. Let us examine a feature of clan systems that has undoubtedly been transmitted from tribe to tribe regardless of principles of filiation.

East of the high Plains of the United States an overwhelming number of clans are totemic. This holds equally for the Iroquoian, Muskoghean, Algonquian, and Siouan families. The very same animal species—Bear, Deer, Turtle, Wolf—serve as labels in all of them; and they figure no less among the matrilineal Seneca than among the patrilineal Omaha. The distribution of totems is largely continuous, so that the paths by which they traveled from tribe to tribe are clear. Their cropping up again and again is not due to some vague general psychological tendency, for in the high Plains a radically different scheme of clan nomenclature confronts us. It, too, has spread widely, at least from Alberta to Oklahoma. This area, like the East, harbors Algonquians and Siouans, but they name tribal subdivisions very differently from the custom of the eastern members of the same families.

The Crow actually resemble their fellow Siouans of Nebraska less in this respect than they do the Gros Ventre of Algonquian stock. Characteristic Crow names are Sore-lip lodge, Greasy-inside-the-mouth, Tied-in-a-knot, Kicked-in-their-bellies; and Gros Ventre parallels include Ugly-ones, Those-who-water-their-horses-once-a-day and Those-who-do-not-give-away. The Algonquian Blackfoot have subdivisions interpreted as clans by some writers; by others as loose bands. However that be, the problematical units are dubbed Solid-Topknots, Fat-roasters, Short-necks, Small-robes, Liars, and the like. Farther south, the Arapaho of Wyoming and Oklahoma have subdivisions that are unequivocally only bands; they are called Sagebrush men, Red-willow men, Blood-soup men, Ugly people, Ridiculous men.

In other words, the one area uses animal species as labels of tribal subdivisions; the other prefers sobriquets. Broadly speaking, adjoining tribes have similar or even identical nomenclature; the degree of resemblance varies with geographical nearness, which proves more significant than linguistic affinity. Undoubtedly, then, the systems of nomenclature have spread within their respective ranges by migration of peoples and borrowing.

But this undisputed fact has little bearing on the historical relations of the structural units themselves. The matrilineal clans of the Crow are not genetically related to either the Arapaho bands or the patrilineal Gros Ventre clans even though all three bear similar names. In the same way, the diffusion of the name Turtle from matrilineal Iroquois to, say, patrilineal Algonquians (or vice versa) does not prove a genetic tie between the units themselves. For how is such a relationship to be conceived? Assuming that Algonquians in a pre-clan condition become familar with Iroquois matriliny, what is it they discover? Subdivisions bearing animal names. Noting and fancying the latter, they might readily enough introduce a corresponding nomenclature for their bands or whatever other units they had. But by no mechanism conceivable would an alien who observed a matrilineal alignment of kin be prompted to concoct a patrilineal one for his own people. Countersuggestion cannot operate here, for the supposed transmuter lacks the abstraction *we* call "unilateral rule of descent." He may approve and hence borrow a matrilineal arrangement observed by him; he cannot conceivably say to himself, "This is merely one sample of unilateral descent; I will try out its opposite."

In other words, matriliny and patriliny are to be treated as distinct realities. Whether one of them can evolve into the other, as was once generally assumed, will have to be discussed again later on. At present it is enough to state that their basis must lie in totally different cultural conditions.[8]

THE ORIGIN OF PATRILINY.—Under this head fall two separate questions: How can patrilineal kindred be segregated as a distinct group? And how would this lead to the combination of two or more patrilineal units into the usual form of patrilineal clan system?

As Tylor recognized long ago, coresidence is a potent factor; and Steward has plausibly suggested that where men dominate economically, patrilocalism would be the rule. But patrilocalism is not enough: it might produce merely a joint family with loss of females on marriage;

whereas the essence of a patrilineal lineage or clan is that members of both sexes permanently remain in it. To be sure, in a few instances we learn of otherwise typical clan systems in which a wife assumes her husband's clan name, as is reported of the Reddi (Hyderabad). However, this tribe, despite its primitiveness, has been in some ways affected by the higher Hindu civilization; what is more significant, being a matter of direct observation, is that even here membership in the natal clan is preserved, though latent, for it governs the selection of a second husband.

Spier has reconstructed the possible evolution of a patrilineage. The Havasupai occupy one permanent village from April to October. A typical subgroup is a joint family made up of a man with his wife and children, and his adult sons with theirs, each elementary family in a separate but neighboring house. Temporarily there may also be a married daughter with her husband, since a son-in-law stays near his wife's father for a year or so before returning to his own father's camp. Farmlands belong to the subgroup, *daughters as well as sons retaining their rights to a share* without, however, having the males' privilege of transmitting it to their offspring. As Spier contends, this is the essence of patriliny. If those with common property rights came to feel as a distinct unit, they would form a patrilineage, whose existence might later be accentuated by a name or other emblem. Close blood relatives on either side would be barred from intermarriage from the start; as the patrilineal descent group crystallized, those bearing its label would fall under the exogamous rule even if only remotely related, whereas the kinship with corresponding persons on the mother's side would be forgotten. In short, patrilocal residence plus patrilineal inheritance would result in complete patriliny.

In this conjectural scheme the position of the daughters is all important. They, too, inherit farming rights, and they retain contact with their natal group. Were it otherwise, there would merely be a parallel to the Yugoslav or ancient Roman joint family. In ancient Rome a daughter was on principle excluded from the inheritance, as she also ceased to take part in the paternal cult. That is precisely what the Havasupai arrangement prevents, so that the extended family can blossom into a lineage.

This likewise holds in Australia with its patrilocal hordes. Here also the females' tie is not ruptured. A married daughter travels fifty miles to visit her mother, her local patriotism is as strong as her brothers', and on dying she is buried in the territory of her birth.

The Ona case is less certain. The tribal area is split into thirty-nine named and sharply circumscribed hunting territories, exploited by patrilineally linked males. Exogamous sentiment is so strong that, for fear of possibly overlooking a remote relationship, men travel great distances in search of a wife. Are, then, these hordes clear-cut lineages? Perhaps, but we remain in doubt because it is not certain how definitely females remain associated with their native districts. They are evidently not compelled to lose the old affiliation in Roman fashion, for widows are known to have settled again in their old homes after their bereavement. Perhaps the data are best interpreted as a patrilineal system in the very process of taking shape. In another part of South America, the northwest Amazons country, the end goal has been reached. The consistently patrilocal Witoto of that region live in communal houses, sometimes assembling well over a hundred patrilinear kinsfolk. Since all those born into a settlement of this type share a patrilineally inherited name, they remain united by this common token.

When two or more lineages have crystallized in this fashion within the same district, their fusion into a village or tribe of intermarrying lineages is easily understood. As Gifford has shown, that has actually occurred in central and southern California. The Miwok once comprised eighty exogamous landowning patrilineages. Hard pressed by white settlers, they were driven out of their ancestral homes and came to amalgamate in villages, where they retained their individuality, thus assuming the part of several unilateral kins of a typical clan system. Other Californians achieved the same result even before Caucasian contact.[9]

THE ORIGIN OF MATRILINY.—As consistent patrilocal residence and patrilineal property interests foster the alignment of patrilineal relatives, so consistent matrilocal residence and matrilineal property interests tend to produce a matrilineal descent group. Obviously it would be necessary for the husband to remain with his wife's group for good, not merely in the initial stages of wedlock; otherwise the children would not become definitely attached to the maternal side of the family. Although information on relevant South American conditions is inadequate for a decisive conclusion, it is interesting that in the one Guiana tribe with matrilineal clans, the Arawak proper, the groom, after a visit to his mother's, "soon returns to his father-in-law's place where he takes up his permanent abode." These people are not unique in this respect, but there are not a few South American tribes which practice only temporary matrilocalism and have remained clanless.

As it was necessary to explain how females could become attached to the male core of a patrilineage, so it is essential to suggest a way of aligning males with the female core of a matrilineage. Where matrilocal residence implies merely that the husband lives with his in-laws, but remains in his home village, he can easily keep up contacts with his own kinsfolk. A Hopi or Canella man thus pays constant visits to his mother's household. The failure of so many South American tribes to achieve matriliny despite matrilocal residence may be correlated with the frequent necessity of a groom's shifting his headquarters to another village. The strictly matrilineal Bororo and Canella, on the other hand, marry without change of settlement.

However, some matrilineal peoples are patrilocal, though not so many as once appeared to be the case. The Iroquois, for example, were described as patrilocal on nineteenth-century evidence, but Fenton has unearthed a source going back to 1644 which proves the Mohawk matrilocal at the time of white contact. Again, the matrilineal systems of northern British Columbia have been reckoned as patrilocal, whereas at least one of them is now reported in association with matrilocalism. Similarly, Rivers's categorical statement that all Melanesian couples live with the husband's people is refuted by Powdermaker's observations in New Ireland.

Nevertheless, the residual cases of matriliny among patrilocal peoples make it desirable to have recourse to a possible determinant besides residence. Here an Australian fact reported by Roth merits attention. In certain districts of Queensland, women individually own clumps of useful plants, their claims being inherited by their daughters. The phenomenon is exactly paralleled in one Paviotso region of eastern California, where pine-nut plots "were owned by women and inherited matrilineally." Since women so frequently are responsible for procuring wild vegetable food, it is not surprising that wherever a particular species had scarcity value the patch containing it should be claimed by the sex that alone would exploit it. Precisely as feminine dress is inherited by girls, not boys, so the tracts in question would automatically pass on to daughters, sisters, sisters' and daughters' daughters.

It would still be requisite to bring males into the scheme in order to achieve a matrilineage. If we assume that the woman and her offspring are linked with the plot she owns by a name defining the locality, this difficulty would be overcome. A somewhat analogously oblique connection of *females* with a group is known from the Colorado River region. In every Mohave clan all the women bear an identical name of totemic significance, the clans themselves being patrilineal and nameless. Among the related Maricopa, however, the clans bore names which often passed on to women, "but only after marriage"—perhaps, we may conjecture, as a safeguard against their losing solidarity with the natal clan. My suggestion concerning a possible origin of matriliny is that the women in an extended family acquire rights to a particular plot of seeds, trees, and so on; that this locality has a name borne by, or connected with, the owners; and that the connection comes to be shared by sons as well as daughters.

The factors proposed as effectively bringing about matriliny are, then, coresidence and coproprietorship by the core of a matrilineage, with some mechanism for labeling male as well as female offspring of the women belonging to the nascent lineage.[10]

IMPEDIMENTS.—If unilateral descent evolves so easily, why is it not universal? Because the conditions set forth above are lacking or only imperfectly developed. Offhand the patrilocal Yurok seem an ideal breeding ground for patriliny; yet clans never arose, and blood relationship alone counted. Looking at the facts more closely, we find that these people were not strictly patrilocal: a man unable to pay the full price for his bride had to live in her father's settlement and work under his direction, thereby losing status for himself and his children. Very nearly one quarter of all marriages—85 out of 356 known cases—turn out to have been contrary to the norm. Failing consistency with respect to patrilocalism, the Yurok were naturally unable to develop a strictly patrilineal scheme, while the aberrant cases were far too infrequent to set them on the road toward matriliny.

The Semang present somewhat different phenomena. These food gatherers live in minute settlements, which resemble the Yurok villages in being inhabited largely by blood kindred, but differ in being impermanent. The patrilineages have a definite territory to roam in, and within it adult males owned clumps of trees. How far the women continue belonging to their natal horde is not clear. Apart from an initial two years' period of service for his father-in-law, a husband takes his wife to his paternal horde. The population of a camp is often composite: one settlement of only fifty-four inmates living in seventeen windscreens turned out to include members of four distinct kindred groups, each spatially segregated within the camp. In another settlement fifteen windbreaks belonged to natives of the dialectic group called Jehai, while apart from them lay the dwellings of an old man and his sons, who spoke the Sabubn language. These had married Jehai wives and settled with their in-laws, but periodically went off on their own.

Since there is uncertainty about the permanent affiliation of the females, we cannot be sure whether the dominant group in a camp is a lineage or only a joint family. If the former, the first settlement mentioned would parallel the amalgamation of Miwok lineages into a village community. But the Semang alliances seem to lack permanence. A small body of visitors turns up, is allowed to linger without being really welcomed, then flits away again.

Finally, economic conditions may militate against the assemblage of unilateral kindred beyond the elementary family. The Chukchi, the Eskimo, the Yaghan live so precariously that only a handful of persons can keep together for any length of time. Unless that condition is overbalanced, as in Australia, by connecting a larger company with a tract of land, there will be no sizable social unit.[11]

INDEPENDENT CENTERS.—No one asserts that all the recorded kin systems have originated independently of one another. To take the five tribes of the Iroquois Confederacy, all had matrilineal clans; the distribution of clan names was as follows:

*Seneca*: Wolf, Bear, Turtle, Beaver, Deer, Snipe, Heron, Hawk
*Cayuga*: Wolf, Bear, Turtle, Beaver, Deer, Snipe, Eel, Hawk
*Onondaga*: Wolf, Bear, Turtle, Beaver, Deer, Snipe, Eel, Ball
*Oneida*: Wolf, Bear, Turtle
*Mohawk*: Wolf, Bear, Turtle

Add that the first three tribes certainly grouped their clans in moieties and that the last two in all probability likewise did so, and the evidence for a genetic connection becomes absolute. We are dealing with linguistically related tribes intimately associated with one another and sharing the same general mode of life. Either the basic social structure, then, existed in the tribe parental to all five and was carried away by the several offshoots to be modified by subsequent events, or one of the tribes after differentiating evolved the scheme, which later spread to the others, wholly or in part. Whether (as Morgan believed) the Mohawk and the Oneida lost the clans found among their fellows, or whether (as Fenton has it) the Seneca borrowed the Deer, Beaver, and Heron clans from the Huron, is a detail. Marriage with an alien woman from another matrilineal people provides an easy mechanism for introducing a new clan; and the geographical position of the tribes favored borrowing. In short, any variant of the original pattern illustrates descent with modification.

The question is not whether evolution from a common pattern has taken place, but how far such a hypothesis can be reasonably extended. For instance, we have previously found that systems may travel freely not only among members of the same stock, but among utterly unrelated tribes. At the same time it became clear that diffusion of special features does not necessarily imply diffusion of the essential structural pattern. However, even that may be proved by specific evidence. The Menomini and the Winnebago are both residents of Wisconsin, but the former are of the Algonquian, the latter of Siouan stock. Both have a clan system characterized by (a) patrilineal descent; (b) totemic clan names, of which over half a dozen agree; (c) moieties linked with the upper and lower worlds, respectively; (d) the ownership of name-sets by clans. Where this pattern, much of which also occurs among the Eastern tribes, ultimately took shape need not concern us now; it evidently was not invented independently by our two tribes, whose observed systems are obviously only variants of a single scheme. That only diffusion across linguistic barriers can account for the resemblances further appears when we compare the Winnebago with their fellow Siouans, the Crow, who have a clan organization without a single feature on the Winnebago and Menomini roster.

But precisely how far must unilateral organizations agree to support the theory of a single origin? On this point scholars differ. Morgan, we saw, believed that unilateral descent originated only once in the history of mankind, spreading from a single center, but the archaic form would be uniformly matrilineal. He fully realized the chasm between matriliny and patriliny and explained how at a much later period the rule of descent might change. Kroeber seems to imply a corresponding evolution in the New World when he outlines the course of social developments among American Indians. Swanton had indicated the rudeness of patrilineal compared with matrilineal tribes north of Mexico, and the still greater simplicity of those loosely organized. Building on this foundation, Kroeber assumes clanlessness as the archaic American condition. At some period Middle America, advancing in other phases of life, also evolved patriliny, he contends, and disseminated it in all directions, though without affecting such marginal peoples as the Eskimo and the Yaghan. Subsequently Middle America turned matrilineal and diffused the new principle, but less widely; and finally the central area dropped unilateral kinship altogether, achieving political integration.

This theory does not purport to explain why Middle Americans switched from patriliny to matriliny, a rather serious gap considering the traditional view that the reverse sequence is natural. Moreover, it assumes a minimum of spontaneous creativeness on the part of the simpler peoples: everything beyond the barest elements of culture is derived from a center of higher civilization. This approach has, indeed, much to recommend it if the trait in question involves a difficult technical accomplishment, such as metallurgy, or an extremely elaborate intellectual achievement, such as a calendar system. In the case of unilateral descent, neither of these assumptions holds: the conditions of residence and inheritance spontaneously screen out individuals who make up a unilateral descent group. This happens as easily in Tierra del Fuego as in Mexico, in Arnhem Land as in China. A multiple origin is therefore indicated both for patriliny and matriliny in the New World and a fortiori in the history of all mankind.

How frequently unilateral descent happened is of course hard to say, but diffusion must rest on the sort of evidence that demonstrates the unity of the Winnebago and the Menomini systems. To make the argument concrete, the matrilineal Crow and the Iroquois organizations are to be considered independent of each other until proof to the contrary appears. Of course, it is *metaphysically* conceivable that in some dim past a matrilineal scheme arose somewhere; and that its surviving offshoots diverged to such an extent as no longer to share anything but the bare rule of descent. All sorts of conjectures can be put forth to suggest the paths of transformation. But such fictions do not yield scientific proof. [12]

## General Considerations

RELATIVE CHRONOLOGY OF KINS.—Though half a century ago scholars generally accepted the proposition that all patrilineal peoples had gone through an earlier, matrilineal stage, they did not put matriliny at the very beginning of human society. Morgan explicitly conceived matriliny as a reformatory development that swept away ruder arrangements. And Tylor, in the article on statistical method, declares: "It seems probable that this maternal system arose out of an earlier and less organized and regulated condition of human life." Modern investigators certainly concur in the view that unilateral descent groups arose out of a condition in which descent was not fixed, however different their picture of those early times may be from Morgan's. For reasons already explained, they place the elementary family before the kin, not at the very end of social evolution. Nowadays it seems an historical accident that Morgan laid down the well-nigh universal distribution of the clan at a certain level of culture: he was influenced by what he had observed among the Iroquois, whom he had studied first and most thoroughly; had he begun with the Ute or Paiute or the Andaman Islanders, he would not have scented clans everywhere.

As a matter of fact, it is not easy to correlate clans—rigidly unilateral exogamous kins—with any particular stage of development. They do not occur in Western industrialized nations, but they are still powerful in at least part of so civilized a country as China. On the other hand, the so-called clans of Japanese history do not conform to our definition. The Japanese word *be* that is so translated is, indeed, applied to hereditary groups, but also to corporations of weavers, fishermen, farmers, and the like; and, what is decisive, the oldest historical writings of the country, the Kojiki and the Nihongi, indicate the absence of exogamy. Again, the patrilineal Arab "clans" are proved not to be such by the constant marriage with a father's brother's daughter.

Near the opposite end of the scale, virtually all the Australians have clans, but these do not occur among many of the hunting peoples—the Andaman Islanders, the Eskimo, the Yaghan, the Chukchi. Some stockbreeders, such as the Masai, have the system; others, like the Lapps, are without it; in still other cases, such as the Kazak, the question of the exogamous unit remains unclear. It is a striking phenomenon that tribes in adjoining areas and sharing the same general type of culture often differ radically in this respect. The Kwakiutl of Vancouver Island are roughly on a plane with the Tsimshian, but are without clans; the Arapaho and the Crow are both typical buffalo hunters, but present the same contrast; the Canella moieties are exogamous, those of the Apinayé agamous.

Undoubtedly an intensive study of such cases may reveal the reason for the difference, but a generalizing statement in broad terms seems impossible. At one time the correlation of clans with agriculture seemed promising, but it can no longer be maintained even for the New World, where it was once applied. In tropical South America, innumerable farming populations of various degrees of complexity are without clans; in northern British Columbia several fishing tribes have them; the eastern Pueblos are not exogamous nor were the Pawnee.

We are on safer ground if we drop exogamy in an attempted correlation. Kins of some sort are not the only means of consolidating groups exceeding the joint family, but they are one very effective means toward that end. Accordingly, we may reasonably expect them above a certain level in the absence of economic deterrents and of equivalent devices for integration. Thus, the clanless Arabs and Japanese certainly did have kins, and the same holds for the Polynesians. As the ideal of nationalism, whether in a dynastic or a popular form, grows in strength, the narrower loyalty must yield to the wider, either becoming subordinated or being wiped out. In southern Albania the people lost their clans in the first half of the nineteenth century as a result of the Turkish overlordship, but the system has lingered on in the isolated northern part of the country.

The utility of the kin thus falls mainly into the field of politics and will be reconsidered in connection with the rise of statehood. The clan, of course, shares this function. Its marriage-regulating attribute it shares with the elementary family: mere clan exogamy would not prevent a father from marrying his daughter among the Crow, or a mother from sex relations with her son among the Murngin.

To sum up, unilateral descent groups do not appear at the very beginning of social evolution; and they tend to be overshadowed or even eliminated when political organization is highly developed. [13]

CHRONOLOGY OF MATRILINY AND PATRILINY.—The earlier theorists considered it self-evident that matriliny must precede patriliny, because fatherhood would be uncertain in the dim past. Whether this premise is valid or not, the inference no longer holds. We now know that physiological fatherhood is a matter of supreme indifference to various primitive groups. Other supposed lines of evidence have also proved deceptive.

The occurrence of double descent in a fair minority of cases puts a new complexion on the problem. It would in each instance require a detailed analysis of the entire cultural setting before we could hazard even a probable guess which of the coexisting systems was prior. Emeneau, the discoverer of the matrilineal Toda clans, has done just that. He finds that in South India patriliny predominates until we reach the Malabar coast with some fully evolved matrilineal clan organizations, but more generally there is a tendency, fluctuating in intensity, to bar unions with matrilineal relatives. Contrary to Rivers's assumption, there is no linguistic affinity between the Toda and the people of Malabar, and only generic or superficial resemblances exist between the two cultures. The Toda have apparently seized upon the moderate repugnance to marrying matrilineal kindred that is common in the whole area and have intensified it, the process culminating in a second exogamous scheme. Here, then, matrilineal clans followed patrilineal ones. It is a local development that need not have been duplicated anywhere else, though it explains how double descent *may* arise.

Apart from the complication introduced by the fact of bilinear peoples, the chronological relations of matriliny and patriliny remain a problem. We must distinguish among (a) the imposition of one of these systems by a dominant power; (b) change by borrowing; and (c) the internal evolution of one into the other. Our government tends to introduce our patrilineal rules of inheritance in place of aboriginal matriliny, rules which might undermine the ancient system, though it is remarkable how long the Iroquois, Navaho, and Hopi have preserved ancient custom. Perhaps Islam might somewhat more effectively alter an earlier matrilineal scheme.

Diffusion has admittedly played a large part in the distribution of unilateral organizations. But we may reasonably doubt whether a people actually organized according to one rule of descent would borrow the opposite rule. Given the differential way of regarding relatives from the two sides, such borrowing would involve a total reorientation. A Crow, borrowing Gros Ventre patriliny, would have to drop his aversion from marrying a tenth or putative cousin through the mother and transfer his repugnance to the patrilineal counterparts; his defenders at all odds and his censors would change places unless, as is quite likely, there would be an utter loss of bearings in all social relations. It is rash to declare that anything is impossible, but the process seems highly improbable.

It is true that Boas reported an often-quoted shift from patriliny to matriliny on the northwest coast. What appears from his later description of the facts, however, is something rather different. The Kwakiutl were primarily without unilateral descent, though favoring the father's side, as many loosely organized tribes do. On coming into contact with matrilineal groups to the north, the northern Kwakiutl adopted this mode of reckoning. Matriliny, then, superseded not patriliny, but a loose bilateral system which, to be sure, might under favorable conditions have evolved true patriliny or, like the Yurok one, might not.

The objection that holds against borrowing of an antithetical rule of descent likewise holds against an internal evolution of either system into the other. Morgan suggested that as property accumulated men would not want to have it inherited by their nephews, but by their sons, and saw in this a motive "sufficiently general and commanding" to bring about the change to patriliny. The motive certainly is a real one: in West Africa and Melanesia, in British Columbia and northern South America (p. 52 f.), men demonstrably have tried to get around an existing matrilineal code for the material benefit of their sons. To be sure, new forms of wealth have not been able to sweep away the inveterate matriliny of the Hopi, Navaho, or Iroquois, nor do we know how far the reported paternal efforts quoted just now would actually go toward altering the established system. On the other hand, no comparable motive has yet appeared that would favor an internal shift from patriliny to matriliny. We can, then, fairly state that, *if* a change in the rule of descent occurs, it is more likely to be in the patrilineal direction; but that a change is inherently improbable.

It is otherwise when no crystallized system of unilateral descent is involved, but only certain conditions that are favorable to the evolution of one. The statistics for the Yurok show a prevalence of patrilocalism, but a fair proportion of matrilocal marriages. If general impoverishment should make it necessary for most men to serve for their wives instead of paying the bride price, matrilocalism would, of course, become the norm and *might* set in motion a development toward matriliny.

The conclusion, then, is that a full-fledged matrilineal or patrilineal system does not evolve into its opposite. Contrary to early theories and to some diffusionist doctrines, the two have a distinct history. [14]

THE MATRIARCHATE.—Bachofen, who first treated matriliny in theoretical fashion, conceived it as part of a larger social system—a matriarchate (Latin *mater,* mother; Greek *archos,* ruler) or gynaecocracy (Greek, *gunē,* woman; *gunaikos,* of a woman; *kratein,* to rule). This implied rule of the family by the mother, not the father; control of government by women not men; and the supremacy of a female deity, the moon, not of the male sun. We are here concerned merely with the question whether matrilineal descent is actually correlated with the domestic and political superiority of women.

In the first place, no strictly matriarchal peoples are known ever to have existed. Sporadically, natives tell tales about the former ascendancy of women. The Fuegian form of the story explains petticoat rule as due to the men's ignorance of the masquerade costumes by means of which the women impersonated spirits and cowed their husbands. When men by chance learnt the truth of the matter, a revolution followed that put men at the helm. This is the sort of myth often told by aborigines to account for present usage as the exact opposite of what was customary in the remote past. The historical value of such traditions is nil.

Recent accounts of matriarchal conditions boil down to the fact that some societies recognize certain prerogatives of women that are unusual or contrary to Western law. In this category belongs the Hopi notion that houses must belong to women regardless of how much labor men may have put into their erection or repair. However, we never hear of women as chiefs, and the all-important ceremonials are directed by men. The Khasi women similarly hold all real estate, as well as the family jewels, and at least locally the highest priestly office is held by a woman. Nevertheless, the husband may kill an adulteress, and within the house it is the wife's eldest brother who ranks as the head, not the house-owning wife herself. Again, Iroquois women impeach and nominate chiefs, but no woman is ever chosen for the office.

These are perhaps the most extreme cases recorded; their analysis explodes the notion of any true matriarchate. The sporadic occurrence of feminine rulers, is, of course, wholly beside the point: Queen Elizabeth, Queen Victoria, the Empress Catherine, and Maria Theresa reigned successfully, but without in the slightest degree affecting the status of their female subjects.

But for true perspective it is essential to compare the position of women in the distinctly patrilineal societies. As males are not the downtrodden drudges of termagant wives in matrilineal tribes, so females are by no means the mere toys and slaves of their husbands among patrilineal peoples. Here, too, apparently extreme instances actually refute popular prejudices and lay bare the contrast between theory and reality. Niebuhr, the eighteenth-century traveler previously quoted on Arab polygyny, could discern no great difference in the treatment of women by Moslems and by Europeans: "The women of that country seem to be as free and happy as those of Europe can possibly be." The theoretical right to take four wives was exercised only by "rich voluptuaries" and "their conduct is blamed by all sober men." Legally entitled to divorce a wife at will, "the Arabians never exercise the right of repudiating a wife, unless urged by the strongest reasons." Women enjoyed great liberty "and often a great deal of power in their families." The wife retained control of her dowry, and a poor man might be wholly dependent on his spouse. Niebuhr dismisses as absurd the travelers' tale that all Mohammedan women are slaves. A century and a half later the Seligmans had much the same experience in the Sudan: the Kababish Arab women were anything but obsequious, felt in no way aggrieved, and rather pitied Mrs. Seligman for wearing no jewelry and being obliged to travel without a litter. They had complete disposal of their money and possessions and were often treated with marked respect.

Parallel observations apply to China. Ideologically, woman may be rated an inferior creature, but folk literature teems with tales of henpecked husbands, the Chinese mother is supreme in her household, and at various periods of history some women seem to have exerted a tremendous influence even on public life. It appears, then, that the question of correlation is not at all a simple one. Certainly it is false to accept either rule of descent as a token of unqualified dominance by the ostensibly favored sex.

The question is peculiarly difficult for several reasons. For one thing, there is the observer's personal equation. A naïve American traveler may be outraged by all sorts of things noted abroad. He winces at the arrangement of matches by French parents and is revolted by the sight of a female hod carrier in Austria. It never occurs to him that foreigners have many things to offer by way of countercriticism, and that the average European woman, like her Chinese sister, may be quite contented with her lot. Second, if the recorder has purged himself of his society's preconceptions, what objective criterion is there for deciding that woman's position in a particular community is better or worse than elsewhere? Third, granting that the criterion is known, how easy is it for a stranger to get a fair sampling of the life led by either sex? How much do we know of the intimate relations of our best friends?

To return to the question of patriliny versus matriliny as affecting the position of the sexes, the most promising line of inquiry would be to compare related peoples that differ in the rule of filiation. Further, where possible, we should eliminate the personal equation by considering the same observer's comments on different tribes.

Thus, Nimuendajú, intimately acquainted with a number of South American tribes, was greatly struck with the dominant part played by women among the Palikur, a patrilineal people of Brazilian Guiana. At adolescence the girls begin to put on airs, look down at young men, and henceforth pilfer catches of fish from incoming boats as a matter of privilege. Husbands are conspicuously uxorious, hunting and fishing according to their wives' demands, and a man will miss a chance for lucrative employment if his woman wants him to gather shrimps for her. Even in public affairs women are obviously not without authority, for about 1735 a missionary reports that a sorcerer who had aroused the women's suspicion was killed by them, not by their husbands. Nothing in the division of labor accounts for pronounced feminism: both sexes plant, weed, and harvest; and since fish are as a rule shot with bow and arrow, the task of getting them is a masculine one. Residence is not fixed, but the husband's status is naturally even worse when he lives at his mother-in-law's.

More enlightening than the Palikur case are the phenomena Nimuendajú recorded among the Canella and the Sherente. The Canella, as previously noted, are consistently matrilocal, with women owning dwellings and plantations. This puts the husband at a disadvantage; but since with wedlock he merely shifts dwellings, not settlements, he can in case of conflict return to his mother's and sisters' home, where he plays a significant role. All in all, "neither sex considers the other inferior; the sexes have distinct functions, not higher and lower ones." Only men are councilors and chiefs, but "except in warfare nothing is undertaken without feminine participation." In contrast to this situation, the Sherente husband is in sole control of the home and farm, residence being of course patrilocal, and his wishes prevail. Daughters are trained to be submissive. Yet Nimuendajú saw no instance of a husband's systematically bullying his wife, and one man deceived by his wife, instead of beating her, hanged himself.

These observations among a matrilineal and a patrilineal people of the same stock, offered by the same investigator, are surely suggestive. But we must recall our earlier caution concerning causal connection. Matriliny is not *the* cause of the favorable position of Canella women, when that of their Palikur sisters is even more favorable in a patrilineal community. Matriliny is one descriptive trait that we have isolated from a complex, some other element of which—say mode of residence—may be more important. For a clearer insight into the significance of rules of descent we should require a large series of comparisons like those just indicated for South America. How do the matrilineal Northern Kwakiutl compare with the loosely organized Kwakiutl proper? Is the status of women noticeably better among the matrilineal Crow or Hidatsa than among patrilineal Siouans, such as the Omaha? among their patrilineal neighbors, the Gros Ventre? among loosely organized fellow-Plainsmen, such as the Western Cree or the Arapaho? Corresponding comparisons are necessary in Melanesia, Africa, and other regions. Pending such investigations, any conclusion is necessarily tentative. The indications are that the rule of descent is not highly and only indirectly correlated with the status of the sexes—probably only in so far as the rule is itself connected with the mode of residence. With complete assurance, however, we can assert that matriliny does not automatically involve a matriarchate nor patriliny a patriarchate. [15]

# Chapter 12

# SOCIAL STRATA

I T IS difficult to find an institution that exactly corresponds to associations holding higher or lower status within the same community, society, or state. On the other hand, the psychological motives that favor stratification are easily understood, for they occur everywhere. Consciousness of kind, we discovered (p. 15), tends to be narrowly exclusive; unless strangers happen to enjoy some obvious advantage, they appear ridiculous and inferior. Those Ifugao who grow rice by irrigation methods look with scorn on their fellows to the east who eat only sweet potatoes or mountain rice. If two such groups should become co-residents of the same territory, they would represent subcultures, marked off by peculiarities of dress, behavior, belief, speech. In other words, they would become distinct *classes*. Though the history of Yurok distinctions of this type is not known, the subdivisions of this tribe are good instances of full-fledged classes primarily distinguished in point of wealth. A rich Yurok, however, is at the same time a well-bred person. He speaks little and eats slowly, nor would he stoop to sell food. Conversely, he parries a breach of etiquette with the lofty comment that the offender "comes from poor people and cannot know how to conduct himself."

## *Origins*

In order to understand the process of stratification it is well to consider cases whose history is definitely known. In the early Middle Ages, in an era of insecurity, free French peasants sought the protection of powerful neighbors, thus turning into dependents. What started as a purely personal contract between two individuals was later fixed by the hereditary principle, with the result that the formerly free peasant became a serf.

Swedish parallels are even more instructive. In early medieval times captives in war and their descendants became slaves, but the peasants, who formed the core of the population, were an eminently respectable class. This appears from the stipulation that "a bishop must be a peasant's son," i.e., *not* of low degree. For, oddly enough, it was the lower orders of society that were fixed first in Sweden. Below the peasant proprietors were the cultivators who made a piece of common land arable, the tenants who worked others' fields for compensation, managers, servants, crofters. Ancient codes defined the status of each of these classes. In the thirteenth century slavery began to drop out. A law of Uppland in 1296 declared the child of one free parent of either sex to be free; and in 1335 the king put an end to the institution of slavery for those to be born in the future.

At that time the upper ranks were not yet clearly established. There were royal officials (*jarls*), but their prestige corresponded to the extent of their king's dominions. As their master's realm grew, the *jarls* became men of consequence, and descent from a distinguished man also came to be reckoned honorable. About the second half of the thirteenth century the nascent aristocratic class was in some measure integrated, the crucial point being equestrian military service. In return for the expense of maintaining horses, cavalrymen were exempted from taxes in 1279, thus being elevated above the farmers; and from about 1400 on, no upstart was allowed to rise in the social scale by becoming an equestrian. Thus was created the secular nobility.

When Christianity had been fully established (ca. 1150), the Church grew rich from bequests and donations; moreover, bishops, as the most educated part of the population, naturally served as royal councilors and as spokemen of the upper class. On the other hand, when permanent residences of the traders rose on market sites, towns sprang up, often organized after German models since the merchants were largely of German origin. Artisans appeared as an additional urban group, then royal bailiffs, municipal administrators and churches.

The peasants were never enslaved and at no time was there an efflorescence of feudalism in Sweden: characteristically, the same amount of compensation had to be paid for the killing of any freeman. What is more, the first Swedish parliament (1435) recognized the cultivators as a distinct "estate" along with the nobles, clergy, and burgesses, a system that continued for 430 years. Yet the growth of one higher order of society after another automatically lowered the social status of the peasantry.

It is worth comparing this development with what occurred in Hungary. Here, too, initial slavery was abolished in the later medieval period. A decree of King Louis the Great in 1351 crystallized two classes, commoners and noblemen. A commoner tilled his nobleman's fields, paid taxes, and rendered various services; a nobleman was subject only to the king who bore the sacred crown of Hungary; his duty was to bear arms and defend the country, a function that freed him from taxation. In legal theory all noblemen were at first equal, but actually great estates brought increased power, so that magnates, presently segregated from the mere gentry, formed a Crown council. About 1400, the towns, too, were legally recognized, i.e., a commercial class was established, but the burghers never exerted any deep influence on public affairs. In the eighteenth century there were four estates—the prelates, the magnates, the gentry, and the royal free towns. However, all the urban votes jointly were reckoned equal to only a single county vote, the higher aristocracy thus being dominant in the diet. The peasants remained serfs bound to the soil until in the eighteenth century Joseph II permitted them to go where they pleased and to dispose freely of their chattels. Under the old law neither a peasant nor a burgher had the privilege of bringing suit against a nobleman in person, but could do so only through a county official.

In the Hungarian system the peasant thus occupied the lowest rung; the urban dweller, too, was at a definite disadvantage. The privileged part of the population comprised three distinct classes—the higher clergy, the magnates, and the gentry, the last two having differentiated from an originally single class.

Finally may be cited the history of Russian serfdom. Here, as in medieval Western Europe, the peasant was at first a freeman. But the state, wishing to make sure of larger taxes, bound the cultivators to the soil and expected them to till all taxable lands. This police measure, decreed in the sixteenth century, prevented mobility, but without as yet depriving the farmer of all liberty. However, the cultivators fell into debt servitude to landowners; and when these paid their debtors' taxes, the state granted the creditors some measure of jurisdiction over the peasants. This power increased to such an extent that by the time of Catherine the Great a landowner might sell his peasants as he did his livestock, could torture them, and controlled their marriages. As described dispassionately in Turgenev's *A Sportsman's Sketches,* these conditions continued until the emancipation of the peasants in 1861. Masters, possibly owning 500 "souls" or more, were restrained only by their own sense of right. A landowner allowed grasping agents to exploit and extort tribute from his bondmen. He would slap the peasants' faces at will, seize their property, and order a complaining petitioner to be flogged within an inch of his life. Indeed, not to rely on fiction only, Turgenev's mother had sent two serfs to Siberia for not saluting her with sufficient respect; and in his youth Turgenev paid 700 rubles for a serf girl to whom he had taken a fancy, and had a daughter by her. There were, to be sure, diverse kinds of serfs—household domestics, peasants who according to local custom owed their master so many days of labor, and others who worked in the towns and paid their owner a fixed amount out of their wages. But many "serfs" were clearly in the strict sense of the term "slaves."

## Social Mobility

Class systems are far from uniform in point of social mobility, even the same people radically altering their notions on the subject at different periods. During the last two centuries feudal prerogatives receded, and eminent men of the middle classes acquired titles. Thus, the Duke of Saxe-Weimar added a handle to Goethe's name, and Queen Victoria not only knighted the physicist William Thomson but ultimately raised him to the peerage. Wealth has gained similar honors, as it did in imperial Rome. There even rich slaves gained such influence at court that they were flattered by candidates for office, and a wealthy freedman might take precedence of praetors and tribunes.

On the other hand, descent in the scale may result from primogeniture. Whereas imperial Germany and Austria permitted the father's title to be borne by all the children, England and Spain limit it to the eldest son. In consequence, Winston Churchill, though the son of a lord and the descendant of a duke, is a mere commoner. Evidently this rule prevents a sharp cleavage of classes, for by it the younger sons of noblemen merge into the commoners' stratum.[1]

For the sake of clarity we shall begin our survey of stratification with the most rigid of class systems.

## Castes

HINDU CASTES.—The population of India comprises an indefinite number of graded endogamous kins or "castes" (Portuguese *casta,* lineage). Rooted in Hinduism, the system has affected East Indians of other faiths, even Mohammedans and rude aborigines. A man's caste is considered immutable; only in a future rebirth may he enter a higher one. In theory, but only in theory, there are four castes—Brahmans (priests), warriors, merchants and farmers, artisans and laborers; the first three are sharply set off from the fourth by being "twice-born." That is to say, at the age of about seven the boys of the three upper castes undergo a spiritual birth corresponding to our confirmation and to aboriginal initiation rituals. Henceforth they wear a sacred thread as an external sign of their status. Actually the fourfold division probably never existed and certainly does not hold for any historical period; it is a mere rationalization concocted by the Brahmans. The single district of Poona, with a population of 900,000, was found to have over 120 castes, of which 15 were made up of Brahmans. What is more, though the spiritual leaders of Hinduism are Brahmans, who have succeeded in keeping up the general belief in their superiority, "Brahmans" neither are nor, on the testimony of their sacred books, ever were exclusively or preponderantly priests and sages. Some of them gain their livelihood as cooks, soldiers, shepherds, farmers, scribes, even as masons. The same holds true for the "warriors' caste" and the "merchants." What does apply generally is the unbounded contempt for certain occupations, and these a Brahman would, of course, not engage in. Notable among them is any kind of leather work or any task connected with corpses. For this reason Hindu medical students for a time refused to learn anatomy by dissection.

Foremost among the pertinent religious conceptions is that of pollution. Leather is contaminating; so is contact with those lowest castes popularly called the "untouchables" and "pariahs." In some areas a member of these would not dare approach within 32 yards of a high Brahman and was under obligation to cry out aloud to give notice of his presence. In Malabar an upper-caste member could formerly kill a pariah who crossed his path. In some districts an untouchable dare not enter a shop to make his purchases, but puts the money on the ground and withdraws, the shopkeeper places the desired goods on the ground, picks up the coins, and goes inside, when the buyer is at last permitted to appropriate his hard-bought property. In modern schools the upper castes have persistently fought admission of the children of untouchables on equal terms. These youngsters have sometimes been made to sit apart from their age mates; sometimes the schools admitting them have been boycotted; again the parents have been intimidated, beaten up, and otherwise abused. As late as 1931 O'Malley notes a brutal assault on a pariah woman who had ventured to send her boy to a public school. In rural districts the untouchables are obliged to dwell outside the village and to draw water from separate pools.

Such restrictions are not confined to the lowest of the low. In one section of the country an attendant of a certain grade must not enter the chapel, kitchen, or dining room of a Brahman house. He may touch the bedding and woolen garments, but not cotton ones freshly washed. Even servants of Brahman lineage must submit to rules. They are defiled by contact with mattresses, cloaks, and turbans; if they should touch a shoe or strip of leather, they must purify themselves by bathing.

On the other hand, a pupil who has taken a bath must not turn the pages of a book bound in leather, but gets a servant or younger sibling to do it for him.

The notion of impurity attaches especially to food and drink. Generally only members of the same caste may be messmates or take food of certain kinds from one another. Some victuals, such as beef, and certain beverages are intrinsically foul and forbidden to the self-respecting members of higher castes. Others, in themselves pure, are defiled if offered by an untouchable. A Hindu loses caste if beef merely touches his lips even without being consumed. A Rajput officer is known to have died from thirst rather than take water from a leather-worker; others starve themselves rather than take "impure" food. Hindus obliged to go on voyages have taken the trouble to carry caskfuls of Ganges water, which is so sacred as to nullify pollution.

Contamination requires purifying ceremonies, say, by bathing or by drinking water consecrated by a Brahman's dipping his toe into it. Even involuntary defilement puts a man outside his caste, in which he can be reinstated only after appropriate measures and usually by a feast for his fellows. For apart from anything else a caste is a corporation with juridical powers. It can expel offenders against the code, thereby reducing them to a pitiable state, for the verdict is circulated in neighboring districts and on pain of similar judgments prevents anyone from eating, drinking, or smoking with the culprit, who soon finds his condition intolerable and seeks to atone for his conduct.

As to food taboos, there are many whimsical notions apart from regional peculiarities. A man will accept victuals from a person somewhat lower in the scale if they have been fried with butter and salt, but not if boiled in water. Sugar and pastry are acceptable from all but such untouchables as sweepers and leatherworkers. In the Punjab a Hindu will take pure milk from a Moslem, but not if it is mixed with any water. The regulations bearing on food have proved very irksome in recent decades. In a college at Lahore the cooks struck rather than prepare meals for a low-caste student; in Allahabad it was necessary to provide thirty-seven kitchens for a hundred students. Soldiers in World War I underwent great inconvenience in order to keep up orthodoxy.

Of overshadowing importance in the system is the principle of endogamy. This typically combined with exogamy, which applies to the clans into which a caste is subdivided. It is also tempered with "hypergamy," the rule that a girl may marry either into her own or a higher, but never a lower, caste. This law has at times led to curious arrangements. Girls in the highest caste naturally suffered from a shortage of husbands, since their male peers were free to take wives from lower castes. Accordingly, the Kulin Brahmans of Bengal resorted to polygyny on a major scale. In one case a man disposed of eighteen kinswomen by giving them all in marriage to a Kulin boy ten years of age.

Other matrimonial rules have also been of great importance. An orthodox Hindu must get his daughter married; hence he often arranges a wedding before she is of age, the marriage being consummated after puberty. Further, there is a strong prejudice against the remarriage of a widow, who was formerly cremated on her husband's funeral pyre.

The caste system is so thoroughly entrenched in India that new castes are constantly arising. A section of one caste will devise a differentiation of custom or occupation and then claim a superior status, refusing to eat and intermarry with former fellows. Thus, shoemakers may separate from those who work with rawhide. A low caste will enhance its own self-respect, even if unsuccessful in impressing its betters, by tabooing the remarriage of widows, by lowering the age of marrying off a daugher, or by assuming without true warrant a sacred thread.

Rivers, properly insisting that "caste" and "class" should not be treated as interchangeable terms, restricted the former to the Hindu phenomenon. Though theoretically he would include "such other examples as it is possible to put into the same category," he actually excludes all others. This is an unprofitably extreme position. Obviously the Hindu system is in a sense unique, but so are all complex social systems; indeed, our authorities on the subject not only admit but contend that the Hindu scheme varies enormously from region to region. The unity found in India is merely that of a composite photograph. Rivers lists four criteria of caste—endogamy, hereditary occupation, hierarchical grading, and rules of avoidance between the grades. However, as he presently has to concede, these are not infallible touchstones. Hypergamy qualifies endogamy; occupations do not coincide with castes; the grading differs locally; and so do the rules of avoidance. What is more, all the criteria occur elsewhere, sometimes all of them jointly, as among the Masai. The Polynesians in some respects had castelike phenomena, even though special features, such as primogeniture, counteracted a rigid stratification. Their fussiness about food closely corresponds to Hindu parallels; for example, "persons of different degree of sacredness eat apart." "No one not consecrated or closely related must touch the royal person, and death was the penalty for passing anything over the head of a high chief" [in Tahiti]. In both areas there is the same dread of contaminating contacts along with the need for purifying techniques. Add the existence of a priestly aristocracy suggestive of Brahmans, and Handy's theory of a genetic connection between Hindu and Polynesian culture becomes fairly plausible.

It seems best, then, not to limit the word "caste" to the Hindu groups, but to recognize a continuum of graded classes, with castes merely representing the extreme of fixity. This enables us to draw a useful distinction between the less and the more permeable strata of the same society, and in some instances to speak of the "classes" into which a "caste" is subdivided.[2]

Let us, then, consider castes outside of India.

THE AMERICAN NEGRO.—In the United States the Negro is a pariah. Public opinion everywhere favors strict endogamy, and many states forbid miscegenation by law. The division between whites and Negroes is conceived as absolute, and the faintest trace of Negro blood puts an individual into the lower caste. No more than in India is there a hundred per cent correlation of caste with occupation, but certain callings, such as that of Pullman porter or dining-car waiter, are exclusively or preferably associated with color, while the economically and socially most desirable vocations are closed to all but an infinitesimal part of the Negro population. The Hindu rules of avoidance are closely paralleled in several ways. Even in the North, colored people are extralegally segregated in special districts, and attempts to extend their living facilities precipitate riots. In southern California children are reported striking because of five Negro schoolmates. The South insists on Jim Crow cars and provides every railroad station with separate washing accommodations for the two races. Oklahoma drives the status of the Negro home by allowing Indians to use the white man's waiting rooms. As in India, whimsical variations of behavior crop up. In a Virginia bus headed for Washington, D.C. colored passengers must sit in a special section; but if there is standing room only, Negroes and whites jostle one another in the aisle. In both India and our Southern states, moreover, excessive value is put on all sorts of outward tokens of social distance. Our two castes are not supposed to eat together; and a white ought not to confer the courtesy titles of Mr., Mrs., and Miss on a colored person.

A parallel worth noting is the Negro's acceptance of white standards. As the low-caste Hindu or primitive indigene mimics the upper castes by wearing the sacred thread or deprecating the marriage of widows, so the Negro puts "anti-kink" on his hair to approach Caucasian appearance, sets a high value on a light skin when choosing a colored mate, and adopts Caucasian ideals of chastity.

Finally, there are in both cases rationalizations by the dominant caste to justify superiority. The Brahmans claim higher rank by virtue of their religious sanctity; Caucasians either appeal to a God-ordained difference of status or substitute a scientifically yet undemonstrated organic endowment.[3]

THE JEWS.—Until their emancipation in the late eighteenth century, the Jews were in several respects outcasts. Endogamous by their own and Christian law, set off by their occupation of trading and moneylending, they remained segregated in ghettos. However, their case and that of the Hindus also present notable differences. From the point of view of their hosts, the Jewish status was not immutable, for conversion put them on the common Christian level. If they rarely availed themselves of the possibility, it was because—unlike the Hindu untouchables—they had no sense of inferiority and as "God's chosen people" lacked the urge to mimic their more privileged neighbors.

With emancipation the Jews abandoned this conception along with other parts of the traditional ideology and often intermarried with Christians in Western Europe. Able to enter many callings hitherto closed to them, they, like others, could even advance socially on the strength of services to the Western governments or by professional eminence. As early as 1816 a Rothschild was knighted, and later in the century a daughter of the British branch of the family married Lord Rosebery. Disraeli became the leader of the British Conservatives, prime minister, and a peer of the realm. Under the French republic, Gambetta, also of Jewish extraction, played a corresponding part in politics. Conditions in Germany did not favor such spectacular public careers, but there were many intermarriages and some instances of ennoblement. That assimilated part-Jews suffered discrimination outside the army and the bureaucracy is extremely improbable. Paul Heyse, a noted poet and novelist in his day, was the grandson of the Prussian court jeweler, Salomon Jacob Salomon. Nevertheless he remained for years a favorite "cultural attaché" at the court of King Max of Bavaria and was invited by the Grand Duke of Weimar to join his circle. A cousin of Heyse's married a French count, an aunt had been engaged to a Portuguese duke, who died before the nuptials.

Only with the rise of nationalism in Germany did anti-Semitism grow obtrusive; and later in the nineteenth century the movement assumed a racialist tinge. The adherents of this school conceived the Jews as both innately inferior and immutably hostile to the German spirit; hence their influence had to be combated and suppressed. After World War I this tendency culminated under Hitler, who reduced Jews to a worse than medieval status. He enforced endogamy, treating miscegenation as a crime against the "German race." Jews, ousted from their homes and again segregated in ghettos, were obliged to wear distinctive badges. As our Southerners deny Negroes the courtesy titles of "Mr." and "Mrs.," so rabid Nazis addressed adult and cultivated Jews by the pronoun reserved for intimates, children, and inferiors. In some cities Jews were barred from public parks or forbidden to share benches with "Aryans"—as an untouchable in India must remain at a respectful distance from his betters. Thrown out of employment, they literally became a degraded caste. Characteristically, Alfred Rosenberg, the philosopher of Nazism, bracketed them with "Niggers."

JAPAN.—Until the second half of the last century the Japanese had a rigid class system with two veritable pariah castes at the bottom. The *Hinin* included entertainers, beggars, and executioners. The still lower *Eta* made leather goods and disposed of carcasses, thus corresponding to one of the "untouchable" Hindu castes. A further resemblance lay in the imposition of endogamy and of separate living quarters; even commoners would neither eat nor sit with them.[4]

EAST AFRICAN CASTES.—The Masai blacksmiths are an endogamous pariah caste. Obliged to camp apart from the other Masai, they are treated as a necessary evil; even the indispensable weapons they provide have to be purified before use. Deprived of civil rights, they may be killed with impunity; in fact, several smiths must die for even an accidental killing of a Masai. As usual, caste prejudice is justified by a rationalization: God forbids bloodshed; the blacksmiths manufacture weapons that tempt men to break the commandment; hence they are rightly accursed.

In other sections of East Africa ethnic differences have perhaps produced clearly defined classes rather than castes, but some of the systems known seem borderline cases. Thus, in Ruanda and Urundi there are three strata, distinguishable by physique and occupation. The lowest group consists of pygmylike hunters, the Twa; intermediate are

Negroid, moderately tall Hutu peasants; and dominant is the pastoral Tussi group, extremely tall and of mixed Caucasoid and Negroid blood. As in India, differences in food accompany class distinctions and evoke emotional reactions. The Tussi despise the Hutu for eating mutton, the two upper classes scorn the poultry and egg-eating Twa, and neither would intermarry with them. But between Tussi and Hutu the cleavage is not quite so strict. A poor herder will sometimes marry a Hutu woman, a pastoralist may become a peasant's blood brother; and eminent Hutu have held some of the lesser official positions at court. As a matter of fact, even the hunters are assigned to less honorific offices of chanters in royal processions, policemen, and executioners; and wholly opposed to the Hindu scheme is the organization of a secret society that after a fashion admits members of all three classes. The Ruanda system, then, doubtless has elements of a caste system, but despite hierarchical grading, occupational differences, and a strong endogamous prejudice, there is far less separation of the component strata of the population than among either the Masai or the Hindu.[5]

## Classes and Rank

Group distinctions lacking the rigor of a caste system are widespread, arise from various conditions, and are by no means always hereditary. Though less fixed than castes, such classes are far from equally open in all cases. The Southern Negro caste may itself be subdivided into an upper and a lower class on the basis of economic status and education. Theoretically a poor Negro may advance himself by acquiring wealth and professional training. But practically how easy is it for him to do either? Drucker has convincingly shown similar difficulties for a British Columbia Indian. Here, too, wealth underlies higher status, but whereas modern conditions offer the native a chance to get a small fortune, there were no such opportunities in aboriginal days.

On the other hand, societies that specially prize bravery tend toward a high measure of social mobility. A Bagobo (Mindanao) who had never slain an enemy was a nobody. A man who had killed at least two persons rose to the honorable class of *magani,* allowed to wear a badge of honor in the form of a chocolate kerchief. If he scored as many as six victims, he put on a full suit of blood-red color, led war parties, and assisted at annual ceremonies; and each additional killing increased the slayer's influence.

In North America the Plains tribes had a corresponding system of emblems and titles. A Crow who had captured a picketed horse, wrested a bow or gun from an adversary in a hand-to-hand fight, touched an enemy's body in battle ("coup"), and led a successful raid was dubbed a "chief." Special decorations indicated the nature of a brave's exploit, e.g., a wolftail at the heels of a moccasin showed that the wearer had struck a coup. Those Cree youths who became known as good fighters formed the class of "worthy young men." However, here the hereditary element intruded: a chief's son was soon hailed as a "worthy," whereas the offspring of unimportant parents had to prove his courage beyond any doubt.

Classes less rigid than castes may nevertheless stress their distinctness. In central Albania a hundred years ago, crafts were hereditary and children of, say, masons were expected to intermarry, while an artisan would not take a peasant's daughter for his wife. In modern England, primogeniture precludes caste; but though a Winston Churchill cannot inherit a title, he does belong to the tone-setting class of "gentlemen."

As the Hindu system leads to an indefinite multiplication of castes, so an inveterate feeling for social grades tends to produce ever new distinctions. Within the German culture sphere the doctorate had become one of a large series of honorific symbols. In consequence, students of comparatively new branches of knowledge would not rest until it was conferred upon them. Thus, in 1901 Austrian civil engineers gained the title of "Doctor rerum technicarum" and five years later a mining engineer acquired the inestimable prerogative of putting on his visiting card "Doctor rerum montensium." Since a German doctor's diploma was not executed until the dissertation had been printed, a sop was thrown to the candidate who had fulfilled all other requirements and he was allowed to call himself "Doctor designatus." The qualified (*habilitiert*) lecturer at a university became a "Dr. phil. habil."

Tangible emblems of distinction are prized even in modern democratic and leftist societies. Our order of the Purple Heart or the Soviet Order of Lenin is in ethnographic perspective the counterpart of a Crow Indian's wolftail. Prince Eulenburg records some strange experiences. One of his acquaintances worried himself sick because, after long craving a certain decoration, he had received one of the next lower grade. Another fellow aristocrat, his heart set on the Maltese order, decided to turn Catholic in order to qualify for it. Once the ninety-two-year-old Nestor of the Austrian diet asked the Prince to exert his influence on his behalf: the suppliant, who held some order of the third degree, longed for that of the second.

Modes of address form another symbol of status. We have already noted that Nazis were wont to express their contempt for Jews by refusing to address them by the pronoun of politeness. In Sweden the upper classes came to avoid the pronoun "ni" (you) in mutual address, substituting titles and the third person pronoun. Thus, a baron would not ask the governor, "Have you received a letter?" but "Has the Mr. Governor received a letter?" Only here and there in a conversation was it permissible to slip in a "ni" without giving offense. Similarly, in England a haberdasher or a greengrocer may content himself with the superscription of "Mr. John Smith," but a gentleman is entitled to an "Esquire" after his name.

It would be an error to suppose that these distinctions are fostered only by their obvious beneficiaries. The "Four Hundred" may set the tone, but they are readily imitated and outdone by humbler fellow citizens. The picture Dickens draws in *The Pickwick Papers* of a charity ball in a provincial town is hardly exaggerated. At one end are "the aristocracy of the place," whom everyone else mimics. The lesser officers of the local regiment "devoted themselves to the families of the less important functionaries from the dock-yard." The wives of the solicitors and the wine merchant head another grade, and "by mutual consent" the postmaster is the leader among the tradespeople. An equivalent picture from real life is offered by Eulenburg for the lower ranks of German society. He noted with surprise that his own employees were more punctilious about grading than were masters of ceremony at the imperial court in Berlin. All sorts of nice differentiations were in vogue. A secretary and a "private" secretary, an ordinary hunter and one who held his master's extra gun, were socially distinct, as were valets, stewards, accountants, and what not. So-and-so would have to be the first to lift his hat in mutual salutation, and even the extent to which it was lowered by men of unequal grade was a matter of etiquette. Some of these petty officials would not visit certain others or even hold conversation with them.

Drucker has properly distinguished between rank and class; but though conceptually we must recognize their diversity, in actual life they merge into each other. The purple heart is an individual distinction, but it is conceived as the badge of a military fraternity, a "class." As noted for the Cree, the offspring of eminent parents are *ipso facto* in a preferential position.

In British Columbia that principle is even more explicit. Privileges were transmitted to one's children mainly according to primogeniture, but the rules became so complicated that quarrels regarding individual position were of common occurrence. In other words, questions of precedence loomed large among approximate equals. Polynesia exhibits similar phenomena. Mangareva, for instance, had an indefinite number of shades of dignity, but Laval found only two basic classes, the nobility and the commoners. A plebeian might marry into the nobility, but only after lengthy debates, for such a union was regarded as a misalliance, and though the inferior rose in rank, the blot of his lowly origin was never quite wiped out. The traditions of Mangareva tell of an upstart conqueror who invited a patrician woman to be his wife. "No," she disdainfully snubs him, "I should rather be a fugitive with a noble husband than marry a conqueror of mean extraction." Samoa, where primogeniture is absent, has preserved the traditional yearning for titles, which members of the lineage confer on the men of their choice after much intrigue and logrolling. There is an indefinite number of statuses with honorary designations, and at a kava-drinking feast the relative rank of the participants is shown by the order in which they are served. Here, as in British Columbia, it may sometimes appear that there are no classes, only individual ranks. Actually, there are both, and social rivalry rages among men of roughly equal status, i.e., of the same class. Each chief tried to eclipse the rest by the splendor of his house.

Broadly speaking, caste was rare or absent in Polynesia, notwithstanding excessive emphasis on rank, based on supposedly direct descent from the gods. The extent to which an individual might rise in the scale evidently varied regionally. A suggestive phenomenon is the widespread occurrence of professional classes—priests, housebuilders, shipwrights—intermediate in station between the commoners and the aristocracy.[6]

### Ethnic Groups

As Schrieke aptly remarks, "Nationalities play the role of classes in the American social structure." Not that our social organization can be viewed wholly from this point of view, as shown by white tenant farmers of Anglo-Saxon stock, but "ethnic minorities" do form social classes, often with distinctive occupational trends, a fact which itself reacts on status. There is a constant interaction between social grade and form of employment. If Negroes come to be employed preponderantly as porters of sleeping cars, whites cease to apply for the job; in Europe, where Negroes are rare, porters are of course white.

Immigrants to the United States have generally come from their homeland for economic reasons; thus they start with lower standards of living and underbid the native-born in the labor market—whence the bitter resentment over and above the suspicion due to campanilismo. Successive groups of immigrants develop corresponding economic animosities, as when Italian and Spanish stevedores superseded the Irish on the docks of the lower west side of New York City.

The several factors that enter into the grading of minority groups are illustrated by the history of Irish and German immigrants. The Irish had the double advantage of English speech and of physical resemblance to older stocks. Relatively early arrivals, they adapted themselves before late-comers to the American standards of living; when crowded out of jobs at hard labor by Italians and other groups, the Irish automatically rose in the scale. In a Massachusetts town where (in 1930) they numbered 3,943 against 9,030 old Yankees, the Irish characteristically held proportionately more political offices, though only half the number of "high control" positions. The Germans furnished an unusual percentage of educated immigrants and a disproportionate number of physicians, druggists, and musicians. Yet it is noteworthy that the Know-Nothing party of the 1850's was specifically directed against these two advantageously situated nationalities.

The Germans and the Irish in the United States illustrate an important point that is sometimes overlooked. Classes within the same major society need not all be hierarchically graded, even though that may be the most common situation. Certainly neither the Germans nor the Irish would admit their inferiority to the other group. And what holds for ethnic minorities applies equally well to classes of identical nationality. So far as I know, the only author who has drawn attention to this fact is Professor Myrdal. As he remarks, a medical man, an army officer, and an artist may well enjoy roughly similar status and meet as peers in ordinary social intercourse. Nevertheless, their interests and attitudes are so distinct that it is best to recognize "several parallel social status continua."

Ours is by no means the only country in which juxtaposition of diverse stocks has occurred. The resulting conditions have already been discussed in part. They obviously depend a great deal on such factors as the numerical relations of the several groups, their comparative military or cultural potency, the respective ideologies. Until recently a handful of Englishmen have been able to control three hundred million East Indians; and in Ruanda the better-organized herders lord it over ten times as many peasants.

In caste-ridden India even rude aborigines tend to adapt their notions to the common class-consciousness. On the Nilgiri Plateau there are four tribes speaking mutually unintelligible Dravidian languages—the meat-tabooing, buffalo-breeding Toda; the millet-growing Badaga; the Kota, who grow millet for themselves, eat meat, and serve all the tribes as artisans and musicians; and the Kurumba, who are dreaded as sorcerers. In consonance with Hinduism, though the faith remains essentially alien to them, these four tribes have evolved a symbiosis, yet with a minimum of social contacts. The Kurumba, at the bottom of the scale, are requisitioned to practice magic, but are rarely allowed to enter the villages of the other tribes; as soon as they appear, Kota women and children flee inside their homes. The Kota, a step higher, are essential in Toda ceremonials that require music; but if any of them get close to the sacred dairy, it is necessary to go through a rite of purification. Indeed, because of the low status of musicians in the Hindu scheme, some Badaga have recently tried to eliminate Kota music from ceremonials. The strictness of caste also limits the otherwise normal diffusion of traits through imitation of one's betters. A few Kota who mimicked the Badaga headgear were beaten up for trying to get beyond their natural station.

This example indicates that assimilation, which where possible obviates difficulties of social relations, may be prevented by specific circumstances. The question, obviously of both theoretical and practical importance, merits special treatment.[7]

ASSIMILATION.—In the United States pertinent questions have generally been discussed under the caption of "the melting pot." At one time enthusiasts assumed that the American scene would automatically transform immigrants, or at all events their offspring, into the semblance of the Anglo-Saxon majority. This oversimplified conception of the phenomena ignored several obstacles to a rapid metamorphosis. The several ethnic groups had by no means the same background; hence assimilation might be expected to be far slower for some than for others. Again, such differences applied even to immigrants from the same country, not all of whom might seek assimilation. Finally, "Old Americans" themselves might discourage assimilation by their attitudes toward particular groups.

Here, again, we must note that our country is not the only one that has to cope with the problem of minority groups. In Yucatan, for instance, there is a juxtaposition of whites and of Indians. Ignoring local variations, the emphasis in class distinctions is no longer on the difference between races but on cultural diversity. The Indian by race is accepted on equal terms so far as he bears a Spanish surname and dresses in civilized costume. However, significantly, where the Indians do not mix with whites, they experience no sense of inferiority.

To return to the United States, the advantage of those stocks which resemble the Anglo-Saxon physically need not be further enlarged upon. Even "passable" Negroes merge into the general population without difficulty so long as their origin remains undiscovered.

There are two questions of basic importance for all members of minority groups: Do they *wish* to be assimilated? Does the majority (or dominant minority in some countries) welcome assimilation to its norms?

It has been too lightly assumed that all immigrants crave absorption into the American people. We should recognize broadly three distinct types of immigrants within the same stock: those eager to assimilate; those intent on preserving their cultural tradition against Americanization; those envisaging a blend of their social heritage with that of the United States.

Undoubtedly the first type is numerically strong. An enormous percentage of all immigrants have come here to better their material conditions, and these represent the poorer layers of their homeland. Enabled to improve their standard of living, brought for the first time into contact with sanitary plumbing and other tokens of an advanced technology, they have often been dazzled by new gadgets and look down with scorn upon "the old country." Their major concern is to shed every vestige of their distinctness, to lose the nickname of a "greenhorn." If they return to the native land, their pockets jingling with money, they boast tactlessly of the wonders of America and treat their stay-at-home cousins as country bumpkins. For such as these a Tourist Bureau in Stockholm found it desirable in 1924 to issue a folder of advice on "Something a Swedish-American ought to observe and know while visiting Sweden." The first paragraph warns against speaking English or sprinkling Swedish conversation with English phrases. The second reads: "When you meet Swedes, do not talk about America and conditions there unless you find a *real* interest in the subject."

Our Scandinavians in large measure represented this first type, being in the main humble folk who left the fatherland to escape military service or to improve their lot; some were dissenters from the State Church; others resented existing social discrimination. They knew little of the higher achievements of Scandinavian culture, and even the colleges they founded in the United States were in no sense centers for the propagation of Scandinavian thought, art, and literature. Indeed, of all these the typical immigrant was profoundly suspicious. The pastors, often bigoted emotionalists, deliberately blocked their parishioners from such heretical or at least profane endeavors. In 1870 many Swedish-Americans would not honor Christine Nilsson because public singing seemed too worldly an affair; and one congregation split over the proposal to organize an orchestra, the violin being regarded as the devil's own instrument.

Yet this very narrow-mindedness was also consistent with the stubborn retention of such fractions of Scandinavian culture as the immigrants knew and valued; and this implied stern repudiation of some things characteristically American. One Lutheran minister declared that the charge of hard-hearted, un-Christian intolerance was one to rejoice over, since "truth must be exclusive over against falsehood and error." The "godless," i.e., nondenominational, public school was a special object of denunciation; and one Norwegian leader at a Lutheran college "could find nothing more severe to say in condemnation of a person than that he was 'Americanized.'"

If such were at times the sentiments of the less cultivated, those steeped in the spiritual and intellectual atmosphere of the Old World were bound to react with equal violence to a greater number of irritants found in their new homes. It is wrong to suppose that the educated immigrants are the most readily assimilated. On the contrary, bringing with them sharply defined dogmas on political, religious, and social issues, they are precisely those least likely to project themselves sympathetically into the life of any alien people. When, as frequently happened, they were further exacerbated by financial difficulties, disillusionment would turn them into savage and often absurdly uncomprehending critics.

Educated Germans, Forty-Eighters and those of similar convictions, furnish striking examples. For instance, having conceived vehement views on the subject of Church and State, they would on the slenderest grounds scent sinister designs for an established church in America. About 1870 one Friedrich Schünemann-Pott, speaker of the German Free Congregation of San Francisco, was incensed by a presidential

Thanksgiving proclamation and thus expressed his indignation: "The swallow-coated king and prospective bishop of a future State Church, His Excellency, the Rt. Rev. Ulysses Grant, has once more condescended to fix in a proclamation. . . . a general 'Thanksgiving Day' for the country, which was dutifully celebrated by all present or future good and faithful subjects. According to a trustworthy rumor another proclamation is being prepared in the provisional ministry for ecclesiastical, educational, and medical affairs, fixing January 5th as the day on which all the inhabitants of the country shall be baptized or circumcised, unless reliable certificates prove that one of the procedures has already been executed on them." In a later issue of his journal the author reverts to the theme: "Of a fine Sunday President Grant took the Japanese embassy during their stay in Washington to a Methodist church. One can hardly suppose that he did it only in order to set a horrible example. . . . now apparently the Methodist Church seems to be officially the Washington court Church."

This is very heavy humor. The point for us, however, is that an educated man was capable of such abysmal lack of insight into the culture of a country in which he had lived for several years. The reason is clear. Schünemann-Pott's vision was clouded by doctrinaire convictions imbibed in Europe and mechanically transferred to the New World.

On a much higher plane, corresponding bias, precluding assimilation, appears in the letters of Friedrich Kapp (1824–1884). Kapp, who had participated in the revolutionary movement of 1848–1849, fled from Germany to New York, where he successfully practiced law, but increasingly resented the American atmosphere. In writing to his intimate, the philosopher Ludwig Feuerbach, he expressed sentiments that may be regarded as typical of a whole class. He strongly advises his friend against coming to America: "A German peasant who turns farmer cannot make a more fortunate choice; an academically educated man degenerates spiritually, rarely prospers materially, and at best creates a carefree future for his children. . . . Your fame as a writer would rather hurt than help you. . . . If you are through with Europe in every, in *every* respect, if you are convinced that it has nothing whatsoever to offer you, then come here; otherwise under no condition."

The nature of Kapp's discontent is easily analyzed. Like many Continentals, he not only deplored the lack of interest in the arts and philosophy, but found the Anglo-Saxon basis of American life singularly repulsive. The public opinion of an uncultivated majority was worse than Czarist despotism. American politics stressed legalism to the detriment of abstract principles; our Constitution seemed "petrified," our political parties simply "silly." Kapp did not discriminate between sincere piety and bigotry or hypocrisy; and lay cults revolted him by their crudity. The American, he gathered, was the slave of parsons and, even more than the Englishman, "a Protestant Jew." Superstitiousness to the point of imbecility, insensitiveness to higher values, stupid nationalism—these constitute Kapp's indictment against the people of his adoptive country.

In these acrid comments, often acute and justifiable in themselves but without insight into the historical conditions of a pioneer civilization, Kapp consciously reacted against the extravagant eulogies which more naïve fellow immigrants were lavishing on the United States. Never content with his intellectual environment here, he finally became reconciled to Germany after her unification, returned there, entered public life, and was elected into the Reichstag. He represents, of course, the extreme of unassimilability, but his case is far from unique. It is true that the sophisticates are numerically weak among immigrants, but since the leaders of any ethnic group are largely recruited from them, their potential influence is out of proportion to their numbers. The question is not whether they are wholly wrong. But their very insistence on perpetuating transatlantic ideals, however valuable in themselves, serves to distinguish their followers in speech and mores from the bulk of the population, maintaining them as a separate class within their ethnic group.

Once more we must try to see a phenomenon in wider perspective. It is not only Germans in the United States who spurn identification with Anglo-Saxon Americans. Italian newspapers, whose writers in part know no English and have no American friends, describe Americans as "artificial, unscrupulous, money-crazed, hypocritical." Campanilismo, with its intransigence even in the minutiae of folkways and with regard to intangible attitudes, everywhere militates against genuine assimilation. To take peoples of the same speech, an educated Englishman is repelled by much that he sees in America, and Americans rarely are thoroughly acclimatized in Britain or even in eastern Canada. Similarly, North Germans who settle, say, in Switzerland or Austria or Bavaria often grow restive. In Switzerland they become conscious of political sentiments hostile to their patriotic susceptibilities; in Austria or Bavaria a transplanted Protestant would feel out of touch with the Catholic atmosphere. Further, a Northerner reacts to the South Ger-

mans' muddling along much as most of us do to the Latin-American
policy of "mañana." The unskilled immigrant laborer or barely literate
peasant is, of course, suspicious of anything different from his own
folkways, but his suspicions are spontaneous and grow dormant when
he is materially well off. The alien sophisticate, on the other hand, has
clear-cut touchstones for appraising all unfamiliar ideas and behavior,
and his doubts are not so easily allayed.

The third type of immigrant reaction is best illustrated by Ole
Edvart Rölvaag (1876–1931), the author of *Giants of the Earth*. Born in
the Lofoten Islands, from which he did not emigrate before his twenti-
eth year, he became the authentic interpreter in fiction of Norwegian-
American life. In his position he is equally remote from the immigrant
who dreads above all the stigma of a greenhorn and from Kapp with
his mordant criticism of American life. Rölvaag is thoroughly friendly
to the United States, but retains a nostalgic pride in the values imported
from Norway. "It is a mistaken belief," reads the motto of one of his
books, "that the immigrant has no soul." His spiritual values should
be cherished as long as possible, ultimately fusing with the dominant
ideals of Anglo-Saxon America and preserving them from a monoto-
nous standardization. What is more, in his essays and private letters,
Rölvaag, perhaps more poignantly than anyone else, has described the
strife between immigrant parents and their American-born children.
If the conflict of generations may arise in the most favorable circumstances, it is intensified to the point of tragedy when through contact
with American associates the young folks imbibe notions contrary to
all their elders deem sacred, when they are unable or ashamed to talk
freely in the only tongue their parents fully know, when they look
upon father and mother as rather absurd old fogies.

Rölvaag's discussions raise the vital question of what *kind* of
assimilation is desirable. He argues for a gradual absorption of ethnic
units both from humane considerations on behalf of the older generation and in the interest of the adoptive country. The Norwegians he
envisages would linger on as a hyphenated class in America, apprecia-
tive of what is good in the country, but proudly conscious that they
are donors as well as beneficiaries.

It is, then, clear that the old notion of the American melting pot
is unsound, for—irrespective of whether all foreign elements can be
assimilated or not—many immigrants do not want to be melted down,
preferring somehow to preserve their identity.

So far we have considered only one side of the problem—the attitude of the nondominant ethnic units. Of equal importance is the position of the stock in control, which likewise may or may not desire assimilation. It may prefer to keep all newcomers (or the vanquished indigenes) as hewers of wood and drawers of water. In some East African states that is precisely what the ruling herders have done in their treatment of the conquered peasantry. Some American writers, regarding certain ethnic stocks as innately inferior, would like to limit them to menial occupations and to relegate them to a position of social inferiority.

More generally, some groups, such as the Japanese, are often viewed as unassimilable and hence, in the nature of things, as a class apart. This attitude inevitably has strengthened the class-consciousness of the older immigrants and later that of their American-born children (the nisei). As Schrieke and Embree have shown, our naturalization laws blocked the older people who might have desired Americanization. The second generation who went to school in the United States and were not sent back to Japan for a prolonged stretch of years acted precisely like any other second-generation group. They had to deal with two diverse ideologies and, for the most part, inclined to that of their white schoolmates. Neither the Japanese language schools, which never succeeded in giving a perfect knowledge of the ancestral tongue, nor the teaching of parents could counterbalance the influence of age mates. When, however, it became clear after Pearl Harbor that efforts toward Americanization were futile, many nisei naturally compensated for their frustration by seeking contact with the land of their ancestors, where at all events race would not bar them immutably from recognition as equals. A close parallel is presented by those Jews who had regarded themselves as fully assimilated Germans, but whom Hitler's persecution drove into the arms of Jewish nationalism.[8]

## Slavery and Serfdom

Slaves are defined as "human chattels" and are popularly distinguished from the partly free "serfs" of medieval Europe. Actually both terms have had a variety of meanings at different periods and as applied to different peoples. That Russian "serfs" were often treated as chattels has already been pointed out. Both concepts, if viewed historically, once more illustrate the fluidity of social units and conditions. In consequence none of the customary criteria can be regarded as infallible.

What can be considered an established fact is that the serf's status, so far from being uniformly superior, was often distinctly worse than the slave's. As Eduard Meyer has pointed out, in antiquity a slave was sometimes able to gain wealth, whereas the medieval "serf," or "villein" and the *colonus* of late Roman times "was born into his class and with his descendants was unable ever to get out of it." Thus, if the word "caste" were to be extended to these phenomena at all, it would more properly designate the serf's rather than the slave's status. However, this would depend on the particular culture and period under consideration. In other words, "slavery" is a blanket term that denotes diverse social and legal positions, which hinge in large measure on the economic context. Thus, among the same people a native slave sold or pawned to appease his family's creditor is commonly much better off than a captive in war; and the domestic slave is likely to enjoy a better lot than the member of a plantation gang. As a rule, we must guard against generalizing from particular cases. Though before the Civil War a Southern Negro could not hold property, this prohibition is emphatically not a universal one. The Ashanti, for instance, definitely recognized a slave's claim to ownership.

Some concrete illustrations will provide a fairer picture of the institution.

Lobi slaves were invariably foreigners bought at intertribal markets for from 40,000 to 160,000 cowrie shells. The purchaser took his chattel home and sacrificed a beast to the family god, asking him to protect the slave and to keep him from fleeing and from practicing sorcery. Master and man then ate the flesh of the victim. Thereafter a male slave would work with the men of the household, a female helping in the kitchen. The owner was permitted to sell his bondsman, but rarely did so; and he was not supposed to kill him without cause. Slaves generally received good treatment, some becoming rich enough to buy their freedom and even slaves for themselves. The master fed his slave as though he were his own son, bought him a wife, sometimes even made him marry one of the owner's kinswomen. The children, who could not be sold, inherited their father's property to the exclusion of the master. Altogether, Lobi slaves enjoyed very definite rights.

In Southern Nigeria, too, where slaves were largely prisoners of war or criminals sold by alien tribes, they were normally treated kindly. A British administrator holds that the majority, who were used for household service, were happier than "many of the wage slaves in modern civilized countries." They emphatically were not a lower caste, for they exerted influence in the family and married freeborn women, who suffered no loss of status from the union. In 1857 the sister of a king was married to a slave. Indeed, a slave frequently acted as his master's agent and enjoyed greater confidence than a relative. He could even rise to the chieftaincy. A slave woman was often taken to wife by her owner. In many tribes the children of a slave were free. The slave had, indeed, to work for his master; but since much of his time was his own, he often earned considerable wealth, of which only a third to a half fell to his master's share. Thus, here again a slave could not only grow rich, but acquire slaves himself. He wore the same dress as freemen and was not mutilated in token of his position.

Naturally there were disabilities. The harder and disagreeable work did fall on slaves; some tribes, but by no means the majority, forced them to live in separate compounds, and some permitted a master to kill his slave with impunity. Worst of all, the victims of human sacrifices were largely recruited from the slaves.

The so-called pawn slaves of the area were not slaves at all, but persons contracted by themselves and their families to work off a debt. They were released as soon as the obligation was liquidated and even as pawns retained a freeman's status.

To take a third African example, in Uganda likewise slaves were obtained in raids or wars, so that the majority were foreigners. They could be sold or killed by their owner, but it should be recalled that in an African autocracy no one's life or property was safe. The king of Uganda had the power to have any chief put into the stocks or killed. In these circumstances the slaves' insecurity differed only in degree from a free subject's. By and large, an African slave was incomparably better off than a Masai blacksmith.

In the one North American area where slavery flourished in aboriginal times, viz. in coastal British Columbia and Washington, the social status of the slave was unquestionably inferior to that of his African counterpart. Intermarriages between commoners and slaves "were in theory quite impossible, and in earlier days could at best have been but rare." Slaves owned no property and stood outside the social life of their owners, who were at liberty to beat, sell, or kill them at will. The disgrace of being a slave was such that a vindictive Tsimshian would kidnap a member of an influential lineage from his own or a neighboring tribe in order to cover it with ignominy. One chief humbled a powerful lineage of his tribe by twice marrying one of its women and each time selling her into bondage. Her kinsmen twice redeemed her, but were impoverished by the ransom paid. It was difficult to wipe out the stain of having once been enslaved. Though spinsterhood was most uncommon, one Tsimshian girl who had been redeemed from servitude and adopted by a clanswoman remained unwedded because no man would degrade himself so far as to take her to wife. Even among the Quinault, near the southern margin of this culture area, the solitary instance Olson discovered of a male slave's marrying a free woman is regarded as a blot on her family's reputation: "It is a subject to be mentioned only in whispers—or to be thrown in the face of a member. . . . in a bitter quarrel."

In classical antiquity the nature of slavery changed with the type of economic organization. In the Homeric age the majority of slaves were females who, apart from satisfying sexual desire, joined other women in domestic tasks, including such craft activity as had not yet become specialized. At this period of Greek history, and in most parts of the Near Orient permanently, there was no economic need for slavery on a large scale. *That* developed only when industrialists had developed so as to require "the cheapest laborers possible, whose strength could be completely exploited, who were completely in the palms of their hands." Henceforth kidnaping and slave trading were systematized, spreading from Chios to the rest of the Hellenic world. Where economy remained on the more primitive level, as in the interior of the Peloponnesus, slavery, too, remained as before; but in the great industrial centers of the fifth century B.C.—Corinth, Athens, Syracuse—the number of slaves greatly increased. In mining, only slaves were put to work, but artisans and shopkeepers also came to use them; and though intensive exploitation in agriculture was exceptional, it occurred to some extent as industrialists acquired land. However, the equivalents of our factories were the main centers for slave labor.

In Rome the situation differed. As the republic conquered larger and larger areas, capitalists invested wealth largely in land and craved rural labor. Free tillers were too expensive, whereas the constant wars brought thousands of captives, who all but replaced the free yeomanry of old. When prisoners of war no longer sufficed, raids were organized against citizens of Greek and Oriental states as well as against barbarians. During the two centuries before Christ, the era of large slave markets and of brutal abuse of the laborers, slaves were put to work on the land in gangs. The empire, establishing general peace, blocked the supply of slaves from outlying parts of the realm; and many masters set their slaves free as more humane sentiments asserted themselves.

Custom permitted the slave to acquire and bequeath property, and with his master's consent he could enter craft guilds.

The slave trade of modern times notoriously developed with economic requirements of cheap labor. As Eduard Meyer cynically remarks, Roman capitalists utilized the pre-existing institution of slavery for their ends, but had there been no such thing they would have found some other way to procure the laborers needed "and would have found the legal form therefor." Their counterparts in later periods were not less ingenious. Mohammedans were not supposed to enslave coreligionists, but Sunnite raiders justified their kidnaping of Shiites on the ground that these were at bottom only pagans. There was a corresponding excuse for Negro servitude in the early history of Virginia; and in Brazil the Portuguese raided Indian settlements on the ground that the natives were cannibals. The inborn inferiority of certain races cropped up as a later rationalization of Western policy.[9]

## General Considerations

In considering social stratification we have to reckon with several deep-seated human drives. The desire to excel one's fellows, though apparently repressed by a few peoples, such as the Pueblos, is intense in most societies. Ability in a direction favored by a society lends personal eminence, and a powerful sense of kinship tends to make the distinction hereditary. The trend has been found noticeable even in comparatively democratic tribes. It is noteworthy that, contrary to an old dogma, the clans of a people are often not equivalent. Among the Menomini and Winnebago, for instance, the chief is necessarily from a particular clan; the Hopi link ceremonial offices with such and such clans; among the Sherente, the Sun moiety claims precedence over that associated with the Moon. In Uganda, clans serve specific functions: the Mushroom people are bark-cloth makers; another clan takes care of a sacred drum; the Tailless Cow people are the blacksmiths; the Leopards are exempt from enforced labor for the king, devoting themselves to the custody of a temple. Actually, in many cases it is even a special lineage of the kin that holds the title to honors: when the head of a Ganda clan dies, his successor is chosen from his own section of the clan.

Clans with specific functions are not identical with classes, but they contain the germs of class differentiation. The same holds for ethnic differences, which often actually lead to diverse classes and even castes, though they are consistent with only a mild sense of separateness.

Classes, though usually graded, are not always so: in European parliaments or diets, the "lords spiritual" and the "lords temporal" were distinct estates; and of two sharply distinguishable ethnic units—say the Irish and the Germans in the United States—neither need be inferior to the other nor to the general population.

Subjugation of one people by another naturally depressed the conquered, as in parts of East Africa, but as European history demonstrates, this is certainly not the only source of stratification. For the Masai blacksmiths, Cline has thrown out a plausible suggestion. East African pastoralists disdain any form of useful work not connected with livestock, and a Masai gains glory only in warfare. But the very conditions of ironwork isolate smiths from the normal routine of Masai life. They must live near sources of ore and fuel, hence are less migratory than the other Masai, a fact which implies that they cannot perpetually pasture cattle, of which they accordingly own very few head. Further, since they supply the weapons needed for raids, they cannot constantly engage on these ventures, from which they alone are discouraged. With disabilities in both cattle breeding and war exploits, the smiths thus lack the only opportunities for distinction open in their society and have come to be definite outcasts. Generically, the case of the Jews at certain periods is parallel. In the Middle Ages and later, their exclusion from agriculture and crafts isolated them from the preponderantly rural orientation of European populations and drove them into usury, a calling not likely to gain the favor of their neighbors. In imperial Germany, with her high value on military affiliation, Jews were precluded from rising in the army, a restriction which automatically reacted on their status.

Stratification is often wholly irrational, i.e., from the point of view of the general interest, sometimes even from that of the upper strata. At times, as in the Hindu system, it is wholly capricious. It is nonetheless clear that in many instances one group economically exploits another. But here again the assertion of power is more significant than rational utilization of the depressed class. The East African herder drives his cattle ruthlessly over the subject peasants' fields, but because of his ideology he fails to reap the maximum profit from his ascendancy.[10]

# Chapter 13

# SODALITIES

SINCE the concept of sodalities is merely a convenient lumber room for a great variety of associations, we cannot link it with a particular institution or with any one psychological motive. Aims and functions change in these associations, and their very composition may be revamped. They arise in response to certain needs, whether sentimental, social, economic, or religious, and are inevitably affected by coexisting institutions and folkways. Thus, the Omaha Indians had three feasting societies which united, respectively, mature men, young men, and boys. But since in the southern Plains, rank was somewhat affected by heredity, it was possible for a member of the older groups to send his son as a proxy, thereby altering the constitution of the mess. The Ibo of Nigeria hold markets which demand some supervision. Since they regard buying and selling as feminine affairs, it is naturally a women's committee or society that lays down the rules for a market and decides all pertinent questions.

Because sodalities must answer potentially general human needs in particular social environments, we cannot expect uniformity throughout the world. Actually, the distribution of these associations, or of any particular variety of them, is exceedingly irregular. The Chinese have not only cooperative loan societies, merchant and craft guilds, but also associations for visiting the sick, watching the crops, praying for the dead, making pilgrimages to sacred mountains, and building village temples. Even beggars organize corporations in all the cities, blackmailing people into alms at weddings or funerals on pain of having the solemnities broken up by a disturbance. Nothing comparable occurs among the pastoral nomads to the north, though in part the Turks and Mongols of the area are far from simple peoples. That mere complexity cannot be the decisive factor is demonstrated by the African phenomena. West Africa is honeycombed with secret societies and clubs, whereas South and East Africa rarely have anything but age divisions. Yet the Shilluk and especially the Ganda have a well-knit political organization along with the refinements that accompany such features. In Oceania the Banks Islands parallel West Africa in the multiplicity of their sodalities, but other Melanesian groups, as well as Polynesia, have a very meager assortment. America yields similar contrasts. It is true that in the rudest tribes, those of the Basin and Plateau, sodalities dwindle down to nothing, whereas the Pueblos and coastal British Columbia spawn them. But the Plains Indians are hardly inferior to the Pueblos in this respect, and on the northwest coast, where all the tribes are more or less on the same level, secret societies are most highly developed in the south, markedly petering out in the direction of the Alaskan panhandle. To draw comparisons in Europe, Germany —notwithstanding a mania for founding and joining all sorts of voluntary associations that precipitated a special word, *Vereinsmeierei*—never paralleled the development of upper-class clubs, often with political aims, so characteristic of England in the seventeenth and eighteenth centuries. The lack is, of course, to be traced to the total structure of social life in Germany, which inhibited such growth. In primitive areas we must also look for the explanation of corresponding differences in the surrounding social atmosphere.

Since sodalities represent a congeries of diverse associations set off by negative rather than positive criteria, they defy logical classification. Indeed, given their marked fluidity, classification of that sort would wrest asunder phenomena that are genetically related. We shall therefore content ourselves with describing and discussing a few definable categories that recur with considerable frequency.[1]

## Men's Tribal Societies

Often all the adult men of a group form a club that excludes women. The separation may be more or less formal, the implied attitudes vary from a desire to escape temporarily from feminine company to a veritable hostility, but uniformly there lies at the bottom of the division a sense of sex solidarity. The tendency persists in civilization. The Anglo-Saxon barroom and the modern Greek café are men's clubs; university faculty clubs restrict ladies to special dining rooms; some denominations segregate the sexes in divine worship.

TRIBAL CLUBS.—A spontaneous manifestation on the order of a general store gathering in an American village was noted by Nordenskiöld in the Gran Chaco. In several settlements the Ashluslay Indians grouped their huts around a central plaza, where the men alone would assemble in the shade of a tree or under a sunscreen. The observer rightly put this arrangement into the same category as the more formal clubhouse of northeastern Bolivia. There Chacobo bachelors, married men, and male guests sleep in a single dormitory swept by women early in the day, but otherwise avoided by them. The inmates also lounge, drink manioc beer, weave baskets, and manufacture their weapons in this structure; in other words, they spend most of their time there.

Specific folkways inevitably color the rules of the men's house without altering essential principles. In Buin the "chief's hall" is a club barring all but old women, and even them except sometimes for brief periods. The members disport themselves much like their Chacobo brethren, but in addition the hall has a sacred character, being dedicated to a spirit, who receives offerings at the fireplace. Here, too, the natives celebrate festivals in honor of the dead, hold councils, and assemble when summoned by emergency signals. The club of Northwest Californians exhibits additional traits. Though a men's and grown boys' winter dormitory, it is also heated for a ceremonial Turkish bath, hence figures in the literature as a "sweathouse." It foreshadows social discrimination, for though the membership includes all full-fledged male citizens, slaves and "bastards," i.e., men whose mothers were inadequately paid for in marriage, are barred.

Sometimes a bachelors' hall and the men's club merge. A dwelling set aside for the unmarried youths may be used by benedicts after their marriage. But since this by no means holds generally, the bachelors' hall will receive distinct treatment.[2]

TRIBAL SECRET SOCIETIES.—In the cases cited, the shift from the maternal home to the adult men's quarters is not marked by a definite solemnity. Further, except possibly in Buin, sex solidarity does not imply conscious antifeminism. In the instances now to be described, both these factors enter. A boy is initiated into adult status by a rite or a series of rites; he learns of a secret that he must not, often on pain of death, divulge to the uninitiated, i.e., to any woman or to the younger males. Thereafter he enters the organized men's company, which at times exploits and terrorizes the women. Typically initiation is prerequisite to marriage.

Parenthetically we note that initiation occurs also in other contexts. Conspicuous in masculine secret societies of limited membership, it likewise figures in some women's sodalities and may betoken the status of marriageability without implying admission to a tribal society. The Canella, for instance, have to undergo an initiation before taking a wife, but the ritual merely welds together those who jointly undergo it; it does not advance them into a tribal society, for none such exists.

To return to men's tribal societies, they are conspicuous in several discontinuous areas—Australia and Melanesia; West Africa; in California, on the Rio Negro, and in Tierra del Fuego. In view of the remoteness of these regions from one another, the resemblances they exhibit are rather surprising.

The Kiwai, who inhabit an island near the mouth of the Fly River (New Guinea), bar women from sacred ceremonials. At puberty begins a boy's initiation, which proceeds by a number of stages, one of which qualifies for wedlock provided the candidate has taken an enemy's head. Especially significant in the ritual series is the Ghost Dance. Some men in disguise impersonate the recently deceased, the women being ordered to bring food for the entertainment of the ghosts. At night the performers make weird noises and throw mud at the houses in order to frighten the women. At a certain stage of initiation the novice's maternal uncle carries him to the beach, washes him free of feminine smells, and takes him to the dance ground; on the way the boy is supposed to be beset by ghosts, a form of hazing. Initiation also gradually releases the novice from certain food taboos hitherto observed.

In another section of New Guinea the Bukaua men mystify and terrorize the female population throughout a long boys' initiation festival, which includes circumcision. A demon, the women learn, craves their sons' flesh, but by bringing plenty of food they can appease the monster, who will regurgitate the youths he has swallowed. The hoax is bolstered up in various ways. According to the men's tale, the ogre bites or scratches the lads, which explains the marks from circumcision. Bull-roarers are whirled through the air, and the horrible sound produced thereby is supposed to be the demon's voice. The tyros themselves undergo a severe test. Their seniors lead them, blindfolded, to their several months' retreat, where concealed guards frighten them with sounds and weapons. Just before the operation the men produce an awe-inspiring din by shouting, swinging bull-roarers, and rattling shells. When the novices finally discover the truth, they are forbidden—on pain of horrible punishments—to breathe a word to the uninitiated.

The Poro of Liberia has already been described as a society uniting men and the boys graduated from the bush school. The youngsters have normally been circumcised before they are secluded, but as novices they get the Poro design scratched into their bodies as a lasting badge. During their course there is no coddling. A pupil must obey implicitly, no matter what demands are made on his patience. He lies naked on the ground, sleeps uncovered, is beaten and made to exercise vigorously. At the close of the period the Grand Master appears in the village with his retinue and the newly initiated. On this occasion all women, strangers, and as yet uninitiated boys must hide. The new members are treated as reborn, bear a new name, fail to recognize their closest relatives, go astray in their native village, and pretend to have lost all memory of any past experiences. Membership is lifelong.

Several traits of this organization merit emphasis. The Grand Master is, in theory, a supernatural being who can kill and revive people. No woman dare look at him lest she turn blind. All members must aid one another as soon as a request is uttered in the Poro's name. Thus, they form a definite unit as against all women, young boys, and Negro outsiders. The duped women, as in New Guinea, have to provide victuals for the maintenance of their sons in the bush. On the other hand, the total picture differs in at least two respects from the Papuan equivalent. For one thing, there is a feminine counterpart, the Sande, from which men are as rigidly barred as women are from the Poro. Again, the Poro is, indeed, a men's tribal society, but it also contains a secret society in the narrower sense of the phrase. For the four years' course by no means teaches the novices the deeper mysteries to be known. These belong to the older members, who thus form a higher grade or, what comes to the same thing, a secret society within the Poro.

The Ona of Tierra del Fuego, too, illustrate typical features. They initiate only boys, whom they train ethically and vocationally, and by the most rigid discipline. The pupils fast, are permitted little sleep, must sit in uncomfortable positions, and remain silent when not spoken to. If disobedient, they are cuffed and vilified. The women are regaled with a version of the usual cock-and-bull story: spirits, mostly malevolent, have come demanding food, which the women are asked to supply. A small number of reputedly good actors impersonate these supernatural beings in masquerade costumes. Some of them terrorize the women, beating them and snatching away the skin coverings of their huts. In order to lend verisimilitude to their story the men go to great lengths, pretending that they, too, are being abused and causing their blood to flow by way of proof. At the close of the festival the women are told that the spirits have departed.[3]

## Secret Societies

Secret societies with a limited male membership evidently are akin in spirit to the masculine tribal society; instead of excluding only women and young boys, they also debar a portion, possibly most, of the male population. The older Poro members, we saw, are virtually a secret order within the tribal society. It is not, then, surprising that characteristic features are common to both the tribal and the secret sodality—initiation rites, masquerading antics to mystify the outsiders, sound signals to warn off possible intruders. More perplexing is the fact that widely separated peoples use the bull-roarer as the device for frightening and keeping away the uninitiated, Australians, Papuans, West African Negroes, and South Americans all believing that the female sex must not view or handle this sound-producing toy. The idea is, of course, quite fanciful, so that were the paths of diffusion easily imaginable no one would doubt that it had traveled from a single center. As it is, the problem remains unsolved.

One trait that many secret societies share with the tribal associations is their intransigent antifeminism. The Mumbo Jumbo society of West Africa has a mummer impersonating a forest spirit who chastises adulteresses. As soon as the women catch sight of this figure, they take to their heels and hide. Initiates must solemnly swear never to divulge the secret to a female. In Nigeria young maidens are known to have been killed for unwittingly trespassing on the grounds of a cult organization—no wonder that Mr. Basden's innocent impersonation of Santa Claus threw girls into a panic.

Nevertheless, it will not do to think of secret organizations solely from this point of view. In West Africa we find women's associations that are by no means only pale reflections of the men's. Of the Sande organization in Liberia we are told: "As the women must not see the Grand Master of the Poro, so the men must not cast a glance at the headwoman of the Sande or catch a glimpse of anything that occurs in the Sande, lest they expose themselves to the magic of the Sande. After dismissal from the school the women keep all knowledge of their order as secret from the men as vice versa." The Ekoi sorority has an even more potent defender in a female deity who in crocodile shape avenges her followers' grievances, seizing the offending husband of a suppliant wife. Naturally women cannot rely on physical force to protect themselves against men, but fall back on supernatural means.

Moreover, the rigorous sexual dichotomy insisted upon by Schurtz is far from universal. The Dyoro society of the Lobi, which exhibits many of the most characteristic traits of masculine secret organizations, hardly discriminates against females. The formal initiation involves segregation of the novices, who are frightened with tales of a beast that will devour them and whose voice is suggested with a bull-roarer. The pupils sleep on the bare ground, eat little and in uncomfortable postures, and receive new names. Returning from their retreat, they act as though newborn, hence wholly devoid of knowledge previously acquired, so that they utter only inarticulate noises and put food into their ears. But practically throughout the festival there is no separation of males and females. Even the bull-roarer may be looked at by both sexes, though only boys may handle and whirl it.

What happens occasionally in Africa is not at all unusual in America. In addition to a wholly masculine tribal society, the Pomo have a sodality that welcomes shamans of either sex. Winnebago women enter the sacrosanct Medicine society, enjoying most, though not quite all, of the privileges of membership. In the Tobacco society of the Crow, the sexes are on a complete basis of equality, women cooperating with their husbands and potentially filling the most important ceremonial offices. Pueblo women are associationally far less conspicuous than the men; nevertheless here, too, absolute cleavage is lacking. The Cochiti women should never know that the spirit-impersonating masqueraders are merely their tribesmen, but they freely enter any of the curing organizations. At near-by Santa Ana, women may even appear as mummers—probably, as White reasonably argues, because the masculine masqueraders' tribal society has been refashioned into a curing organization. In the western villages of the area the masqueraders may include a few laywomen, and one of the Zuñi clown groups has passive female members; women belonging to curing organizations occasionally doctor, and many of them are in "the nonmanagerial part" of various ceremonial bodies. The Hopi even have three women's societies. To be sure, male associates conduct their altar ritual; but the issue is not whether women play an equal role with men, but simply whether men and women can unite in sodalities.

Finally, the exclusion of women from a men's sodality is by no means necessarily a symptom of a profound, eternal, inescapable sex conflict, as Schurtz seems to think. One would hardly expect a woman in a fraternity of blacksmiths or hunters or war raiders, whether such groups practice secret rites or not. Even the deliberate exclusion of women from an association may go back to the widespread fear of menstrual pollution rather than to mutual antipathy.

The political aspects of secret and other associations are best dealt with jointly in connection with the development of the state.[4]

## Exclusive Clubs

Without necessarily laying claim to any secret knowledge, a men's tribal club readily passes into the more exclusive type of sodality foreshadowed among the Yurok. An obvious motive for organizing such a group is vanity, the urge to segregate oneself from the common herd. One means of gratifying this craving is wealth. In order to be clubbable, a tribesman must pay an entrance fee; or degrees are introduced with, as a rule, progressively higher entrance fees. The riffraff are thus shut out or limited to the lowest ranks of the order. Plutocratic snobbishness is marked in West Africa and Melanesia.

The Ibo men's club excludes slaves as well as women. It recognizes many grades, of which the lower ones are partly hereditary; the remainder require payments, all fees going to members of the grade. The lowest rank has for its badge a corded string for the waist and the ankles; usually boys enter at an early age, paying a fee of ten pounds. The entrance dues of the second grade amount to twenty pounds and entitle the novice to a new name. Most substantial citizens are content with the fourth stage, few even trying to advance further. Candidates for the fourth grade pay from fifty to ninety pounds and must appease any initially hostile member of the group. They acquire a nine-foot staff and a large ivory horn as symbols of their dignity and enjoy distinctive prerogatives, such as the use of a carved stool. Essentially the sixth grade, Awzaw, stands foremost; candidates pay at least a hundred and twenty pounds to get in, not counting incidental expenses for music and the sacrifice of a horse. No one may aspire to membership before his father's death. At this level there are great material benefits. The Awzaw are the real rulers of the people, gain a special honorific title, are immune from bodily assault and exempted from the duty of manual labor. In part of the area this grade is related to religious conceptions. The initiate has to observe food taboos; the senior member must be a priest; and sacrifices to the novice's ancestors are obligatory.

The club of the Banks Islanders, a similarly plutocratic affair, coexists with secret ghost organizations, which at a certain stage a native must have joined before advancing in the club. Nevertheless, the two types of sodality are essentially distinct. The secular association occupies a house that serves as dormitory, refectory, lounge, and workshop, but unlike the Chacobo equivalent it is not simply entered when a boy is considered old enough. Payments are prerequisite; accordingly, an infant may be initiated by aid of a rich relative, whereas a poor youth continues eating with the women until a compassionate kinsman rescues him from this ignominious plight. As among the Ibo, no one can rise without increasingly greater pecuniary outlay; hence the majority of these Melanesians, too, remain in the middle ranks. Each grade has its own fireplace in the club, and at a candidate's entrance there is a common ceremonial meal within the grade joined. Encroaching on a compartment superior to one's own was formerly punished with death. Again in harmony with Nigerian notions, the Banks Islanders confound the chief's status with that of a member of the highest grade.

Some primitive peoples stress other features than wealth and hence define clubbability in other terms. Each Plains Cree band had a single Warrior society which owned unique insignia, songs, and dance steps. Those among the unorganized younger braves who had distinguished themselves were sooner or later invited to join the Warriors. Though admission was expensive, the primary qualification was bravery, and it was through his war raids that a young man would normally procure the booty required for the initiation payments. Suggestively enough, the principle of admission was occasionally modified: a good hunter or one whose family distributed many gifts might enter without having scored in warfare. During the season that permitted large encampments the Warriors put up a special lodge in the center of the settlement, and there the members ate, slept, and danced. Their chosen headman directed dances, and the society policed the camp and guarded its line of march.

This is the simplest form of the system of military organizations typical of the North American Plains. Most tribes had not one military club, but a whole series, individual sodalities being related to one another according to different plans. Thus, all the Arapaho organizations were graded by age and all were under the general direction of the old men in the highest society. By way of contrast, the Crow counterparts were so many coordinate sodalities, so that it was possible for intense rivalry to develop between certain ones.

In this context it is worth casting a glance at the rise of clubs in Western civilization, which are nowhere so markedly developed as in Anglo-Saxon countries. Of course, they did not start by contraction of the whole male population of England, but as spontaneous assemblies "of good fellows, meeting under certain conditions," as Dr. Johnson put it. The late medieval rhymester and bohemian Thomas Hoccleve is credited with being the earliest ascertainable organizer of a club of this type in 1400. During Queen Elizabeth's reign Ben Jonson was conspicuous as a rallier of distinguished literary men at the Mermaid and the Apollo, the latter inn providing a separate room, or even floor, for the club.

The inn of the earlier period was eclipsed as a center for masculine reunions by the British coffeehouse, the first of which opened in Oxford in 1650, soon to be followed by an endless string in London. An entrance fee of a penny was to exclude the common herd. The frequenters indulged in literary or political conversation, soon adding dice and cards to their pastimes. In 1697, Bianco, an Italian who later anglicized his name, founded the chocolate house that subsequently blossomed into the famous White's Club. Having an eager patronage, he raised the admission to sixpence, permitted only the choicest tobacco for snuff, and reserved special quarters for favored guests. His widow provided the customers with English and Continental newspapers and further catered to polite society by procuring tickets for masquerade balls when these entertainments were particularly popular. By 1736 there was a strictly private club at White's, with a book of rules and a list of members that included several earls and a duke. Subsequently a rival club, Brooks's, sprang up directly across the street, one of the two organizations becoming a center for Tory, the other for Whig politicians.[5]

## Age Classes

BACHELORS AND SPINSTERS.—As explained, the bachelors and married men may be united in a common dormitory, or the youths' dormitory may continue to serve as a men's club, but this is emphatically not always the case. Often there is a sharp line of demarcation between unmarried and married males, militating against sexual solidarity.

Until a Sherente boy receives a certain kind of girdle he is free to stay in or away from the bachelors' hut; thereafter residence in it is obligatory until marriage. The division is deemed so important that a bachelors' dormitory is put up even in a temporary encampment. Normally it stands in the center of the village. Within it one tribal moiety claims the northern, the other the southern, half of the structure; and the space from west to east is divided among four economic associations (p. 308). A boy of the Sun moiety and the Krara association thus finds himself in the second section from the western door and on the north side of the dwelling. Female relatives bring food, but no wantons are allowed in the sleeping quarters and an unchaste boy is instantly expelled. For three or four years a youth stays in this dormitory, gradually passing through several age grades, each marked by a special emblem, until he has entered the sixth class at about twenty years of age, when he is allowed to marry.

In startling contrast to the puritanical Sherente, other tribes link bachelors' dormitories with ostentatious premarital license. Thus, in Chota Nagpur (India) the Oraon have separate boys' and girls' dormitories. A lad enters at eleven or twelve and passes through two grades of three years each, when he advances to the last, in which he remains until marriage at, say, twenty. The group is under a head boy and a sergeant-at-arms, who compels the inmates to take part in dances, punishing recalcitrant ones with a whip that forms his emblem of office. The novices receive instruction and perform magic in order to ensure success in the chase and in procreation. They go on hunting trips, by privilege appropriate certain fruits once a year, cook for the guests at a wedding feast, magically drive away cattle disease, and establish friendly relations with lads from other villages. The younger boys fag for their seniors, performing the necessary menial tasks, and fetch girls from the spinsters' hall with whom the boys of the two upper grades consort. "If a girl does not agree to have a mate from amongst the boys . . . , she is 'cut' by the older girls who refuse to dance with her or otherwise mix with her, until she agrees to do what she is told." The attachments formed tend to last for a considerable period, couples are acknowledged as lovers, and an interloper would be fined by the head boy. However, the companionship rarely leads to marriage.

In essentials this arrangement is duplicated in Luzon, except that children may sleep in the bachelor dormitory of their respective sex at a much earlier age, possibly at four. In the circumstances visits are often innocent enough, but there is also a good deal of sexual intercourse.

"Bachelors' hall," though a convenient blanket term, is evidently highly ambiguous. A boys' dormitory that is shared by the married men differs fundamentally from the type that sharply sets off bachelors from benedicts; and in turn a bachelors' club designed to prevent sex relations prior to marriage is the very opposite of an arrangement that fosters premarital cohabitation. Here is another example of the need for viewing any sociological phenomenon in its total setting.

On the other hand, parallels to some of the arrangements described appear among European peasants, single young people of both sexes forming definite complementary groups whose mutual relations recall Oraon conditions. Bulgarian maidens gather in sewing bevies, where they are visited by their swains, as graphically described in Ivan Vazoff's novel *Under the Yoke*. Spinning bees of the same order were in vogue in Sweden. What is far more significant, bachelors and spinsters of the Swedish peasant class were until recently organized as clear-cut age classes with characteristic patterns of mutual behavior. In Dalarna and other conservative provinces it was held indecent for the unmarried of opposite sex to be seen chatting together in the daytime, but by way of compensation nocturnal visits were an accepted feature of social life. Confirmation was regarded as a rite of initiation; accordingly the old stagers mercilessly mocked the youths during their period of instruction, haughtily calling them "the pastor's pigs." In one Dalecarlian village the newly confirmed had to attend a bachelors' meeting on pain of being fined for truancy, paying a "wooer's tax" for the status of "big lads," who were entitled to join in collective courting. Anyone who tried to do so before this formality was locked up in a pigsty. The group elected a grand master, who presided and received assessments, while some literate member served as secretary. The last session of the sort was held as late as 1899. The club had written statutes, which regulated the youths' behavior: they were prohibited from wantonly breaking windowpanes or stealing apples, and so forth.

The Swedish bachelors furthermore placed themselves in conscious opposititon to the older generation. As an organized group they would avenge an injury to one of their number by playing practical jokes even on affluent and prominent peasants. At weddings a ceremonial fight between bachelors and benedicts symbolized the antithesis of the two status groups.

In short, the bachelors in Swedish villages formed an age set conscious of its distinctness from, and in a sense opposition to, both younger and older males; and they played a recognized part with regard to a parallel group of maidens.[6]

AGE-CLASS SYSTEMS.—The existence of a bachelors' unit does not necessarily create a permanent bond, but often such a tie is established very early in life by a common rite or by joint segregation. To the instances previously cited may be added some characteristic examples.

The Habbé of Nigeria, like the Oraon, permit boys to leave their home before puberty and to live together outside the village. There girls visit them, in subsequent years becoming their sex partners. The boys choose badges and a divine patron, organize hunts and fishing trips, and establish affiliation with similar groups in neighboring villages. Those circumcised during a three- or four-year period form an age society. If one of its members wishes to marry, its chief acts as go-between. He also orders all associates to till the fields for the prospective parents-in-law and to build a hut for the groom and bride. Each sodality has passwords and at times fanciful rules; for example, a fine may be imposed on a mate who sits down or eats before being so ordered. When a member of the group travels, he is at once admitted to the local chapter. Altogether, fellowship in circumcision organizes a lifelong mutual aid society of coevals.

An arrangement of this sort frequently occurs in West Africa for both sexes. South Nigerian communities sometimes recognize as many as twelve and more classes, the first starting at about four years of age. They often serve distinct public functions, e.g., the fourth class must clean the town, the fifth remove trees, the sixth fight enemies, the seventh settle all serious questions. The plutocratic factor so strongly marked in the area sometimes invades the obviously more ancient age principle, enabling the rich to buy a place into one of the older groups for themselves or their children.

The Yakö offer special interest because they have both an informal sorting out of boys and girls, respectively, in sets of age grades and also a subsequent ceremonial acknowledgment of a new boy's set at four-year intervals. The new set comprises those youths who have married or become marriageable since the creation of its immediate predecessor. In each ward of a village there are from seventeen to eighteen masculine classes, ranging in age from seventeen to over seventy. For the girls there is no equivalent solemnity, though the sets are similarly formed. Particular groups of either sex may be called on to render public services. At weddings and funerals of members a small group of intimates within the age set play a prominent part.

As previously indicated, age classes are conspicuous in parts of Brazil. Among the Canella, an informal age grouping crystallizes through a ceremony—in this case by joint initiation—after which in former times the youths collectively married their fiancées. There is a definite organization with two official leaders, who conducted their class in the wars of the past and have the exclusive right to call the group together. There are no feminine equivalents, but every class has two girl associates. Each of the four youngest age classes occupies a distinctive site in the central village plaza. These classes build houses for villagers engaged in communal business, assist people in harvesting when requested by the tribal council, and organize innumerable races; they also figure prominently in Canella ceremonial, which is preponderantly secular. When the time for retirement arrives, members of an age class pass into the council, still preserving their group identity, and a junior class supersedes them in the plaza.[7]

## Economic Sodalities

The societies hitherto considered are not primarily concerned with practical issues, though these often enough intrude sooner or later. Sodalities run the gamut from a disinterested union of kindred souls or a glee club to so unsentimental and rationalistically oriented a thing as a stock company. We now turn to samples of the latter type, or rather approximating it through a primary, or at least ostensibly primary, concern with economic interests. Actually we soon discover that the primitive fusion so often encountered throughout human history crops up even there, being relegated to the background only in so aggressively tough-minded an era as the present.

EUROPEAN GUILDS.— The merchant guilds that sprang up in England soon after the Norman Conquest sought the monopoly of trade in everything but foodstuffs. The craft guilds about a century later began to gain corresponding privileges for artisans, so that a London weaver could not legally ply his craft until he had joined the appropriate "mistery." In 1474 the Southampton tailors petitioned their municipality to shut out competitors coming from other towns. The economic motive naturally communicated itself to English and Continental journeymen whose brotherhoods strove for higher pay, even by means of organized strikes.

But even within the framework of these medieval sodalities other aims intertwine with the economic. The French fraternities (*confréries*) sometimes paralleled the craft corporations, but often they professed religious and charitable ends, celebrating holy services, aiding masters who were financially embarrassed, and attending to the funerals of the membership. Indeed, the avowed object of English journeymen's unions during the fourteenth and fifteenth centuries was to make sacred offerings for deceased brethren and sisters or some similar pious task. To be sure, the masters denounced these professions as merely a transparent mask for selfish aims, which in many cases probably enough they were. Nevertheless, in the late Middle Ages the masters' corporations themselves concentrated on spiritual benefits, notably by providing services for deceased members. As Ashley explains, burghers not wealthy enough individually to endow "chantries," i.e., masses for their souls, would do so cooperatively. It also happened that a rich citizen founded a chantry and left its care to his guild, thus allowing all to share in his spiritual gains. In this fashion, then, guilds and religious brotherhoods came to be closely connected, at times even indistinguishable, even though the earlier craft organizations had been preponderantly secular.

SAMOAN GUILDS.—The mingling of practical and ideological aims is, of course, to be expected among aborigines. Superficially, the Samoan guild of canoe- and housebuilders resembles a modern trade union. But it is far more than that. Supposedly founded by the god Tangaloa, the society, Sa Tangaloa, claims high social status and maintains its prerogatives with the jealousy of a prima donna. A Samoan chief being in no sense politically dominant, the builders, who consider themselves his peers in rank, are able to defy him. If he proves niggardly in his food offerings or other payments, they strike in the midst of a job, and since all the chapters of the guild are connected, the employer is left in the lurch, unable to get the house or the canoe completed until he appeases the offended workers. Even without taking this step, canoebuilders would vent their spleen in revenge for an imagined slight by casting a spell on the boat to make it unlucky.

In 1927 Dr. Buck happened to attend an incipient strike. At a village feast connected with one stage of housebuilding a deadly affront had been offered to the guild—one of the fowls presented to the workmen had not been cropped. "The prestige of the Sa Tangaloa was at stake." "They were the descendants of gods, the companions of kings ...." An old builder declared that in the good old days his guild would have departed at once. "His voice quavered with emotion." The chief's spokesman apologetically explained that the insult was wholly accidental. The representative of the guild superciliously replied that "such things were not done"; in view of the assurances made, his associates would generously overlook the incident, but if anything like it should occur again "they would not be so lenient." In expiation the villagers offered a fine mat, which the builders accepted, and all was well.

SHERENTE SODALITIES.—In Brazil apparently economic sodalities combine a variety of other activities. Four Sherente associations are in part strictly utilitarian. They engage in collective hunts, the kill being distributed among the members; make clearings for each household of the membership in turn; and aid in harvesting. Each society owns clumps of the two species of palm most useful for their edible fruits and basketry materials; in the old days encroachment on these property rights would have provoked a fight. But other than economic activities appear. In warfare the associations form the tactical units. Further, each arranges races between some of its members against the rest. Oddly enough, each owns a set of feminine names, which are formally conferred on the girls. Finally, when an eminent man dies, his fellow members direct a commemorative ceremony. Thus, an association is at once economic, military, sportive, social, and religious in nature.

A DAKOTA WOMEN'S GUILD.—The religious element astonishes us by cropping up frequently in unexpected situations. Expert Oglala Dakota quill embroiderers have a sort of sorority, meeting for an exhibit of their handicraft, enjoying a feast, and exchanging gifts. But this is not quite like a garment workers' five o'clock tea. The society, it is said, was founded by the supernatural Double-Woman, who first revealed how porcupine quills could be worked.[8]

## General Considerations

Sodalities vary so greatly in their positive traits that no single formula can do justice to all the relevant phenomena. The concept is of some utility in bringing home the fact that individuals associate irrespective of whether they belong to the same family, clan, or territorial group; and that such associations play a dominant part in the social life of many peoples, rivaling and sporadically even overshadowing other ties. To have first emphasized this neglected fact is the lasting merit of Schurtz (1902) and of Hutton Webster (1908). At the time of their publications, unilinear schemes of evolution were still in vogue, and they could not escape the influence of this intellectual current. From this point of view, Wilhelm Schmidt's theories (1924) are preferable, for they assume a multiple development.[9]

HISTORICAL SCHEMES.—In fairness we must admit that Schurtz and Webster recognize the restricted distribution of phenomena which on their general principles should be universal. Webster may speak of "secret societies which have everywhere arisen on the basis of the puberty institutions," but presently he cites the Maori as having neither such organization nor puberty rites for the common herd. Schurtz takes pains to point out that closely related and neighboring groups often develop along quite different lines; that "at present the men's house in typical form appears essentially within the Malay race and its relatives"; that on higher levels masculine gregariousness may *independently* create phenomena similar to those found among savages and accordingly not to be conceived as survivals of ancient forms; that secret societies need not be *directly* linked with age classes and their offshoots. Yet both authors, retaining faith in their evolutionistic formulae, do not interpret concrete cases in the light of their specific context, but distort them into line with their respective schemes. Likewise the force of an admission is soon nullified by an antithetical proposition, even when not technically contradictory. Only a few pages after Schurtz has conceded that modern secret societies need not be *immediately* connected with earlier ones, he writes: "With slight reservations we may say that every contemporary secret organization can be traced back to forms that have developed in the transformation of age-classes into secret associations."

Let us consider the two evolutionary schemes. According to Schurtz, the masculine urge to congregate with congenial spirits produced in the first place three age classes of boys, bachelors, and married men. Outstanding among the classes was the bachelors' group, which came to segregate itself in a special house. At this point several distinct "short evolutionary lines" are suggested. A common development is toward a bachelors' *and* married men's house, yielding a sodality of all adult males. If favored classes of the community bar slaves and humbler tribesmen, an exclusive club results; and that in turn *may* under favorable circumstances grow into a secret organization.

Webster operates largely with the same two factors—sexual solidarity and age grouping. However, he reverses the position of the secret society and the social club, regarding the latter (as well as the magical fraternity) as a degenerated secret society. The secret society has as its forerunner the whole company of initiated males, from which it evolves by an undemocratic sifting of the original membership.

Both systems concentrated attention on a few broad principles that helped envisage the jumble of raw ethnographic data. On the other hand, they apparently felt that a neat scheme absolved them from studying concrete phenomena in terms of their setting. When Schurtz read about Plains Indian military age societies, they at once fell into the preconceived groove for age classes, which according to his system come earliest. Yet, he discovered, they were not *pure* age classes since payments are required for admission. Well then, they must have been in a state of transition toward exclusive clubs and secret societies. It does not occur to him that the age classification observed here might have been introduced later. Obviously he cannot be blamed for ignoring what was not known when he wrote; but actually it turned out that military sodalities had been arranged according to two main plans. Either they were more or less coordinate or they were graded by age. Now, it was precisely the age societies that demanded payments, and the ungraded ones that dispensed with them, which is contrary to the system and indicates the danger of schematism.

Again, it is obvious to Schurtz that a large number of age divisions must be merely a refinement of the simpler grouping into boys, bachelors, and married men. We shall see that this does not follow and that a series of many age classes may readily arise in other ways (p. 314 f.).

Webster, confronting the same data in the light of *his* formula, regards the military societies as decadent masculine tribal societies: by dropping all secrecy they assumed their observed character. But it is a gratuitous assumption that all North American tribes, let alone all primitive peoples of the world, once had tribal societies initiating all males.

Schmidt, in turn, errs in not consistently adhering to the principle of multiple evolution, that is, of strict historical method. He assumes a limited number of independent complexes which have severally traveled over much of the globe and sometimes, at later periods, influenced one another. For present purposes only two of the basic complexes require discussion. According to Schmidt, one basic combination is that of patrilineal totemism with boys' initiations, whence age classes and bachelors' halls. Another complex includes secret societies, though not in its earlier stages. Schmidt conceives the following sequence. By inventing agriculture, women became economically dominant and inaugurated not merely matriliny but a matriarchate. They minimized or abolished boys' initiations in favor of girls' puberty rites and lorded it over men, both in the household and in public life. Ultimately, however, the worm turned: men clandestinely organized secret societies and by a revolution turned the tables on womankind.

Something of the sort had, indeed, been adumbrated by Schurtz in passing. He, too, envisages economic motives. Hunting as a masculine monopoly ensures masculine ascendancy, he argues. As it recedes and farming turns into the basis of existence, men become dependent on women, a relationship men try consciously to temper, partly by emphasizing military activity, partly by "the secret societies with their mystical, apparently irresistible power." However, it is Schmidt who has fully elaborated this idea.

For an evaluation of the method it suffices to consider how Schmidt interprets admittedly negative instances. Why, for example, are men's houses so rare in North America, where patrilineal totemic groups are common enough? The answer is that "they have been superseded by clubhouses of the secret and dancing societies." Obviously this is an auxiliary hypothesis advanced to justify the scheme, not a conclusion based on direct evidence. Again, Schmidt with laudable candor admits that

North American secret societies seldom intimidate women; "on the contrary, not infrequently there is organic collaboration of men and women." By way of explanation he suggests (a) that this may be a survival from the totemic period; (b) that the matriarchate was strong enough to inhibit exclusively masculine secret societies. Objections spontaneously suggest themselves. Why did not the matriarchate of other areas exercise a similar effect? Where in North America is there evidence of a true matriarchate? What is there in the patrilineal totemic complex as conceived by Schmidt that would favor the observed cooperation of the sexes? If, as he puts it elsewhere, the rise of age classes weakened the importance of the family and of women, why should the sexes collaborate more or less as equals because of an aftereffect of patrilineal attitudes? Finally, as with Schurtz and Webster, the discussion of Plains Indian military clubs reveals the dangers of schematism. The age societies of the region are supposed to be age classes transformed into social clubs by the impact of secret societies upon age classes. The fraternities of the Pueblos are interpreted along similar lines, i.e., by the mixture of patrilineal puberty rituals with matrilineal secret societies.

Evidently auxiliary assumptions of this sort could be used to prop up *any* a priori scheme; they cannot be accepted as demonstrations of its validity. Schmidt soundly rejects unilinear evolution, but the course of history is too involved to warrant generalizing methods for reconstructing it. We shall not determine it except with the aid of intensive regional comparisons and of documented historical facts. These will yield conclusions on a sounder foundation and not without theoretical import.[10]

HISTORY.—Whenever there is adequate information, there is evidence of a remarkable fluidity in the character of sodalities, a fact properly stressed by Schurtz himself. Some relevant facts may be added to those which have already been cited.

Continental masonic lodges are traceable to the British order consolidated in 1717, but regionally they were in time radically altered. For example, the profession of a supernatural love of humanity strongly appealed to the Germans of the classical period, so that Lessing, Herder, and Goethe joined the ranks. Yet as early as 1778 and 1780 Lessing published dialogues on freemasonry in which the lofty ideals of the brotherhood are sharply contrasted with the snobbishness and flummery that had invaded German lodges. Again, originally atheists were excluded and the society abstained on principle from political strife. In Anglo-Saxon and northern countries these policies remained in force, so that

Protestant royalty did not scruple to enter the association. In Southern Europe and Latin America an entirely different development occurred. In 1877 the French offshoot known as the "Grand Orient" removed belief in God as a qualification for membership, and henceforth masonry in states of Romance speech has been identified, at least by outsiders, with infidelity and leftist trends. The Habsburgs prohibited it in Austria, and Mussolini in Italy—a fact difficult for an American to grasp.

A different type of political function can be shown to become linked with craft guilds. Under Turkish domination the Bulgarian associations of that category were the only ones tolerated by the government, which found them indispensable as purveyors to the Sultan's court and army. As a consequence, these guilds assumed tasks that had nothing to do with their craft but which the state ignored. They maintained the highways, arranged for what schooling was feasible, and crystallized Bulgarian national sentiment against the influence of Greek priests. Similarly, under the empire, the Chinese merchant and craft guilds not only regulated business and exercised jurisdiction over their members, but also kept streets and drains in order, organized fire brigades, and attended to poor relief. Bulgarian and Chinese conditions evidently favored an extension of sodality functions in similar directions.

Private societies, then, ostensibly serving industrial purposes, may come to envisage public needs. The guilds of Western and Central Europe exemplify other transformations as well. In about 1400 "the Fraternity of Taylors of Bristowe of the Gild of S. John the Baptist" was converted from a religious brotherhood into an industrial craft union, though retaining its religious features. But though "primitive fusion" was common enough, it would not be correct to derive all rationalistically oriented craft organizations from pious motives: we must also reckon with "craft associations which had not grown out of religious fraternities."

The historical fact that sodalities need not traverse identical stages even within a single culture area has important applications for aboriginal data. Without specific indications to that effect, we are not warranted in assuming that a secular club is a decadent form of a mystic cult society, as Webster assumes. Certainly there is no reason to deny that such changes have sometimes taken place, but it is wholly possible that (a) secular societies may *subsequently* assume a religious flavor; (b) they remain what they have always been.

To make the matter more concrete, disguises are used in various parts of Melanesia, Africa, and America to awe the uninitiated. But among the Canella the Mummers form no tribal or secret society; they are simply one of several secular men's associations, to whose general pattern they conform. Thus, they have one leader and two girl associates, and transfer of membership is matrilineal. The costumes "are wholly secular, completely lacking religious or esoteric significance"; they "are not taboo to anyone and inspire no fear, least of all in the tribeswomen, two of whom themselves wear them . . . . Masquerading is a jollification for the villagers, nothing more." Conceivably the Canella at some time picked up the practice from a tribe that attached a more serious meaning to it, but that is an idle conjecture. We know that White's Club in London grew out of the meetings at a chocolate house, not out of an esoteric brotherhood. Why not credit primitive peoples, too, with so simple an urge as that for entertainment and company?

Age grouping, also, is quite another matter when viewed historically, i.e., with reference to its setting, and when interpreted by a preconceived scheme. Schurtz deserves the greatest credit for recognizing age as a basis for social divisions, but he was under the sway of the idea that "the widespread system of three age-classes" was preponderant. That is to say, the male population is basically divided into boys, bachelors, and married men, the females into corresponding groups. Finding ten masculine societies among the Hidatsa, Schurtz leaps to the conclusion that "obviously the intercalation of new dance societies, noticeable as incipient among the Mandan, has greatly increased the number of groups." It is, indeed, quite true that the Indians of the northern Plains repeatedly enlarged their system of associations by buying or imitating the ceremonial complexes of neighboring tribes. A society already owning one set of regalia and dance appurtenances might purchase an additional one and later sell either set separately to a younger group that had none, thus establishing a new company defined in terms of its ceremonial privileges. But no evidence exists that the tribes in question were ever split up into Schurtz's three hypothetical grades. The Masai, the Yakö, the Canella are all divided into many age classes without a sign that these blossomed out of an original trinity.

To be sure, the Masai have three status grades that correspond to Schurtz's scheme, but of these only the circumcised bachelors form a positive social unit; the "boys" are simply those not yet circumcised, the "elders" those who have passed out of the single warriors' dormitory.

The latter can no more be considered an association than can the sum total of American citizens who have graduated from grammar school. A social bond unites only those who have been circumcised during successive four-year periods. Fellow initiates are lifelong members of a sodality, sharing a class name and pledged to entertain one another on visits. Thus, there is at any one time an indefinite number of age classes, limited only by Masai longevity, which might make it eight or ten. The collective entrance into a certain status by successive groups of approximate age mates is the crucial factor.

The Canella phenomena are especially illuminating. Like Yakö children, juvenile playmates unite in spontaneous groups "long before the formal recognition of a set and a man's age set membership has in fact been already established in childhood." Beginning possibly at six years of age, Canella boys pattern themselves on the youngest of the four officially recognized, athletically active age classes with meeting places in the plaza. When the youngsters enter the scene as an acknowledged class, the oldest of the four groups leaves to enter the council, so that there are always four in the large central circle.

It might seem that we have here a threefold division of the male population—uninitiated boys; an intermediate stratum embracing the four sports clubs; and the council of elders. But this consonance with Schurtz's scheme is only apparent. The councilors are married, but so are the majority of the athletes, seeing that they take wives immediately after their initiation is completed. The eastern pairs of plaza classes are pitted against the western in races, but in no sense is the quartette an association with a sense of solidarity. It is the companies of little boys who first assembled in mimicry of their seniors that persist as true sodalities. They are coevals because juvenile playmates are bound to be such, more or less; and because they continue to stick together as they advance in status, a fairly large number of rough age classes results *without* previous trisection of the male population.

Oddly enough, a threefold age division crops up in the Plains area only in an inconspicuous and insignificant fashion. The three feasting societies of the Omaha (p. 294) play so minor a part in the people's life that one of the two large monographs on this tribe fails to note them at all. Among the Crow the Fox society recognized a subdivision of mature men, an intermediate, and a young group; but there was no *tribal* age classification.

What such observations suggest is that age is indeed a genuine factor for social grouping, but that it may arise at any stage, need not affect more than a portion of the people in question, and may lack deeper significance.[11]

SODALITIES AND SOCIAL LIFE.—The immense advance due to Schurtz is at once apparent when we consider how different social life would become if we eliminated sodalities. Blot out church organizations, the Y.M.C.A. and the Y.W.C.A., bridge clubs, literary and scientific societies, Rotary lunches, Masonic lodges and Elks, trade unions, corporations, Daughters of the Revolution, Democratic and Republican party organizations, and the scene certainly alters very radically. We can also approach the matter differently by comparing primitive tribes poor and rich in sodalities. How narrowly circumscribed are the social relations of a Ute or Paiute, whose sodalities are minimal or lacking, when placed alongside such a people as the Ibo. A Paiute has duties toward his kindred and claims upon them, he has somewhat more tenuous bonds with nonrelated coresidents, but that exhausts the roster of his possible social relations. The Ibo individual has potentially many additional ones. A freeman is almost certain to belong to at least one of the lower clubs; and though his wife may not join him there, she shines in reflected glory as he advances to the middle or to the highest of the series. Apart from such secular activity a man may enter the secret Ghost society. A woman may belong to the women's committee for her village, to all intents and purposes a club that regulates feminine affairs, including everything pertaining to the markets, and that is consulted by the chiefs whenever matters affecting both sexes are at issue.

The broadest function of sodalities was clearly grasped by Schurtz. By making cooperation a reality beyond the narrow confines of the blood tie they pave the way, in principle at least, for a wider integration, whether in the form of a state or of a supernational religion.[12]

# Chapter 14

# THE STATE

J URISTS, historians, political scientists, and philosophers have all debated the nature of the state, often with widely divergent conclusions. We conceive it as the association corresponding to law, both sharing as their diagnostic feature the monopoly of legitimate physical force, i.e., of force which the community concerned recognizes as properly exercised. An Eskimo group in which a bully can wrest away from a fellow resident any possession he craves, maiming him with impunity (p. 161), has neither law nor statehood because the exhibition of force, though accepted unresistingly, is not acknowledged as proper. On the contrary, when the king of Uganda orders a chief to be executed at his pleasure, this is wholly "constitutional," hence a sign of how the people define acceptable coercion. The state, then, embraces the inhabitants of a definite area who acknowledge the legitimacy of force when applied by the individuals whom they accept as rulers or governors. This statement does not prejudge the question whether coercive authority is concentrated in one or more agencies.

For purpose of exposition, juridical matters have been discussed under the head of Law. Other questions could not be satisfactorily treated before such topics as sodalities. In the present chapter we shall deal with the territorial tie, separatism and expansion, the relation of sodalities with statehood, and a number of correlated problems.

## *The Territorial Tie*

In his epoch-making book on *Ancient Law* (1861) Maine contended that in early societies kinship was "the sole possible ground of community in political functions," whereas "the idea that a number of persons should exercise political rights in common simply because they happen to live within the same topographical limits was utterly strange and monstrous to primitive antiquity." In this form the proposition is antiquated. It exaggerates the correct view that kinship has played an enormous part in the social life of aboriginal and archaic peoples. That the territorial tie is never wholly negligible is proved a fortiori by two extreme instances of kinship-dominated tribes, the Ifugao and the Yurok.

In his earlier work on the Ifugao, our principal authority, Dr. Barton, represented their legal and political life as resting solely on consanguinity. Yet on his own evidence coresidents and Ifugao strangers were not treated alike in native law. A thief, for instance, from the same village was merely fined, whereas an outsider would be killed. A later publication reveals other discriminations in favor of contiguous groups. An Ifugao fights people from neighboring districts, but he will not take their heads. Barton now explicitly states that the local unit, though vague in aboriginal consciousness, is "extremely important"; indeed, in exceptional conditions it even overshadows kinship solidarity. To take an actual case, during a period of interregional strife a man who was smarting under ridicule for his lack of prowess deliberately killed a first cousin from the hostile district.

The Yurok, too, once seemed without a "definite community sense within a village," though admittedly "town mates, impelled by bonds of association or imperiled by their common residence, would sometimes unite with the group of individuals with whom the feud originated." Further inquiry had led to an explicit revision of earlier impressions: "The bonds of co-residence were evidently fairly strong, though they did not transcend those of kinship."

Both tribes share a suggestive feature—an informally sanctioned go-between who adjusts difficulties within the settlement. In other words, neutral neighbors are concerned about disputes between persons not necessarily related by blood either to each other or to the rest of the community. Since the intermediary lacks coercive authority, he certainly does not represent a "state," but the societies employing him must be credited with one criterion of the state, viz., a measure of territorial solidarity.[1]

## Separatism and Expansion

Separatism is the political counterpart of campanilismo. It denotes similar resistance to wider integration, but in the sphere of organization rather than of feeling. That campanilismo tends to prevent the political collaboration of persons who view one another with suspicion is obvious. Accordingly, any number of groups closely akin in race, speech, and custom have persistently recoiled from uniting except at most in loose alliances for temporary ends.

The Maidu, for example, numbered about four thousand in pre-European times, but each village was independent of every other. In at least one section of their area the tracts belonging to a settlement were marked off by boundary lines, which were patrolled by sentries to guard against trespass. The system resembled that reported in the seventeenth century for the Vedda of Ceylon, where encroachment on a neighboring group's territory led to fighting.

However, extreme separatism may imply not so much hostility as an incapacity for integration. The Semang, though averse to warfare, have no national sentiment. Their total population of about two thousand is split up into half a dozen dialectic groups ranging from one hundred to eight hundred individuals; yet the local group that corresponds closely to a political unit is much smaller. A typical encampment visited by Schebesta comprised fifty-four persons in seventeen dwellings. Even so minute an aggregation may include more than one lineage, sometimes even members of distinct dialectic units. However, though tolerated, the strangers remain a distinct body, spatially segregated from the majority.

It is natural, but not justified, to correlate separatism with general backwardness. To be sure, for major integration technological advancement is prerequisite. Without an adequate system of communication the Roman Empire is unthinkable. The Inca realm, "the largest area ever united under one government in aboriginal America," extended from Ecuador to northernmost Chile and was inhabited by possibly six million people. As an indispensable condition for administering so vast a territory there were roads—two longitudinal arteries with transverse connecting roads; suspension bridges crossing wide rivers; and a postal service by means of runners, who carried government messages from and to Cuzco, the capital. However, the reverse proposition would manifestly be incorrect. Advanced knowledge and economy are not enough to weld millions of people into a nation. The star example is ancient Greece, split into a hundred dwarf states, which neither Athens nor Sparta was ever able to make into a Hellenic commonwealth. Separatism proved too strong. "Thus, at the very time when Greek culture had attained its peak and grown ripe for a prospective world culture," writes Meyer, "the Greek nation was condemned to utter impotence."

Campanilismo can be overcome by special conditions, say a propagandist faith, religious or patriotic. But a sizable state presupposes more than community of feeling. In most cases it has been created by conquest. Macedonia, ancient Rome, modern Prussia are stock illustrations. Growth of the United States has been in part peaceable, but over 900,000 square miles came to us through the Mexican War. Recent colonial empires have as a rule arisen from the subjection of native peoples.

To turn to aboriginal states, the Peruvian Empire was not a league of Quechua, Aimará, and other Andean Indians; the lords of Cuzco had successively invaded and incorporated into their dominion one alien group after another. As for the much-vaunted Aztec Confederacy, it never even remotely approached the Andean achievement. The three towns of Texcoco, Tenochtitlan, and Tacuba did combine for the temporary despoilment of common enemies, but without permanent merging of interests. For many years two towns, both within the present city limits of Mexico, remained entirely independent of each other; and during the Spanish siege in 1520 the Texcocans helped the Spaniards against their "ally," Tenochtitlan. North of the Rio Grande the Creek and the Iroquois Confederacy are interesting enough as nascent efforts beyond the usual aboriginal separatism, but they hardly loom large in global perspective. When De Soto, in 1539, entered what are now our southeastern states, the Creek confederacy may not have been in existence, and it certainly grew very considerably after white contact. Centralization of power was not accomplished until the rise of the mixed-breed, Alexander McGillivray, in the last quarter of the eigtheenth century, and after his death in 1793 "no man appeared of sufficient force and tact to take his place and the government seems to have slipped back, at least in part, into the ancient channels." In any case the population involved was large only in comparison with the average Indian tribe: it was of the order of 15,000 to 20,000. Similarly, the Iroquois League requires deflation. Morgan dubiously sets the maximum population of the federated tribes at 20,000, "if they ever reached that number"; Hewitt's figure is 16,000. After getting firearms they certainly raided far and wide, from New York southward to Tennessee and South Carolina, westward nearly to the Mississippi. But we can hardly accept Hewitt's statement that "their dominion was acknowledged from Ottawa river to the Tennessee and from the Kennebec to Illinois river and Lake Michigan." According to Fenton's convincing conclusion, there was never anything like an "Iroquois empire," and the united tribes never "effectively controlled the enormous territory that they claimed to have subjugated." How loose was the union even within the league appeared at the beginning of the American Revolution, when each member was allowed freedom of action. "All the tribes, with the exception of the Oneida and about half of the Tuscarora, joined the English."

Other continents exhibit similar phenomena. Oceania is markedly separatistic, notwithstanding much warfare and a mental set that elsewhere has fostered powerful monarchies. Even in New Zealand, where nature offers two large land masses with a population possibly far beyond Captain Cook's estimate of 100,000, the political unit did not exceed several thousand.

Negro Africa is commonly credited with large states having a central government. Rulers over a hundred thousand people are not rare, and several kingdoms, such as Uganda, had a population of over a million. Though the course of development in many cases is unknown or merely legendary, what we do know supports the view that large countries originated in conquest, as holds typically for Ruanda and for several other East African areas where immigrant pastoralists subjected the indigenous farmers. Dahomey was founded by conquest in 1625. In the early part of the nineteenth century, Shaka, overthrowing one people after another in Southeastern Africa, made a petty tribelet, the Zulu, into a powerful nation.

Compared with either Oceania or America, Africa does stand out for the number of its large states. But a word of caution is necessary. If instead of trying to set Africa off from other ethnographic areas we study Negro political life by itself, a rather different picture emerges, even for the very region conspicuous for its great autocracies, West Africa. In 1931 the Lobi on French soil numbered 69,484, but politically every aggregation of a few houses is distinct, and their inmates regard with hostile eyes similar hamlets on the opposite side of the valley. Of a hundred of these autonomous "villages," only 3 had over 500 inhabitants; 55 had fewer than 125; 4 less than 25. Even after the establishment of French administration each local group jealously guarded the territory it claimed for exploitation and fought encroaching fellow Lobi. "The altruism of these populations is limited to a small group of kinsfolk and neighbors."

Extreme though it may be, the Lobi instance is not unique in West Africa. The 10,000 Talis are divided into some 25 composite clans, each of which is the largest local group "capable of exhibiting social cohesion." On the coast, each of the 6 Gã towns is an independent republic. In the wooded regions east of the Niger there are many small and mutually independent groups. Parallels crop up in the east. The 200,000 speakers of the Nuer language are politically divided, the largest unit within which disputes are settled by arbitration ranging anywhere from a few hundred to 45,000, with the mode somewhat over 5,000. Among the western Anuak, a village of from 50 to 1,500 residents forms the governmental unit.

This is not to deny that large-scale amalgamation can occur without conquest; but that is obviously not a common process. Separatism, indeed, is so strong that it reasserts itself even after being overcome. The Mongol empire created in the early thirteenth century collapsed in 1368, and even before that date outlying portions of the realm had turned into virtually independent states. The same holds for the provinces of China during much of her history. Within modern imperial Germany, Bavaria remained a hotbed of particularism; and the British dominions are autonomous to such a degree that South Africa came perilously close to withholding support to the mother country during World War II.

But though conquest is the readiest means of expansion, it is not at all an obvious idea. We have seen that Yurok feuds do not lead to the defeated party's subjugation; as a matter of fact, the principle that every injury should be paid for makes the victor economically the loser (p. 31). To an Australian a given tract seems so intimately tied up with a horde that he does not dream of dispossessing a worsted group. Some of the most warlike peoples in the world have shown no talent for systematically expanding their territories and consolidating their gains.

Separatism, then, is even harder to overcome than campanilismo. Campanilismo blocks peaceable expansion, and subjection of an enemy, which seems so easy a way toward political aggrandizement, is foreign to the folkways of many peoples. What is more, except in highly favorable circumstances, the centrifugal trend is so strong that it can nullify a consolidation once achieved. Skillful political leadership seems a condition antecedent to that accomplishment.[2]

## Chiefless Societies

Though minute communities are at times controlled by the iron will of a recognized leader, they are often without a headman or have only a titular one lacking authority. The Eskimo and the Chukchi, the Paiute and the Yurok, the Fuegians and the Ifugao have no chiefs, though as everywhere in the world a strong personality can make its influence felt.

A large Shoshonean village was likely to have at its head a man of experience who directed pine-nutting trips for those "who cared to cooperate. His authority, however, was not absolute. Any family was at liberty to pursue an independent course at any time." Even such leadership as existed was dispersed and ephemeral: special economic tasks that called for joint effort were supervised by the men best qualified. This held particularly for communal rabbit hunting. The leader of an antelope drive, however, gained his temporary status by a vision. A village headman might combine several functions of this type, but they ceased with the activity in question.

The economic motive is also prominent among the reindeer-breeding Lapps. Each *sit* (p. 28) has a leader, who serves without emoluments. He is not formally chosen, but emerges naturally by virtue of his competence, and his term of office lasts as long as his acknowledged superiority. Enjoying a good deal of informal authority, this headman adjusts quarrels, arranges for the tending of the herd, and allots tasks to the fellow members of his group. But he in turn is guided by their advice, and anyone is free to dissociate himself from the *sit*. However, a seceder is likely to be cross-questioned when he applies for admission to another *sit* and may be rejected if his reasons for shifting his allegiance prove unsatisfactory.

In the simple societies just passed in review such leadership as exists is closely correlated with the mode of life. Seasonal activities (p. 23) bring with them calendric differences in social arrangements. Where the unit shrank to the proportions of a household or two for a part of the year, formal direction became for that period superfluous. On the other hand, when special circumstances demand it, even the Fuegians can rise to the occasion. At an Ona initiation festival, with two hundred or more participants and spectators, there develops temporary coercive authority. The father of the oldest novice assumes the direction of the proceedings and has the right to deputize others. More significantly, the entire body of initiated men—the men's tribal sodality—is in complete control. They bully and haze the candidates, send them on strenuous errands or exhausting marches, and punish the unruly with blows and abuse. The women must bring meat for the initiates and are intimidated in various ways. Tall masqueraders appear in their midst, beat them, and draw away the leather coverings of their huts. In short, for the time being, the men's tribal club exercises a monopoly of constraint upon the rest of the community, which submits to its dictation.

To sum up, many of the simpler peoples are without statehood, at least for a large part of the year; headmen are generally without coercive powers; on the other hand, nonce authority can develop with need even where normally wanting and may then be vested in persons other than "chiefs," such as the members of the Ona sodality.[3]

## Sodalities and the State

Implicitly Schurtz's theory of men's societies is also a theory of the origin of the state. If the men of a community unite irrespective of blood relationship, their company represents the fighting part of the total population, which at a pinch can physically control the community and defend it against outsiders. Sodalities thus appear as a step toward territorial or political unification.

However, there are sodalities and sodalities. The Dakota quill-embroiderers' guild is certainly not fit to found a state, nor are many masculine societies. If a handful of Omaha Indians who have seen visions of buffalo spirits cure a patient and perform a dance, these activities neither consolidate the tribe nor evince any compulsive powers.

Exclusively male associations do not by any means necessarily align all men in a single company. There are often series of mutually independent sodalities, whose rivalry militates against local unification. Thus, the Fox and the Lumpwood societies among the Crow stole each other's wives in the spring and constantly tried to outdo each other in warlike deeds. About 1820 similar competition between the Dogs and the Foxes very nearly precipitated a feud. Such activities need not, of course, end in an open schism, but they are potentially disruptive—hostile to a centralization of authority where the sodalities under discussion are the most prominent executive arm of the state.

Here, again, discrimination is required. Dual or multiple sodalities may coexist without strife, especially if there is some coordinating agency. The Arapaho, like the Crow, had military societies, but theirs formed one graded whole headed by the seven old men at the top who "embodied everything that was most sacred in Arapaho life." In these circumstances a flare-up between any two organizations could hardly develop into a serious conflict.

"The monopoly of legitimate force" does not necessarily imply that all such force must be concentrated in a single individual or group for *all* purposes. As the church renders to Caesar the things that are Caesar's, so a people may well recognize the supremacy of diverse agencies each in its own sphere. In the United States the President and the Supreme Court have separate functions, and the several states retain definite sovereign rights, though not the right of independently waging war or coining money. It is only a totalitarian government, such as Nazi Germany's, that insists on controlling all of the social life of a people from a single center.

MILITARY SOCIETIES.—Relevant facts are graphically illustrated by the Cheyenne. These Plains Indians are ostensibly governed by a self-perpetuating Council of Forty-Four, headed by five priests, with two tilers below them, and the other thirty-seven undifferentiated in status. Among the priests, one, representing the culture hero, stands foremost as the holiest tribesman, yet without distinctive political power. Every ten years there is a turnover of this council, but during his term of office a member is unimpeachable. On the other hand, this does not place him above the law. When in 1879 or 1880 the head priest, Little Wolf, a leader of the greatest distinction, shot Starving Elk, he retained his rank, but went into exile like any ordinary murderer and remained "a man apart" even after his return to camp. Another councilor was severely flogged for a criminal assault. The qualities regarded as essential for the office are revealing: equanimity and generosity. A councilor ought never to get angry, even under the greatest personal provocation; and he gained honor in proportion to the gifts he presented to needy tribesmen.

All this, so far, suggests nothing of coercive authority. The councilors—we had best avoid calling them chiefs—are mature, wise, benevolent men who enjoy the esteem of their people but do not seem to rule. Nevertheless their functions are not altogether unrelated to the management of a state. For when the bands reunite after their dispersal in the wintertime there are two occasions, camp-moving and the tribal hunt, when the council appoints officials who exercise unmistakably coercive authority, viz., one of the six military societies. The Dogs or Foxes or some other sodality police the march and the chase, not sparing physical force if required to restrain or punish a recalcitrant culprit. Theoretically they even have the right to kill him, but this hardly occurred since the Cheyenne, unlike other Plains tribes, considered homicide within the tribe not merely a crime but also a sin that demanded a rite of purification. For such a deed the council banished the offender, and in case of need the police enforced the sentence. In actuality this has been unnecessary, for the culprit always obeyed.

So far the military societies seem merely like our Army executing the orders of the President, or like a constabulary body under a board of forty-four police commissioners. But the matter is not so simple. For one thing, there are ceremonies pledged by some tribesman, whose military sodality as a foregone conclusion, i.e., without authorization by the council, assumes control for the duration of the festival. Second, apart from homicide, which ranks as a ritual offense, the council pays little attention to secular matters. These, accordingly, devolve in large measure on the police society of the season, whose activities depend on the initiative and character of its chief. By a most remarkable rule this head may never serve on the council, though the rank and file are allowed to do so. Thus, Llewellyn and Hoebel are not far from the mark in detecting here a mutual check-and-balance system between civil and military authority.

A police society led by a man of violent character sometimes proved dictatorial and tyrannical, but there is no record of a consequent clash with the council. Moreover, such a society was on occasion capable of assuming the position of a modern government. Sleeping Rabbit, when upbraided for neglectful treatment of his wife by the woman's uncle, Bird Face, severely wounded his monitor while the Cheyenne were on the march. The Foxes, who were in charge—not Bird Face's society— kicked and beat the assailant and made him doctor the victim. There was some agitation for running Sleeping Rabbit out of the camp, but he ate humble pie, pacifying the police with a gift of five horses. That is to say, the Foxes treated the matter not as a private grievance of Bird Face's, but as a crime against the tribe; not Bird Face but the Foxes received the voluntary fine. In short, the sodality, for the time being, stood for the Cheyenne state, inflicting a corporal penalty and pocketing the payment rendered to them— not, as would have happened elsewhere, to the injured party. They were "the people"—or in monarchical countries, "the Crown"— against Sleeping Rabbit.

The Cheyenne military society differs from the government of a modern state in not functioning continuously. Its powers lapse during the cold season, and there is a shift from one sodality to another according to the council's decision. But intermittent as the authority of the Plains organizations is, Provinse is doubtless right in holding that so long as they are in control they are a full-fledged government.

CHINESE GUILDS.—In striking fashion, nineteenth-century China illustrates the partition of governmental powers. Not only were the viceroys to all intents and purposes independent rulers—notwithstanding the theoretical supremacy of the emperor—but in so vital a matter as taxation neither the central nor the local authorities loomed as coercive dignitaries. In 1880 the magistrate of a city proclaimed a new tax on each pig killed. The butchers' sodality resolved not to kill pigs for the time being and seized what pork was exposed for sale. Then the five hundred members shut themselves up in their guild house and prevented the magistrate, escorted by two hundred to three hundred runners, from entering.

Public opinion definitely veered in favor of the guild because of the official's attempt to use force, i.e., to act as a state functionary. Three days later all the shops in town closed. A few days later the magistrate issued an apology to the butchers and the public: "So the officials have all miserably failed in squeezing a *cash* out of the 'sovereign people' of Ssuch 'wan," wrote an English observer. In Hangchow there was a similar teahouse strike in 1889, and the officials agreed to withdraw the tax on tea, contenting themselves with a single payment of $1,500. Again, in 1838 the governor of Canton tried to search all the shops in a street for opium. The shopmen in a body went to the entrance of the street and told the police that under no condition would they allow the search; the governor deemed it wise to abandon his project.

In theory the emperor remained the representative of Heaven, the object of highest veneration, the fountainhead of all power, the absolute executive and legislative authority. In practice a prefect notorious for his cruelty might be lynched with the excuse that he had failed to carry out the emperor's good intentions. Specifically, the great merchant and craft guilds sometimes met official force with force *and were popularly held justified in so doing*. They also assumed positive functions that contemporary Western peoples ascribe exclusively to a central agency, such as the maintenance of roads.

AFRICAN SOCIETIES.—The West African sodalities also present some relevant phenomena. Three basically different situations may be distinguished. The chief or king may dominate the important societies, thus strengthening his control of all subjects with the aid of a closely knit organization. Second, he may be a mere puppet in the hands of a secret society. Finally, there may be divided authority.

The first of these conditions appears among the Kuyu of the French Congo. Here the chief regulates admission to the men's club, personally conducting the initiation, instructing the novices, and presenting them to the sacred images of his deceased parents. He also retains half of the entrance fee. Beyond this association there is the more exclusive Panther fraternity with only nineteen members out of a possible male population of fifteen hundred. The chief acts as head priest, and puts only his kinsmen in the official positions of the sodality. He claims a mysterious affinity with an actual panther, which he impersonates by spotting his face and body when he wishes to punish a neglectful debtor, stealing the culprit's goats or even killing him. By this double mastery over two organizations the chief evidently profits materially and is able to cow his subjects.

In some sections of the area, however, the religious fraternities managed to preserve their independence of the chief, whose power, as in Yorubaland, "was greatly fettered by the society" called Ogboni, which decided all important issues and turned criminals over to a satellite sodality for execution.

The Kpelle arrangements are intermediate. Their paramount chief or king is hardly negligible. In theory supreme, he owns the land, has numerous wives, serfs, and slaves, acts as the court of appeals in litigation, and maintains a small body of professional mercenaries as the core of his army. The subjects farm his fields, build his houses, carry burdens for him, and as tribute surrender part of their kill, all elephants' tusks and tails, and all leopards' teeth and hides. On the other hand, despotism is doubly checked. The Kpelle have an informal tribal club, which assembles in a special structure near the king's residence. There adult male litigants plead their cases, thither the king invites his subjects for an evening's carousal, and there the elders are as likely as their supposed master to suggest desirable measures. If a decisive majority favors some course of action, the king will not oppose the popular will. Even more definitely the grand master of the Poro offsets and even eclipses the royal power. He can call meetings of the sodality which the king is bound to attend, but also has the right of excluding him. Whereas the king is responsible to the elders for his decisions, the grand master has absolute punitive powers and sometimes orders men to be executed by his secret agents. "Where the grand master appears, the king stands in a corner." This proverb is especially applicable to the period of initiation, when the grand master takes over otherwise royal administrative duties. For instance, he may then requisition labor for the maintenance of roads and bridges and arranges for the transmission of news and for transportation. Nevertheless, the king is not ignored even at this time. He helps decide what each tyro is to learn, keeps in touch with occurrences in the bush, and is occasionally referred to as the true head of the Poro.

In short, certain sodalities have shown political potency, to that extent complementing and limiting the power of other governmental agencies. [4]

## Chiefs and Kings

A brief ethnographic survey will help us understand the extent of possible political arrangements. As just explained, these are not necessarily centered in the person of the "chief" or "king," but a discussion of the office brings out some of the essentials in governmental machinery.

American Indians, Polynesians, and African Negroes illustrate some of the most important principles.

AMERICAN INDIANS.—The term "chief" as applied to the ostensible head of American Indian tribes must often be understood in a Pickwickian sense. In strict logic one could draw up a long list of chiefless tribes in the New World. Nevertheless, a difference must be recognized between the Eskimo or the Ona, who recognize no official superior within the community, and tribes with one or more titular heads, invested with honor, if not with coercive rights. Naturally the influence exerted by such a person depends on his ability and character, as well as on coexisting agencies that may prop up or impair his status.

What were the ideal qualities of an American Indian chief? Many tribes emphasize evenness of temper and generosity—neither of them consistent with arbitrary rule. The Hidatsa chief was "a man of general benevolence who offered smoke to the old people and feasted the poor"; his Pawnee counterpart was above all a peacemaker and guardian of the village; a Plains Cree chief sacrificed his property in the interest of public order and would forgo vengeance if one of his own kinsmen was slain. A Winnebago colleague constantly gave away his belongings and interceded between evildoers and their vengeful victims. He went so far as to mortify his flesh to awaken the compassion of the rightfully aggrieved and make them desist, for his sake, from retribution. Even among the Apache, where the chief could order a witch or the breaker of the incest rules executed, "he was powerless forcibly to punish the wrongdoers" in normal disputes. Again, the chief of the Salishans in northeastern Washington "could only strive to direct . . . by oratory and reasoning; he had no dictatorial power." One of his main tasks was "to preserve tranquility within the village"; for that good end he would sacrifice his personal possessions to appease complainants. On the northwest coast there was, indeed, tremendous emphasis on the leader's rank, but we must not identify prestige with power. The Tsimshian chief "is the social and ceremonial figurehead of the tribe, but has very little formalized political power." He had no rights over the people's lives or property; the recipient of gifts from others, he is expected to share accessions to his wealth. Without such liberality he would soon sink in popular estimation. The tribesmen "are by no means passive followers": the lineage elders advise him in all matters of consequence and withhold their support if they see fit. To turn to another complex culture, the Pueblo town chief is "prescriptively a man of peace" who is not expected to fight or hunt. At Zuñi the high chiefs are so inconspicuous that their offices remained unknown to a white trader during a thirty years' residence. The ideal Hopi equivalent was self-controlled, patient, mild; the person chosen on one occasion was "not very forceful," devoid of a reformer's zeal, and for that very reason fittest.

The chief was, indeed, typically the conservator of traditional usage. Eloquence in its championship was another prized attribute of the tribal head. Among the Maricopa he regularly delivered sermons early in the morning, a feature likewise common in South America. Oratory is one of a Toba-Pilaga cacique's most essential qualifications. "Every day at sunset that cacique whose spirit moves him launches into a lengthy improvisation which the others listen to only inattentively without deigning to interrupt their petty labors. The customary topic of these harangues is peace, harmony and honesty, virtues recommended to all tribesmen." Similarly, eloquence and patience are prerequisites for the Sherente official. He, too, lectured the people in the evening. "Stepping in front of the semicircle and resting his hands on the ceremonial lance while rocking his body back and forth, he would impressively and vividly harangue the crowd for possibly an hour. Usually he began by circumstantially explaining the half-forgotten ceremonial of some festival to be celebrated. There followed a lengthy admonition, supported by visionary experiences, to preserve ancient usage. In conclusion he would urge all to live in peace and harmony . . . . The people would listen attentively, but only a minority acted in accordance with his speeches; and neither he nor any other chief had coercive power against recalcitrant tribesmen." Their fellow Brazilians, the Tupinamba, looked upon a falconlike bird as king of the whole family because it "rose early and harangued the other birds, just like the chief daily at dawn in the Tupinamba villages." In a tribe of the Gran Chaco a woman had been the recognized hereditary chieftainess until old age weakened her: "her father taught her to speak."

Naturally the qualities that fit a man to be peacemaker and monitor are also at times combined with a greater measure of authority. But it is remarkable how many of the New World aborigines dissociate any vital power from the holder of the honorific title.

What, if any, are true "state" authorities where the titular chief is unable to command? The rather specialized case of the Cheyenne has already been described. By and large, coercive authority lies with the general body of mature men. The Canella arrangements may be taken as representative. The chief "does not command and punish, but is above all a peacemaker." He displays "a minimum of individual assertiveness" and, though entitled to marks of esteem, works for a living precisely like a commoner. Nor does the council, with whom he cooperates, form a true oligarchy. However, it decrees the death of a suspected sorcerer, who is promptly executed by several men who volunteer for the job.

Notably enough, in the debates of an Indian council—and this probably holds for most primitive groups, as it did in the diet of Poland before her partition in the eighteenth century—decisions were reached not by majority vote, but by unanimous agreement.

Contrary to what might be supposed, tribes conspicuous for their martial spirit rarely, if ever, had military dictators. Generally, their war-fare was in the nature of raids undertaken by an individual brave who thirsted for glory or loot and whose leadership ceased with his expedition. It was thus with the Iroquois and the Crow, the Jivaro (Ecuador) and the Canella. In 1639 a Dutch observer mentions a chief of the northeast Brazilian Tapuya as highly respected in the field, but adds that he "is not thus honored" at home.

On the other hand, relatively often—and among the simplest as well as the most complex peoples—genuine rulers arose by virtue of their religious character. The Botocudo followed the man strongest in supernatural power, the one supposedly able to transform himself, to doctor the sick, and to revive the dead. Inspired prophets successively guided the Guarani on wild-goose chases toward an earthly paradise. Thus secular merges with spiritual superiority, coercion being none-theless real when it rests on the people's conviction that in order to stave off disaster they must obey their shaman-chief, a mouthpiece of divine protectors. The Inca emperor claimed absolute power on the score that he was a lineal descendant of the sun-god. In keeping with the advanced stage of the culture, he enjoyed elaborate outward marks of his lofty status—a fringed headdress, clothing of special quality, a mace with a golden star-head, a wooden throne covered with fine cloth. He kept a large harem and traveled in a litter borne by liveried servants. There was a complicated court etiquette, and at his death his favorite women and some attendants were strangled to accompany him.

A pale reflection of this splendor appeared in a few other South American regions. In Panama, e.g., chiefs ruling over hardly more than a few thousand subjects managed to affect a superior style of living and had themselves carried about in hammocks. The one region in North America that exhibited anything comparable at the time of the discovery is our Southeast. From Virginia to Florida and westward to Louisiana there were Indians who submitted to veritably despotic rule. In 1607, when the English founded their first colony, Powhatan had conquered a number of tribes, but the total population under his sway is not set above 9,000. Yet on a minor scale he was a potentate of the Andean type. His subjects viewed him with adoration: "Not only as a king, but as halfe a God they esteem him," reported Captain John Smith. He was surrounded by a guard of forty to fifty stalwarts, exacted tribute, and had criminals beaten with cudgels, clubbed or burnt to death. Like the Inca, he had many wives and wore decorative clothing. Significant parallels crop up in other sections of the Southeast. In the sixteenth century the bride of a Floridian cacique was brought to him in a litter, and at his death servants were slain to keep him company. Here, too, priestly and secular authority fused. The resemblances with Peruvian conditions were especially marked among the Natchez of the lower Mississippi, a people numbering rather under 5,000. They were ruled by an absolute monarch connected with the solar deity and named accordingly. He was master of his subjects' lives, property, and labor. He traveled in a litter, wore a diadem of feathers, and exacted outward signs of homage; at his death tribesmen were killed.

As Swanton reminds us, theory and practice did not wholly coincide. The Great Sun's authority was curtailed by his council and by the more eminent village chiefs. Similarly, the Inca emperor's lineage and the high priest of the realm shared political power with the sovereign. This, however, is a universal feature of autocracy throughout the world: the power actually held by an executive depends largely on his own personality and on the conditions of the time rather than on his "constitutional" status. Just as the Roosevelts exerted an incomparably greater influence than, say, Warren G. Harding, so Peter the Great was a genuine autocrat, whereas the last of the Czars was only nominally such. The same must apply to aboriginal despotism.

The remarkable thing is not that a Natchez or an Inca monarch was *de facto* limited, but that the pretensions to autocracy could arise at all on American soil, seeing that most of the Indians were egalitarians and, except in special circumstances, resented an encroachment on their individual freedom. [5]

POLYNESIANS.—Sacred chiefs, absent in North America except for the southeastern United States, are the Polynesian norm. Broadly generalizing, we may say that a high chief or king in this area claimed descent from the gods, outranking possible competitors if he could trace his lineage as the eldest son of an eldest son, and so back to the divine ancestor. In order to attain a maximum of purity the Hawaiians favored the marriage of a ruler with his own sister as the only person of strictly equal rank. Because of a Tahitian monarch's sanctity, anything he touched acquired his supernatural quality, hence became unfit for common use, so that a canoe on which he set his foot became his property; correspondingly, it would be dangerous for an inferior Maori to wear a chief's discarded clothing, hallowed as it was by contact with his body. In general, a chief's head was especially sacred; hence to touch it appeared the worst form of sacrilege. A Mangarevan saga forcibly brings home the pertinent attitudes. The offspring of the rightful but dispossessed ruler is trying to visit his grandfather incognito under the guardianship of a faithful servitor, who poses as his uncle. On a crowded raft the prince hopes to escape detection. At first all goes well, but in the course of the journey fellow passengers grow suspicious, discovering a family resemblance to the royal line, and challenge the identity of the guardian's pretended nephew. As the discussion waxes louder and some passengers suggest throwing the king's son overboard, his henchman calmly begins delousing the boy's head, a thing he would never have dared do in ordinary circumstances. The sacrilegious act saves the prince's life: his ill-wishers could not conceive it possible that a follower would ever lay hands on a royal head!

Because of so lofty a conception of the chief's person one might expect general submission to an autocratic sovereign. But as illustrated by this very story and the entire cycle to which it belongs, revolutions were quite possible. In principle, the Mangarevan king was absolute; he monopolized the iron that floated toward his islands with driftwood, he could confiscate a subject's property and order the execution of anyone who uttered a word of criticism against him, the people never spoke to him except at a distance, and he was almost always deified after death. Yet when Te-Magi-tutavake insisted on collecting as his rightful due an excessive part of the breadfruit crop, an ambitious plebeian profited from the general discontent and usurped the throne, ousting Te-Magi-tutavake, who fled, but perished in a shipwreck.

As a matter of fact, the most common and distinctive phenomenon in Polynesia was not absolutism, but the emphasis on rank as the basis for prestige. This appears clearly from the story of the outraged Samoan trade union in its relations to a village chief (p. 308).

A number of typical situations developed on this common base, modified by regional and individual differences. In the Hawaiian and the Society groups there was genuine autocracy, the most sacred, hence highest, person holding simultaneously the whip hand in secular affairs. Here also there was the greatest development of court etiquette. Tahitian sovereigns, "being regarded as gods incarnate by all the others, held suzerainty over them. Their lands were extensive, their dwellings were spacious , . . . and they always had a large retinue of retainers." They also had the exclusive privilege of wearing a royal feather girdle. A Hawaiian monarch wore a choice feather cloak as part of his insignia, and poets laureate recited his pedigree and eulogized his deeds.

Notwithstanding the holy character of the ruler in Hawaii and the Society Islands, it was at times challenged, just as it was in Mangareva. The Tahitian traditions are clear on that point. They tell us of a royal line peacefully reigning at Huahine, when a distant kinsman rose in rebellion and succeeded in establishing a new dynasty. At Porapora a great warrior, Tapoa I, ruled and extended his dominion to other islands, but was finally driven dack to his own, where another renowned soldier, Ma'i, constantly contested his sovereignty until a treaty of peace assigned part of the kingdom to each of the rivals.

Tonga holds special interest, for in the early days of white contact its polity suggested that of Japan before 1867. The Tui Tonga, corresponding to the Mikado, held undisputedly the highest title among the males of the land, which nevertheless was governed by another man, the Tui Haa Takalaua. Gifford's analysis of aboriginal history and legend indicates that in an earlier era the Tui Tonga, like the Hawaiian and Tahitian kings, was both holy and powerful. He commandeered the labor of his subjects for the production of huge truncated pyramids, received the first fruits of his subjects, and had to be treated in most ceremonious fashion in token of homage. However, first one collateral line and subsequently another assumed the actual reins of government. In any case the rule was arbitrary and tyrannical; a great chief owned all the land and could abuse his tenants at will. A remnant of such power has lingered into modern times; during Professor Gifford's visit in 1920–1921, chiefs still occasionally horsewhipped a refractory subject.

An atoll like Tongareva hardly permitted such refinements as Hawaii and Tahiti. In every district the chief was the eldest representative of the senior family. His authority remained limited, though one incident shows how even under untoward conditions a militant personality can assert itself. At one time a man named Turua proclaimed himself chief of all Tongareva and laid claim to all turtles caught by the natives. He was able to enforce this law, but it lapsed after his chieftainship.

Finally, in Samoa prestige did not descend automatically by primo-geniture; hence in view of the general Polynesian mania for honorific titles there was eager competition between possible holders. A title was bestowed by the landowning heads of households, who as a body were to all intents and purposes the rulers, so that they could banish or even kill unpopular chiefs, however lofty in position. [6]

AFRICAN NEGROES.— The caution expressed concerning the size of African political units is doubly necessary when discussing their chiefs or kings. Unquestionably the Negroes have had many autocratic rulers, and in various parts of the continent. When the Portuguese discovered Benin in 1472, the country had a deified ruler, at once spiritually and temporally supreme. Even noblemen were not allowed to look directly at his face and had to walk backward from his presence. He had numer-ous wives, some of whom he bestowed on his noble retainers. He con-trolled a standing army estimated at 20,000 warriors. His palace com-prised many walled-in buildings, and his capital, with its thirty main streets, was said by Dutch visitors in 1670 to equal in size any town in Holland. Corresponding power and splendor characterized the Mang-bettu king. Munza, when Schweinfurth visited him in 1870. Munza claimed the monopoly of ivory and a share in his subjects' crops. He had several hundred wives of several degrees and a special bodyguard. There were many officials: a keeper of weapons, a master of ceremonies, a superintendent of the commissariat, and "an immense number of civil officers and local overseers" in the outlying districts of the realm. The king's establishment consisted of a palisaded series of huts, halls, and sheds accessible only to himself, his retinue, and servants. He ate alone and whatever he touched was too sacred for anyone else to touch. No visitor, even of the highest rank, was allowed, on pain of death, to light a pipe from the fire that burnt before the throne. Whereas a commoner's dwelling was about 20 by 30 feet, the king's exceeded 75 feet in width and 160 feet in length and towered some 60 feet above the ground.

Again, the Shilluk king, sacred because possessed by the divine national hero, was the supreme judge, ruler, and priest. He claimed all booty from raids, derived a great income from cattle fines imposed by the courts, received all elephant tusks and leopard skins, and com-mandeered labor for his personal benefit. A royal bodyguard executed his judgments. Another example from a large number of possible instances is the spectacular rise of the Zulu Shaka from the humble position of limited chief of a petty tribe to that of absolute tyrant over a nation conservatively estimated at over 100,000.

These are undisputed facts, but they are not the only pertinent ones. As elsewhere, men of strong will have sometimes achieved despotic rule in Africa, but this cannot be taken as the norm. Not infrequently the theoretically absolute ruler more or less parallels the Tongan Tui Tonga in the last part of the eighteenth century or, for that matter, the Merovingian kings of France in the eighth. Thus, in the Belgian Congo the Bushongo king is said to be the embodiment of a god and outwardly receives marks of the utmost respect even from his enemies. In reality his status has shrunk to that of a figurehead, and half a dozen councilors are in virtually complete control.

It should also be noted that even where the monarch remains a vital political figure he may be under serious handicaps. For one thing, the code that separates him from the common herd may not only prove irksome to himself, but also preclude his exerting a direct influence on the majority of his subjects. The rulers of the Oyo in Yorubaland never appeared in public except on stated occasions, being confined to their palaces by established etiquette. Further, among the Shilluk the very holiness of the monarch becomes his undoing. They believe that a dire calamity would befall the entire people if the divine hero inspiring him were housed in a weak body; hence in historic times all kings have been suffocated as soon as they grew feeble. Obviously, malcontents could easily discover signs of senility in a hated ruler who was only temporarily ill.

African autocracy, then, had its drawbacks. Despite all reservations, its relative frequency remains remarkable, but it must not be exaggerated. Probably more truly representative is an intermediate condition that for want of a better name may be put into the category of "limited monarchy." That is what investigators find in South Africa. The typical Bantu chief is, indeed, rain-maker and judge as well, receives tribute in kind and labor, and claims part of all court fines. He is greatly revered by the populace and his deeds are eulogized by minstrels. But by way of reciprocity he has obligations to discharge. Precisely because of his riches, he is expected to feed the needy and to reward his braves; a niggardly chief is deserted by his subjects. What is more, he is curbed by a small conclave of kinsmen and confidants, as well as by the general assembly of clan headmen; and no chief would normally venture to override the wishes of the majority.

To turn to another aspect of the question, West Africa, the center of great and at least apparently despotic kingdoms, is also the region in which secret or other sodalities at times eclipse the chief and are able to depose him. What is more, in the same area, as well as in other sections of the continent, there are tribes as devoid of official agencies as the Ifugao and the Yurok. The markedly separatistic Lobi are also notably lacking in anything remotely resembling a state. They have neither chiefs nor councils of elders. To be sure, a district priest makes offerings to the Earth deity when a new market is founded or when his group migrates. But though his sacred functions invest him with prestige, his coercive powers are nil; as a conciliator, he seems a precise replica of the Yurok or Ifugao go-between. Sometimes African legal procedure obtains even in the absence of chiefs, but the Lobi have no true judges—merely an informal assembly of the priest and the old men, whose sentence there is no official to execute. Only the culprit's kindred, afraid that disobedience might prejudice the deities, prevail upon him to bow to the verdict. A final though not the only other available example may be cited in the Nuer of the Anglo-Egyptian Sudan, whose "leopard-skin chief" is only an intermediary of Ifugao type. When a murder has occurred, he gets the slayer's relatives to promise an indemnity and persuades the victim's kindred to accept it.

To sum up, Negro Africa has autonomous political units no larger than a Semang camp, and these units may be as wanting in coercive authorities as a Yurok village. Africa presents us with the entire range of phenomena, from tiny separatistic communities to large states with a population of over a million, from anarchic settlements to kingdoms under the sway of an absolute tyrant.[7]

## General Considerations

PARALLELISM AND CONVERGENCE.—As Thurnwald remarks, political systems are each unique; yet they reveal certain common features, because, politically, human beings tend to behave more or less alike in similar situations. Accordingly, this phase of culture probably offers more definitely authenticated examples of parallelism than any other.

This statement does not imply unilinear evolution. We cannot argue that peoples starting from the same basis are bound to reproduce similar forms of government. For example, economic conditions are admittedly of enormous significance, but even authors taking a favorable view of economic determinism find that it leaves observed differences unexplained. The economy of the tropical forest peoples of South America is virtually identical, Kirchhoff finds; yet "the differences in social structure . . . . cannot be brought into causal relations with the technical side of economy." Similarly, Swanton points out that in the southeastern United States the Indian tribes erected divergent governmental systems "upon an economic base practically identical." Some exploited the theocratic absolutism of Inca type, but the Choctaw had a weaker central government with less inequality, and the Cherokee were a loose confederation of towns led by the heads of the seven clans. Corresponding observations apply to the Ge stock in Brazil. Within it the means of getting a livelihood hardly vary, but whereas other members of the family are inveterate separatists, the Sherente have somehow developed less parochial a sense of solidarity. It is not sufficient for unification, but at least several of their settlements do cooperate.

The reverse approach has proved more promising and can be extended to the present problem. Isolating a specific economic factor, we can sometimes correlate it with certain aspects of political organization. The Eskimo of Nunivak, occupying an exceptionally favorable habitat with an ample food supply, founded settlements of over a hundred people, whose social life is not nearly so formless as that of their northern and eastern congeners. To be sure, Nunivak "chiefs" are far from being rulers, but they do bear an honorific title, which to some extent they transmit to their sons. Even if the model of near-by Indian tribes has had an effect, the economic differentia remains significant, for the title is bestowed for conspicuous liberality, which would be impossible under Arctic conditions.

It is, then, fairly easy to prove *divergent* evolution—descent with modification, due to an economic (or conceivably some other definable) difference—but the *same* base also yields different superstructures. In what sense, then, does Thurnwald's proposition hold?

Concerning the general course of political development, a few propositions seem clear. In the earliest period large and differentiated units are inconceivable because an economic and technological basis was lacking. The earliest communities must have been tiny, egalitarian groups corresponding to a Semang or Eskimo camp. Such a community was in the main a body of kindred, but coresidence knitted them into a significant unit, so that blood and contiguity must be reckoned with from the start. Disciplinary authority must have existed in the familial sense. The problem, then, could be formulated as follows: How did the miniature communities grow in size? How were differences of status added to the inevitable ones of age and sex? How was the coercive authority strengthened and extended?

These questions have in a measure been answered, and it should be clear why parallels are likely. It is because the number of solutions is limited if put into abstract form, and further limited by conditions in the world of reality. Thus, expansion can be due either to peaceable union or to forcible incorporation, and for large-scale aggrandizement the latter is obviously more expeditious. Further, when a conqueror has subjugated a foreign group, he may either—on the principles of campanilismo—segregate them as an inferior class or assimilate them to his other subjects. If the ruler is an autocrat, differences of rank disappear, because his elevation is such as to level all normal distinctions by comparison. Again, it is in the nature of things that a large population must be governed by proxy; whence the appointment of viceroys, chiefs, headmen according to the size of the administrative units. Such posts are naturally filled with members of the ruler's family or with trusted henchmen. Crisscrossing such developments are widespread human traits—vanity and power-madness, for instance—which are bound to appear with fair regularity and lead to recurring manifestations. Thus, the rivalry of royal brothers or of other close relatives overrides family bonds and evokes similar disturbances in Negro Africa, in the Inca empire, in medieval Europe.

A few special developments merit closer scrutiny. How does a leader acquire genuinely coercive control, possibly even without deliberate planning? Three instances from wholly diverse cultures illustrate the process.

In Fiji it happened that individuals fled from their home district to another where the chief exercised only limited authority over his people, but did have the right to assign wasteland for farming. Accordingly, the newcomers would apply to him for an allotment. This, however, at once put them into a different category from the native commoners, who owned their cultivations, making the aliens directly dependent on the chief. But this greatly enhanced the chief's status with reference to his traditional subjects, since now for the first time he could command retainers not allied to the other commoners, men who to him alone owned their very means of livelihood and hence were ready to do his bidding.

In the rise of Kazak and Mongol khans a comparable phenomenon was conspicuous. Soldiers of fortune who for some reason had broken away from their original allegiance would attach themselves to some outstanding chief, officer his army, and act as his bodyguard, as masters of the hunt, ambassadors, and advisers in civil affairs. These nököd, as the Mongols called them, paved the way for a primarily territorial unification since they came from alien kinship groups; and as a khan conquered other tribes these trusted retainers were predestined to be "appointed not only military commanders but governors directly responsible to the khan."

A medieval European parallel is pertinent. In conflicts of emperors with the papacy the former were handicapped by the obedience all Western Christians owed to the Pope. Frederick II lessened this disadvantage by transferring 16,000 conquered Moslems from the Sicilian mountains to Apulia, where they founded a regular colony, forming a troop directly responsible to him and immune to excommunication.

In these three instances, rulers gained physical means of coercion through the accession of outsiders whose political ties within the territorial unit were exclusively with the ruler.

The religious motive, already discussed, merits further consideration. Rude societies are essentially democratic, yet even in them a person believed to be favored by supernatural beings is able to dominate. In more sophisticated conditions a chief who aspires to absolute power claims supernatural descent, hence a divine or semidivine character. As Eduard Meyer convincingly shows, Alexander the Great's demand that Macedonians and Greeks, no less than conquered Orientals, should prostrate themselves before him and add him to their gods had a definite meaning. The king craved a form of absolutism that could be defended only if he were divine, hence no longer subject to the laws, but in his person their embodiment. This claim, Meyer concludes, is essential to absolute monarchy; hence it is bound to turn up wherever that form of government has evolved. The Andean and the Polynesian parallels support his proposition.

The artificiality of the claim likewise precipitates numerous correspondences in widely distant regions and periods. In Mangareva and in Peru, in the Holy Roman Empire and in medieval Japan, it is recurrently punctured by rebels who ousted and killed the supposedly divine monarch or made him into a man of straw.

In all this, however, there is nothing inevitable. For example, a given chief may or may not grasp the possibilities inherent in a devoted bodyguard; Alexander's claim to be divine met with initial antipathy in Greece, and it was a historical accident that the king was strong enough to overcome resistance.

Similar developments in this department of culture can also come about through diverse antecedents. Conquest is a frequent factor in expansion, but matrimonial arrangements—witness the history of Austria, Spain, and Portugal—can bring about the same result. Even federation has proved effective in the United States and, on a smaller scale, in Switzerland.

Classes likewise arise by different channels, as their history in the United States, Sweden, France, and Russia sufficiently indicates. In East Africa peasants subjugated by herders became a lower class. Here we even find a curious analogy to European feudalism: the chief of the ruling pastoralists, now king of a sizable population, claims in principle all the subjects' livestock as a medieval monarch claimed all their land.

This last instance suggests that the similarities to be reckoned with are not identities; such they cannot be, for they are inevitably involved with significant traits rooted in the unique culture of which they are part. Thus, an African chief who has conquered a million people duplicates the rise of European autocrats. But a Negro chief is also invariably a judge and naturally retains judicial attributes as a king that his European counterpart would lack. Further, the typical African monarch has specific magico-religious functions, such as rain making, which his Western colleagues do not aspire to, though generically their supposed ability to cure scrofula by the royal touch falls into the same category. [8]

NATURE OF THE STATE.— Many writers have conceived the state as something independent of its constituent individuals and superior to them, as having purposes of its own to which all individuals are in duty bound to submit. Radcliffe-Brown has rightly spurned this view as a philosophical fiction, and Anton Menger has even more trenchantly exposed its absurdity. As Menger puts it, "state" simply epitomizes the sum total of human beings residing within the dominion of the same supreme authority, and it is simply the arbitrary will of the persons wielding that authority which dictates the objects and activities of "the state." The notion that the might and magnificence of one's state legitimately require individual sacrifices ignores the fact that in reality the demands in question are those of limited groups of beneficiaries. In this connection Menger quotes a conservative German political scientist who "consistently contends that in the most important political questions God shares the views of the Junkers east of the Elbe"; and Menger drily adds that "this odd assumption cannot at bottom be refuted by authenticated historical facts."

The opinions of Eduard Meyer, the eminent historian of ancient civilizations, merit greater consideration. The state, he contends, is the equivalent of the herd among animals, but, in contrast to other species, man always lives as a member of several concentric or overlapping associations. Among the several associations one, however, is supreme, demanding that all groups and individuals within its sphere subordinate themselves to its will and purposes and, if necessary, it forces them to do so. Above all, there is "the consciousness of the eternity of the association." "This dominant form of association, whose essence involves the consciousness of a complete, autonomous unity, we call the state." It is the historically primary form of human community, whose development was made possible only through it. Proceeding to anthropological illustrations, Meyer cites the marriage rules of the Australians. Such regulation is more than mere usage; it is a *law* enforced by the strict punishment of every transgressor. That, however, implies a state organization. It is the state that creates the family, not vice versa.

This argument exhibits a commendable desire to see the social phenomena of aborigines and of civilized people as a continuous whole. Whether the term "state" should be applied to certain manifestations, or whether one should rather speak of a prior condition revealing elements out of which a full-fledged state could develop, would be a mere matter of taste, were it not for Meyer's dogmatic assertion that the state is everywhere the antecedent of other associations. That is, on any reasonable definition, highly dubious and certainly incorrect on Meyer's. He is right in seeing state activity in our sense when an Australian horde punishes what it considers incest, for here a "law" is being preserved by physical force directed against the offenders. But what warrant is there for assuming the consciousness of a permanent association? As Radcliffe-Brown shows, it happens that several hordes combine for a religious celebration and *for the time being* constitute a political unit possessing a repressive technique for use against criminals. But the hordes need not be the same at successive assemblies; a particular horde is successively part of differently constituted major units. Where, then, is the consciousness of a permanent association on which Meyer puts such emphasis?

The Australian instance is by no means isolated. Even in Africa there are parallels. In the Northern Territories of the Gold Coast, 35,000 Tallensi live without forming an integrated whole, and no subdivision is circumscribed by definite boundaries. Each so-called tribe merges into others, so that an intermediate community has equal ties with the tribes on either side of it.

As for the criterion of compulsive authority (in which Meyer's and our definition coincide), that also has been found wanting in some communities. Let us recall what Egede and others report from the Eskimo. Other instances abound. In 1914 a woman in the Coronation Gulf district, when taunted by another for being barren, stabbed and killed the scoffer; about a year later a man sharpening his knife was jeered at by a neighbor for his lack of skill and drove the tool into the other man's stomach, saying, "Now see if I can't make a knife." Neither murderer was punished. In another case the slayer fled from the victim's relatives, but a year later the natives' opinion was that he could then return with impunity: "The murder had taken place long ago, they said, and no one wanted to remember it or to wreak vengeance ...."

It is quite true that periodically there is general consensus that So-and-so is an incorrigible nuisance and must be eliminated. In Baffin Land a man named Padlu had taken away another's wife and killed not only the husband, but two of his would-be avengers. Finally, the murderer's neighbors agreed to get rid of Padlu and authorized an outsider from a neighboring tribe to shoot him. Birket-Smith has aptly summarized the facts by declaring that "there is never any question of *judicial action*, whether the infringement springs from the individual or the community. It is either a simple act of vengeance . . . or, if the whole community joins . . . it is for the purpose of securing quiet and order." Such fitful meting out of punishment is certainly not consistent with the notion of a permanent state that above all wills its self-preservation. We are dealing with an assemblage of human beings long cowed by a bully until they are jointly less afraid of him than of the possible consequence to themselves due to his unchecked brutality.

The Eskimo have traveled a long way from the hypothetical precursor of the human species, and if they lack statehood we can hardly credit it to the subhuman level. What, then, shall be said of "the origin of the state"? The potentially lasting use of physical restraint in a way sanctioned by the community must have grown gradually out of uncrystallized and transient forms of reprobation by kinsmen and coresidents. As mere custom ripens into law when someone, with general approbation, does something positive about its breach (p. 156), so the sporadic exertion of force in such circumstances develops into an enduring agency. The Cheyenne military societies, compared with their equivalents in neighboring tribes, prove instructive in this respect (p. 325). Precluded from evolving into a permanent government by the seasonal breakup of the people, these organizations nevertheless illustrate a marked step toward the extension of force. Instead of acting only in narrowly circumscribed conditions, they have come to take on novel tasks and to function more frequently than, say, the Crow police sodalities.

Within Western civilization there is, of course, much documentary evidence on the embryonic stages of statehood. The Icelandic commonwealth that evolved in the Middle Ages had a parliament (*Althing*) and a "Lawman" chosen by it through a unanimous vote. But the *althing* had no means of enforcing the laws it passed; and the Lawman was not an executive, though he presided in court and at the legislative assembly. All he was qualified to do was to recite the entire code, and his office expired with the session. He rendered no judgment and inflicted no penalties. He was homologous with the Ifugao go-between, not with a contemporary judge or executive.

How a state in the modern sense can arise out of such dim foreshadowings is demonstrated by the first national movement in Norway under Harold Fairhair. The earlier separatistic kings had been limited not only in the extent of their territory but also in their authority. A loyal subject followed the leadership of the king in repelling an attack on his territory, but hardly beyond that. Harold Fairhair (d. 933), inspired by Charlemagne's example, subjugated these local kings and either ousted them or transformed them into tax collectors, merely royal appointees, not feudal lords. He made defeated enemies swear an oath of allegiance to himself, regarding them as traitors if they repudiated the obligation and as military henchmen if they fulfilled it. He claimed all of Norway by right of conquest and accordingly demanded rent from the traditional landowners. To combine Hardy's and my own phrasing, Harold for the first time applied force within Norway as it had previously been applied by Norsemen to alien countries only. Those who spurned his principles emigrated to the Scottish islands, and later to Iceland; those who submitted helped to form the first pan-Norwegian state.[9]

THE LOCUS OF COERCIVE POWER.—Nowhere is the discrepancy between theory and reality more striking than in the sphere of government. Shilluk and Ankole kings are described as absolute. They are masters of their subjects' lives and property, marry the women they covet, confiscate any livestock they crave, dismiss officials arbitrarily. The list of their prerogatives sounds impressive. However, there is another side to all this, and analysis shows that actually they are not absolute by any means. For one thing, until recently nearly every monarch died by violence, the Shilluk monarch being suffocated, his colleague in Ankole poisoned as soon as they showed signs of physical decline. But who decided when this happened? If an unpopular Shilluk king had a running nose *that* might be reckoned a sufficient ground for eliminating him; so would the charge of waning virility by a vindictive wife. Moreover, in both the kingdoms under discussion royal duties balanced the prerogatives, and there were very real checks to apparent absolutism. For example, in Ankole the king's sister or mother could veto a death sentence pronounced by him; and though it is all very well to say that a king could appropriate any chief's live-stock, the sufferer was likely to rebel. Whether an autocrat can *safely* do what he is in principle authorized to do hinges on his personality, on the will power of his enemies, the compulsive mechanisms he is able to control at the moment.

Japanese political conditions prior to the so-called restoration in 1867 are usually brought under the formula that an impotent Mikado enjoyed the highest outward honors, while a military commander, the Shogun, actually ruled. This is an oversimplification. It is true that for several centuries the Mikado had ceased to exert any influence on the management of the country. For a long period many petty lords, independent of one another or any national head, controlled their respective districts until Iyéyasu (died 1616) as military head conquered most of the land and divided much of it among his adherents. Sup-posedly the Shogun's vassals, these barons (daimios) became virtually independent under Iyéyasu's successors. However, developments were such that within a baron's demesne the decisive factor was an oligarchy of the poor but vigorous sword-bearing gentry, who degraded their theoretical superior to the status of a nobody, determined his policies, and prescribed what he should say on public occasions.

In modern and contemporary Western states, the amount of coer-cive power actually held by the responsible government and the amount constitutionally vested in it are two different things. There is, moreover, another consideration—the amount they can arrogate with the approval of either coordinate branches of government or of the people who count. Theodore Roosevelt boasted that he had illegally taken the Panama Canal Zone for the good of the United States, forestalling possible congressional opposition. He would not, of course, have gone to the lengths of Hitler, creating a rump legislature that would pass an enabling act. The American mores would have been too strong to sug-gest that course to him as either proper or safe. But he rightly felt that for what he did do he would not be impeached and that he would gain strong popular support. Other presidents, such as Jefferson and Lincoln, showed similar defiance of the judicial rather than the legislative branch of government. But any known American president would hesitate to use his coercive powers as commander-in-chief of the armed forces to oust Congress. Even if he had any such desires, he would suppress them, wondering whether so extraordinary an order might not be challenged by his military subordinates.

In other words, true sovereignty and paper sovereignty are quite different. A statesman often stakes his fortune on some policy whose outcome alone can show what measure of power he has really had. Menger wisely remarks that sovereignty is not determined by some paragraphs in a country's constitution: "In reality what is decisive for possession of the supreme actual power is not whether the sovereign is entitled to exercise some constitutional authority, but precisely the opposite fact, whether if necessary he can impose his will upon the system of law."[10]

IV.  SOCIAL ORGANIZATION IN ACTION

# Chapter 15

# THE CROW INDIANS

T HE preceding chapters have treated human institutions and associations. It is now necessary to see how individuals live within the social structure imposed upon them. In a general work this can be exemplified for only a few peoples, but the reader is urged to make a similar synthesis for any other culture, aboriginal or advanced, with which he happens to be familiar. It is naturally impossible to cover the range of possible variations even for a single society. Apart from personality differences, there are those of status. A Siberian shaman does not play the same role as a layman, an African potentate has a very different set of social relations from a commoner's, and even in the simplest communities the social ties of women are qualitatively, if not also quantitatively, distinct from men's. The function, then, of synthetic sketches must be merely suggestive, stimulating corresponding efforts —possibly with other individuals of the same societies—rather than trying to exhaust the possibilities.

The following chapters consider human beings in four diverse cultures, selected because the material on them is reasonably ample and because they illustrate essential points.

## Social Organization

The Crow Indians, forming with the Hidatsa of North Dakota a branch of the Siouan linguistic family, are living on a reservation within their old territory in eastern Montana. In 1833 their number was set at about 3,500, but a recent figure is in the neighborhood of 2,000. There were two politically distinct, though friendly bands, the River Crow along the lower Yellowstone, and the Mountain Crow farther south, ranging at least in the winter into Wyoming. All Crow lived mainly by buffalo hunting, the only planting activity being the cultivation of their sacred tobacco.

Under normal conditions the individual Crow was hardly restricted in his actions except by tradition and public opinion. Hereditary classes were unknown, but the greatest emphasis was put on individual distinction. This rested primarily on glory in warfare, i.e., on the performance of four types of creditable deeds—the wresting away of a bow or gun from an enemy; touching an enemy (= the "coup" of French-Canadian voyageurs); cutting loose a horse picketed within a hostile camp; and leading a successful raid. A man who could claim all four of these enjoyed the honorific title of "chief," and the totality of such chiefs determined band policy. One of them would act as head of the camp, but without dictatorial powers in normal conditions, and he probably served only so long as the people enjoyed good luck under his leadership. He decided when to move the camp and where; and every spring he appointed one military society to exercise the coercive powers usual in special circumstances among Plains Indians. At the great Sun Dance ceremony, however, the supreme control was vested in the owner of the medicine bundle, who also designated the sodality to police the spectators of the festival.

Kinship and religion were the two conspicuously potent Crow institutions. The tribe embraced thirteen matrilineal clans, found in both bands, which bore such names as Sore-lip lodge, Whistling Water, Filth-eating lodge, Greasy-inside-the-mouth. The obligations to a clansman usually overrode those to the band or tribe, precipitating at times blood feuds, which the chief and police tried to stave off by conciliation. For economic reasons, sometimes from pique, the men of a clan would move off with their families for a period of time, but, with hostile peoples all about, such segregation might prove fatal. Membership in a large body of kindred gave security, which was sometimes abused; traditions tell of gangster tyranny. Correspondingly, no insult struck home more tellingly than to be twitted with having no kindred; it meant that one was reckoned a nobody exposed to sadistic maltreatment. A person in such a situation was likely to fast and seek a vision in order to gain a supernatural blessing that might restore his mental equilibrium.

Although descent was matrilineal, the patrilineal kindred were extremely important. They included the censors if a person had outraged decency, for his joking-relatives were the children of his father's brothers or their classificatory equivalents. On the other hand, patrilineal uncles and aunts were publicity agents for one's creditable exploits. By way of reciprocity, they, above all others, had a moral claim on gifts if their clansman's son had gained wealth by some lucky fluke, which ordinarily meant that he had captured loot from the enemy.

Warfare cannot be separated from religion, for every successful raid was supposedly inspired by a supernatural apparition or audition. The object of prayer was largely military good fortune. The Sun Dance was in fact a prayer for revenge upon a hostile people; and though the Tobacco Dance, the other great ceremony, explicitly served only the general welfare, its performance was full of martial allusions.

The military sodalities, to one of which every man belonged, were wholly secular clubs, each with its peculiar costume, dance, songs, and traditional behavior. About seventy-five years ago the Foxes and the Lumpwoods were rivals, trying to outdo each other in bravery and to steal each other's wives during a limited period in the spring (p. 97). Notable in each sodality were a few "officers"—not managers, but young men who accepted distinctive regalia, thereby pledging themselves to special bravery for the season. Thus, the bearer of a hooked staff would under no condition flee in battle—unless he wished to become ever after the butt of scathing mockery.

The concern with war involved women no less than men. A girl, as well as a boy, bore the name given by a great man to commemorate one of his exploits. A woman who had lost her son would goad some warrior to avenge his death. Wives gained honor from their husbands' records, publicly exhibited their men's shields, and danced with the scalps taken. Even young children were steeped in the militaristic obsession: boys learned to strike game animals as though they were enemies, and, for want of a scalp, their female playmates danced with the hair of a coyote. A youth who had never been to war was jeered at as a mollycoddle.

The boys constantly had it impressed upon their minds that "old age is a thing of evil, it is well for a young man to die in battle." It was customary to point out how vulnerable human beings were in contrast to strong or eternal natural phenomena, the implication being that men can hardly expect to live long: "Earth and sky are everlasting; men must die." The notion naturally ran counter to the instinct of self-preservation; and individuals responded to it according to their psychological makeup: there were shirkers, lip servers, believers, and rapturous enthusiasts. Inevitably the *average* Crow was exposed to strong conflicts, for not everyone could be born a hero. Yet the passion for being admired as a paragon of courage overcame many a man's inborn revulsion from death.

There is the story of Went-down-a-bank-on-a-white-horse. "I do not want to be old," he declared, "I don't want to be a coward, I don't want to be afraid of anything . . . I'll do something to die." He went on four war parties and dug himself in in a pit. The enemy surrounded him, but each time he leapt out, and drove them back. He scoffed at his fellow Crow as cowards. One day, after a dance, he rode his white horse, put blinkers over its eyes, and deliberately ran it beyond the edge of the bank so that he and his mount were smashed to death.

Indeed, the deliberate desire to die—apart from the comparatively prosaic endeavor to stand one's ground—was sufficiently common to be pressed into a fixed mold. A Crow frustrated beyond all hope would affect a special kind of sash, then suddenly appear in camp, shaking a rattle, singing a distinctive song, and "talking crosswise," i.e., expressing the contrary of his obvious meaning. Then everyone would know that he was a "Crazy Dog"—a man who had vowed to die before the end of the season. His next of kin would begin to weep and wail in anticipation, but the crowd cheered him and young women, lured by the glamour of heroism, would thrust their favors on him. The motives for becoming a Crazy Dog varied. Spotted-Rabbit courted death because he could not get over the loss of his father, but the best-known instance of recent times had a more typical basis. Young Cottontail had gone on a raid and been wounded incurably in the knee. His career was blocked. "Whenever young men went afoot on a raid or hunting, whenever they undertook anything he was handicapped and felt envious." So, when a Dakota war party was reported coming he boldly advanced against it, attacked, and was instantly killed.

The foregoing are merely some high lights of Crow culture, introducing the biographical facts about Gray-bull, one of my informants.

## Gray-bull and Crow Society

Gray-bull's earliest memories, dating back to possibly 1850, indicate the setting of Crow life before the western Plains were pacified. He was about four years old when a party of Dakota killed twenty-three Crow, including three boys who were chasing calves. The camp rallied to drive the marauders back, killing about ten of them and capturing two of their women. The next winter a man and his family separated from the rest of the Crow, and the Piegan killed them all. The following summer a party set out against the Dakota, who killed eighteen Crow and captured three of the women accompanying them. In the battle one Crow showed his mettle. Secure in his belief that he could not be wounded, he dismounted while his companions were driven back and killed a Dakota brave assumed to have claimed the same gift.

As a little boy, Gray-bull hunted birds and chased butterflies. He played at target shooting and later took part in such juvenile pastimes as stealing meat that the women had hung up for drying and which the thieves then feasted on. As he grew older, he began to take part in war raids. Now he was able to make fun of the lads who had not yet had that experience; he would abuse them roundly, telling them that they were not males, but women.

Going on a war party was not unmingled joy. A novice had to fag for the old stagers, carry their provisions and fetch water, in return for which they would mercilessly send him on wild-goose errands. Worse than that, there were real hardships. Once a party remained without food for five days, and when they finally sighted buffalo they were so weak that they had to walk with canes.

At this point we must mention Gray-bull's clan connections. From his mother he had inherited affiliation with the Filth-eaters, while his father was a Whistling Water. When he struck his first coup, his fellow clansmen gave him his manhood name, for until then he was known as Last-bull. They renamed him for a famous warrior of his father's clan, who was still living and who received a horse as remuneration. The incident demonstrates the dual relationship of any Crow, his maternal kindred always on the alert to protect and advance him, the patrilineal relatives also willing to help, but predestined to get any gifts in the offing.

A medicine man fitted out Gray-bull to go on the warpath with a tooth from the skull of a great chief, White-cub. It had given a former owner conspicuous good fortune, and Gray-bull, too, was lucky, so that he got together a herd of from seventy to ninety horses. The medicine man once sent him out to satisfy an old woman begging for revenge because her son had been slain by the enemy. So Gray-bull set out and his party killed four Piegan. They celebrated a triumphant return, at which every brave who had struck a coup was lauded in song by some clansman of his father's, for which the panegyrist received gifts from the warrior's own clan. In the course of time Gray-bull again and again distinguished himself, cutting loose three tethered horses, capturing three guns, striking three coups, and leading three successful parties. Ranking as a chief, he was now entitled to decorate his moccasins, leggings, and shirt with hair; when others trudged afoot in a parade, he might ride on horseback; at any great gathering he could get up and recite his deeds.

Long before Gray-bull had attained such eminence he had joined the Fox sodality. One spring the four old men who were managing the affairs of the organization offered a pipe to various members who might fill the position of death-defying standard-bearers. The young men, Gray-bull among them, were very coy and shrank from the office on the plea that they were afraid of not being strong enough. At last, Gray-bull's comrade seized him by his bang and forcibly made his lips touch the mouthpiece. Thus he became a staff-bearer, but escaped injury in that position.

The episode illustrates once more the conflict between theory and practice. All these youths had had it dinned into their ears from infancy what a splendid thing it was to die young, but even as unchallengeably brave and ambitious a youngster as Gray-bull was liable to an attack of "cold feet" and had to be literally dragooned into a highly honorific position fraught with danger.

The comrade mentioned was a friend chosen in boyhood for special intimacy after the Crow fashion. Such cronies exchanged gifts, shared sweatbaths, went on raids together, and assisted each other in every way. The bond could even override other loyalties. The behavior of Gray-bull's comrade, then, must be interpreted in this light. It was not a gesture of hostility, but of eagerness to make his friend a distinguished man.

In later years, when the Fox and Lumpwood societies declined, Gray-bull joined a club recently imported from the Hidatsa, the Crazy Dog society (not to be confused with the suicidal Crazy Dogs). They and the likewise modern Hot Dancers became rivals after the model of the Foxes and Lumpwoods, and Gray-bull took an active part in the ensuing wife-kidnapping.

Like every young blade, Gray-bull had his share of philandering. When but twenty-two years old, he married his first wife, who had come to his home after he got back from a raid. She bore him a son, who died. Finding a boy in the tribe who exactly resembled the dead one, Gray-bull adopted him, though the lad remained affiliated with his natal clan (never belonging to that of Gray-bull's wife). Gray-bull raised the adoptive son until the youth married and rejoined his real father. When Gray-bull had been married some four years, his wife raised a row because he had been out on a berry-picking party with another young woman. She angrily told him to marry her rival, so he threw her belongings out of the tent, and she departed. Then he went to his sweetheart's home and married her.

This second wife was a pretty woman, who had had a previous lover from the Lumpwood society, the rival of Gray-bull's sodality.

When Gray-bull had received his staff from the Foxes, there was the usual brief period of mutual wife-abduction. By the rules of the game the Lumpwood who had once had Gray-bull's wife for a mistress was allowed to kidnap her, and he now claimed his right. The woman clung to Gray-bull, but it was entirely against the Crow code for a husband to offer resistance in such a situation, so he ordered her to go with her former lover. "If you have ever been married," he told me reminiscently, "you know how this felt." He was disconsolate, he could not sleep for four nights, brooding over his loss. At last he painted himself, dressed up, and went to the dance ground, casting about for Lumpwood women he might steal in retribution. He found one, who willingly accompanied him. In the customary way her abductor's relatives gave his captive a fine dress, decorated with 500 elk teeth, and painted her up. Her husband was beside himself with grief, got himself up in Crazy Dog attire, and stayed in his lodge, singing the death chant. One night he came to Gray-bull's tent, shook his rattle, and thrust his hand inside. Because of the ferocity of Crazy Dogs, Gray-bull was terrified and promised to return the woman. He did so, but as soon as she arrived the Lumpwood tore off his sashes and fled. Thus he became an object of contempt among the Crow.

These incidents are revealing in several ways. Gray-bull loved his wife, but the canons of Crow gentlemanliness were deeply impressed upon him, so he conquered his feelings and made no attempt to restrain her abductor. From the native point of view this proved that "his heart was strong." By way of contrast stands out the sham Crazy Dog, whose failure to carry out an obligation once assumed made him a butt of ridicule for the remainder of his days. It is again interesting to note here how in the second episode Gray-bull, brave as he was, could turn coward, on this occasion being evidently hypnotized by the aura that surrounded the Crazy Dog office.

For these first two wives no property was paid, since their moral character did not qualify them for that honor. But it was otherwise with Gray-bull's last wife, despite the fact that she was his brother's widow. It was his own mother that suggested the match to him, and after some hesitation he consented. Then a horse and other gifts were dispatched to her family. He went to her home to consummate the marriage, feeling bashful at first because of her chastity. "Men," he told me, "would buy a woman who was not lewd. The Lumpwoods never came to the door of my tipi to take away my last wife. That is the sort of wife we paid for." She was an accomplished as well as a virtuous woman, having gained secret obstetrical knowledge by paying a horse to the man who had first procured it through a vision. Once she successfully treated a patient whom two other native doctors had vainly tried to help, and the grateful relatives paid her a horse, a blanket, some other goods, and some money.

Gray-bull's contacts with religion illustrate how that institution was intertwined with kinship, as well as with other social relations. Gray-bull once joined a war party led by White-stripe-across-his-face, who had been adopted into the Tobacco society by Bell-rock. It redounded to a person's glory to adopt new members, and with this idea in mind the captain allowed Gray-bull to keep a horse he had stolen from the enemy under his direction. Gray-bull coveted the leader's war medicine and asked whether he might receive that if he allowed the captain to initiate him. White-stripe-across-his-face agreed and that summer adopted Gray-bull and his wife. The couple, aided by their kindred, paid him thirty-three horses for the privilege of membership, Gray-bull himself contributing ten.

The joint adoption of husband and wife was a regular custom and incidentally illustrates that among the Crow there was nothing comparable to Melanesian sexual dichotomy. Couples lived together, ate together, and in large measure joined in ceremonial. For instance, painting the face of Tobacco dancers was a prerogative ultimately derived from a vision, hence had to be paid for. Gray-bull purchased the right to certain styles of painting from his own mother, giving her a horse, a shirt, quilts, and money as compensation. Subsequently, when decorating dancers, he was assisted by his wife, who painted the women.

Initiation into the Tobacco sodality automatically brought new relationships. His sponsor became Gray-bull's "father" and was addressed accordingly, while Bell-rock logically enough became his "grandfather" and Bell-rock's wife his "grandmother." By way of preparation Gray-bull had to learn songs from four men who also became his "grandfathers," except for one who, being only of Gray-bull's age, figured as a "father." By and large, Gray-bull would look on approximate contemporaries in the society as his siblings, on older fellow members as parents. These bonds were far more than nominal. Whenever Gray-bull thereafter returned from a successful raid, he would bring horses to Bell-rock and White-stripe-across-his-face; even on ordinary occasions he might present them with the whole of a buffalo, receiving from them gifts in return. Gray-bull himself came to adopt "children" into the society and even in recent years would periodically give a ceremonial daughter some money.

Gray-bull was not of the stuff of religious leaders, but he entered wholeheartedly into his people's beliefs and usages. Thus, after a planting it was customary for a member to lie in the Tobacco garden in the hope of hearing sacred songs through supernatural favor. Gray-bull did so, and learnt a song about the Tobacco which he still sang at the dance in 1911. He was told at the garden never to eat the manifolds of a buffalo or cow and faithfully obeyed the command for the rest of his days.

He had other revelations. His grandfather had owned a bird medicine that was granted him in a personal vision, and before dying he had ordered Gray-bull's mother to pass it on to her son when he had grown to a man's estate. She did so, and he went fasting with it. A bird appeared to him, and in the vision enemies vainly tried to shoot it. Thus, Gray-bull got the gift of invulnerability. For another experience he was prepared by a father's clansman, who received four gifts for his labors. Gray-bull saw a gray horse in his vision, captured such a one on a raid, and thereafter accomplished great deeds on this mount. He commemorated the experiences by bestowing on his grandson the name "Chief-with-the-gray-horse." Even in the last years of his life Gray-bull kept on dreaming of battles and of horses captured by him.

There were other contacts with the spirit world. A maternal uncle once gave him a necklace connected with the Moon, who subsequently appeared to him in a dream and taught him a song. Gray-bull used the tooth from White-cub's skull on four expeditions. On these war parties, White-cub would speak to him, giving him advice, so that Gray-bull captured horses and other booty. From his stepfather he inherited a potent rock of odd shape; another he found himself and soon after came to own 120 head of horses.

Gray-bull was a generally esteemed Crow of the old school, saturated with the traditional customs and beliefs of his people. Once only, when a young man, he had badly fallen in tribal estimation by engaging in a fight with a chief—a disgraceful thing according to the native code of honor. His joking-relatives did not fail to make the most of this opportunity. "That one is likely to strike us," they would say on catching sight of him; "there's that fighter, get out of his way, he might hit you."

Gray-bull had a sense of humor; he nearly split his sides with laughter when I performed my version of a Crow dance and once when I asked his dog in Crow why it was barking. His intelligence appeared in lucid accounts of every phase of aboriginal life. Even in the narration of folk tales, a field in which he claimed no distinction, he proved competent and widely informed.

The foregoing account shows the multiple social ties possible in a comparatively simple hunting culture. Gray-bull has the universal connections with his elementary family plus the bonds with matrilineal and patrilineal kinsfolk as defined by the Crow. We see how constantly these turn up in his life, as helpers, mentors, eulogists, recipients of presents. He acquires new ties when as a boy he chooses a comrade, and later he becomes a husband and father, enters the Fox sodality, and when that is obsolete, the Crazy Dog society. He joins war parties, membership in one of which leads to initiation into the Tobacco society by the captain; whence multiple new relations follow as a logical consequence. Successive marriages establish bonds of affinity with distinct clans, others would follow in the wake of his children's and his siblings' marriages. Thus, he comes to have fairly specific relations with a very large proportion of his tribesmen.

## *The Woman's Angle*

A society that stresses warfare is bound to have a masculine cast, but this unquestionable fact is easily exaggerated. Again we meet the danger of looking at a people solely in comparison with others, solely to determine diagnostic features. Contrasted with Semang, Paiute, or Hopi, the Crow are certainly a militaristic tribe. But if we view them with reference to their total adjustment to life, fighting recedes into its proper niche. After all, the first business of these Indians, as of others, was to provide the means for daily existence; important as warfare loomed in their consciousness, it was not literally all important. That human beings put the frills of existence above its core, that they grow intoxicated with fictitious values, is a familiar phenomenon, and Plains Indian life teems with illustrations. But there was another side to this, and not merely with regard to practical necessities. No Crow man was on the warpath continually, and when not raiding he found plenty of indispensable employments nearer home. He had to hunt unless his family were to starve, he must repair his arrows and tend horses; and his wife cooked, dressed skins for clothing, put up the tent, collected such plant food as there was. To relieve the humdrum existence, both sexes, jointly or alone, had their diversions—dances and sport, games of chance, and at night, storytelling. In this daily routine that actually made up a great part of life woman's activities were not a whit less significant than man's.

Naturally, as in every militaristic culture, whether it be that of the North American Plains or of modern Prussia, the ideological super-structure bore heavily on women. It might thrill them to the core to hear how a son or husband had wiped out a whole tentful of Cheyenne, but it was not so pleasant when sooner or later retribution was visited upon a near kinsman. And it was not only the enemy that brought grief. How did Crow women feel about that fortnight's licensed libertinage in the spring, when Foxes and Lumpwoods broke up many happy homes? A woman absolutely above suspicion of unchastity, like Gray-bull's last wife, might breathe freely when the rival societies reorganized for the season, but others could not be sure of remaining with their husbands even if they had settled down to an exemplary conjugal and maternal role. Strikes-at-night gave a graphic account of the average woman's reactions.

My husband was a great warrior. He was a Fox. The Lumpwoods and the Foxes were stealing each other's wives one season while my husband was on the warpath. Before I had married, another man had courted me with gifts of beef and horses, but I married Bull-weasel's father. Now this suitor came with other Lumpwoods to get me. I was afraid they were going to take me by force, so I sneaked away to the hills, where a woman was mourning her dead son. Another woman came with me for the same reason; she was the mourner's sister-in-law. It was she who planned the way to escape. "My sister-in-law," she said, "goes out every morning to fast; let us go with her." We all got mourning blankets and early every day we went out together up the hills, where no one could find us. We were not so far but that we could hear the Lumpwoods hallooing and see them searching for women to steal. When the "showing-off" ceremony was done, we saw the abductor take the stolen woman to his home. We fasted and watched up there all day. We had no water. In the course of the day the mourner's relatives came to bring her food and water. Then we two others hid, begging her not to tell about us. When the relatives had gone, we all feasted on what they had brought. At night we returned to camp with the mourner. Mourners then slept in very small tents, deprived of all decoration. We slept in such tents and sneaked out with the mourner early the next day.

My husband returned with Big-ox's war party, and I saw him looking for me. The people told him I had fled in order not to be taken away. He never came near me because he did not wish to be present when I should be kidnapped. One night I stealthily approached him. He told me that if the Lumpwoods came for me while he was present he would let me go, but if I hid it would be well. I thought that if the camp were moved during the period of wife-kidnapping I should have no way of escape. They really did move. My husband painted me all up, and I rode his horse. Now they planned to catch me, but my husband's sister warned me and told me to go with her, saying that then they would not take me. The Lumpwoods were in the rear of the line of march, riding abreast and making a show of six Fox women they had captured. I was riding with my sister-in-law when the Lumpwoods approached. My sister-in-law would not let me run away, but they were coming fast and I got scared and broke away. Some tents had already been pitched by the Crow in the van, and I ran into the lodge of a woman whose husband was a Fox. She helped me unsaddle my horse, turned him loose, and covered me up with rawhide bags. There I lay. I heard the Lumpwoods outside. They had taken the wife of a man who had been living with her peacefully for several years. He got furious and was going to kill her with an arrow as she was being shown off. He let fly and barely missed her. The Lumpwoods all scattered. They took revenge on the Foxes by cutting up their robes into strips and pounding their horses' feet.

Towards evening we heard a shot. We saw a man running back and forth, raising a blanket and throwing it off several times to indicate how many Crow had been killed. He did this three times, then we could not count any more. We thought the main band had been wiped out. We learned that they had had war parties out in two directions and that all the warriors had been killed. The woman who had been shot at by her husband had lost two brothers. Our whole camp mourned.

Thus the wife-kidnapping ceased, and I escaped.

Possibly the narrator is truthful in her claim that the onetime suitor had never been her lover, hence had no right to lay hands on her. For sometimes might was right. Other informants tell of men feigning a past intimacy so that they could wrongfully abduct a woman. Thus a young wife's situation was doubly hazardous, seeing that she could never rely on her husband to protect her. Strikes-at-night's husband, like Gray-bull, made it clear that he would not defy the code, however much he suffered from it. As the case of the other husband shows, a responsible man had his fellow members to consider, all of whom would bear the brunt if he resisted the kidnaper. Except for the paragons of virtue, then, no woman was secure. Having young infants did not save her; they would be taken along with herself. What is more, she could not hope for a new stable union, for the kidnaper usually dismissed his prize soon after the capture. Nor could she expect to rejoin her true husband after the interlude, for on this point again the code was inexorable: a man who took back a wife under these conditions stood disgraced for life.

No wonder that Muskrat, a woman who had admitted having once been "young and free" in her actions, disapproved of the custom. She did not, to be sure, suffer in the usual way, for her husband was a Fox and all her brothers were Lumpwoods. However, her husband kidnaped at different times nine Lumpwood wives, though he soon got rid of them; only the eighth seems to have been a domestic problem.

Crow women of the old school, then, had a hard lot. They were forever mourning their husbands or brothers or sons; and at home they were exposed to the blatant virility of their tribesmen. Yet the women who had lived in the buffalo-hunting days preferred them to the pedestrian security of a modern reservation. The reason is clear: the old life had a tang that is drained out of contemporary conditions. For the impeccably chaste there was the supreme honor of serving in a sacred capacity in the Sun Dance. The skilled skin dresser could earn kudos and ample pay. An average woman might shine from the reflected glory of her husband. Visions and ceremonial activity were open to both sexes. Muskrat, an intelligent and well-informed, though extremely vain old woman, smugly recited her past triumphs in Crow society. She would dream of a bear, send out invitations for a big feast, and get presents from her guests. She had visions that enabled her to doctor broken bones and other ailments. She had held the highest post in her branch of the Tobacco society and adopted many novices. For the old-fashioned Crow woman the days of the war parties and the military societies, for all their tribulations, had a rich content. "I know the songs [of the Goose Egg Dance]," Strikes-at-night told me, "and sometimes I sing them, and they bring back memories of the past that make me feel sad." [1]

# Chapter 16

# THE BUINESE

## *Social Organization*

IN BOUGAINVILLE, one of the Solomon Islands, the district of Buin is inhabited by about 7,800 natives. Several centuries ago Melanesian marauders from the south conquered the Papuan indigenes, introducing some new elements of culture, but adopting the speech of the old population. Thus arose an upper and a lower stratum in the remodeled society of Buin. However, the conquerors brought very few of their own women, so that it was not practicable to maintain endogamy. In consequence, only the chief's successor could normally marry a mate of equal status. In the course of generations intermarriages multiplied: a chief's widow would take for her second husband some commoner, her junior daughter would be given to a half-Papuan, and so forth. Buinese of partly upper-class descent naturally stood socially above those who had no such relationship, received favors from their patrician kinsmen, and in turn formed their chief support, being appropriately styled their "pillars." Thus, there evolved three classes—chiefs, freemen, and the subject ·bondmen. The symbol of a paramount chief is a pretentious assembly hall, furnished with large tomtoms and decorative posts. It serves as a typical tribal clubhouse taboo to women. The main pillar represents the owner's war god, Orómrui, to whom a chief would formerly dedicate the skulls of commoners. On his first visit, in 1908, Professor Thurnwald found as many as sixty of these offerings in one hall. Less elaborate public buildings are put up by the chief's relatives and other vassals. These, too, generally controlled bondmen, since a chief was likely to allot several to faithful followers.

These developments materially altered the previous structure of society as it can still be observed in other sections of Bougainville. The neighbors of the Buinese are not stratified, are divided into matrilineal totemic clans, practice matrilocal residence, and grant a wife a good deal of domestic authority, e.g., in the arrangement of marriages. These positive features automatically went by the board through the happenings in Buin. Since most of the women belonged to the subject stratum, the conquerors naturally attached more importance to the father's line, regulating succession to office accordingly; and, as usual, the lower classes imitated their betters. Exogamy broke down; and though totems continue to be passed on by the mothers, the status of women has greatly deteriorated. A potter is no longer free to dispose of the vessels she has manufactured; her husband sells them, adding the money received to his hoard, to be expended for purposes of his own. When a widow remarries, her first husband's heir at once claims the payment offered to her father. On Buinese theory, the deceased mate had purchased her labor services, which would be lost by the new union; hence his kindred are entitled to an indemnity. By the patrilineal principle that has gained ascendancy, the bride price, then, should go to the dead man's son, to be shared with his brothers and other patrilineal relatives.

Of course, invasion did not completely transform social life—for one thing, because some customs were doubtless common to indigenes and invaders. This may apply to cross-cousin marriage, which continues to be the ideal form; in 1934 about a third of all unions for five generations back conformed to this principle. Nowadays, however, the theory is often sacrificed to other considerations: a wealthy commoner no longer tries to have his son take to wife a cross-cousin, but casts about for the daughter of a chief so as to enhance his prestige.

The desire to shine socially has, indeed, become one of the dominant factors in Buin life. As in most of Melanesia, a man advances his standing by playing the host at pork feasts. Women never participate in these, but the task of raising pigs for the purpose devolves on them, a wife's skill at the job being one of the most highly prized feminine accomplishments. It is customary for a chief to farm out suckling pigs to commoners, compensating them for their wives' trouble in feeding them. Characteristic of the prestige economy of these people is the notion that pigs are to be exchanged for shell money, and vice versa. This is a constantly recurring theme. When two paramount chiefs hold a fraternization festival, the celebration ends with the transfer of ten large pigs by one of the new confederates, who in return receives a thousand fathom of shell money. About a year later the process is reversed, the recipient of the pigs on the previous occasion now presents his partner with an equal number and gets back his shell money. After a chief's death his heir distributes part of the legacy in shell currency among his vassals and commoners, who take pride in providing him with a sizable porker in return. On the other hand, inherited pigs are given to men who reciprocate with presents of shell money, which the heir promptly uses to buy new pigs. Thus he may accumulate as many as fifty pigs for the memorial feast nine months or so after his predecessor's cremation and eclipse his peers by the extravagance of his offerings.

There is similar emulation in matrimonial arrangements. An ambitious upstart who has received shell money for his daughter will send back more than the traditionally proper number of pigs. The groom's father must then return supplementary fathoms of currency, and this rivalry continues until the resources of one competitor are exhausted and the other triumphs as his social superior.

Rank naturally affects the amount of the bride price. In one settlement a bondman's daughter could be bought for 100 to 200 fathom, a vassal's for 200, the junior daughter of a great chief for from 200 to 300, while his eldest daughter might fetch up to 400 fathom.

Politically, the Buinese are markedly separatistic; even a great chief of the old days had only a handful of freemen and possibly fifty bondmen. An eminent chief and his allies might gather together an exceptional army of five hundred, but ordinarily an engagement with a hundred braves on each side was referred to as a major battle. Like the Yurok, the Buinese paid damages for the injuries inflicted, the sufferers receiving, say, 100 fathom for every man slain. Furthermore, there was never an accession of territory, so that the economic advantages from victorious warfare were nil.

It is necessary to distinguish between nominal and real chiefs. All of a chief's sons claim the title, but it remains an empty one unless the claimant is able to put up a clubhouse and give a feast there, those who accept his invitation thereby recognizing him as a chief. These lesser chiefs are essentially nothing but prominent heads of households. Far less numerous and correspondingly more powerful are the "great chiefs"—or they were so before the colonial administrators restricted their functions.

However, even a great chief was far from being a despot. In the first place, we must distinguish between his position toward the middle class and that toward the lowest stratum. The latter, to be sure, labored under serious disadvantages. Whereas a bondman who so much as trod the trail used by women of the chief's household suffered death, his daughters were at the chief's disposal, becoming either his own or his guests' concubines. The father received as compensation two fathom of currency. Economically the bondmen depended on their chief since it was his prerogative to allot fields to be cultivated by them. One of the greatest liabilities of the rank resulted from the chief's eagerness to conciliate his war god. For that purpose he ordered a retainer bearing the glorious title of "the slayer" to kill a bondman of the district, or of some adjoining one, so that still another skull could be consecrated to Orómrui. For all that, the bondman was not quite so badly off as the foregoing statements may suggest. He was not prevented from gaining wealth, and in so plutocratic a society this implied that he could rise in standing. Whatever may have been a chief's theoretical claims, he was careful not to transgress certain limits. A malcontent driven beyond endurance might flee into the bush or even desert to the side of a rival chief. Thus, the mutual relations normally rested on reciprocity: the chief claimed a bondman's daughter, but not without payment; he allowed bondmen to share in pork feasts; he lent them currency required for ceremonial or matrimonial purposes; he kept them in good humor by liberal compensation for services rendered.

A freeman's status was, of course, far higher, so that at times the great chief must have been no more than the first among equals. However, his actual authority varied with his personality. One old chief, Cibelau, whom Europeans called "the king of Buin," terrorized even other chiefs of the district, treating them as though they were his bondmen and deliberately defying the norms of generosity. Thus, he would accept a large pig valued at 100 fathom and return only 10 fathom in exchange. This example leads us to the general topic of individual adaptation to Buinese society.

## Individual Buinese

A stratified society presents complications lacking among the Crow. For anything like a complete picture we should have to know the careers of representative men and women belonging to each of the three classes. The data available hardly suffice for so ambitious an aim, but Mrs. Thurnwald's biographical information on various Buinese personalities is of great value.

Buinese society is not only conspicuous for its stratification, but also for a marked class consciousness. Moriai, a freeman, insisted on the chasm between his own and the bondman's status. Were it not for the support given by his class, he argued, chiefs would be impotent. Freemen did, indeed, fight for a chief and render him tribute, but all services were wholly voluntary. A nineteen-year-old girl was indignant because Mrs. Thurnwald had failed to inquire about her celebrated matrilineal kinsfolk, who included the great chief Cibelau himself. Yet there is no suggestion of a caste system on the Hindu plan. We constantly meet with plebeian connections of great chiefs, with men of the lowest stratum who have attained eminence. Kolekai, a mere bondman, became rich, got together as many as thirty pigs, and managed to take to wife the daughter of a great chief. Long before democratization could be laid to white influence, Kocikai became a chief's "slayer," accumulated so much wealth that he bought chief's daughters for his two oldest sons, and himself was able to afford three wives—a rare and remarkable instance of polygyny within the lowest class.

Individual differences are as noticeable in their social effects among the upper ranks. Moaci, paramount chief of Kugumaru, is descended from a line of distinguished predecessors still mentioned with reverence despite the fact that some of them had married the daughters of freemen. For lack of a cross-cousin, Moaci took to wife a more remotely related girl of his own station, later marrying an additional young woman of the middle class. He adheres to ancient usage, continuing to live in a secluded homestead rather than in the street favored by the colonial officials, and enjoys general esteem: at an assembly no one ventures to take the floor until he has expressed his views, nor does any member of his retinue expect him to engage in physical labor. Nevertheless, he has lost in actual power, if not in prestige. Though the white administration has recognized him as village bailiff, it subordinates him to Lea, a socially inferior native. Moaci retains ten vassals and fourteen bondmen inherited from his father, but no longer really controls the latter group. A rather languid, unaggressive personality, he fails to assert himself against the cunning and unscrupulous Lea, whose knowledge of English and whose mental alertness made him the favorite of the white man's government.

In the neighboring settlement of Laitaro, the chief, Mamoko, likewise the scion of a great lineage, presents rather different traits. He retains six vassals and twenty bondmen, inherited an ample legacy of pigs and currency, and skillfully uses his means to preserve his status. His dependents continue to breed pigs for him and to render other services, but in return he entertains them at sumptuous feasts. He is also popular as their banker, helping his people when anyone of them has to buy a wife or would otherwise be unable to celebrate the traditional wake in honor of a dead relative. In contrast to Moaci and others among his peers, Mamoko does not stand aloof from his subordinates, but assists them in carrying loads or in other manual labors. In his makeup, too, he is not like other chiefs, forgoing their distinctive decoration. His democratic ways and his lavish banquets reconcile the people to his blunt and domineering manner. Unfamiliar with English like Moaci, he has nevertheless made a much better adjustment than his colleague. However, he was loath to give ethnographical information.

Lea, the village bailiff of Kugumaru, has already been mentioned as Moaci's rival. For years the servant of a British official, he became fluent in pidgin English, an accomplishment highly prized by the white administration. Thus the son of a middle-class man and a bond-man's daughter was put at the head of a district comprising 19 settlements with a population of 2,000—one much greater than had ever been ruled by the greatest of aboriginal chiefs. To be sure, his coercive authority is only vicarious through his status as the white police superintendent's deputy. Nevertheless, his manifold duties involve much responsibility and power. He reports infanticide, marriages of immature girls, maltreatment of bondmen; supervises the collection of the poll tax and the repairing of bridges and roads; and undertakes the construction of settlements in accordance with governmental decrees.

Quite apart from the consequences of his official position, Lea is an astute businessman who manages to extract profit from transactions with poor bondmen. If one of them requires shell currency for a bride payment or money for the poll tax, Lea advances him 10 fathom for raising his little pig, which Lea subsequently sells for 100. In this fashion he has made himself the richest man in Kugumaru and periodically gloats over putting the old aristocrats to shame. When paid 400 fathom for his daughter as bride of a chief's son, Lea sent back pig after pig beyond the required number, forcing his son-in-law's father to compensate him with shell money until the chief no longer knew how to procure more of it. On every occasion he ostentatiously displays his wealth, paying for swine in advance or gorging his guests with pork and sago. Chiefs, as well as their middle-class vassals and their bond-men, have become Lea's debtors, and everyone is obliged to admire the upstart's liberality.

Yet Lea remains a marginal man. He never feels quite secure. Suspecting theft, he padlocks his door, contrary to general practice. Professing an enlightened attitude toward native superstitions, he still dreads entering a medicine man's tabooed forest and is afraid of being magically poisoned. He is painfully aware of not having inherited a single bondman; and neither his official powers nor his affluence makes him forget that the old chiefs look down upon him. Nor can he quite overcome his inferiority complex toward the men of high rank. Though he has eclipsed Moaci in riches and by virtue of his superior bailiff's status, he dares not affront him by openly divorcing the old chief's niece, much as he has longed to do so since falling under the spell of a second, shrewish wife, who veritably henpecks him.

That such truckling to women can occur in a society which treats the female sex as inferior is significant. How individual gifts can surmount barriers due to theoretical disabilities is demonstrated by the personality of Kidou. Descended from a great chief, she was married at puberty to a matrilineal relative who was a vassal of her father's. Not long after her marriage she began to go into trances and prophesied that she would soon become a doctor. A remotely related medicine man whose son had refused to take over his father's calling instructed her, teaching her to recognize the spirits and to understand their speech. She inherited her mentor's guardian spirits and the ability to rescue the souls of people snatched away by demons. Kidou has risen to preeminence in the profession: when her male colleagues are at a loss in the treatment of a patient, they appeal to her for aid. At home she eclipses her husband and has been able to veto a son-in-law favored by him, substituting the man of her choice as their daughter's husband. Most remarkable of all, Kidou is allowed to enter the men's clubhouse. Yet as recently as 1914 any woman attempting to do so would have been promptly killed, and even twenty years later most females would hurry past the assembly halls. In short, exceptional capacity can override deep-rooted disabilities even in a society that so definitely discriminates against women. [1]

# Chapter 17

# THE SHILLUK

THE Shilluk are a Nilotic people of the Sudanese family, inhabiting mainly the west bank of the Nile between 10°40′ and 9°25′ northern latitude. In 1869 the famous explorer Georg Schweinfurth set their number at 1,200,000, settled in 3,000 villages that almost merged into one another to form a single continuous area of occupation. Wars and slave raids, however, reduced the population, so that in 1903 a census put it at only 60,000, inhabiting 1,200 villages. For the period imme-diately following World War I, Hofmayr suggests the reasonable figure of 120,000.

As explained in the chapter on the State, the Shilluk while under aboriginal conditions were governed by a theoretically despotic king, but contacts with higher civilization, especially with the Anglo-Egyptian administration, wrought great changes. In the following account the native organization is described as though ancient patterns were still in full swing.

## *The Social Foundation*

The Shilluk farm, breed livestock, hunt, and fish. Sorghum is the staple crop; originally only women cultivated it, but more recently men have shared in the work, though they are mainly concerned with cattle herding. They derive relatively little practical benefit from their stock, for the cows yield little milk and animals are not slaughtered as part of the normal routine. Nevertheless the Shilluk are passionately devoted to their beasts. As a delicate compliment they address an intimate as "My ox" or "My cow"; spend hours massaging an animal's hump or artificially twisting its horns for embellishment; and even celebrate their cattle in eulogistic songs. Since there is no regular butchering, hunting and fishing remain important as the sources of flesh diet. Except for the blacksmiths, the Shilluk are hardly artisans in an economic sense: the woman who makes pottery and the man who thatches roofs still devote most of their time to tasks connected with getting or preparing food. Apart from farming, the women fetch water and firewood, clean the house, and tend to the meals. As a proverb puts it, "Women are born to cook"; and from early childhood girls eagerly compete with one another in basic culinary accomplishments. Subsequently, at wed-ding feasts they show off their art, trying to eclipse their rivals. On the other hand, only men take care of the cattle, which are herded and milked by boys and youths.

This fairly, sharp division of labor does not go with the rigid social dichotomy common in Melanesia. The sexes join in dances and other amusements; even in the ceremony held in honor of deceased men the women play their part, beating the drum and bawling their laments, while the girls perform a dance.

Every individual belongs to his father's clan, a unit that generally bears the name of an animal or a plant. The totemic species include the shad, pike, ostrich, giraffe, gourd, and tamarind. A few clans bear such designations as "rope" and "hearthstone."

Children are not weaned until about two years of age; and since the parent must remain continent so long as the infant is nursed, the men naturally desire an additional wife. There is extremely little discipline for youngsters, especially in the case of a favorite child. When about five years old, a boy joins other lads, sleeping henceforth in the village byre. He learns to tend and to milk livestock, at first herding only goats, later cows. Girls also sleep by themselves in special huts, often supervised by matrons. These young women have their diversions, telling stories and propounding conundrums to one another.

There is no circumcision rite to mark a boy's coming of age; the Shilluk abhor the custom and constantly make fun of neighboring peoples who practice it. The only formality in vogue at puberty is the lad's admission to the warriors' dance. As soon as his father sanctions it, a son joins in the performance, henceforth becoming a person responsible for his actions and a member of the army. For a while he is likely to go wandering through the length and breadth of the Shilluk territory. He soon turns his thoughts to marriage, for without a mate a man is of little consequence. A poor boy is hard put to it to acquire a wife in competition with wealthy elders. So he starts courting and casts about for cattle to offer in payment for a bride. Periodically disease and raids greatly reduce the total number of livestock in the land, setting the traditional price far beyond an ordinary suitor's means. Recognizing the difficulty, King Kuikon, who reigned from 1876 until 1882, made himself very popular with the younger generation by reducing the amount to a single cow together with four or five sheep and a lance. However, a few decades later the price had again risen to the old level of ten head.

A girl undergoes no ritual at puberty, but must abstain from milk. Matrimony now looms on her horizon and her parents may permit her some freedom of choice. A slender youth who dances well, has killed an enemy, and can catch plenty of fish will find favor, for the Shilluk are passionately fond of dancing, esteem bravery, and prize few dishes as much as a fat fish or fish soup. On the other hand, vitriolic songs deride a lazybones and poor provider. A girl will make a confidante of her mother, who usually takes her part against the father if he is bent only on getting a maximum of profit out of his daughter's nuptials.

A youth who has come to an understanding with a girl sends an older kinsman as go-between to ask the parents for the hand of their daughter. As indicated, the mother is by no means negligible in these transactions. The contracting parties agree on the bride price and the groom sends the first installment, thereby cementing the engagement. Henceforth he must treat his prospective parents-in-law with extreme awe, never speaking with them outdoors and avoiding their home. He visits his fiancée only once a month, and then in some stranger's house, where he may converse with her of an evening, but must not dance with her. The young man is now expected to work continually for her parents, bringing them fish, meat, and other supplies. He is in a constant state of anxiety lest her family break the engagement, which would mean the loss of these minor gifts. Periodically his girl's kindred invite his friends to a drinking spree, where they dun the guests for such head of cattle as have not yet been delivered. In a very large percentage of cases the betrothal is dissolved, usually because the young man is unable to pay the entire stipulated price. However, some young women break the tie from sheer fickleness and jilt several suitors before settling down to wedlock.

When five male and five female head of cattle have been conveyed to the bride's parents, the marriage is consummated after certain ceremonial acts. These include a mock fight between the bride's and the groom's friends, followed by a mutual washing of hands by the young couple, which seals the bond. For three or four days the newlyweds stay in the bride's village; then she is taken to the groom's. Divorce is common, either because the wife has entered the marriage unwillingly or because her parents insist on extra payments if some of the cattle paid them die off. Since plagues have afflicted the livestock in recent times, such supernumerary demands work a grave hardship on most young men. Economic difficulties explain why polygyny, however strongly desired, occurs in only 30 per cent of all cases, and in the overwhelming majority of cases is limited to bigamy.

Contrary to popular impressions of Negro matrimony, a Shilluk wife enjoys an excellent position in society. She may leave her husband; she does not resent a second wife, who may be her own sister and whom in any case she welcomes as a helper in the housework; she may, indeed, be beaten if refractory, but not with a stick; and a husband striking her during her pregnancy would expose himself to severe punishment. However, a barren woman stands disgraced and is divorced, her parents being compelled to restore her bride price.

A strange custom obliges a woman who has just been delivered to confess all her past amours to the midwife. She hardly ever refuses to do so, for there is a strong belief that this would cause her and the infant to die. The lovers revealed by this confession pay the husband an ox or a sheep. Instead of resenting his wife's past love life, he rejoices both over the property her avowal will get him and over his newborn child: If no child blesses a union, he permits one of his half brothers to have sex relations with his wife; any issue from such intercourse legally belongs to the husband and would inherit from him, not from the begetter.

The eldest son inherits his stepmothers. Indeed, because it is so difficult to acquire wives, a man will sometimes share his wives with his son, except, of course, the young man's own mother.

Some of the relevant social facts are illustrated in an account of the daily routine by a Catholic missionary on the basis of years of observation. It is briefly summarized in the following paragraphs.

## The Daily Routine

Before sunrise the women of a homestead begin to pound their grain. After a while the men rise and dash into the warm cowshed, inspect their beasts, and powder themselves with native cosmetics, while the boys clean the byre, collect cow dung for fuel, and attend to the stock. A woman enters with lukewarm water, and the males superficially wash their faces. While the men are still lounging, the women and girls are pounding or grinding cereals or brewing beer. At about nine o'clock a cook brings a pitcher of water for rinsing the mouth and sets down a pot with hot porridge, which the men consume in company. The woman squats by herself, then once more offers water for cleansing. If the adults have left part of the breakfast unconsumed, the boys have their innings; otherwise they go to the kitchen and appeal to the women there.

After the meal, the company breaks up: the youngsters drive the livestock to pastures; some men go to the fields with their hoes; would-be dandies strut about in their finery; those more seriously minded plait baskets or twist cords in their huts. The dwellings are arranged in the form of a circle, and in the center of the enclosed space there is a sacred tree supposedly connected with the village and the ancestors of the residents. In its shade the elders are accustomed to sit, discussing their traditionary lore and current events as well as bewailing the tribute they are compelled to pay. Sometimes, too, court sessions are held in this public forum.

Suddenly three visitors from another settlement arrive and seat themselves before the old residents without saying a word. After a prolonged silence the headman of the village begins the conversation by uttering the names or the totem of the oldest guest; then each of the hosts in turn greets each of the visitors individually. Only after these amenities a hide is spread for them to sit on. To come to the point at once would be regarded as the height of churlishness; accordingly everybody engages in several hours' talk concerning trivial matters: one man raves about the delicious fish eaten on some past occasion, another waxes expansive over his hunting trophies, a third mimics the absurd mispronunciation of Shilluk words by foreigners, still others make fun of the local dudes or criticize the indecent behavior of the young women.

Everyone knows perfectly well that the newcomers are trying to arrange a match with a local belle, but only after endless talk about totally irrelevant affairs does the senior visitor take out a parcel of rods, which he lays down in order of their size. They denote the cattle and other stock which the prospective groom is able to pay. The matchmaker pleads his client's case and exaggerates his riches. He particularly mentions all the suitor's sisters—the more the merrier, for the bride prices to be fetched by them will bring wealth to their family. At last the intermediary feels that he has done his duty and departs with his companions.

While the elders congregate under the sacred tree, the younger males assemble and gossip some distance outside the village, where the blacksmith plies his trade and his apprentice manipulates a bellows. Unlike some Africans, the Shilluk highly esteem a blacksmith, an expert craftsman ranking with a chief.

Toward sunset everyone goes home, the herders driving the cattle back and shielding them from mosquitoes by a smudge. The boys milk cows and goats, then stable and tether them. Now is the time—about seven o'clock—when the natives partake of the second and last meal of the day, the sexes again eating separately. After dinner sociability and entertainment once more reign supreme. The elders resume their discussions under the sacred tree, lovers have their trysts, young men and women play games or perform their dances, and minstrels compose their songs—very likely in honor of some beloved cow. Finally everyone goes to sleep.

## Social Groupings and Ties

The foregoing sketch indicates some of the essential ways in which a Shilluk individual is socially classed. There is no sex dichotomy, but in eating and working the division of men and women is clear enough. The men's assembly under the village tree brings in the additional factor of age, since only mature males come together there. Seniority appears in another way: seniors and superiors must be addressed by the polite pronominal form corresponding to French *vous* or German *Sie*. Modes of address, as usual, are tinctured by the pervasive influence of kinship. When villagers meet they call each other by suitable relationship terms, whether a relationship exists or not.

But the social structure is greatly complicated by two further factors that have so far been deliberately ignored—the class system and the political organization of the country. Intimately connected with each other, the two vitally affect the individual Shilluk's life.

Politically, the country is divided into four major and two minor provinces, the governors of the former being also the electors of a new king and serving as royal councilors. Within each province the various districts have their chiefs, and in each district there may be from five to twelve villages with their respective heads. In the chapter on the State the king's office has already been briefly described. We shall revert to the subject presently, for royalty seriously modifies the course of the subjects' lives; and on the other hand, the king's private life is an extreme deviation from that of the normal Shilluk. For the present we need merely recall the strange tempering of absolutism with grave disabilities.

As for classes, four may be recognized. First come the kwaret, i.e., the male and female descendants of kings, living and dead. Each ruler prides himself on the number of sons who may succeed him, and of the traditional kings one named Nyakac (1780–ca. 1820) was prized happy beyond all others because four of his sons actually came to ascend the throne. The second rank is that of the oror; these are kwaret whom the monarch degrades for reasons of his own to the status of mere noblemen. The third class comprises the bulk of the population, the commoners. Finally, there are the slaves, either commoners who have fallen into debt or foreigners acquired in trade. Both are treated remarkably well, literally as members of the family, the former even being allowed to marry women of the commoners' rank.

It should be noted that by this scheme chiefs are not by virtue of their office blue bloods, but simply executives and judges. Even the provincial governors are not hereditary patricians, but are elected by the people and then ratified by the king; the monarch himself chooses his ministers. In other words, apart from the ruler, office and rank need not coincide.

## Modification of the King's Social Life by Royal Prerogatives.

As a sacred person inspired and possessed by the legendary demigod and culture hero, Nyikang, the king cannot but exert a great deal of influence. Economically he exploits all commoners: they are obliged to put up the huts he needs or to provide the necessary materials for them and surrender to him the most valuable indigenous and imported articles. Customary law even permits him to confiscate a nobleman's cows; King Kwatker (1863–1870) twice took away all the kwaret Ayang's stock. Court trials form one of the principal sources of the royal revenue. Characteristically, the fine for murder is paid to the king rather than to the aggrieved; Kur (1892–1903) clandestinely promoted rather than suppressed blood feuds in order to increase his supply of cattle, thus easily making himself the wealthiest stockowner in the land.

The ruler's judgments are executed by his bodyguard, an indefinite number of young men who form his constant retinue, collect taxes and debts, and oppress the populace. Kings have commonly played favorites in the execution of legitimate judgments, indefinitely delaying it on behalf of their friends and mercilessly hastening it from animosity or sheer whim.

In his capacity of high priest the king wields tremendous power, for the people believe that he can make rain, thereby putting a stop to a prolonged drought and thus staving off a famine. Fadyet (1903–1917) was still able to intimidate his subjects by threatening to withhold precipitation. In such an emergency it is only the king who may decree a human sacrifice.

The monarch has often directly changed the private lives of his subjects. In order to have the maximum number of sons he marries many wives, choosing any girl he desires. This is sheer loss for her family, for he does not pay the customary price, and if the young woman is betrothed he simply orders that the engagement be broken, which means that installments of the bride price must be returned to the fiancé.

Some laws promulgated by past kings have influenced the fortune of his subjects to their advantage, as when Kuikon (1876–1882) reduced the bride price or when Aney (1820–1825) abolished a cruel blood-letting test of the royal wives that was supposed to show whether or not they were sterile.

To repeat, notwithstanding the loftiness of the ruler's status, serious liabilities attach to it, and even privileges unchallenged in the abstract have actually precipitated revolt. Thus, Ayang, when deprived of his cattle, swore vengeance against King Kwatker, and betrayed him to the Egyptian government. Again, the very sanctity of the king's office leads to his violent death. Any ailment is held inconsistent with his rain-making powers and offensive to the indwelling Nyikang; hence he must be suffocated. Again and again we note a curious stress on the monarch's responsibility to the people. All indications to the contrary notwithstanding, the ruler is not literally an autocrat. At his coronation, for instance, the chiefs in turn lecture him at length on his duties, and in response he promises to be just and to protect the weak.

Above all, the king's private life is traditionally fixed in a manner that precludes normal development of human relations. A newly chosen king is prohibited from retaining his wives, who must not accompany him to Fashoda, the capital; he dismisses them with gifts and occasionally pays them a visit, but creates a new harem for himself, with his predecessor's wives as a core. To this legacy he adds women from many villages and is rather expected to wed one of his half sisters—in contrast to the otherwise general incest rules. After becoming pregnant, the wife remains in Fashoda for five months, then returns to her native village, whose chief is in duty bound to protect her. Like ordinary women, a royal spouse must confess all her love affairs after her delivery before she is permitted to receive her child. Neither she nor the infant may approach the ruler during the nursing period. Then the mother presents her offspring to the royal presence; a boy receives cows, a girl minor gifts, then he or she returns to his village, growing up without seeing either father or mother, for the latter must remain at the capital until her next pregnancy. After she has given birth to two or three children the king appoints her as the attendant of some temple, where she spends the rest of her days unmarried. At death she is properly mourned, and a son of hers who comes to ascend the throne is likely to erect a sanctuary in her honor.

Kwaret of either sex are brought up by their mother's parents or other kinsfolk. They are marked off by an external sign from their playmates: unlike other Shilluk, persons of royal blood retain all their lower incisors. From childhood on, they are likely to treat their companions in a haughty manner. A princess must remain single, since there is no one of equal rank for her to marry. Moreover, a conceivable husband could not make the payment that alone validates a union, since it would have to be rendered to the king. He, however, is supreme lord over everything; hence it would be logically absurd to pay him out of his own wealth. Since Kur's reign a princess is permitted to choose a lover, but not to bear children. Her influence in the village is considerable, and sometimes she is even elected its chief.

A young prince early plays a prominent role among his age mates, arbitrarily deciding difficulties after the royal fashion. But as a youth he begins to travel up and down the land and to court popularity. Since there is neither primogeniture nor any other fixed rule of succession, an eager competition develops among all princes so far as they are not excluded from the throne because of being left-handed, maimed, cross-eyed, or imbecile. The attempt of the princes to curry favor with their prospective subjects again demonstrates the fact that the people, appearances to the contrary notwithstanding, do count for something in the Shilluk scheme. It is true that the four (or six) provincial governors are technically the electors and choose the future king from among the large number of candidates, i.e., all physically and mentally fit sons of kings, but in their choice they are largely influenced by popular preference.

The traditional upbringing of a possible king precludes close sentimental ties with his parents or siblings. Usage also impairs the relations with his harem. Inordinately jealous, the king kills any unauthorized male intruder into the palace grounds. Unrestrained when out of sorts, he flogs his wives cruelly, and Kur is even said to have killed one of them in a fit of rage. On the other hand, the wives, numbering from thirty to sixty, have means of revenge. They may compass their royal husband's death by charging him with decrease of virility or otherwise plot against him with rival princes. Typical is the murder of Nyidok (ca. 1845-1863). During an indisposition he was visited by one wife, who pretended to fan him, but as soon as she heard her fellow conspirators, she vigorously struck the king's temples with her brass ring, and the entering noblemen promptly suffocated him.

From every point of view royalty thus has a distinctive social life. The ordinary Shilluk woman marries and becomes an object of contempt unless she bears children; a woman of royal blood ought not to marry and must under no circumstances bear a child. Princes, as well as princesses, fail to establish the bonds a commoner has with his parents or his siblings; brothers are essentially conceived as rivals and enemies; a half sister becomes a spouse. The king rides roughshod over the feelings of his parents-in-law—relatives whom everyone else treats with peculiar reverence. He cannot watch his children grow up, he must by immemorial usage divorce the wives acquired before his accession and cannot permanently keep any that he marries subsequently. Custom permits him to maltreat his wives unchecked, but by way of compensation they turn into the means for his destruction.

## Comparison of Crow, Buinese, and Shilluk Organization

Each of these peoples considered shares the essentials of its social structure with a fair number of other tribes within the same area. The Cheyenne, the Dakota, the Hidatsa, the Blackfoot systems of military sodalities have many conspicuous resemblances to that of the Crow. Buinese ideas of prestige in association with pork feasts are widely spread over the whole of Melanesia and such outlying parts of Indonesia as Alor. As for the Shilluk, the polity of several East African monarchies not only conforms to the same general pattern of autocracy tempered with assassination, but duplicates even details in the ruler's mode of life.

Is it possible to bring our three samples into relation to one another? If so, it will certainly not be by way of a simple scheme of unilinear evolution. Economically, the farming and pig-breeding Buinese are above the Crow hunters and below the farming and cattle-raising Shilluk. But each of the three societies has complexities of its own not paralleled in the others. The sodalities of the Crow and the Plains Indian ideology of war are not steps toward the prestige economy of Buin, and the strata of the Buinese are by no means logical and inevitable antecedents to the Shilluk class organization. Certainly there are resemblances as well as differences, but they are of the most general type: sex, age, kinship play their respective parts as they do in all human societies, though, of course, not in the same way.

Turning to the social adjustments of the individual, we find that he is nowhere free in an absolute sense. Education imposes on the Plains Indian no less than on the Melanesian or the African certain standards by which he gauges his own and others' conduct, irrespective of his original nature, and by which others judge him. A cowardly Crow, a stingy Buinese, a childless Shilluk woman inevitably descend in the estimation of their tribesmen. On the other hand, the extent to which one's positive traits count in raising one's status varies radically in our three samples. No one can rise to the kingship, no one can be promoted to kwaret status among the Shilluk; the Buinese scheme is less rigid, but even in recent times the successful upstart does not quite "belong"; only among the Crow the inborn qualities of bravery and liberality permit a man to rise to the pinnacle of tribal esteem.

Nevertheless, this is an oversimplified picture. An orphaned Crow may become the great chief of his generation, but he does not start unhandicapped. The *average* poor boy will always be less secure socially than an equally endowed lad with powerful kinsmen to support him. On the other hand, in the stratified Buinese and Shilluk societies uncommon gifts make for an uncommon career. A Buinese woman outshines her medical colleagues, a commoner becomes the chief's trusted assassin-in-ordinary. Among the Shilluk the very selection of a king from among the possible incumbents is in the last analysis due to his personal traits, and we have seen that some rulers have had some consideration for the general welfare. Further, Hofmayr assures us that the longevity of a king depends on his popularity; it is a monarch who has incurred the general displeasure that is likely to be plotted against before the normal time. The governing of so large a population also requires a variety of royal servants whose selection must again hinge on their abilities and characters, whether they are the royal ministers or the stool pigeons who keep their master informed of what is going on among his subjects.

The significance of individual worth (according to any existing norms) may thus be greater or less from a social point of view, but it is never a negligible quantity in any society.[1]

# Chapter 18

# IMPERIAL AUSTRIA

Complex societies may be studied from the same point of view as simpler ones. For many of them ample evidence is available, so that it is possible to trace their evolution through long periods. For present purposes it suffices to consider a single country, imperial Austria, beginning with the attempt of the Habsburg family to unify their possessions in the eighteenth century and ending with 1914. We shall take up the state, nationalism, and the social classes, finally noting how individuals fitted themselves into the existing social structure. The discussion of political history serves merely as a background for the picture of society.

## *The State*

The idea that a particular ethnic group should have a state of its own, uniting all its members, is fairly recent. It certainly did not exist when the Habsburgs rose to prominence in 1273, with Rudolf of that line having been chosen emperor of the Holy Roman Empire. They secured territories in the Netherlands, in Italy, in Hungary, and claimed the loyalty of the inhabitants as a dynastic matter, irrespective of whether they were of the same stock or not. Sometimes the Habsburg patrimony was split up among members of the line; then it would be united again.

By the feudal system the ruler dealt with the common people only indirectly; his direct relations were with the "estates" (*Stände*), i.e., the nobility, who were in immediate control of the peasants. The estates came to rival the monarch in point of sovereignty, but only within the particular dominion—say Styria or Hungary—in which they had established themselves. Such a "crown land," as it was afterward called thus was a dual state. Theoretically, the monarch was supreme, but his coercive powers might be matched and challenged by the estates, who raised armies of their own. At the opening of the Thirty Years' War (1618–1648) the Bohemian aristocracy defied the emperor, rising in open revolt. In this particular case the estates were crushed, but elsewhere they continued to stand on their hereditary privileges and deprecated any attempt of his majesty to centralize his power by imposing an imperial bureaucracy on and over them.

However, in the long run this dual system broke down. When threatened by a foreign invader—notably by the Turks—the estates of a single dominion were rarely strong enough to repel the attack; hence they would apply for help to their neighbors, as Carniolan nobles did in 1528. Unfortunately for them, such aid might be withheld. In 1667, Styria, when asked to assist Carniola, declared that it was *His Majesty's* business to defend his lands; in 1707 Carinthia and Carniola refused a similar request of the Styrians, and with this incident the practice of seeking support from fellow estates ceased.

This condition of affairs paved the way for centralization of power by the Habsburgs. Not to go into detail, they did away with ancient customs barriers within their realm and introduced over at least part of it a uniform code of laws. Centralization was marked by such steps as abolishing a separate administrative board for Bohemia (1749), which henceforth was governed by the same Viennese officials in charge of the Alpine lands. However, this tendency failed of complete realization. When Joseph II (1765–1790) tried to make it prevail in Hungary, the nobles resisted with such vehemence that he felt obliged to restore the traditional laws of that country.

In short, Austrian despotism, too, was hemmed in by other social forces, the restraining agency in the case quoted being the Magyar estates.

The French Revolution brought the concept of a liberal, democratic nationalism opposed to dynasticism. This new idea spread rapidly over a large part of the continent, reaching such diverse peoples as Germans, Czechs, and Norwegians. After the downfall of Napoleon, European statesmen of the old school restored the dynastic principle, but were no longer able to exterminate national feeling. The revolutions of 1848 in Germany and Austria were inspired by democratic, national ideals. Aided by Russia, the Austrian troops crushed the uprising, and the government sought to centralize authority once more in the new emperor, Francis Joseph, throwing all symbols of democracy into the discard. Political associations ceased, the only organizations that escaped suspicion being Catholic fraternities sanctioned by a bishop. Professional judges took the place of juries, the lower classes were once more subject to flogging. Unenlightened police inspectors gained the right to censor plays, books, and newspapers. Large bodies of stool pigeons dogged the footsteps of political liberals and even spied on cabinet ministers. Reputable authors groaned under the incubus of heresy hunters before and after 1848. The classical dramatist of Austria, Franz Grillparzer, a fervent patriot and believer in a centralistic Habsburg state, wrote a tragedy brimful of loyalty to the dynasty, yet a censor prohibited its performance until by chance the empress discovered it and had the ban removed.

A constitution came in 1867, limiting the monarch's sovereignty, yet some of the absolutistic features of the earlier period continued indefinitely. Political meetings became permissible, but the police inspector in attendance had the right to dissolve them if he regarded any of the speakers' utterances as subversive. At the turn of the century, leftist editors continued to be haled into court and to jail on flimsy charges. In 1897, when Mark Twain stayed in Vienna, he was amused at the censorship in vogue. Parts of newspaper articles would be pronounced unpublishable and whole issues might be confiscated.

However, as the estates had once restricted the authority of the ruler, so in the nineteenth century other social forces had to be reckoned with. Foremost among these was precisely that mixture of democracy and nationalism which had apparently been destroyed by the victorious monarchical armies in 1848. Francis Joseph felt himself to be a *German* prince and remained intransigent on one point: all army commands, whether addressed to Ruthenians, Magyars, or Viennese, had to be issued in German. On other matters he and his family were anything but consistently pro-German. Indeed, there was a time early in his reign when "German" was suspect as allegedly synonymous with "liberal." For instance, Prince Friedrich Schwarzenberg, though he fancied himself as a writer of German verse, advised his sovereign to rely on Magyars and Slavs rather than on German Austrians. At all events, the emperor and his ministers constantly temporized, now yielding to one ethnic group, now conciliating another. Habsburg princes all studied at least Magyar and Czech; Crown Prince Rudolf acquired Polish in addition; his mother read Jókai in the original Magyar. Archduke Franz Ferdinand's undisguised loathing for the Hungarians, it was hinted, went back to his troubles in learning their formidable tongue. In other than linguistic ways Magyars, Czechs, and Poles were in turn favored and appeased.

Francis Joseph yielded to mass agitation in two memorable instances. In the eighties and nineties Dr. Karl Lueger, at one time a liberal and a democrat, began to arouse the petty bourgeois against Jewish capitalism and Jews generally. Gifted with a remarkably magnetic personality, he became the idol of innumerable Viennese, organized the Christian Socialist party, and was elected mayor of the capital. In this office, however, he had to be confirmed by the emperor. Francis Joseph, who did not take kindly to demagogues, refused to ratify the people's choice, but when they elected Lueger again and again the monarch bowed to their will. He was no longer an absolute sovereign.

Still more remarkable was Francis Joseph's active promotion of universal manhood suffrage in 1907. The constitution he had belatedly granted in 1867 had, indeed, formally abolished autocracy. There was henceforth a parliament (*Reichsrat*) with an elective lower chamber and a partly hereditary, partly appointive senate. On the face of it the former would be a potential check to the latter and to the emperor. Actually the dice were heavily loaded against the rank and file of the people. In 1893 the senate comprised 21 archdukes, 66 hereditary peers of aristocratic lineage, and 125 lifelong members appointed for merit. Since the numerical strength of this body was not fixed, any government could enlarge it with supporters of its policies. Further, the lower chamber could not be a popular safeguard because of property qualifications so formulated as to disfranchise two thirds of the Austrian males. The qualified voters, again, were divided into classes with unequal voting privileges. Sixty-three great landed proprietors elected the same number of deputies as 2918 urban or 10,592 rural voters; a single landed proprietor was politically equivalent to 46 townsmen or to 168 peasants. The Socialists had long inveighed against the iniquity of the system, and in 1907 the agitation finally led to universal and equal manhood suffrage. The result was startling: the Socialists, hitherto represented by only 11 deputies, now captured 87 out of a total of 516 seats.

Manifestly this had not been the goal desired by the imperial government. In supporting democratic suffrage it simply recognized a shift in the actual balance of power within the monarchy. Even the lower classes could no longer safely be treated as subjects who owed blind obedience.

This meant, of course, abandoning strictly monarchical logic, but that is the common fate of absolutism. In the last analysis, even the Shilluk king proved to depend on his popularity. He was elected from among a number of potential princes, all of whom had pushed their candidacy by making friends among the people in the hope that pressure would thus be exerted on the theoretically independent four electors. And the very duration of a reign hinged on the king's pleasing his subjects, who were then less likely to pretend to notice his physical decline.

Among the social agencies that no Austrian government could ignore stood the Church. In 1910 almost 78 per cent of the people in the entire monarchy were Roman Catholics. Since the vast majority of Protestants and Orthodox Christians lived in the Hungarian half of the state, the proportion of Catholics in Austria proper was over-whelming—over 90 per cent. However, this preponderance was significant for the present theme only because the modern state and the Catholic Church are what they are. To compare with primitive conditions, all Crow Indians shared the same world view, but neither Crow faith nor Crow coercive agencies overlapped in their interests in certain problems that Western states and religions both regard as vital, notably marriage and education. Here, then, it is possible for a conflict to arise. Everything hinges on which of two mutually exclusive ideologies a state supports with its coercive machinery. Thus, in 1888 a clerical deputy launched a bill wholly defensible on Catholic principles: it rested on the premise that the public schools ought to give religious instruction; and it proposed that the Church exercise supervision over all the instruction offered. Since part of the population baptized into the Catholic Church had grown secularist, the bill was vigorously opposed. We are not concerned with the merits of the dispute, but merely with the fact that religious associations may be strongly concerned with the way in which a state arranges certain matters; and that when strong they may determine, or at least affect, policy. This is not a peculiarity of Catholicism; among Norwegian immigrants in our country the "godless" public schools of America were a target for severe criticism.

Distinctive of the Church-State relationship in Austria and other Catholic countries is the *international* character of the established faith, whose head resides in Rome. Hence borderline issues cannot be settled without reference to an authority outside the territory over which the state claims supremacy. In so far as the state accepts the decisions of that authority, then, it surrenders its sovereignty.

When Joseph II extended his centralist programme, he maintained that no such concession was possible, that Austrian priests were merely state officials. Among other things he gave the monopoly of clerical training to the state seminaries founded by his mother; he forbade the publication of papal bulls by priests without the monarch's permission; he even regulated the details of religious service, stipulating how many candles were to be lit on weekdays and on holidays. These laws, which date back to the early 1780's, were revoked by Francis Joseph in 1850. Five years later a further step was taken. Austrian bishops argued that obligations were binding only through an agreement with the Holy

See; hence a concordat with the Pope was recommended and concluded. The minister for worship and education acquiesced in the contention that not only the dogmas and ethics but also the constitution of the Church had been divinely revealed, that accordingly the state was in duty bound to recognize these laws. The concordat thus gave to the bishops jurisdiction over matrimony and the supervision over public education; they were recognized as supreme censors, whose judgments on literary products were to be executed by the state. These latter extensions of Church power did not last beyond 1870, whereas the decrees of 1850 remained in force.

These modifications are instructive concerning evolutionary factors. Joseph II was affected by two influences—the craving for a maximum of sovereignty, and the ideas current in the period of West European enlightenment. Francis Joseph, on the other hand, had been tutored by the subsequent Cardinal Rauscher, was a devout Catholic, and after 1848 was especially prone to hail the Church as a stabilizing influence. But by 1870 anticlerical elements had crystallized their antagonism to the concordat and succeeded in abrogating it.

This seesawing is characteristic of all statesmanship. The state pretends to an absolute power within its territorial limits and of course theoretically its army could coerce submission to any decision by the commander in chief. In reality, statesmen are loath to resort to the final argument of military force. What if the army should mutiny? What if passive resistance should nullify the law? As a consequence, the men in control restrain themselves. To revert to a primitive parallel, the head of a Plains Indian police sodality *could* wipe out men who resolutely resisted his orders, but he does not always consider it worth while. If a couple of desperadoes should kill several policemen before being themselves overpowered, the people at large might blame the leader for his intransigence and he would lose prestige. No governor or president in the United States lightly calls out troops against strikers or demonstrators because the results cannot be foreseen and some of the possible reactions within the population are distinctly unpleasant. In imperial Austria the emperor and his cabinet did not as a rule feel able to carry out a particular policy that happened to be congenial to them —say, an absolutistic, ultramontane, pro-German programme. They were aware of too many contrary currents to be taken into account, and these appeared at one time weak, at another strong. Hence the granting of a constitution in 1867, hence the vacillation in clerical policy, hence the sporadic concessions to nationalistic and other popular demands. The politician, whether in an autocracy, a limited monarchy, or a democracy, has to guess what he can "get away with," to compute as best he can the resultant of the forces, the pressure groups, at a particular moment.[1]

## *Nationalism*

By conquest, marriage, and diplomacy the Habsburgs came to rule diverse ethnic groups. In 1910, German—the language of the dynasty—was thus the mother tongue of only 23.5 per cent of the Austro-Hungarians, not exceeding 35.8 even in the Austrian half of the monarchy. Thus, in the empire as a whole the Germans did not greatly predominate over the Magyars (19.5 per cent) and were decidedly outnumbered by Slavs (47.5 per cent). Together with three million Rumanians, the Germans, Magyars, and Slavs made up 97 per cent of the population.

Actually, the ethnic situation was far more complex than is suggested by these figures. For minute differences in dialect suffice to rend people asunder (p. 15) and even where speech is alike, campanilismo finds other grounds for division. Accordingly, the Slavs never formed a natural social unit. The three and a half million "Ruthenians" (Ukrainians) of Galicia were not at all in harmony with the five million Poles whose nobility dominated that crown land. Bohemia had Slovak as well as Czech inhabitants. The Catholic Croats had little sympathy with the Orthodox Serbs, though both spoke the identical language. In addition to Magyars, Czechs, Slovaks, Ruthenians, Poles, Slovenes, Croats, Serbs, and unassimilated Jews, we must further reckon with some three quarters of a million Italians, an ethnic group that had played a much greater role in the earlier part of Francis Joseph's reign, when Lombardy and Venetia were still among his possessions.

This motley population is reflected in the very names of Austria's leading statesmen—Goluchowski, Chlumecki, Bilinski, Dunajewski, Czernin, Korytowski, Andrassy, Burian von Rajecz, Lonyai, Giovanelli. Any list of men in other walks of life tells the same story. In 1918 two of the three vice-presidents of the Anthropological Society of Vienna were Vatroslav v. Jagic and Josef Szombathy. The author of the standard biography of Empress Elizabeth is Egon Caesar Count Corti; and no writer is more typically Viennese in his dialect and his themes than one Vincenz Chiavacci.

The last instance indicates how thoroughly Italians, like other nationalities, could be assimilated. This was due to the confluence of two conditions: before the growth of nationalism non-Germans strove to partake of the advanced culture of the dominant nationality; and, on the other hand, dynasticism welcomed loyal subjects irrespective of their origin, whence the vast host of Italian, Croat, Czech, Polish, and Hungarian generals and courtiers. With some of the assimilated individuals, solidarity with the ruling family or with German culture survived into the era of uncompromising nationalism. Svetozor Boroevic von Bojna (1856–1921), a Croat field marshal in World War I, sincerely grieved over the collapsing fatherland and issued orders that the nascent Slovene government be treated as an enemy. At Prague in 1910, a Czech fellow physicist of Einstein's was as rabidly anti-Czech as any Sudeten German.

These are isolated survivals from the period of German ascendancy. The shift in general attitude during the nineteeth century was truly extraordinary. In the decades before World War I the Magyars were among the most rabid nationalists, deliberately bent on Magyarizing the Slavs, Germans, and Rumanians within Hungary. Yet in 1800 only the common people spoke Magyar; the diet, the courts, the more educated classes used Latin; in about 1820 a German traveler still noted that though one occasionally heard Hungarian speech, a visitor to Buda or Pest (these had not yet been united) might well imagine himself in Germany. By 1890, however, Magyar had definitely come to prevail in the capital: of 486,671 residents 146,144 spoke only Magyar; 58,658 only German; 210,180 both languages; 11,139 only Slavic. After World War I the younger generation was often totally ignorant of German.

As for the Czechs, Prague is the seat of the oldest *German* university (1348), the Czech counterpart being founded as late as 1882. When Hoffmann von Fallersleben, the "arch-German" poet of the subsequent national hymn of the German Empire, visited the capital of Bohemia in 1834, he consorted on the most amicable terms with the leaders of national Slavic studies. In the later Austrian parliament some of the Czech deputies proved orators who could vie with the best speakers of German stock in the use of the Teutonic tongue. However, by the eighteen seventies the linguistic issue had grown into a fighting matter, so that patients bound for Karlsbad and stopping at Prague would vainly ask residents for street directions even if the persons addressed understood German as well as the questioners.

German Austrians reacted toward other ethnic groups within the empire as any dominant group is likely to react. Campanilismo claimed its usual victims: the stage Jews, Czechs, and Croats corresponded to our stage Jews, Irishmen, and "Dutchmen." But full-fledged assimilation bore the customary fruit. There was social intercourse and intermarriage, and even the less enlightened petty bourgeois no longer spurned a Jiricek or Kövesshaza whose Viennese brogue sounded authentic. As for the tone-setting upper circles, they early recognized that the monarchy had ceased to be a German state, and courted now the Magyars, now the Czechs, now the Poles.

Royalty and aristocracy have always been international in their matrimonial arrangements. They have had to be because suitable mates are few, the choice being further narrowed when husband and wife are expected to be of the same faith. Thus, a Catholic prince might seek a wife in Galicia or Hungary or abroad. Princess Pauline Metternich's father, for instance, was the Hungarian Count Sandor de Slavonicza, and Crown Prince Rudolf married a Belgian princess.

On lower planes amicable accommodation, however, came to be restricted by nationalistic intransigence. The Hungarians, who had become virtually independent by a compromise with Austria in 1867, rode roughshod over Slavic and Rumanian fellow subjects and in part resented even the slender thread that tied them to Austria. The Czechs, when once roused, naturally saw no reason why they should be denied the autonomy granted to the Magyars. The southern Slavs felt oppressed by the Magyars, who opposed universal suffrage in Hungary precisely because it would have jeopardized their rule. Among the Austrians proper, a small, but violent and vociferous contingent turned aggressively pan-German. Madly enthusiastic about the successes of Prussia in the War of 1870, they repudiated the Habsburgs and envisaged a union of all Germans under the Hohenzollerns. Baron Georg von Schönerer, the leader of this strange crew, was a worthy forerunner of Hitler. He preached a racial anti-Semitism, militantly defied the Catholic Church, and led his bullies in hand-to-hand brawls with political adversaries.[2]

The several nationalities thus grew into mutually hostile groups. But most of them were far from homogeneous, being stratified in the usual European fashion.

## Social Classes

THE ARISTOCRACY.—The aristocracy included the imperial family, princes, counts, and barons of ancient lineage. Officials and other men more recently rewarded with a patent of nobility are rather to be grouped with the upper middle class.

Undoubtedly the aristocracy was exclusive, but this trait is easily exaggerated. From the Habsburgs down, the blue bloods varied enormously in their accessibility. Contrary to what has sometimes been alleged, this holds even for their ladies. The Princess Alexandrina Dietrichstein did bar everyone from her home unless she deemed him of adequate hereditary status, but the equally exalted Princess Pauline Metternich freely opened her doors to artists and literati. Betty Paoli, a poor poetess, became the companion of Prince Karl Schwarzenberg's widow, whose noble intimates continued to maintain relations with her.

The pinnacles of society often patronized art and scholarship. In 1776 Joseph II founded the Burgtheater, for a long time one of the great European dramatic centers. His mother had Mozart play before her as a six-year old prodigy, and one of her younger sons, the Elector of Bonn, sent Beethoven to Vienna for musical training. There princes and countesses vied with one another to aid a genius none too easy in personal intercourse and never likely to truckle to rank.

Creative achievement in art and science thus sometimes took precedence of ancient lineage and military eminence. A princess once knelt before Beethoven to make him play. Grillparzer, the national poet, was a crusty, petulant old man when the Baroness Marie von Ebner-Eschenbach, daughter of Count Dubsky, wife of a lieutenant field marshal, made his acquaintance and paid him periodic visits. Immersed in a Spanish drama, he might insist on reading her a whole scene in the original despite her plea that she understood not a word of Castilian. Yet she was only too happy to put up with his whims. Deeply revealing are her reminiscences and diary entries on the subject: "With Grillparzer; he received me most cordially; I am proud and happy. . . . That I was permitted to have social relations with Grillparzer, to hear him speak, to tell him of my great and infinite admiration for him, makes me rich for the rest of my life." One day the old poet, touched by a considerate gift the baroness had brought him, went so far as to kiss her. "I felt," she writes, "as though I had been consecrated,—quite blissful and quite solemn. I really cannot say whether I walked, ran, or soared down the staircase." That is how the educated nobility regarded literary eminence.

Of course, not all aristocrats were educated. Some archdukes were monomaniacs about hunting wild game, others were notorious debauchees. Some noblemen wanted, above all, to preserve their privileged position. In this respect historians note a significant chronological change. The aristocrats of the eighteenth century still partook in large measure of its freethinking and humanitarian atmosphere. Their sons, horrified by the terrors of the French Revolution, recoiled from all modernistic ideas, turned into staunch believers, and strove to prop up their ancient prerogatives. As late as 1910 Archduke Franz Ferdinand bewailed the passing of feudalism and absolutism, contending that nevertheless "the nobility, with the Emperor at the top, must play the first part and primarily determine all affairs of the realm."

This was not an unnatural position for the reactionary heir to the throne. The aristocracy accepted the sentiment only with reservations. They were, after all, the descendants of the estates that had often opposed their will and their privileges to the ruler's. About the middle of the century they used to resent the appointment of untitled imperial officials by the centralizing government and cast longing glances in the direction of the Prussian Junkers, who claimed administrative and military posts as a foregone conclusion. Many of these die-hards had exalted notions of their dignity. On his deathbed Prince Alfred Windisch-Grätz attired himself in his field marshal's uniform so as to receive the papal blessing in proper style. Nor did he fail to address a posthumously published letter to his regiment: "I have always felt a lively sympathy with it in this world, so in the hereafter, if possible, I shall keep informed of its deeds and fortunes."

Men of this calibre were united by an international class solidarity. They felt with their fellow grandees of Hungary and Bohemia rather than with the German-speaking middle class, who then still seemed tainted with liberal ideals.[3]

THE UPPER MIDDLE CLASS.—Below the blue bloods, the untitled or only recently ennobled officials, the professional men, businessmen, and bankers jointly formed "the second society," an upper middle class. It included many assimilated Jews, largely coincided with the intellectual elite, and on the whole was a close counterpart of the equivalent strata in the German Reich. On the positive side this class shared with the educated aristocrats a reverential attitude toward learning and the arts. Men of this category—not professional scholars, virtuosi, or littérateurs necessarily, but educated bankers or businessmen—constantly amazed foreigners with the extent and the accuracy of their knowledge. They interlarded conversation with snatches from Horace, spoke with circumstantial detail of El Grecos they might never have seen, and discriminatingly criticized public monuments, plays, or the performance of a classical opera. Yet there was nothing miraculous about it. Precisely as a youthful Crow imbibed the notion that a man should die young, so virtually from the cradle a Viennese lad of the circles in question absorbed certain tastes, acquired a certain sensitiveness.

Stefan Zweig has graphically depicted how he and his high school cronies diverted themselves at fourteen or fifteen, when the average American youngster thinks of baseball or putters about with his radio set. Not a lonely prodigy, but some two dozen of his set would regularly attend every important performance at the Burgtheater or the Opernhaus. They cared not a fig about economics or politics, they would have been ashamed to engage in sport, but they caught on with lightning speed if a score had been cut and discerningly compared one conductor's interpretation with another's. In the rest of life they were content to muddle along in the approved Austrian way, but art was real and serious, and in that sphere negligence was intolerable.

Zweig's statement thus displays the reverse of the medal. Incipient aesthetes would grow up impotent to cope with reality, inept when confronted with practical issues of the first magnitude. The same man who could pitilessly dissect a bungling piece of sculpture never thought at all on social questions. Of course, this meant that in the majority of cases he naïvely absorbed predilections and prejudices of his class. To him peasants and shopkeepers were beings of a lower order. He wished them well, but hardly stooped to concern himself with their problems. The existing system of society he accepted on the principle of "Whatever is, is right"; at all events, it was not his business. A beneficiary of the "liberal" laissez-faire principle, he hardly ever inquired into the ethical foundations of an economic regime that were being questioned not only by the Socialists, but by conservative Catholic reformers. He dearly loved a handle to his name, whether he could rightly claim it or not; would call an untitled equal "Herr *von* Strohmeier" in the hope of being similarly honored in return; and rather resented it if the superscription on an envelope represented him as only *Wohlgeboren* (well-born) instead of *Hochwohlgeboren* (highly well-born).

THE LOWER MIDDLE CLASS.—As urban as the upper middle class, the petty bourgeois formed in every other respect its exact antithesis. They included various callings and ranged widely in economic condition. The majority were mechanics and craftsmen, janitors and cab drivers— in short, the urban plebs. So long as things went well, they were the easygoing Austrians of popular fiction and song, willing to live and let live. They would sample the new wine in a suburban inn to the music

of zithers, watch the Punch and Judy show in the Coney Island
section of the big park, while away hours at a game of tarock cards with
their bosom friends. "By sports like these were all their cares beguiled,"
and that set them off from the superrefined aesthetes of the upper
strata. If possible even more naïve in accepting the existing regime,
they fostered an inordinate local patriotism and looked down with
good-humored smugness on the outsider—the Jewish peddler, the
Italian salami vendor, the Slovak tinker.

Industrialism, however, bore its usual fruits in Austria. The old-
fashioned master carpenters, tailors, and what not, unable to compete
with advanced modes of production, grew economically insecure, and
struck out blindly against capitalism, progress, intellectuals, Jews—all
of them more or less synonymous terms to an undisciplined intelligence.
The Rothschilds were prominent bankers, their coreligionists had been
active and sometimes unscrupulous entrepreneurs, so the harried
burgher, inflamed by sincere fanatics of the Schönerer type (p. 388) or
by spellbinders, like Lueger, who aspired toward prominence in public
life, came to trace all modern ills to the Jews. And, precisely as later
among the Nazis, anti-Semitism went hand in hand with a revolt
against culture. Psychologically this was intelligible. We have seen that
the middle-class intellectuals were on the whole uninterested in reform.
But even those who did enter the arena rarely spoke the language of
the common people, who secretly resented them as snobs or at best as
alien spirits. American parallels abound: voters prefer the back-slapping,
baby-kissing boss of a corrupt party machine to the virtuous and
gentlemanly head of the Citizens' League. When in the eighteen
eighties and nineties Lueger and other silver-tongued rabble rousers
began to deride the cultivated classes and flattered the plain citizen as the
core and backbone of the nation, the urban mob had its hours of
triumph.

Public life thus sank to the same level of degradation that a
generation later marked pre-Nazi Germany. Mark Twain vividly
describes scenes he witnessed in the Austrian parliament of 1897, when
the riffraff had sent men of their own kind to represent them, such
deputies naturally transferring to the legislature the language and
behavior of the gutter. Filibusters, pan-German and otherwise,
obstructed business by banging their desks, defied the chairman, abused
their opponents in the vilest billingsgate, and engaged in hand-to-hand
fights until the police forcibly dragged them from the chambers. Such

demeanor remained typical in the Austrian parliament, the Lower
Austrian diet, the municipal council of Vienna. The delegates from
the petty bourgeois ranks ostentatiously flouted whatever smacked of
culture and science. "One should not learn only from books," scoffed
one of their number, "those are copied by one Jew from another!" And
when an opponent quoted from Tolstoi, the same wiseacre replied,
"Tolstoi is an old boob!" Lueger, incorruptible in money matters and
sincerely devoted to his native city, rose largely by pandering to such
mob psychology and even subsequently maintained his popularity by
baiting the intellectuals. Once he declared that "so long as scholars
cannot produce a single blade of grass, they are bunglers!" In the
diet his adherents launched a campaign against the university, tried
to hinder vivisection, and accused a famous ear specialist of having
illegally despoiled corpses of their ears for research material. The
professors felt obliged to issue a resolution protesting against "the
malevolent and insane attacks . . . against the medical faculty and the
medical profession."

Evidently the cleavage between the upper and the lower middle
class was a radical one. They stood for totally different norms, their
social ties were of a different order.[4]

THE WORKING CLASS.—Imperial Austria had still another urban
class—the proletariat. This appeared on the scene somewhat tardily, for
industrialization set in later than in other Western countries and never
attained the same proportions as in Germany. As a class the workers
were organized by Socialist propaganda.

In general, Austrian Socialists followed the doctrines and the
tactics of their German comrades. They were internationalists and
secularists by principle. In the abstract they avowed complete neutrality
in matters of religion; concretely they opposed the Church and any
clerical party as props of the government. Enthusiasts for popular
enlightenment, they denounced every attempt to curtail the period
of compulsory schooling, set themselves against Church supervision
over education, and resented any restraint of the freedom of investigators. Their leaders fought valiantly to give the workingman a taste
of art and literature, and to acquaint him with the results of research.
The veritably worshipful attitude of the proletariat toward learning
sharply contrasted with the contempt for education felt by the petty
bourgeois and affected by their leaders. In the strictly political sphere,
the Socialists fought for extension of the suffrage, opposed militarism,

and strove for an amicable understanding among the laborers of all ethnic groups within the empire, whose lot they sought to ameliorate by social legislation.

It might be supposed that on several of these issues the Socialists could have effectively collaborated with other parties. This, however, was rendered impossible by the orthodox Socialist position that theirs was a proletarian class movement intrinsically hostile to other classes. Not a whit less than the petty bourgeois faction did the Socialists repudiate Liberals and Jewish high finance: both were advocates of laissez faire, which implies ruthless exploitation of workingmen. When a comrade in the Reich advised support of progressive bourgeois, Dr. V. Adler, the leader of the Austrian party, replied that none such had ever existed as a class in Austria. On the other hand, the Socialists would not collaborate with reformers who combined their programme for betterment with dynastic loyalty or patriotism.

Theoretically, then, the workingmen of all nationalities were to be a solid phalanx against the rest of the population, against aristocrats, professional men and capitalists, petty bourgeois, and peasants. The leaders sought to solve the ethnic problem on the Swiss model, each nationality being permitted to retain its language and culture. The Czech, the Magyar, the Slovene, and the Rumanian proletarian were all brethren in their fight against a common enemy.

But this wholly economic and rationalistic approach foundered on the rock of ethnic solidarity. An incident that occurred in 1907 is typical. The Czech Socialists demanded that in a certain Viennese electoral district with a majority of German voters, but a large minority of Czechs, the party should nominate a Czech rather than a German candidate; and they were indignant and restive over a contrary decision by the party management. For the time being the breach was healed, but in 1911 nationalism triumphed: notwithstanding heroic efforts on the part of the leaders, the majority of the Czech Socialists broke away and joined the Czech bourgeois. Nationality proved a stronger bond than common economic interest.[5]

THE PEASANTS.—In 1910, 50 per cent of the population in the Austrian half of the monarchy, i.e., 14,400,000 persons, were still employed in agriculture or related pursuits as against 5,200,000 in industry and mining, and 1,200,000 in commerce and transportation.

The relative figures, however, varied greatly according to nationality. The preceding census (1900) credits the Germans with only 33.5 per cent agriculturists and 38.3 per cent industrial workers, the Czechs with 43.1 and 36.5 per cent respectively. But for the Poles, the figures are 65.6 and 14.8; for the Serbo-Croats, 86.9 and 4.6; for the Ruthenians, 93.3 and 2.5 per cent.

The rural population, however clearly set off from the other strata of the realm, was itself far from uniform. Apart from ethnic differences, there were socioeconomic subgroups within the same nationality. An old-fashioned Styrian farmer scorned hawkers of flax or wool, could make his own carts and tables or put on a horseshoe; but he depended on itinerant rural weavers, tailors, and shoemakers for his clothing and footgear. Any sizeable homestead, moreover, had graded inmates—the farmer and his wife ranking above the hired help, who again included foremen as well as ordinary laborers, cow girls, and scullery maids. At kermess, the festival in honor of the local patron saint, when everybody was likely to foregather for the celebration, the peasant proprietor would clinch his bargain for the next year with such servants as he needed. In remote Alpine tracts a century ago thirty florins a year (about twelve dollars) and everyday clothing were reckoned good wages.

However isolated, the Austrian peasant could not live wholly unaffected by progressing civilization. Church and state both made their demands and altered his original nature. Typically, he was a devout Catholic and a regular churchgoer. Here lay an abiding source of conflict between him and the freethinking intellectual or proletarian town dweller. Accordingly, though he personally might live in sin, he valued the sacrament of marriage and put those born out of wedlock into a lower category. On the other hand, the state asked for taxes and conscripts, and the young men who served in the army acquired a new intellectual horizon.

Legally, the peasant's status altered with the times. Joseph II had abolished serfdom, and the Revolution of 1848—abortive otherwise—did away with the obligation to work for the gentry gratuitously. The mental set of the class, of course, was not immediately changed thereby, nor was the contempt felt for it by the other classes. Yet there was another side to the ancient conditions. Some peasants looked back wistfully to the good old days when a patriarchal baron helped out with seed corn in the hour of need, whereas later they were on their own and had to deal with an inhumanly impersonal taxgatherer.

Because of its antiquity the peasantry exhibits more parallels to primitive usage than do other classes. As in other parts of rural Europe, age and sex grouping come to the fore. Like a Shilluk, a young Styrian addresses an elder peasant—sometimes even his father's hired help—by the pronoun of politeness, i.e., of the second person plural. More significantly, a veritable stratification by age appears in the solidarity of the bachelors as against the married men. Tied up with this association are the gatherings for amusement of a Saturday evening, culminating in premarital courting (cf. p. 304). At midnight an individual lad sneaks off to knock at the window of some lass he admires, probably one with whom he has previously made a pact for mutual services—she washing his clothes, while he puts nails into her shoes. At first the girl is coy, but finally she opens the window far enough to permit conversation and caresses.

As in the primitive world generally, marriage is a matter of convenience rather than of romantic love, and in Styria the commune would not allow a farm hand to marry unless he had a little homestead of his own or three hundred florins in cash. Thus there, as in Africa, economic factors may favor extramarital relations.

Kinship, besides determining the transmission of property, regulates visiting; it is more particularly affinities or godparents and godchildren that periodically call on each other in Styria. Education, always important, formerly had a very different meaning from schooling (cf. p. 193). The peasant's children learned the economic tasks proper to each sex as well as the old established folkways. In rare instances a boy of studious inclinations might be sent off to be trained for the priesthood. But a century ago even literacy was an unusual accomplishment in the remote uplands. Peter Rosegger, the peasant author, describes a typical episode. A hired woman on his parents' farm, who had a son in the army, wished to write him a letter. She had to send for a scribe, a tailor who lived an hour's walk from the nearest village. Illiterates did own one book—a gaily illustrated almanac with holidays marked in red and distinguished by accompanying drawings. Thus, an infant on a cushion indicated Christmas, a flying dove Whitsunday, a yellow pyx with the consecrated bread Corpus Christi. Indeed, religion was to the peasant as vital an institution as to a Crow or a Shilluk. To quote Rosegger, "The countryman brings everything into relation with his church. His whole life gains shape only through the church." Taking a concrete instance, this writer traces a villager's career from the baptismal font through his first confession and communion, his services as assistant at mass and as bell ringer, as choir boy and candle lighter. He was of course married in church and had his offspring baptized there. He continued to fulfill sundry functions, playing the flute, carrying the flags in summer processions and finally, as one of four elders clad in a ceremonial cloak, he would accompany the priest to the altar on the great holidays with special candles.

The social ties of the rural population are clearly very different from those of the militantly anticlerical, antitraditional urban proletariat; but they also differ widely from those of the petty bourgeois. Each stratum of the total population of the monarchy represented a distinct cultural complex.[6]

## Class Interaction

At the same time the several strata could not remain impervious to mutual influences. Diffusion occurs among adjacent subdivisions of a population as it does among totally unrelated neighboring tribes. Thus, the Buinese middle class mimic the chiefs' pork feasts, and the Austrian middle class affected baronial titles, the proletariat emulated the cultural interests of the educated classes. Nor is the direction of diffusion uniformly from the top downward. The Buinese conquerors took over the Papuan language of what became the commoners' stratum; and the Austrian aristocrats, when not on their good behavior, were prone to lapse into cockney Viennese.

Such borrowing does not imply a leveling of all differences. What is possible in an unstratified society is not possible in a well-established class system. The poorest orphaned Crow could become a great chief or shaman, but only a Shilluk prince could ever ascend the throne and there was no promotion from the commoner's to the nobleman's status. Even in Buin the successful middle-class upstart remained an upstart in the sight of the old-style chiefs. In Austria, to be sure, caste lines were not absolute. Intelligent aristocrats preferred to associate with their peers by taste and capacity rather than by birth. Mere university professors were appointed to the senate chamber. Sporadically even endogamy broke down, as when the Archduke Johann (1782–1859), the sixth son of Leopold II, married the daughter of a postmaster. Jewish extraction prevented neither the Rothschilds from gaining a baronetcy nor J. E. Veith from serving for fourteen years as the cathedral preacher at St. Stephen's. However, there were limits to promotion. No more than a Shilluk of the rank and file ever entered the nobility could an Austrian Lincoln become an archduke, let alone head of the state; nor is any Jew known to have been promoted to the higher military ranks.

## The Economic Factor

During Francis Joseph's reign Austria experienced the changes typical of Western Europe. Peasants who had raised crops and bred livestock to support their households began to produce for the market. Their sons were lured to work in the towns for higher wages than they could hope for at home. The factories created an urban proletariat; and capitalism squeezed the petty bourgeois into straitened circumstances. The changes that resulted in the life of the family and in class feelings have been commented on in previous chapters. In Austria, however, the ethnic differentiation gave a distinct flavor to some of these developments.

It has been forcibly argued that ethnic conflicts themselves were only masked economic conflicts. "National hatred," writes Bauer, "is transformed economic class hatred." Through historic accidents the Germans preceded other nationalities in industrialization; hence they had the first capitalists, and these exploited workingmen irrespective of their origins. In Bohemia the Czech standard of living was inferior to the German; hence Czech peasant immigrants in the towns worked for smaller wages, a differential which inevitably called forth the animosity of the German workers. Later, German towns were invaded by Czech shopkeepers and craftsmen, who entered into competition with their German colleagues and inflamed their wrath. The growing industrial centers also lured Czech professionals, who thus became the economic rivals of German physicians and lawyers and by virtue of their higher education figured as spokesmen of their less articulate fellow nationals. Even administrative jobs in the post office, the state railroads, and the courts came to be increasingly in Czech hands. Germans, so the argument runs, protested against being crowded out by Slav newcomers, phrasing the economic clash in ethnic terms.

Doubtless this is a fruitful approach. Its validity can be supported by parallels from other areas. In the United States, as in Bohemia, capitalists have sought profits by importing cheap labor from countries with a low standard of living. Here, too, native workers either lost their jobs or were reduced to a lower standard of living, hence rose in wrath against Irish, Portuguese, Southeast European competitors (cf. p. 18). As a rule, selfishness in this instance also did not appear in its naked form as a struggle over wages, but was glossed over to appear as a struggle of higher against lower types of humanity. Here is an example of a true evolutionary sequence with like consequences following like antecedents.

However, this is not the whole story. The purely economic interpretation ignores or minimizes disinterestedly irrational motives. As a Melanesian sells property at a loss or gives away pigs not in order to increase his wealth, but to gain prestige, so even modern civilization harbors motives besides the lust for profits. Bauer himself cites example after example of Austrian struggles over prestige and ideals, in short, over nonrational symbols. So far as their material interests went, the Czechs might have gone on sending their sons to the old German university of Prague, but it became a matter of national honor to have a Czech sister institution. Magyar policy was largely built on the principle that the aristocracy must preserve its ancient prerogative of exploiting commoners, whether Magyar or of ethnic minorities, and of remaining free from taxation. But the Magyars had a chance to barter tax exemption against still more valuable economic concessions and refused to yield as a matter of pride.

However, as already suggested, the most convincing proof lies in the conduct of Austrian Socialists. Contrary to the profession of internationalism, contrary to the dogma that proletarians of the world must unite against all other classes of society, the Socialists of Austria have repeatedly abandoned the principle in favor of national ideology. In 1905 a group of Jewish "comrades" seceded from the Polish Socialist party in order to found an organization of their own. In 1907, we have seen, the Czech Socialists vigorously protested against the nomination of a German candidate for the house of deputies; in 1911 the tie with fellow Czechs proved stronger than that with workingmen of alien speech. In 1914, much as the Austrian Socialists regretted the war, the preponderant majority considered it necessary and a matter of duty to fight for their native land. Like the Socialists in Germany, France, and England, they proved that patriotism could be stronger than economic solidarity.

Fully recognizing the potency of economic ties, we must conclude, then, that they provide only one basis among others for social grouping.[7]

## The Individual in Austrian Society

In a population of many millions the problems that confront the individual are too manifold to be adequately represented by a few biographical sketches. All that is practicable within brief compass is to indicate some typical forms of adjustment to the foreordained social conditions, above all, to the dominant facts of class and ethnic differentiation.

As pointed out, the Austrian philosophy of life was not a democratic one. There was a widespread feeling that people had best remain in the station in which Providence had placed them. There was not the general American belief in education as a right and a cure-all. In the late nineteenth century, proposals were still brought before parliament to reduce compulsory schooling from eight to six years; textbooks even in the elementary classes were free only to certified paupers. Thus, the average Austrian of lowly background could not rise with the ease proverbial in the United States. But just as an exceptional Buinese woman could excel all contemporary shamans, so Austrian peasants and proletarians did from time to time achieve great things.

Peter Rosegger (1843–1918), whose authentic accounts of Styrian custom have been quoted in this book, was the scion of a long line of peasants on his father's side, and his mother's father had been a charcoal burner. He himself was rather weakly for coping with the barren mountain soil, so after six years of irregular primary schooling, he was apprenticed to an itinerant tailor. On his wanderings he made the acquaintance of all sorts of peasant mountaineers, who became the models for the characters of his novels and tales. He began to write for his own satisfaction, and helped a popular composer to collect Styrian folk songs. An editor began to take an interest in the young man, and found patrons who provided for secondary instruction. Later, periodicals began to publish his writings, and gradually he was recognized as an outstanding regional author.

More spectacular is the history of Thomas Masaryk (1850–1937), the founder of the Czechoslovak Republic and its first president. He was the son of a Slovak teamster born as a serf, who had married a former housemaid. The father could read, but was unable to write. Apprenticed to a blacksmith, Thomas was befriended by a teacher and a priest; he attended the German high school at Brno and later the University of Vienna, laying the foundation for a scholarly life.

Both careers illustrate that an able individual with character could transcend his adverse environment, but they also prove our point that a class system need not raise unsurmountable barriers. There was diffusion from one subculture to another; without that, Rosegger and Masaryk would have remained illiterate or barely literate plebeians. In Masaryk's case there was also diffusion from another ethnic culture.

Without the German tongue, without the German higher education imbibed at Brno and Vienna, Masaryk could never have become a scholar. A wealthy Slav, of course, might have studied in Paris or Oxford; for a poor Slovak provincial, the German language and the capital of the monarchy were the obvious steppingstones in intellectual progress.

In both instances, the influence of the early social environment never ceased. In spirit Rosegger remained rooted to the soil. He clung to the old peasant life, mourned over its dissolution by industrialization, preached a return to the old values, and found in the horrors of World War I a justification for his faith. As for Masaryk, the bondsman-teamster's son, once educated to perceive the social system clearly, was likely to react against it; and since ethnic and class distinctions fused in his native province, he naturally grew up both a democrat and a national leader.

Here the nicer shadings of personality must be noted. Masaryk was a Czech patriot, but he was also a man of probity. When he was a young professor at Prague, a battle raged over certain manuscripts that purported to prove that literary culture had attained a high level in the Middle Ages among the Bohemian Slavs. Scholars exposed the hoax, and as an honest man Masaryk sided with them. Incredible as it may seem nowadays, chauvinists denounced him for this as a traitor to the Czech cause, but he never faltered in his contention that patriotic claims must not rest on falsehood.

The struggle between ethnic and other loyalties, of course, occurred also among the German Austrians, as instanced by the life of Engelbert Pernerstorfer (1850–1918). Like Masaryk, he was predestined to be the common people's spokesman, for he was the son of a tailor, whose widow was hard put to it to support her family. As ardently pro-German as Masaryk was pro-Czech, Pernerstorfer thrilled over the unification of Germany, but always placed the people's welfare above dynastic interest. He worked to preserve German speech wherever it was threatened with extinction in border areas, helped to organize school associations, and launched periodicals for that end. At first he collaborated with Schönerer, but when that Pan-German grew indifferent to labor and concentrated on anti-Semitic propaganda, Pernerstorfer seceded, founding a democratic monthly to defend sound nationalism without detriment to other ethnic groups. In the early nineties German voters were likely to acknowledge his pro-Germanism while shaking their heads over his Socialistic bias, whereas Socialists were inclined to accept him as one of their own "if only he were not a nationalist." Convinced that sane Germanism was consistent with internationalism, he formally joined the Socialist party in 1896. Fifteen years later he was able once more to prove his rectitude. The Italians within the monarchy desired a university of their own. When the German School Association bitterly opposed the request, Pernerstorfer gave up his membership. Like Masaryk, he was not a 200 per cent nationalist. He thus preserved the esteem of other ethnic groups, and at his funeral a Czecho-Slovak deputy pronounced one of the obituary eulogies.

The upper middle class, too, had its deviates. Purblind as the majority were in their social vision, exceptions did occur. Anton Menger (1841–1906), an eminent jurist who had dropped the hereditary *von* to which he was entitled, developed an anti-Marxian Socialist system of his own and mercilessly exposed the legal disadvantages of the laboring class. His colleague, Ernst Mach (1838–1916), a physicist-philosopher now recognized as a precursor of Einstein, was an advanced progressive interested in popular enlightenment and in the alleviation of proletarian misery. As an appointive member of the senate, he supported a shorter working day for striking miners and, though paralyzed by a stroke, had himself carried to the legislature at great inconvenience to himself in order to register his vote.

Finally, it is rewarding to consider several members of the imperial family. Here we must note that, like their African counterparts, the Habsburgs were subject to an inexorable ceremonial code. When the Archduchess Sophie, Francis Joseph's mother, was on her deathbed, it was imperative for the family and the entire court to assemble around it. At court functions questions of precedence were of primary importance. It is interesting to see how the Emperor's mother, his wife, he himself, and his two successive heirs adjusted themselves.

Archduchess Sophie, sister of King Ludwig I of Bavaria, was Empress Elizabeth's maternal aunt before she became her mother-in-law, but it would have been difficult to find two temperaments less alike. The older woman was the archetype of the well-meaning dragon —a devoted but possessive mother, a domineering mother-in-law. Energetic, narrow-minded in her political and religious views, she was thoroughly conventional and held violent prejudices against everything that smacked of modernism. For years after her eighteen-year-old son's ascent to the throne in 1848 she was the uncrowned leading spirit of the Viennese court. For her the Habsburg etiquette was an ideal set of rules, precisely to her taste.

Sophie's sister's daughter had evidently inherited more from the paternal side. Elizabeth's father, a wealthy Bavarian duke, was an easygoing character given to horseback riding and banquets, but also to literary efforts of indifferent quality. He was far from exclusive in his social relations, one of his intimates being the founder of a popular comic periodical. Elizabeth had an uncontrollable urge to act naturally that forever ran counter to the regnant Viennese etiquette. Even as a fiancée she was rebuked for addressing her prospective mother-in-law— her own aunt—by the singular instead of the plural pronoun deemed proper in writing to an older lady. After marriage she chafed under the constant surveillance of Sophie and her retainers, who made innocent behavior the target of acrid criticism, if not of malicious gossip. Elizabeth not only loathed restraint but held views of life and society that were anathema to her mother-in-law and the more conservative members of the court. Sensitive, interested in literature, progressive in her political sympathies, she enjoyed the company of authors and scholars. Characteristically, she developed a veritable cult of Heinrich Heine, ignoring his Jewish origins, the bitter things he had said about German princes, his mockery of revealed religion. A pocket edition of his lyrics was her constant companion; she filled her palaces with portraits and busts of him, paid a visit to his aged surviving sister in Hamburg, and had a wreath deposited at his grave in Paris. Once, lying awake in bed, she even had a vision of him. When her son wished to please her with a Christmas gift, he surprised her with a package of her favorite's letters.

Such tastes were totally foreign to her pedestrian though loving husband, and they contributed to the popular conception of her as "queer." Eccentric she certainly became. Once she slipped off in disguise to a masquerade ball, struck up a harmless acquaintance with a personable young man, and carried on a prolonged correspondence with him incognito. She carried her athletic tastes to extremes: a passionate horsewoman, she spent hours in the saddle and amazed British huntsmen by her intrepidity and verve when riding to hounds. Inordinate in everything, she developed a mania for endless hiking that wore her companions to a frazzle. During her visit to Cairo the secret police charged with guarding her found it impossible to keep up with her afoot and took to a carriage. Her restiveness carried her on constant travels to distant parts—to Madeira, to Ireland, to Corfu.

To the staid courtiers at Vienna these were all senseless antics intolerable in an empress. Actually they formed the natural response of an ingenuous, imaginative, high-strung personality to an uncongenial, boring environment. The situation was, of course, aggravated by the rift between the young woman and her tyrannical mother-in-law, who for years kept Elizabeth from bringing up her older children in her own way. To Francis Joseph, sober, quite indifferent to the arts, conservative in all his thinking, punctilious in matters of traditional etiquette, in the beginning madly in love with his beautiful wife, yet since infancy under Sophie's thumb, Elizabeth's behavior must have been often trying and at times a torture. He was frequently torn by conflicting loyalties to his mother and to his wife, must have been constantly embarrassed by the Empress's repeated and prolonged absences. In large measure, doubtless, he found it hard to understand what was bothering her: the traditional regime of palace life suited him exactly.

Crown Prince Rudolf (1858–1889) resembled his mother more than his father, but seems to have been emotionally close to neither. A tendency toward nervousness was doubtless increased by early training, for his first educator, an old general chosen by Sophie, believed in a Spartan technique. By way of hardening the six-year-old he would pretend that a wild boar was about to charge until the boy was frightened out of his wits. At last Elizabeth laid down an ultimatum and forced a change of tutors.

Rudolf proved remarkably precocious and somehow acquired ideas most anomalous for a Habsburg prince. At fourteen he astonished his Magyar teacher by declaring that man was nothing but an improved breed of animal; that the aristocracy and the clergy had always worked hand in glove in order to keep the masses stupid and easily manageable; that with few exceptions the social elite was merely an abscess on the body politic. He subsequently enjoyed instruction at the hands of eminent scholars, traveled to England with the great economist Karl Menger, developed a deep interest in natural science, history, and geography, and contributed to ornithological journals. He also gave the impetus to the preparation of a monumental twenty-one-volume work on the Austro-Hungarian monarchy (1885–1902). Like his mother, he was free of nationalistic, class, or racial bias. True to his early notions, he later joined in the publication of an anonymous pamphlet virulently denouncing the Austrian aristocracy. He hobnobbed with naturalists, scholars, and liberal journalists, and felt deeply touched by an honorary doctorate conferred by the University of Vienna. During the last seven years of his life he was on friendly relations with Moriz Szeps, editor of a progressive daily, to which

Rudolf clandestinely contributed news items and articles. His correspondence with Szeps reveals his political principles. He deprecated any nationalistic chauvinism, such as Schönerer's, as a return to bestiality, as a victory of fleshly instincts over the ideas of equality and cosmopolitanism. In the middle class he recognized the core and backbone of a modern state.

Such sentiments did not endear him to the reactionary statesmen and aristocrats, while his religious freethinking and political progressiveness estranged him from his devout and conservative father. He discovered no adequate means for realizing his ideals, grew restive and dissolute, and finally committed suicide.

His cousin and successor as heir apparent, Archduke Franz Ferdinand (1863-1914), shared nothing with Rudolf except an inordinate fondness for hunting. He had an all-absorbing will to power, coupled with an exalted view of his station and generally reactionary tendencies, and was morbidly suspicious. Relentlessly vindictive, he mistrusted and hated Magyars, Italians, Jews, liberals, and Socialists. He took no interest in the arts and scented freemasonry in the Academy of Sciences. As heir to the throne, he was given high military responsibilities, but so far as possible he meddled in civil affairs and did not scruple to assert privileges that did not rightfully belong to him. With the matter-of-courseness of a Polynesian chief, he would taboo traffic arteries when it suited his convenience in the chase, or draft the Imperial and Royal Engineers to construct highways leading to his estates—at the public expense. In internal politics he favored changing the dual monarchy into a trialism, with the Slavs as a counterweight to the hated Magyars. His foreign policy was to build up a sort of Holy League of Austria, Germany, and Russia as a bulwark against progressive tendencies. Although his piety and his conservatism put him into the same general category as his uncle, he thoroughly alienated Francis Joseph by his arrogant meddlesomeness. After the initial shock of his nephew's assassination, the old Emperor, it is credibly reported, felt relieved.

It might be conjectured that Habsburg traditionalism would have suited Franz Ferdinand perfectly, yet in a crucially important matter he flouted it. Having become infatuated with a Bohemian countess, he declined matches with ladies of his own status and threatened to commit suicide if the emperor withheld his consent to the unsuitable marriage. At the same time he refused to abdicate his rights as heir apparent in favor of a younger brother. Reluctantly Francis Joseph yielded, but in accordance with Habsburg family law his nephew had to renounce all claims to the throne on the part of his offspring. The Emperor conferred on the countess the title of a Princess Hohenberg, but there were things even he could not do, had he wished to. Against the stone wall of Habsburg etiquette the ambitious Archduke and his spouse vainly battered their heads. At any ceremonial function the newly made princess had to yield precedence to every princess to the status born, while her husband marched at the head of the procession with an archduchess at his arm. And there was absolutely no way to prevent the princely families of ancient rank from snubbing the Archduke's wife as an undesirable intruder. Because of these galling humiliations Franz Ferdinand absented himself from the court whenever he could.

How an individual adapts himself into his social order evidently depends both on himself and on the nature of the order. It is not justifiable to base value judgments on the success or failure of the adjustment. Such verdicts are bound to be subjective and must hinge on the judge's feelings about the worthiness of the social structure in question. Within the framework of the Austro-Hungarian monarchy, Masaryk, as a democrat and a Czech nationalist, was an obvious misfit. By destroying the framework and creating the Czechoslovak Republic, he established new norms and became their perfect embodiment. An empirical science, such as anthropology, must leave the problem to philosophy, whether the monarchy to which Masaryk failed to adjust was superior or inferior to the government which he founded. For corresponding reasons neither Archduchess Sophie's acceptance nor Empress Elizabeth's rejection of Viennese court folkways suffices to grade them as human beings.

In the face of his environment the individual is neither omnipotent nor impotent. So long as the social organization remains, the restrictions it implies remain in force. Masaryk could never have become head of the state in the dual monarchy. Franz Ferdinand, with all his obstinacy, could never have made his wife an empress or his sons his successors without a *coup d'état*. But, as our examples from Austria and from Buin show, there is in any society a gamut of possibilities any one of which may be realized in accordance with the individual's endowments. Some botch their opportunities; some make their lives into a harmonious work of art; the majority achieve a modicum of satisfaction.[8]

# APPENDIXES

# LIST OF TRIBES AND THEIR LOCATIONS

Admiralty Islanders, Melanesia
Ainu, Japan
Algonquians, a family of tribes widespread in the United States and Canada
Alorese, Indonesia
Andaman Islanders, Bay of Bengal
Angami Naga, Assam
Ankole, East Africa
Anuak, Anglo-Egyptian Sudan
Apache, s. w. United States
Apinayé, lower Araguaya, Brazil
Aranda (or Arunta), Central Australia
Arapaho, Wyoming
Araucanians, Chile
Arawak, Guiana
Ashanti, West Africa
Ashluslay, Gran Chaco
Aweikoma, s. Brazil
Aymara, Peru and Bolivia
Aztecs, s. Mexico
Badaga, s. India
Bagobo, Mindanao
Bahima, East Africa
Bairu, East Africa
Bakuba, Belgian Congo
Banaro, New Guinea
Banks Islanders, Melanesia
Bannock, Idaho
Bantu, southern half of Africa
Beninese, West Africa
Blackfoot, Montana and Alberta
Bogo, Ethiopia
Boloki, Belgian Congo
Bororo, Matto Grosso, Brazil

Botocudo, south of Rio Pardo, Brazil
Buinese, Solomon Islands
Bukaua, New Guinea
Bushmen, Kalahari Desert, South Africa
Bushongo, see Bakuba
Canella, Maranhão, Brazil
Carib, British Guiana
Caribou Eskimo, west of Hudson's Bay, Canada
Carrier, British Columbia
Cayuga Iroquois, New York State
Chacobo, n. e. Bolivia
Chenchu, Hyderabad, India
Cherokee, s. e. United States
Cheyenne, Montana
Chibcha, Colombia
Chiricahua, s. e. Arizona
Chiriguano, Gran Chaco
Choctaw, Mississippi
Choroti, Gran Chaco
Chuckchi, n. e. Siberia
Cochiti, New Mexico
Comanche, Texas and Oklahoma
Copper Eskimo, Coronation Gulf, n. Canada
Cree (Plains), Manitoba and Saskatchewan
Creek, s. e. United States
Crow, Montana
Dieri, South Australia
Dravidians, s. India
Ekoi, West Africa
Eskimo, from Alaska to Greenland
Gajo, Sumatra
Ganda, Uganda, East Africa

409

Ge, a large family in Brazil
Gheg, n. Albania
Gilyak, lower Amur country
Gold, Amur country
Gros Ventre, Montana and Alberta
Guajiro, n. Colombia
Guarani, Paraguay
Habbé, Nigeria
Haida, British Columbia
Haisla, British Columbia
Havasupai, n. Arizona
Herero, Southwest Africa
Hidatsa, North Dakota
Hopi, n. Arizona
Hottentot, Southwest Africa
Hutu, Ruanda, Belgian Congo
Ibo, Nigeria
Ifugao, Luzon
Iglulik Eskimo, west of Baffin Land
Inca, Peru
Iowa, Iowa
Iroquois, New York State
Jagga, Mt. Kilimanjaro, East Africa
Jehai, Malay Peninsula
Jicarilla, s. e. Colorado and New Mexico
Jivaro, Ecuador
Kababish, Anglo-Egyptian Sudan
Kaingang, *see* Aweikoma
Kalmuk, European Russia, Caucasus, Dzungaria, n. w. Mongolia
Kansas, Kansas
Kariera, West Australia
Kayapo, Araguaya and Xingu drainage, Brazil
Kazak, Central Asia, Turkistan
Ket, Yenisei area, Siberia
Khasi, Assam
Kikuyu, Kenya, East Africa
Kiwai, New Guinea
Koryak, n. e. Siberia

Kota, s. India
Kpelle, Liberia
Kurds, Turkey
Kurumba, s. India
Kutchin, n. w. Canada
Kutenai, n. Montana and Idaho, s. e. British Columbia
Kuyu, French Congo
Kwakiutl, British Columbia
Lacandon, Yucatan
Lango, East Africa
Lapps, n. Norway, Sweden, Finland, Russia
Lengua, Gran Chaco
Lesu, New Ireland, Melanesia
Lobi, upper Volta River, West Africa
Maidu, central California
Mandan, North Dakota
Mangarevans, Polynesia
Mano, Liberia
Maori, New Zealand
Maricopa, Arizona
Marquesas Islanders, Polynesia
Masai, Kenya and Tanganyika, East Africa
Menomini, Wisconsin
Miwok, central California
Mohave, Arizona and California
Mohawk Iroquois, New York State
Mohegan, New England
Mossi, French Sudan
Murngin, North Australia
Muskoghean, s. e. United States
Nambikuara, Matto Grosso, Brazil
Natchez, Mississippi
Navaho, n. Arizona
Nootka, British Columbia
Nunivak Eskimo, s. Alaska
Nupe, n. Nigeria
Ojibwa, Minnesota to North Dakota, adjoining Canadian region

Omaha, Nebraska

Ona, Tierra del Fuego

Onondaga Iroquois, New York State

Oneida Iroquois, New York State

Oraon, Chota Nagpur, India

Osage, Missouri

Ostyak, w. Siberia

Oya, Yorubaland, s. Nigeria

Paiute, Nevada

Palikur, Brazilian Guiana

Pangwe, West Africa

Paviotso, Nevada

Pawnee, Nebraska

Penobscot, Maine

Pilaga, Gran Chaco

Pomo, central California

Ponca, Nebraska

Pueblo, Arizona and New Mexico

Quechua, Peru and Bolivia

Quinault, Washington

Rangi, Tanganyika, East Africa

Reddi, Hyderabad, India

Sakai, Malay Peninsula

Salishans, a family of tribes in n. Washington, n. Idaho, British Columbia

Samoyed, w. Siberia

Semang, Malay Peninsula

Seneca Iroquois, New York State

Sanpoil, n. e. Washington

Seri, Mexico

Shawnee, S. Carolina, Tennessee, Pennsylvania, Ohio

Sherente (or Šerente), Rio Tocantins, Brazil

Shilluk, Anglo-Egyptian Sudan

Shoshone, Idaho, Wyoming, California

Shuswap, s. British Columbia

Sinhalese, Ceylon

Society Islanders, Polynesia

Solomon Islanders, Melanesia

Soyot, s. Siberia, Tannu Tuva

Tahitians, *see* Society Islanders

Tali, northern territories of the Gold Coast

Tamanak, Orinoco country, South America

Tapuya, n. e. Brazil

Tete de Boule, w. Quebec

Tewa, New Mexico

Thonga, Portuguese Southeast Africa

Tikopia, Polynesian enclave north of Banks Islands

Timbira, n. e. Brazil

Tlingit, n. w. British Columbia and Alaskan panhandle

Toba-Pilaga, Gran Chaco

Toda, s. India

Tolowa, n. w. California

Tongans, Polynesia

Tongarevans, Polynesia

Trobrianders, east of New Guinea

Tsimshian, n. British Columbia

Tungus, Manchuria, e. Siberia

Tupi, family widespread in South America

Tupinamba, e. Brazil

Tuscarora Iroquois, North Carolina; later, New York

Tussi, Belgian Congo

Twa, Belgian Congo

Uro-Čipaya, Lake Titicaca, Bolivia

Ute, Nevada, Utah

Vandau, Portuguese East Africa

Vedda, Ceylon

Vogul, w. Siberia

Wapishana, central Guiana

Washo, California, Nevada

Winnebago, Wisconsin

Wolof, French Sudan

Xosa, Southeast Africa
Yaghan, Tierra del Fuego
Yakö, s. e. Nigeria
Yakut, e. Siberia
Yana, California
Yaruro, Venezuela
Yekuana, in Orinoco basin, South America

Yokuts, San Joaquin Valley, California
Yoruba, s. Nigeria
Yukaghir, n. Siberia
Yurok, n. w. California
Zulu, Southeast Africa
Zuñi, New Mexico

# CHAPTER REFERENCES

## *Note on Bibliography and Chapter References*

The Bibliography lists all titles with dates, distinguishing by letters the several publications of one author published in the same year. Thus: Sée, H. 1929 (a); 1929 (b); 1929 (c). Abbreviations used for serials, handbooks, encyclopedias, and symposia are given on pages 427–428. Where a paper takes up only part of a volume or bulletin, the length of the article is indicated, except for very brief encyclopedia articles. E.g.,
Denig, Edwin Thompson.
1930. BAE–R 46:375–628.
In other cases the paging is omitted.

The numeral after B or R gives the serial number of the Bulletin or Report, e.g., BAE–R 37 = 37th Report of the Bureau of American Ethnology.

The chapter references give author and date, with letter where necessary to distinguish publications of the same year, but omit the date if the author has a single title in the Bibliography. The number of a volume is set off from the pages by a colon. Because of two editions of Lewis H. Morgan's *Ancient Society* with differing pagination, that work is cited by chapters.

### I. PRINCIPLES OF GROUPING

[1] Krige, 36–38, 88, 100. G. H. D. Cole 1921, 25–46, 196 f. Hiller. 17–21. MacIver 1937, 4–18. Schurtz, 14 et passim.

[2] Durham 1909, 36. Nopcsa, 59. Linton 1936, 480: id. 1940, 882. Warner, 5 f. 102, 125–137. H. Thurnwald 1937, 182–198. Rivers 1914 (a), 1:63. Radin 1923, 237. Wissler ed. 1912–1916, 79.

[3] Spier 1933, 324. Goodwin, 428. Arensberg and Kimball, 56, 131. Lowie 1943, 634. Nimuendajú 1946 (a), 90 et seq., 112. Merker, 48, 71 et seq., 86, 90, 92. Hollis, XVI, 262 f., 291, 303, 312.

[4] Durham 1928, 151. Radcliffe-Brown 1931, 41. Steward 1936 (a). Krige, 34 f. Gluckman in F and E-P, 28. Forde 1941, 114. Wm. E. Lawrence, in Murdock ed. 1937, 319–354. Lowie in Wissler ed. 1912–1916, 152. Bascom, 46.

[5] Maine, 124 ff. Barton 1919, 14 f. 75. Lowie 1927, 51–73. Radcliffe-Brown in F and E-P, XIV.

[6] Warner, 291. Nimuendajú 1942, 43; id. 1946 (a), 63, 77, 92, 95. Old Testament, I Samuel 18:1–4. R. S. and H. M. Lynd, 272–312. Warner and Lunt 1941, 301–355. Warner and Srole 1945, 254–282.

[7] Ware, 155, 159. Ph. H. Williams. Sartorio. Stephenson, 258, 273, 303, 313. Blegen 1940, 75, 77, 122, 329, 568 f., 582 ff. Philipp Fürst zu Eulenburg-Hertefeld, 1:14 f., 118, 123 ff. Haller, 22 f., 64. Phillips, 269. Lane, 2:275, 281, 284, 289. Lindgren, 605 et seq. Myrdal, 911. Kennedy, 139, 161 ff.

## 2. CONTEMPORARY CIVILIZATION AND ECONOMIC DETERMINISM

[1] E. Lederer in ESS 1934, 14:553 et seq. Lin Yutang, 23 et seq., 172–181, 186. Chen Han Seng, 4. Arensberg, 38–46, 62–69, 71 et seq., 146–173. Arensberg and Kimball, 107 et seq., 282–308. Thomas and Znaniecki, 1:95, 106 et seq., 122, 159, 188. Embree 1945, 43, 59, 124, 222, 259. Schrieke ed. 1929, 1–9. H. Thurnwald 1935, 82–97; 1937, 43–47. Tomašić 1942, 249 et seq.

[2] Sée 1929 (b), 432 f., 497. Groves and Ogburn, 1–77, 440–452.

[3] E. R. A. Seligman in ESS 1931, 5:344. R. Thurnwald 1931–1935, 3:4 ff. Sée 1929 (a), 100 f., 123 f.; id. (b), 136 et seq., 152, 367; id. 1929 (c), 91 et seq., 127, 137. Jones, 2:305. Durkheim. Mauss. Warner, 4, 20, 138 f., 378. Llewellyn and Hoebel, 74, 110, 148. Mandelbaum 1940, 203 f., 225. Hudson, 27, 29 f. Hook in ESS 1933, 10:217 et seq. G. D. H. Cole 1938, 266–269. Plekhanov. Schmidt and Koppers, 638. Herskovits, 447 et seq. Ashley 1914, 2:261 et seq., 338, 352 et seq.

[4] Steward 1938, 44–49, 230–239, 246–262. Bogoras, 544–556, 569 f., 598 et seq., 637, 642 ff., 674 et seq. Lowie 1945 (b). Buck 1932, 9, 51, 53, 58, 62, 68 ff., 106, 108, 113.

[5] Kroeber 1925, 22 et seq., 27 f., 32, 40 ff., 49 et seq. Roscoe 1915, 77–79, 103. Du Bois 1936. Powdermaker 1933, 223 ff. L. Thompson 1940 (a), 84 f. Thomas and Znaniecki, 1:164 f., 190.

## 3. LAWS OF EVOLUTION

[1] MacIver 1937, 412. Radcliffe-Brown 1940.

[2] Tylor 1889 (a). Morgan 1876, pt. I, chap. 1; pt. III, chap. 6.

[3] Tylor 1865, 4.

[4] Schmidt 1937, VII, 10; id. 1935, 244–256. Schmidt and Koppers, 264 et seq., 476, 542 ff.

[5] Committee on Historiography, 110, 136 f. Radcliffe-Brown 1941. Eggan, 69.

[6] Tylor 1889 (a).

[7] R. Thurnwald 1931–1935, 2:83 f., 215. P. A. Talbot 1926, 430, 678.

Krige, 33, 168. Radcliffe-Brown 1931, 96, 98. Driberg, 174.

[8] Tylor 1889 (a).

[9] Gifford 1922, 258 ff. Lowie 1917, 91. Fürer-Haimendorf 1943, 113.

[10] Tylor 1865, 286.

[11] Shimkin, 155 f.

[12] Murdock ed. 1937, 445–470; id. 1934 (b), 294; id. 1947. Simmons 1945, Table VI, p. 267; id. in Murdock ed. 1937, 495–517. Swanton 1929, 382–388. Cooper in Steward ed. 1946, 2:703 f. Turney-High, 134. Loeb 1926, 243, 245.

[13] Parsons 1924; id. 1939, 5; id. 1936, 229 ff. Nimuendajú 1946 (a), 77–84; id. 1942, 16–33.

[14] Mach 1906, 449. Pearson, 98.

[15] Radcliffe-Brown 1931, 109, 138.

[16] Evans-Pritchard 1938.

[17] Chen and Shryock, 629 f. Feng 1936, 59–66; id. 1937, 175.

[18] Boas 1938 (a), 226. MacIver 1937, 479 et seq.

[19] Labouret 1931, 254. Santa Cruz, 2. Boas 1916, 425 ff. Malinowski 1926, 100–111.

## 4. KINSHIP

[1] Lévi-Strauss 1945, 52.

[2] Huebner, 43, f. Laval, 235 f. Gifford 1929, 22, 26. Lowie 1935, 31. Rivers 1914 (a), 1:50.

[3] Krauss 1885, 625–643. Roscoe 1911, 19.

[4] Emeneau, 169. Murdock 1940. Radcliffe-Brown 1931, 8. Forde 1939.

[5] Deloria, 42, 68, 92. Firth, 268. Warner, 4, 7, et passim.

[6] Lowie 1935, 248.

[7] Morgan 1871, 142 f., 276 f. Aginsky 1935 (a). Davis and Warner 1937, 291–313. Rivers 1914 (b), 76 et seq. Kirchhoff 1932, 43–52, Lowie 1929 (b).

[8] Spier 1925. Gifford 1922, 27, 142 f., 148 f. Birket-Smith, 296. Boas 1940, 368. Gusinde 1937, 788, 794.

[9] Spier 1925. Nimuendajú 1942, 24; id. 1946 (a), 105.

[10] Gillin, 82 et seq. Gifford 1922, 147 ff.

[11] Kroeber 1917, 86. Gifford 1922, 254. Seligman 1918, 123. Rivers 1914 (b), 67.

[12] Harrington. Lowie 1924, 287 ff. Freire-Marreco. Kroeber 1917, 53. Lowie 1929 (a). Boas 1916, 492–495; id. 1940, 360–367. Olson 1940, 184 f. Durham 1928, 151.

[13] Rivers 1914 (b), 93 f.

[14] Radcliffe-Brown 1924, 542–555. Lévi-Strauss 1945, 44–53.

[15] Rivers 1924, 65 f. Eggan, 79. Mead, 245 f.

[16] Wilson, 24 ff., 45 f. Lowie 1935, 18–32, Radcliffe-Brown 1941, 9–17.

[17] Murdock 1934 (a). Titiev, 17 ff., 25–28. Kirchhoff 1932, 58. Nimuendajú 1946 (a), 50, 78, 84 f., 96, 108, 111, 124, 153. Radcliffe-Brown 1924. Simmons 1942, 67, 76, 144, 148, 150, 188, 198 f.

[18] Warner, 93 et seq. Firth, 209–226, 268. Gifford 1929, 22 et seq. Krige, 26 f. Eggan, 53.

[19] Gifford 1929, 17 ff. Boas 1940, 384–396.

[20] Labouret, 248. Lowie 1929 (a), 383 f. Titiev, 29.

[21] Titiev, 22. Goodwin, 229. Labouret, 260 f.

[22] Warner, 75. Steward 1938, 194, 197, 245. Lowie 1917, 39. Eggan, 42, 51. Firth, 221, 331. Reichard, 72. L. Thompson 1940 (b), 58. Goodwin, 230.

[23] Warner, 92. Eggan, 56. Lowie 1917, 49. Malinowski 1922, 62 ff. Kirchhoff 1931, 183.

[24] Wissler 1911, 12. Lowie 1917, 49, 80. Kroeber 1902–1907, 11. Labouret, 252.

[25] Lowie 1935, 30 f. Lin Yutang, 148. Eggan, 55. Goodwin, 268. Krige, 30 f. Jochelson 1933, 126. Shimkin, 155 f. Radloff, 1:314, 480. Hudson, 45 f. Warner, 101 f. Driberg, 159. Schebesta, 63, 184, 215, 224. Seligman 1911, 68. Reichard, 71. Lowie 1917, 48. Gusinde 1937, 658 ff., 1239, 1269. Steward 1938, 240. Radin 1923, 135. Nimuendajú 1946 (a), 125.

[26] Reichard in Boas ed. 1938 (b), 446–449. Olson 1936, 91. Lowie 1917, 91. Barnett, 134. Gifford 1922, 259. Speck 1940, 206. Lowie 1920, 101 et seq. Radin 1923, 133. Skinner in Wissler ed. 1912–1916, 738, 769, 800. Ray, 139.

## 5. MARRIAGE

[1] Burgess and Locke, 511–515.

[2] Wissler 1911, 8 f.; id. 1918, 232, 239 f. Lowie 1935, 47. Nimuendajú 1946 (a), 130 f.

[3] Nordenskiöld 1912, 86, 88. Métraux 1937, 382. Buck 1932, 34 f. Firth, 568 f.

[4] Parsons 1939, 108, 168. Nimuendajú 1946 (a), 129; id. 1939, 83. Wissler 1911, 10 f. Llewellyn and Hoebel, 202. Roscoe 1911, 261–264. Labouret, 286 ff. Gutmann 1926, 200. Forde 1941, 71 f., 102 f.

[5] Mathiassen, 211. Birket-Smith, 295. Warner, 64, 306 ff. Lowie in Wissler ed. 1912–1916, 228, 290. Wissler, ibid., 413, 415.

[6] Nimuendajú 1942, 29–31, 50. Jenness 1922, 158. Boas 1888, 580. Gusinde 1937, 538 et seq., 617, 676 f.

[7] Schebesta, 104–109, 225. Lantis, 233. Granqvist, 28, 41 f., 92.

[8] Bogoras, 578 f. Radcliffe-Brown 1931, 37, 102. R. Thurnwald 1921, 16–19, 40–45. Granqvist, 111–117. Warner, 57 f.

[9] Krauss, 250 f., 254 et seq. Tomašić 1945, 475. Firth, 538 et seq. R. Thurnwald 1931–1935, 2:105 et seq., id. 1921, 46. Schmidt and Koppers, 206. Lowie 1935, 186 et seq.

[10] Radin 1923, 138. Lowie 1917, 46. Kirchhoff 1931, 126 ff., 133 f. Nordenskiöld 1912, 212. Bogoras, 579 et seq., 609 f. Schmidt and Koppers, 269 f. Kroeber 1925, 29.

[11] Granqvist, 118–155. Lowie 1917, 46, 75. Kroeber 1925, 29. Driberg, 154 et seq., 174. Forde 1941, 71 f. Labouret, 290. Michelson, 6. Du Bois 1944, 84–93. Murdock 1934 (b), 250 f. H. Thurnwald 1937, 81. Thomas and Znaniecki, 1:118 Arensberg and Kimball, 109 et seq. Gutmann 1926, 84–142.

[12] Junod, 1:200, 207, 243. Ward, 30. Herbst, 20 f. Yule, 1:253. Medina, 280. Kirchhoff 1931, 98, 154. Nimuendajú 1942, 26. Sapir 1916. Steward 1938, 56, 84, 91, 99, 109, 117, 121, 164, 176, 216, 244. Gifford 1916, 186. Dorsey 1884, 251, 261. Opler in Eggan ed. 204–208.

[13] Kirchhoff 1931, 101. Reichard, 62 ff. Lévi-Strauss 1936, 279, 282. Durham 1909, 20 ff., 98. Goldenweiser 1933, 274. Shimkin. Aginsky 1935 (a); id. 1935 (b), 45. Strong 1929 (b). Hallowell 1930. Rivers 1914 (a), 1:184, 294. Malinowski 1929, 1:103, 534 f. Hoernlé, 21. Labouret, 261. Seligman 1911, 64 f., 96 f. Forde 1941, 15. Maenchen, 84. Kirchhoff 1931, 99, 155; id. 1932, 63–67. Boas 1916, 440. Jenness 1943, 526. Métraux 1937, 384. Gifford 1922, 86 f., 247–256. Mead, 354 f.

[14] Burgess and Locke, 626–647. Embree 1945, 124. Birket-Smith, 1:294. Thalbitzer, 1:65, 72. Titiev, 38–43. Lowie 1935, 50 f., 55 f. Schebesta, 105. Seligman 1911, 100. Du Bois 1944, 88. Waller, 525–588. Nimuendajú 1946 (a), 119 f.

[15] Niebuhr, 2:214. Hudson, 49. Nimuendajú 1946 (a), 104, 120. Cooper 1941, 52–57.

[16] Osgood, 143, 148. Petrullo, 223. Steward 1936 (b); id. 1938, 117, 151, 164, 195 f., 242 f. Birket-Smith, 294. Mathiassen, 211. Jenness 1922, 160. Schmidt and Koppers, 312 ff. Rivers 1906, 477–480, 515 et seq. Marshall, 194 ff., 203–232. Handy 1923, 101.

[17] Thalbitzer, 15, 67. Mathiassen 1928, 20, 210 f. Birket-Smith, 67 f., 294. Jenness 1922, 42, 161, 165 ff. Egede, 97. Warner, 77, 157 ff., 473. Firth, 132, 414 f., 565 f. H. Thurnwald 1935, 10 f., 23–28. Driberg, 67,

154 f., 163. Labouret, 261. Roscoe 1911, 95. P. A. Talbot 1926, 429. Du Bois 1944, 29, 100, 110 ff., 495, 502. Ward. Lowie 1917, 46, 49, 74. Opler in Eggan, 204. Hudson, 54. Forde 1941, 77–81, 97 f., 99 et seq. Krige, 181.

[18] Morgan 1876, pt. 3, chaps. 1, 3. Howitt, 163–167, 177–187. Radcliffe-Brown 1931, 103. Bogoras, 602 et seq. Malinowski 1913. R. and C. Berndt, 51.

[19] Malinowski 1926, 13. Warner, 72, 96. Radcliffe-Brown 1931, 78. Nimuendajú 1946 (a), 129. Wissler and Duvall 1908, 160 f. Du Bois 1944, 108 f. Firth, 415. Tomašić 1945, 470. W. S. and K. Routledge, 149. Driberg, 139, 164.

[20] Arensberg and Kimball, 46–49. Warner, 129 f. Roscoe 1911, 403 et seq., 426.

## 6. PROPERTY

[1] Philbrick 1938, 1–42; id. 1939. MacIver 1945. Hallowell 1943. Hohfeld, 28–30. Hoebel 1942 (a). Bekker, 51 f.

[2] Lowie 1928 (a). Seligman 1911, 112 f. Lévi-Strauss 1936, 287 et seq. Radin 1923, 200 f. Dorsey 1884, 227 f. Warner, 147. Wissler 1912, 276 f. Rasmussen 1929, 157–168. Lowie in Wissler ed. 1912–1916, 225 f., 244–247. La Flesche, 70. Thalbitzer, 2:159, 167. Koht and Skard, 17.

[3] Hill, 21–24. Morgan 1876, pt. IV, chap. 1. Nimuendajú 1946 (a), 59 f. Blackwood, 18 f. Gutmann 1926, 302 et seq., 413 et seq. Krige, 176 f. Laval, 223 f., 284 et seq. Forde 1931, 366–383. Titiev, 16, 60–64, 79, 181, 200, 201 f. Thomas and Znaniecki, 1:158. Arensberg and Kimball, 109 et seq., 140 ff. Rosegger, 32 f., 147–154, 346. Krauss, 64–128. Tomašić 1942, 229–261. Adamic, 214. Buck 1932, 58 f. Kroeber 1925, 744.

[4] Radloff, 1:414–420, 452. Hudson, 33–35. Lowie 1945, 447–454. Hoernlé.

[5] Denig, 476 ff. Kroeber 1925, 8, 14, 34, 395, 398. Lowie 1939, 303. Steward 1938, 254. Speck 1915; id. 1940, 104, 203–215. Cooper 1939, 66–90. Jenness 1932, 124. Schmidt 1937, 141–154, 290. Davidson, 18–46. Drucker. Dixon, 225 f. Seligman 1911, 7, 106 et seq. Schebesta, 78 f. Birket-Smith, 260. Roth 1906, 8 f. R. Thurnwald, 1910 (b), 27. Spott and Kroeber, 182–199.

[6] Tregear, 127–136. Rivers 1914 (a), 1:55, 58. R. Thurnwald 1910 (a), esp. 350. Spier 1928, 233. Hill, 23.

[7] Nordenskiöld 1912, 35. Métraux 1937, 398. Nimuendajú 1946 (a), 111, 157. Du Bois 1944, 63. Rattray 1929, 33, 38, 40. Gutmann 1926, 441.

[8] Warner, 63, 70, 147–149. Nimuendajú 1946 (a), 126. L. Thompson 1940 (b), 207 f. Linton 1936, 142 f. Lowie 1935, 221, 248 f. Jenness 1922, 90 f. Lantis, 254. Boas 1888, 582. Gusinde 1937, 980 ff.

[9] G. D. H. Cole in ESS 1932, 8:35 et seq. McMurray, ibid.; 1934, 14:436 et seq. Rivers 1924, 87. Warner, 30, 146–149, 198. Kroeber 1902–1907, 317. Llewellyn and Hoebel, 213. Steward 1938, 74. Spier 1933, 60, 156, 240, 303 f. Boas 1888, 580 f., id. 1907, 485 f. Jenness 1922, 92. Lantis, 227 f. Labouret, 253–256. Gusinde 1937, 1109. Nimuendajú 1946 (a), 158. Hudson 35 f., 81 f. Weeks, 193. Roscoe 1911, 270. Rivers 1914 (a), 1:55. Lowie 1935, 13, 262 f., 299 f. Krige, 180 f. Gifford 1929, 144. Irle, 87, 145. Jenness 1943, 489. Parsons, ed. 1936, 1:XXXVI. Murdock 1934, 238. Sapir in Parsons, ed. 1922, 307. Arensberg and Kimball, 109. Vinogradoff 1920, 1:274–295. Solem, 169 f., 297 f. Loeb 1935, 263. Gurdon, 68, 83. Jochelson 1910, 109. Frazer, 429–566.

[10] Ihering, 175–232, 408–425. Philbrick 1938, 31. Gifford 1929, 124, 171.

7. LAW

[1] Vinogradoff 1928, 2:360. Weber, 3 ff. Bekker, 47. Radcliffe-Brown in ESS 1933, 9:202 et seq. R. Thurnwald 1931–1935, 5:2. Seagle, 275–290. Llewellyn and Hoebel, 24–27. Hoebel 1942 (b). Sellin in ESS 1931, 4:563 et seq. Kirchwey, ibid., 1931, 4:569 et seq. Lobingier, ibid., 1931, 4:662–667.

[2] Koht and Skard, 24 f. P. A. Talbot 1926, 576–579. Gluckman in F and E-P, 28, 31. Gutmann 1926, 246, 562, 575, 688. Giles, 75–106. Pirenne et al., 48–54.

[3] Torday and Joyce, 76. Kropf, 93, 178. Roscoe 1911, 13, 133 et seq. Gusinde 1937, 1025. Wissler 1911, 24. Jenness, 1922, 94–96. Birket-Smith, 264–266. Mathiassen, 209. Rasmussen 1929, 131–144. Boas 1901–1907, 117 f., 467. Egede, 90. Lowie 1935, 5, 9 f., 11 f. Kroeber 1928. Barton 1919, 15, 65 f. Vinogradoff 1920, 1:364. Warner, 162. Bogoras, 663. Gutmann 1926, 240, 245, 598.

[4] Vinogradoff 1920, 1:344–369. Llewellyn and Hoebel, 117, 321. Kroeber 1925, 20–22. Spott and Kroeber, 182–199. Gutmann 1926, 14 et seq., 590 et seq., 619 et seq., 687; id. 1909, 13 ff., 19. Krauss, 39. Durham 1928, 162 et seq. Nopcsa, 23 et seq. Tomašić 1945, 462–465.

[5] Gutmann 1926, 615 et seq., 669 et seq. P. A. Talbot 1926, 619, 640 f. Barton 1919, 96 et seq. Du Bois 1944, 324. Lowie 1935, 217. Llewellyn and Hoebel, 151 f.

[6] Parsons 1939, 65. Irle, 140 f. Métraux 1937, 391. Roscoe 1911, 22–24, 259, 264–266. J. O. Dorsey 1884, 288 f., 363. Llewellyn and Hoebel, 104. Titiev, 65 f. Gutmann 1926, 240 et seq., 688. Gluckman in F and E-P, 38. Hofmayr, 166, 169. Tomašić 1945, 462–465. Barton 1919, 81 f. Vinogradoff 1928, 2:46–172; id. 1920, 1:312 et seq. Bogoras, 667 f.

[7] Llewellyn and Hoebel, 169 et seq. Malinowski 1926, 13 et seq. Menger, 108, 149, 228. Huebner, 16–32. Seagle in ESS 1934, 13:153 et seq. Devereux, 553–584. Maine, 356. Chiavacci, 180 f. Oberg in F and E-P, 130. Allison Davis et al., 498–538. P. A. Talbot 1926, 762 f.

## 8. RELIGION

[1] Driberg, 55. Warner, 248 f. Swanton 1946, 137. Leem, 460. Reuter-skiöld, 59, 68. Scheffer, 101, 115 f., 122, 148. Roscoe 1911, 95 f., 276.

[2] Radin 1923, 290 et seq. Lowie 1919 (a), 416 ff. Dorsey 1884, 225. Irle, 87–89. Warner, 159, 244 et seq. Nimuendajú 1942, 16 ff., 84 et seq. Gayton 1945.

[3] Koht and Skard, 86–90, 79. Blegen 1931, 15, 30 et seq. Stephenson, 14 f., 91. Friedländer, 941 et seq. Radin 1923, 388–426. Métraux 1931. Spier 1935. Mooney, 672–680. J. O. Dorsey 1884, 347 ff. Kawaguchi, 429 f. Conybeare, 69–75. Nadel. Westermann 1921, 4, 12, 228–290. Harley.

[4] Bell, 178 et seq. Yoe, 7–10, 62 f. Parsons 1939, 42, 81, 428 ff., 537 f. Roscoe 1911, 72, 102, 262. Labouret, 286 f. T. Henry, 235. Gutmann 1909, 88 ff. Nimuendajú 1946 (a), 78, 107. Kluckhohn, 54, 58 f., 78. Buck 1936, 3. Simmons 1942, 325 ff. P. A. Talbot 1912, 13–88, 165–202, 230–241.

[5] Gusinde 1937, 1091 f. Kluckhohn, 63 et seq. Seligman 1931, 1–21. Hofmayr, 179. Buck 1936. Gifford 1929, 48 et seq., 82. Embree 1945, 12 et seq. Torday and Joyce, 53, 59 et seq. Nimuendajú 1946 (b), 93–115. Gayton 1930. Malinowski 1922, 64 f. Pobiedonostsev, 78 f., 258, 304 f., 308. Steinmann and Hurwicz, 20, 59, 68 f., 73 f., 76, 144 ff., 151, 224, 237–240. Gluckman in F and E-P, 31. Audrey I. Richards 1935. Nadel.

[6] Métraux 1944, 333. Laufer.

## 9. EDUCATION

[1] Paulsen 1910, 55 et seq. Mead in ESS 1931, 5:399–403. Counts, ibid., 5:403–414.

[2] Radin 1945, 70 f. Warner, 6, 261, 271 f., 283, 288 f., 292, 325, 392. Tregear, 225–228, 374–382, 498 et seq. Gusinde 1937, 754, 852–860, 865 et seq., 900 et seq. Stannus, 246–277. George W. Ellis, 49–56. Teit, 587–590.

[3] Warner, 98. Seligman 1911, 90. Nordenskiöld 1924, 209. Routledge, 124. Pettitt, 6–39. Parsons 1916. H. Thurnwald 1935, 65. Tessmann, 2:287–293. Du Bois 1944, 47–51, 64–69, 238, 244 f., 251, 262, 412 f., 415. Knabenhans. Opler, 44 f., 63.

[4] Du Bois 1944, 51, 135. Pettitt, 47 et seq., 62 et seq., 75 et seq.

⁵ Opler, 38 et seq. Gutmann 1932, 1:84. Titiev, 17, 25. Nimuendajú 1942, 49 f. Loeb 1935, 250. Berndt, 86. Livingstone, 115. Embree 1941. Kapp, 1:334. Raum, 245, 275, 286, 368. Lambrecht, 170.

⁶ Beckwith 1919, 319. Opler, 40, 47, 89, 120. Gusinde 1937, 742, 901 et seq., 744, 868 et seq. Raum, 256 et seq. Tessmann, 2:287–293. Sahagun, 380–408, 458–464. Pettitt, 151 et seq. Gutmann, 149 f., 175, 213 ff. O'Neale, 10–13. Lowie in Wissler ed. 1912–1916, 187. Tylor 1889 (b), 1:72. Radin 1923, 166 et seq.

⁷ Nydahl, 109, 113. Gluckman in F and E-P, 46.

⁸ Ware, 319–345. Irle, 100. Conybeare, 284–291. Mach 1923, 313–355. Turi, 26, 250. Paulsen 1902, 151. Hardy, 207. Luella Cole, 453 et seq., 596 et seq. Menger, 217 f. Boas 1916, 444.

## 10. THE FAMILY

¹ Rivers 1924, 13 et seq. Radcliffe-Brown 1941, 2. Nimuendajú 1946, 125 f. Le Play, 6:386–441. Lévi-Strauss 1945.

² Schmidt and Koppers, 147 et seq. Radcliffe-Brown 1931, 4, 6, 11 ff., 103, 107. Seligman 1911, 86. Gusinde 1937, 779 et seq., 970 ff. Nimuendajú 1946 (a), 59 f., 83 f., 106 f., 125 f. Richards 1939, 110 et seq., 120–123. Kirchhoff 1931, 88 ff., 104 ff. Westrup, 5–23, 102 et seq.

³ Warner, 72. Burgess and Locke, 574–579. Gutmann 1909, 95. Radcliffe-Brown 1931, 99 f. Hearn, 88–101. Rosegger, 32, 129 f. Arensberg and Kimball, 107–115. Thomas and Znaniecki, 1:106 et seq. Arensberg, 43 et seq. Westermann 1921, 58–68, 401–406. Nimuendajú 1942, 29 f., 50. Spott and Kroeber, 143–149. Du Bois 1944, 89–95. Bloomfield, 124 et seq. Embree 1945, 161 f. Kaberry, 154.

⁴ Waller, 457–485. Rosegger, 146 et seq. Arensberg and Kimball, 115 et seq., 123 et seq. Kaberry 54, 71.

⁵ Oberg in F and E-P, 158. Soga, 23 ff. Hoernlé, 22. Malinowski 1929, 36. Goldfrank, 59–63. Hanks and Richardson, 14 ff., 22, 25. Warner, 61. Titiev, 22. Nimuendajú 1942, 57. Lowie 1917, 38 f., 93. Eggan, 51. Goodwin, 224. Sapir 1910, 95. Kaberry, 71.

⁶ Wittfogel, 12. Rosegger, 32. Salomon and Baum, 222 et seq. Du Bois 1944, 94, 251, 398, 412, 413 f., 415, 422 f., 430, 454 f., 502, 515, 517, 529, 531, 534. Mommsen. Goodsell, 294 ff. Arensberg and Kimball, 117, 125. A. E. Watson in ESS 1931, 5:198–206.

## 11. UNILATERAL DESCENT GROUPS

¹ Gifford 1929, 29–40; id. 1926.

² Rivers 1924, 19 ff. Tylor 1865, 278, 282. Morgan 1871, 139; id. 1876,

pt. II chap. 2. Lowie 1920, 111. Powell, LV. Richards 1934. Kirchhoff 1931, 117. Kroeber in Steward ed. 1946, 2:903. J. H. Rowe, ibid., 2:252–256, 262 f. B. Mishkin, ibid., 2:441. H. Tschopik, ibid., 2:539, 544. Beals, Tozzer, 26, 62 f., 99 f. Roys, 31–48. Soustelles, 325–344. Spinden, 186. Vaillant, 108.

[3] Morgan, 1876, pt. II, chaps. 2 and 6. Titiev, 58. Dorsey 1897, 230 ff. Nimuendajú 1942, 17, 23. Labouret, 218 ff. Warner, 33 ff.

[4] Steinitz. Swanton 1908, 430, 434 f.; id. 1946, 663. Colbacchini, 1–30. Lévi-Strauss 1936. Nimuendajú 1939, 21 f.; id. 1946 (a), 79 et seq. Radcliffe-Brown 1931, 6 et seq. Warner, 29–33.

[5] Barbeau. Hutton, 45, 109, 150 et seq., 193. Lowie 1943, 633 f. White, 142 ff. Lévi-Strauss 1944. Parsons 1924. Olson 1933. Métraux 1932, 192–196.

[6] Morgan, 1876, pt. II, chaps. 2 and 6. Soga, 23 ff. Lowie 1929 (b), 324 ff., 336. Strong 1929 (a), et seq.; id. 1927. Gifford 1926. Gayton 1945. Boas 1940, 316–323. Roscoe 1911, 6, 138 ff. Labouret, 51. Rattray 1932, 425–451.

[7] Murie in Wissler ed. 1912–1916, 549 et seq., 642. Lévi-Strauss 1943 (a); id. 1943 (b). Bose, 29. Hutton, 45, 109, 150 et seq., 193. Rivers 1906, 507. Gayton 1945. Goodwin, 119 f. Thomas and Znaniecki, 1:87 et seq. Delafosse, 3:105 f. Hudson, 13, 98–105. Hoernlé, 12. Soga, 18 f., 25.

[8] Morgan 1876, pt. II, chap. 15. Olson 1933. Swanton 1906, 166–173; id. 1905; id. 1946, 654–661. Kroeber 1908, 147 f. Wissler 1911, 21. Kroeber 1902–1907, 7.

[9] Steward 1936 (a). Fürer-Haimendorf 1945, 161. Spier 1922. Westrup, 103 et seq. Fenton, 204 ff. Gifford 1926. Kaberry, 132, 176. Gusinde 1931, 302, 319, 419, 425. Kirchhoff 1931, 170–176.

[10] Kirchhoff 1931, 149. Roth 1924, 669. Murdock 1934. Steward 1938, 52. Kroeber 1925, 741. Spier 1933, 187. Lowie 1919 (b). Rivers 1914 (a), 2:126. Powdermaker, 32. Fenton, 204. Bachofen.

[11] Waterman and Kroeber. Schebesta, 59–69, 78 f., 92 f., 104–109, 225.

[12] Morgan 1876, pt. II, chap. 2. Fenton, 204 f., 217 f., 227. Skinner 1921, 47 et seq., 372 f. Radin 1923, 190 et seq. Olson 1933. Schmidt and Koppers, 78 et seq. Kroeber 1923, 355–358.

[13] Chamberlain, LI, 58 f., 173, 304, 312. Aston, 1:22, 43, 104, 324, 350, 375; 2:31.

[14] Murdock 1940. Emeneau, 173–175. Boas 1940, 356–378. Morgan 1876, pt. II, chap. 14.

[15] Bachofen. Gurdon, 66 et seq., 76 et seq., 82, 93. Goldenweiser 1912,

464–475. Niebuhr, 2:212 et seq. Seligman 1918, 150 f. Lin Yutang, 143–146. Nimuendajú 1926, 33 f., 78–82; id. 1946 (a), 113, 125 f.; id. 1942, 32 f.

## 12. SOCIAL STRATA

[1] Barton 1938, 118, 121, 123, 138. Kroeber 1925, 39 f. Bloch in ESS 1931, 6:203 et seq. Fahlbeck, 139, 142, 178–189. Ö-UM 1888, 5:142–148, 225–228. Mavor, 58 f., 81 f., 91 f., 203, 225.

[2] Senart, 1–107. Rivers 1924, 143–156. O'Malley. Handy 1927, 43 et seq., 135–158, 317 ff.

[3] Myrdal, 57–67, 667–688. Warner, Buford, and Adams, 14 et seq. A. Davis et al., 1–58.

[4] Lowie 1945 (a), 86 et seq. Heyse, 160, 170–287. Embree 1945, 23 f.

[5] Merker, 110, 170, 196, 207, 246. Arnoux 1912, 273–395, 529–558, 840–875; id. 1913, 110–134, 754–774. Czekanowski.

[6] Myrdal, 700–705, 1129–1132. Drucker, 63. F. C. Cole, 96 f. Mandelbaum 1940, 224 f. Hahn, 43 ff. Philipp, 2:156–160, 326 f. Thomas, 94 et seq. Richardson, 122. Boas 1940, 360 f. Laval, 143, 223. Buck 1930, 5, 157, 164. Beckwith, 307–312. Handy 1923, 36.

[7] Schrieke 1936, 93. Ware, 130. Warner and Lunt, 221–226, 373. Myrdal, 676. Mandelbaum 1941.

[8] Redfield, 58–85. Stephenson, 204, 346, 379, 410, 423 f., 441. Blegen 1940, 162, 241–276, 524 f. Schünemann-Pott 1871, 119; id. 1872, 219. Bolin, 188–210. Jorgensen and Solum, 218, 253, 396 f. Sartorio, 42 f., 50. Schrieke 1936, 23–45. Embree 1941, 142.

[9] Knight in ESS 1934, 13:667 et seq. B. J. Stern et al., ibid., 1934, 14:73–92. Meyer 1924, 171–212. Rattray 1929, 33, 38, 40. Labouret, 373 ff. Roscoe 1911, 14 f., 259. P. A. Talbot, 693–707. Garfield, 271–274. Olson 1936, 97 ff. Murdock 1934, 239 f. Sapir 1915, 355–374.

[10] Skinner 1913, 10, 22. Roscoe 1911, 136, 140, 151, 167. Cline, 114, 140.

## 13. SODALITIES

[1] J. O. Dorsey 1884, 342. Basden 1938, 334 f. A. H. Smith, 136 et seq. Courant, 55 et seq., 68 et seq.

[2] Nordenskiöld 1912, 33; id. 1922, 86–90. R. Thurnwald 1910 (a), 316 ff. Kroeber 1925, 80 ff. Goddard, 15 f., 56 f.

[3] Landtman, 171 et seq., 327 et seq., 344. Lehner in Neuhauss, 3:397–485. Westermann 1921, 228–290, 342 ff. Gusinde 1931, 803–1083.

[4] Loeb 1926, 338–389. Park, 1:39 f. Basden 1921, 225 et seq. D. A. Tal-

bot, 194. Westermann 1921, 270. P. A. Talbot 1912, 13–88, 165–202, 230–241. Labouret, 414–436. Radin 1945, 70; id. 1923, 360. Dumarest, 146, 174 f., 189. White, 137–142. Parsons 1939, 114, 131, 137. Schmidt and Koppers, 275–283.

[5] P. A. Talbot 1926, 771 et seq. Basden 1921, 255–265; id. 1938, 133–146. Rivers 1914 (a), 1:61, 64, 87, 126 f. Speiser, 65 et seq. Codrington, 101–115. Mandelbaum 1940, 224–230. Kroeber 1902–1907, 151–229. Escott, 20 et seq., 28–38, 77–118. Timbs, 92 et seq.

[6] Nimuendajú 1942, 49 et seq. Chandra, 211–273. Barton 1938, 9 f. Lambrecht 170–173. Wikman, 17–21, 34 ff., 61 et seq., 139 et seq., 348 et seq.

[7] Desplagnes, 157. P. A. Talbot, 543–561. Forde 1941, 6–10. Nimuendajú 1946 (a), 40, 70, 77, 86, 90–95, 112 f., 122.

[8] Ashley, 1:68–123; 2:68–189. Sée 1929 (b), 111–115, 146 f., 259 f., 353–360. Stair, 65 et seq., 147. Buck 1930, 82–96, 414–417. Nimuendajú 1942, 52 f., 60–64, 100 ff. Wissler ed. 1912–1916, 79, 92 ff.

[9] Schurtz. Webster. Schmidt and Koppers.

[10] Webster, 75, 82 f., 121, 131. Schurtz, 151 et seq., 205, 212 f., 335, 348, 352 f. Schmidt and Koppers, 118, 243 et seq., 248, 275 et seq.

[11] F. H. Hankins in ESS 1930, 10:177 et seq. Kalpaktschieff. Nikoloff. Morse. Giles, 75–106. Ashley, 2:137, 151, 325. Nimuendajú 1946 (a), 90–95, 112 f., 212. Schurtz, 84, 159. Wissler ed. 1912–1916, 28, 188, 842, 955–984. Forde 1941, 9.

[12] Basden 1938, 130, 137, 141, 209 f., 335, 366 et seq., 370 ff.

### 14. THE STATE

[1] Maine, 124–128. Barton 1938, 8, 31, 33 f., 40. Spott and Kroeber, 182–191. Kroeber 1925, 14.

[2] Dixon, 206, 225 f. Seligman 1911, 7. Schebesta, 13, 59, 104. J. H. Rowe in Steward ed. 1946, 2:185, 202–209, 229–233, 269–273. Meyer 1924, 1:213–264. Vaillant, 211 et seq. Swanton 1928, 323 et seq.; id. 1946, 121 ff., 153 f. Hewitt in Hodge ed. 1:617–620. Morgan 1876, pt. II, chap. 6. Fenton. Labouret, 3, 9, 13, 50 f., 56, 130–136, 216, 240–246, 367, 391–394, 441 f., 461. Fortes in F and E-P, 239–271; id. 1936. Field, 72, 212. P. A. Talbot 1926, 562, 599 f., 603, 606, 608. Evans-Pritchard 1940 (a), 123, 147, 152, 162, f., 172, 181; id. in F and E-P, 272–296; id. 1940 (b), 9, 25, 38–51, 62 et seq.

[3] Gusinde 1931, 421, 829, 911 f., 929, 953, 1042; id. 1937, 838 ff., 850. Steward 1938, 246 f. Solem, 185 ff. Mandelbaum 1940, 204, 225.

[4] Wissler ed. 1912–1916, 74, 182. Kroeber 1902–1907, 207 f. Llewellyn and Hoebel, 67–131. J. H. Provinse in Eggan, 365. Giles, 75–106. S. W.

Williams, 1:380–403, 498, 506. Poupon, 53, 88, 397–435. P. A. Talbot 1926, 762. Westermann 1921, 41, 73, 86, 102, 107.

⁵ G. A. Dorsey and Murie, 113. Lowie 1917, 18 f. Mandelbaum 1940, 221, 231 f. Radin 1923, 209 f., 227. Goodwin, 178 f. Ray, 111. Garfield, 182 ff. Spier 1933, 158. Parsons 1939, 15 et seq. Stephen, 139. Métraux 1937, 390; id. 1928, 179. Nimuendajú 1942, 13 ff., 82; id. 1946 (a), 161, 239 f.; id. 1914. Nordenskiöld 1912, 228 f. Morgan 1876, pt. II, chap. 4. Swanton 1946, 641–654; 1911, 100–108. Rowe in Steward ed. 2:257 et seq.

⁶ Handy 1927, 43 et seq., 136–149; id. 1923, 44–55. Laval, 136 f., 138 et seq., 145. T. Henry, 101, 229, 258, 261. Beckwith, 310, 312. Gifford 1929, 48–100, 122–127, 171. Buck 1932, 43–54. Stair, 65–91, 128.

⁷ P. A. Talbot 1926, 155, 562 et seq., 576–579. Schweinfurth, 2:1–64. Hofmayr, 139–182. Gluckman in F and E-P, 25–55. Torday and Joyce, 53 et seq. Schapera ed. 22–28. Labouret, 215, 353, 368–372, 384 ff., 400 ff., 477 f. Rattray 1932, 425–432. Evans-Pritchard in F and E-P, 272–296; id. 1940 (a), 123, 147, 152, 162 f., 172, 181.

⁸ R. Thurnwald 1931–1935, 4:253 f., 301 et seq. Lantis, 246–249. Kirchhoff 1931, 86 f. Nimuendajú 1942, 9 f. Swanton 1930. B. Thomson, 59 f. et passim. Hudson, 59 f., 91 f. Meyer 1924, 1:295 et seq., 439.

⁹ Menger, 157–163. Radcliffe-Brown in F and E-P, XIX, XXIII. Fortes, ibid., 239 et seq. Meyer 1925, 3–35. Jenness 1922, 94 ff. Egede, 90. Boas 1888, 582, 668. Birket-Smith, 264 ff. M. W. Williams, 275 et seq., 290. Hardy, 30 et seq.

¹⁰ Oberg in F and E-P, 138 ff., 143. Hofmayr, 177, 179. Satow, 34–40. Menger, 164 et seq.

## 15. THE CROW INDIANS

¹ Lowie 1935, esp. 3–72, 172–214, 274–296; id. in Parsons ed. 1922, 17–33.

## 16. THE BUINESE

¹ H. Thurnwald 1934; 1937. R. Thurnwald 1934; id. 1910.

## 17. THE SHILLUK

¹ Schweinfurth, 1:9–20. Hofmayr, esp. 27–182, 258–364. D. Westermann 1912, Introduction, 99.

## 18. IMPERIAL AUSTRIA

¹ Bauer, 173 et seq. Friedjung, 2:430 et seq. Adler, 10:9–65, 486–499. Mark Twain.

[2] Sieghart. Friedjung, 2:166 ff., 244–296. Ö-UM 1886, 1:91–122; 1888, 5:269–282, 290; 1893, 12:121, 146, 190. Hoffmann, 2:237 f.

[3] Friedjung, 2:244–282.

[4] Zweig, 139 et seq., 152 f. Adler, 11:70, 78, 160.

[5] Adler, 8:9–32, 82–122; 11:291–301. NÖB I, 1926, 3:167 f.

[6] P. Rosegger, esp. 12–38, 78–111, 119–154, 174–182, 277–287, 346–359. Bauer, 208 et seq.

[7] Bauer, 229, 318–331. Adler, 11:260–274.

[8] NÖB 1923, 11–22, 158–177; 1925, 2:17–30, 97–116; 1926, 3:9–33. Čapek. Corti. Kronprinz Rudolf.

# BIBLIOGRAPHY

The following abbreviations are used for serial publications, handbooks, encyclopedias:

| | |
|---|---|
| A | Anthropos |
| AA | American Anthropologist |
| AAA–M | American Anthropological Association, Memoirs |
| AES–M | American Ethnological Society, Monographs |
| AES–P | American Ethnological Society, Publications |
| ALK | Essays in Anthropology presented to A. L. Kroeber |
| AMNH–AP | American Museum of Natural History, Anthropological Papers |
| AMNH–B | American Museum of Natural History, Bulletins |
| AMNH–M | American Museum of Natural History, Memoirs |
| BAE–B | Bureau of American Ethnology, Bulletins |
| BAE–R | Bureau of American Ethnology, Reports |
| BPBM–B | Bernice P. Bishop Museum, Bulletin |
| CU | Catholic University of America, Anthropological Series |
| ESS | Encyclopaedia of the Social Sciences |
| F and E-P | Fortes and Evans-Pritchard |
| FMNH | Field Museum of Natural History, Publications, Anthropological Series |
| GSA | General Series in Anthropology |
| HSAI | Handbook of South American Indians |
| ICA | International Congress of Americanists |
| JAFL | Journal of American Folk-Lore |
| JRAI | Journal of the Royal Anthropological Institute of Great Britain and Ireland |
| NÖB | Neue Österreichische Biographie |
| Ö-UM | Die Österreichisch-Ungarische Monarchie in Wort und Bild |
| PM | Peabody Museum of American Archaeology and Ethnology, Harvard University, Papers |
| PrM | Primitive Man |
| SWJ | Southwestern Journal of Anthropology |
| UC | University of California, Publications in American Archaeology and Ethnology |
| UW | University of Washington, Publications in Anthropology |

Y            Yale University Publications in Anthropology
ZE         Zeitschrift für Ethnologie
Z vgl. R     Zeitschrift für vergleichende Rechtswissenschaft

Adamic, Louis
    1934 The Native's Return. New York.
Adler, Victor
    1929 Aufsätze, Reden und Briefe. vols. 8, 10, 11. Vienna.
Aginsky, Bernard W.
    1935 (a) The Mechanics of Kinship (AA 37:450–457).
    1935 (b) Kinship Systems and the Forms of Marriage (AAA–M 45).
Arensberg, Conrad M.
    1937 The Irish Countryman. New York.
Arensberg, Conrad M. and Kimball, Solon T.
    1940 Family and Community in Ireland. Cambridge, Mass.
Arnoux, P. A.
    1912 Le culte de la société des Imandwa au Ruanda (A 273–395,
       529–558, 840–875).
    1913 Le culte de la société des Imandwa au Ruanda (A 110–134,
       754–774).
Ashley, W. J.
    1913, 1914 An Introduction to English Economic History and Theory.
       2 vols. London.
Aston, W. G. (translator)
    1896 Nihongi. London.
Bachofen, J. J.
    1861 Das Mutterrecht. Stuttgart.
Barbeau, C. M.
    1917 Iroquois Clans and Phratries (AA 19:392–405).
Barnett, H. G.
    1938 The Coast Salish of Canada (AA 40:118–141).
Barton, R. F.
    1919 Ifugao Law (UC 15:1–186).
    1938 Philippine Pagans. London.
Bascom, Wm. R.
    1944 The Sociological Rôle of the Yoruba Cult Group (AAA–M 63).
Basden, G. T.
    1921 Among the Ibos of Nigeria. Philadelphia.
    1938 Niger Ibos. London.
Bauer, Otto
    1907 Die Nationalitätenfrage und die Sozialdemokratie. Vienna.

Beals, Ralph L.
 1932 Unilateral Organizations in Mexico (AA 34:467-475).

Beckwith, Martha
 1919 The Hawaiian Romance of Laieikawai (BAE-R 33:287-666).

Bekker, Ernst Immanuel
 1892 Ernst und Scherz über unsere Wissenschaft. Leipzig.

Bell, Sir Charles
 1928 The People of Tibet. Oxford.

Berndt, Ronald and Catherine
 1945 A Preliminary Report of Field Work in the Ooldea Region,
 Western South Australia, Sydney.

Bettelheim, Anton
 1923-1926 (editor) Neue Österreichische Biographie. Vienna.

Birket-Smith, Kaj.
 1929 The Caribou Eskimos: Material and Social Life and Their
 Cultural Position. Copenhagen.

Blackwood, Beatrice
 1935 Both Sides of Buka Passage. Oxford.

Blegen, Theodore C.
 1931 Norwegian Migration to America. Northfield, Minnesota.
 1940 Norwegian Migration to America: the American Transition.
 Northfield, Minnesota.

Bloomfield, Leonard
 1928 Menomini Texts (AES-P 12). New York.

Boas, Franz
 1888 The Central Eskimo (BAE-R 6:409-669).
 1907 The Eskimo of Baffin Land and Hudson Bay (AMNH-B 15).
 1916 Tsimshian Mythology (BAE-R 31).
 1938 (a) The Mind of Primitive Man. New York.
 1938 (b), ed. General Anthropology. Boston.
 1940 Race, Language and Culture. New York.

Bogoras, W.
 1909 The Chukchee. Leyden.

Bolin, Wilhelm
 1891 Ludwig Feuerbach; sein Wirken und seine Zeitgenossen.
 Stuttgart.

Bose, J. K.
 1934 Dual Organization in Assam (Journal of the Department of
 Letters, 25:Pt.1:29). Calcutta.

Buck, Peter H. (Te Rangi Hiroa)
    1930 Samoan Material Culture (BPBM–B 75). Honolulu.
    1932 Ethnology of Tongareva (BPBM–B 92). Honolulu.
    1936 Regional Diversity in the Elaboration of Sorcery in Polynesia
        (Y 2).
Burgess, Ernest W. and Locke, Harvey J.
    1945 The Family. New York.
Čapek, Karl
    1934 President Masaryk Tells His Story. London.
Chamberlain, Basil Hall (translator)
    1906 Kojiki. Tokyo.
Chandra, Roy Sarat
    1915 The Oraons of Chota Nagpur. Ranchi.
Chen Han Seng
    1936 Landlord and Peasant in China. New York.
Chen, T. S. and Shryock, J. K.
    1932 Chinese Relationship Terms (AA 34:623–669).
Chiavacci, Vincenz
    1910 Aus Alt- und Neu-Wien. Stuttgart.
Cline, Walter
    1937 Mining and Metallurgy in Negro Africa (GSA 5). Menasha,
        Wis.
Codrington, R. H.
    1891 The Melanesians; Studies in Their Anthropology and Folk-Lore.
        Oxford.
Colbacchini, D. A.
    1925 I Bororos orientali. Turin.
Cole, Fay Cooper
    1913 The Wild Tribes of Davao District, Mindanao (FMNH 12:49–
        203). Chicago.
Cole, G. D. H.
    1921 Social Theory. London.
    1938 Persons and Periods. London.
Cole, Luella
    1942 Psychology of Adolescence. New York.
Committee on Historiography
    1946 Theory and Practice in Historical Study (Social Science Research
        Council, Bulletin 54). New York.
Conybeare, Frederick C.
    1921 Russian Dissenters. Cambridge, Mass.

Cooper, John M.

1939 Is the Algonquian Family Hunting Ground System Pre-Columbian? (AA 41:66–90).

1941 Temporal Sequence and the Marginal Cultures (CU 10:52–57).

1946 The Araucanians (HSA 12:687–760). Washington.

Corti, Conte Egon Caesar

1934 Elisabeth, die seltsame Frau. Salzburg.

Courant, Maurice

1901 En Chine. Paris.

Czekanowski, Jan

1905 Forschungen im Nil-Kongo Zwischengebiet (ZE 35:591–615).

Davidson, W. S.

1928 Notes on Tête de Boule Ethnology (AA 30:18–46).

Davis, Allison; Gardner, Burleigh B.; and Gardner, Mary R.

1941 Deep South. Chicago.

Davis, Kingsley and Warner, W. Lloyd

1937 Structural Analysis of Kinship (AA 39:291–313).

Delafosse, Maurice

1912 Haut-Sénégal-Niger. Paris.

Deloria, Ella

1932 Dakota Texts (AES–P 14). New York.

Denig, Edwin Thompson

1930 Indian Tribes of the Upper Missouri (BAE–R 46:375–628).

Desplagnes, A. M. L.

1907 Le plateau central nigérien. Paris.

Devereux, George

1942 Motivation and Control of Crime (Journal of Criminal Psy-
chopathology, 3:553–584).

Dixon, Roland B.

1905 The Northern Maidu (AMNH–B 17:119–346).

Dorsey, G. A. and Murie, J. R.

1940 Notes on Skidi Pawnee Society (FMNH 27:73–119).

Dorsey, J. O.

1884 Omaha Sociology (BAE–R 3:211–370).

1897 Siouan Sociology (BAE–R 15:205–244).

Driberg, J. H.

1923 The Lango, a Nilotic Tribe of Uganda. London.

Drucker, Philip

1939 Rank, Wealth and Kinship in Northwest Coast Society (AA
41:55–65).

Du Bois, Cora
    1936 The Wealth Concept as an Integrative Factor in Tolowa-Tututni
        Culture (ALK 49–65). Berkeley.
    1944 The People of Alor. Minneapolis.
Dumarest, Noel
    1920 Notes on Cochiti, New Mexico (AAA–M 6:137–236).
Durham, M. Edith
    1909 High Albania. London.
    1928 Some Tribal Origins, Laws and Customs of the Balkans.
        London.
Durkheim, Emile
    1912 Les formes élémentaires de la vie religieuse. Paris.
Egede, Hans
    1923 Die Erforschung von Grönland. Leipzig.
Eggan, Fred
    1937 (editor) Social Anthropology of North American Tribes.
        Chicago.
Ellis, George W.
    1914 Negro Culture in West Africa. New York.
Embree, John F.
    1941 Acculturation among the Japanese of Kona, Hawaii (AAA–M
        59).
    1945 The Japanese Nation; a Social Survey. New York.
Emeneau, M. B.
    1941 Language and Social Forms: A Study of Toda Kinship (in
        Spier, Leslie, et al., editors, Language, Culture and Personality,
        58–179). Menasha, Wis.
Encyclopaedia of the Social Sciences
    1930–1935 15 vols. New York.
Escott, T. H. S.
    1914 Club Makers and Club Members. New York.
Essays in Anthropology presented to A. L. Kroeber
    1936 Berkeley.
Evans-Pritchard, E. E. (see also Fortes, M. and Evans-Pritchard, E. E.)
    1938 Some Aspects of Marriage and the Family among the Nuer
        (Z vgl. R 52:306–392).
    1940 (a) The Nuer. Oxford.
    1940 (b) The Political Systems of the Anuak of the Anglo-Egyptian
        Sudan. London.
    1940 (c) The Nuer of the Southern Sudan (F and E-P 272–296).

Fahlbeck, Pontus E.
 1922 Die Klassen und die Gesellschaft. Jena.
Fallersleben, Hoffmann von
 1868 Mein Leben. Hanover.
Feng, Han Yi
 1936 Teknonymy as a Formative Factor in the Chinese Kinship
  System (AA 38:59–66).
 1937 The Chinese Kinship System (Harvard Journal of Asiatic
  Studies, 2:139–275).
Fenton, Wm. N.
 1940 Problems Arising from the Historical Northeastern Position of
  the Iroquois (Smithsonian Miscellaneous Collections 100:159–
  251). Washington.
Field, M. J.
 1940 Social Organization of the Ga People. Accra.
Firth, Raymond
 1936 We, the Tikopia. New York.
Forde, C. Daryll
 1931 Hopi Agriculture and Land Ownership (JRAI 61:357–405).
 1939 Kinship in Umor (AA 41:523–553).
 1941 Marriage and the Family among the Yakö in Southern Nigeria.
  London.
Fortes, M.
 1936 Ritual Festivals and Social Cohesion in the Hinterland of the
  Gold Coast (AA 38:590–604).
 1940 The Political Systems of the Tallensi of the Northern Territories
  of the Gold Coast (F and E-P 239–271).
Fortes, M. and Evans-Pritchard, E. E., editors
 1940 African Political Systems. London.
Frazer, J. G.
 1919 Folklore in the Old Testament. London.
Freire-Marreco, Barbara
 1914 Tewa Kinship Terms from the Pueblo of Hano, Arizona (AA
  16:268–287).
Friedjung, H.
 1912 Oesterreich von 1848 bis 1860. Stuttgart u. Berlin.
Friedländer, Ludwig
 1934 Sittengeschichte Roms. Vienna.
Fürer-Haimendorf, Christoph von
 1943 The Chenchu. London.

Fürer-Haimendorf, Christoph and Elizabeth von
  1945 The Reddis of the Bison Hills. London.
Garfield, Viola E.
  1939 Tsimshian Clan and Society (UW 7:167–340).
Gayton, A. H.
  1930 Yokuts-Mono Chiefs and Shamans (UC 24:361–420).
  1945 Yokuts and Western Mono Social Organization (AA 47:409–426).
Gifford, Edward W.
  1916 Miwok Moieties (UC 12:139–194).
  1922 Californian Kinship Terminologies (UC 18:1–285).
  1926 Miwok Lineages and the Political Unit in Aboriginal California (AA 28:389–401).
  1929 Tongan Society (BPBM–B 61). Honolulu.
Giles, H. A.
  1902 China and the Chinese. New York.
Gillin, John
  1936 The Barama River Caribs of British Guiana (PM 14, no. 2).
Gluckman, Max
  1940 The Kingdom of the Zulu in South Africa (F and E-P 25–55).
Goddard, P. E.
  1903 Life and Culture of the Hupa (UC 1:88).
Goldenweiser, A. A.
  1912 On Iroquois Work (Summary Report of Geological Survey of Canada). Ottawa.
  1933 History, Psychology and Culture. New York.
Goldfrank, Esther S.
  1945 Changing Configurations in the Social Organization of a Blackfoot Tribe during the Reserve Period (AES–M 8). New York.
Goodsell, Willystine
  1915 A History of the Family as a Social and Educational Institution. New York.
Goodwin, Grenville
  1942 The Social Organization of the Western Apache. Chicago.
Granqvist, Hilma
  1931 Marriage Conditions in a Palestine Village (Societas Scientiarum Fennica, Commentationes Humanarum Litterarum, III.8). Helsingfors.
Groves, Ernest R. and Ogburn, Wm. F.
  1928 American Marriage and Family Relationships. New York.

Gurdon, P. R. T.
    1907 The Khasis. London.
Gusinde, Martin
    1931 Die Selk'nam. Mödling bei Wien.
    1937 Die Yamana. Mödling bei Wien.
Gutmann, Bruno
    1909 Dichten und Denken der Dschagga-Neger. Leipzig.
    1926 Das Recht der Dschagga. München.
    1932 Die Stammeslehren der Dschagga. München.
Hahn, J. G. von
    1854 Albanische Studien. Jena.
Haller, Johannes
    1926 Aus dem Leben des Fürsten Philipp zu Eulenberg-Hertefeld.
        Berlin und Leipzig.
Hallowell, A. Irving
    1930 Was Cross-Cousin Marriage Practised by the North-central
        Algonkin? (ICA 23:519–544).
    1943 The Nature and Function of Property as a Social Institution
        (Journal of Legal and Political Sociology 1:115–138).
Handy, E. S. Craighill
    1923 The Native Culture of the Marquesas (BPBM–B 9). Honolulu.
    1927 Polynesian Religion (BPBM–B 34). Honolulu.
Hanks, L. M. and Richardson, Jane
    1945 Observations on Northern Blackfoot Kinship (AES–M 9).
Hardy, G. Gathorne
    1925 Norway. New York.
Harley, George W.
    1941 Notes on the Poro in Liberia (PM 19, no. 2).
Harrington, John P.
    1912 Tewa Relationship Terms (AA 14:472–498).
Hearn, Lafcadio
    1895 Out of the East. Boston.
Henry, Jules
    1941 Jungle People, a Kaingang Tribe of the Highlands of Brazil.
        New York.
Henry, Teiura
    1928 Ancient Tahiti (BPBM–B 48). Honolulu.
Herbst, Hermann (translator)
    1925 Der Bericht des Franziskaners Wilhelm von Rubruk über seine
        Reise in das Innere Asiens in den Jahren 1253–1255. Leipzig.

Herskovits, Melville J.
    1940 The Economic Life of Primitive Peoples. New York.
Hewitt, J. N. B.
    1907 Iroquois (in Hodge, F. W., ed., Handbook of American Indians North of Mexico). Washington.
Heyse, Paul
    1900 Jugenderinnerungen und Bekenntnisse. Berlin.
Hill, W. W.
    1938 The Agriculture and Hunting Methods of the Navaho Indians (Y 18).
Hiller, E. T.
    1933 Principles of Sociology. New York.
Hoebel, E. Adamson
    1942 (a) Fundamental Legal Concepts as Applied in the Study of Primitive Law (Yale Law Journal 51:951–966).
    1942 (b) Primitive Law and Modern (Transactions of the N. Y. Academy of Sciences 5:30–41).
Hoernlé, A. Winifred
    1925 The Social Organization of the Nama Hottentots of Southwest Africa (AA 27:1–24).
Hofmayr, Wm.
    1925 Die Schilluk. Mödling bei Wien.
Hohfeld, Wesley Newcomb
    1923 Fundamental Legal Conceptions as Applied in Judicial Reasoning. New Haven.
Hollis, A. C.
    1905 The Masai. Oxford.
Howitt, A. W.
    1904 The Native Tribes of South-east Australia. London.
Hudson, Alfred E.
    1938 Kazak Social Structure (Y 20).
Huebner, Rudolf (translated by Philbrick, Francis S.)
    1918 A History of Germanic Private Law. Boston.
Hutton, J. H.
    1921 The Angami Nagas. London.
Ihering, Rudolf von
    1899 Scherz und Ernst in der Jurisprudenz. Leipzig.
Irle, I.
    1906 Die Herero. Gütersloh.

Jenness, Diamond
1922 The Life of the Copper Eskimos (Report of the Canadian Arctic Expedition, 1913–1918, Vol. 12). Ottawa.
1932 Indians of Canada. Ottawa.
1943 The Carrier Indians of the Bulkley River, their Societies and Religious Life (BAE–B 133:469–586).

Jochelson, Waldemar
1910 The Yukaghir and the Yukaghirized Tungus (AMNH–M 13).
1933 The Yakut (AMNH–AP 33:35–225).

Jones, William
1919 Ojibwa Texts (AES–P 7, Pt. II). New York.

Jorgensen, Theodore and Solum, Nora
1939 Ole Edvart Rölvaag. New York and London.

Junod, H. A.
1912 The Life of a South African Tribe. 2 Vols. Neuchâtel.

Kaberry, Phyllis M.
1939 Aboriginal Woman, Sacred and Profane. Philadelphia.

Kalpaktschieff, Stoyan S.
1900 Die Zünfte Bulgariens im 19. Jahrhundert. Greifswald.

Kapp, Friedrich
1876 Aus und über Amerika. Berlin.

Kawaguchi, Ekai
1901 Three Years in Tibet. Madras.

Kennedy, Raymond
1942 The Ageless Indies. New York.

Kirchhoff, Paul
1931 Die Verwandtschaftsorganisation der Urwaldstämme Südamerikas (ZE 63:85–193).
1932 Verwandtschaftsbezeichnungen und Verwandtenheirat (ZE 64:41–72).

Kluckhohn, Clyde
1944 Navaho Witchcraft (PM 22, no. 2).

Knabenhans, A.
1920 Die Erziehung bei den Naturvölkern (Mitteilungen der Geographisch-Ethnographischen Gesellschaft, 19:52–90). Zürich.

Koht, Halvdan and Skard, Sigmund
1944 The Voice of Norway. New York.

Krauss, Friedrich S.
  1885 Sitte und Brauch der Südslaven. Wien.
Krige, Eileen Jensen
  1936 The Social System of the Zulus. London.
Kroeber, A. L.
  1902–1907 The Arapaho (AMNH–B 18).
  1908 Ethnology of the Gros-Ventre (AMNH–AP 1:141–281).
  1917 Zuñi Kin and Clan (AMNH–AP 18:39–205).
  1923 Anthropology. New York.
  1925 Handbook of the Indians of California (BAE–B 78).
    Washington.
  1928 Law of the Yurok Indians (ICA 22:511–516). Rome.
  1946 The Chibcha (in Steward, J. H., ed., HSAI 2:887–909).
    Washington.
Kronprinz Rudolf
  1922 Politische Briefe an einen Freund. Vienna.
Kropf, A.
  1889 Das Volk der Xosa-Kaffern. Berlin.
Labouret, Henri
  1931 Les tribus du rameau Lobi. Paris.
La Flesche, Francis
  1921 The Osage Tribe (BAE–R 36:37–597).
Lambrecht, Francis
  1935 The Mayawyaw Ritual (Publication of the Catholic Anthropo-
    logical Conference, 4:169–325).
Landtman, G.
  1927 The Kiwai Papuans of British New Guinea. London.
Lane, E. W.
  1895 An Account of the Manners and Customs of the Modern
    Egyptians. London.
Lantis, Margaret
  1946 The Social Culture of the Nunivak Eskimo (Transactions
    of the American Philosophical Society 35:153–323). Philadel-
    phia.
Laufer, Berthold
  1913 The Development of Ancestral Images in China (Journal of
    Religious Psychology 6:111–123).
Laval, Honoré
  1938 Mangareva; l'histoire ancienne d'un peuple polynésien. Braine-
    le-Comte, Belgium, and Paris.

Leem, Knud
  1808 An Account of the Laplanders of Finmark (Pinkerton, John,
    A General Collection of Voyages, 376–490). London.
Le Play, F.
  1878 Les ouvriers européens. Paris.
Lévi-Strauss, Claude
  1936 Contribution à l'étude de l'organisation sociale des Indiens
    Bororo (Journal Société des Américanistes 28:269–304). Paris.
  1943 (a) Guerre et commerce chez les Indiens de l'Amérique du
    Sud (Renaissance 1:122–139).
  1943 (b) The Social Use of Kinship Terms among Brazilian Indians
    (AA 45:398–409).
  1944 On Dual Organization in South America (America Indígena
    4:37–47).
  1945 L'analyse structurale en linguistique et en anthropologie
    ("Word" 1:33–53).
Lindgren, Ethel John
  1938 An Example of Culture Contact without Conflict (AA 40:605–
    627).
Linton, Ralph
  1936 The Study of Man. New York.
  1940 A Neglected Aspect of Social Organization (American Journal
    of Sociology 45:870–886).
Lin Yutang
  1935 My Country and My People. New York.
Livingstone, Sir Richard
  1945 Education for a World Adrift. Cambridge.
Llewellyn, Karl N., and Hoebel, E. Adamson
  1941 The Cheyenne Way. Norman, Oklahoma.
Loeb, Edwin M.
  1926 Pomo Folkways (UC 19:149–405).
  1935 Sumatra. Vienna.
Lowie, Robert H.
  1917 Notes on the Social Organization and Customs of the Mandan,
    Hidatsa and Crow Indians (AMNH–AP 21:1–99).
  1919 (a) The Hidatsa Sun Dance (AMNH–AP 16:411–431).
  1919 (b) The Matrilineal Complex (UC 16:29–45).
  1920 Primitive Society. New York.
  1924 Notes on Shoshonean Ethnography (AMNH–AP 20:189–314).
  1927 The Origin of the State. New York.

1928 (a) Incorporeal Property in Primitive Society (Yale Law Journal 37:551–563).

1928 (b) A Note on Relationship Terminologies (AA 30:263–267).

1929 (a) Hopi Kinship (AMNH–AP 30:361–388).

1929 (b) Notes on Hopi Clans (AMNH–AP 30:303–360).

1935 The Crow Indians. New York.

1939 Ethnographic Notes on the Washo (UC 36:301–352).

1943 A Note on the Social Life of the Northern Kayapó (AA 45:633–635).

1945 (a) The German People. New York.

1945 (b) A Note on Lapp Culture History (SWJ 1:447–454).

Lynd, Robert and Helen

1920 Middletown. New York.

Mach, Ernst

1906 Erkenntnis und Irrtum. Leipzig.

1923 Populärwissenschaftliche Vorlesungen. Leipzig.

MacIver, Robert M.

1937 Society. New York.

1945 Government and Property (Journal of Legal and Political Sociology 4:5–18).

Maenchen-Helfen, Otto

1931 Reise ins asiatische Tuwa. Berlin.

Maine, Henry Sumner

1884 Ancient Law. New York.

Malinowski, Bronislaw

1913 The Family among the Australian Aborigines. London.

1922 Argonauts of the Western Pacific. London.

1926 Crime and Custom in Savage Society. London.

1929 The Sexual Life of the Savages in North-Western Melanesia. New York.

Mandelbaum, David C.

1940 The Plains Cree (AMNH–AP 37:155–316).

1941 Culture Changes among the Nilgiri Tribes (AA 43:19–26).

Marshall, Wm. E.

1873 Travels among the Todas. London.

Mathiassen, Therkel

1938 Material Culture of the Iglulik Eskimos (Report of the Fifth Thule Expedition, 1921–1924, vol. 6, no. 1). Copenhagen.

Mauss, Marcel

1906 Essai sur les variations saisonnières des sociétés Eskimo (L'Année sociologique 9:39–132).

Mavor, James
   1914 An Economic History of Russia. London.
Mead, Margaret
   1934 Kinship in the Admiralty Islands (AMNH–AP 34:181–358).
Medina, J. T.
   1882 Los aborigenes de Chile. Santiago.
Menger, Anton
   1904 Neue Staatslehre. Jena.
Merker, M.
   1904 Die Masai. Berlin.
Métraux, Alfred
   1928 La Religion des Tupinamba. Paris.
   1931 Les hommes-dieux chez les Chiriguano et dans l'Amérique du
      Sud (Revista del Instituto de Etnología de la Universidad Nacional
      de Tucuman 2:61–91).
   1932 L'organisation sociale et les survivances religieuses des Indiens
      Uro-Čipaya (ICA 25:191–213).
   1937 Etudes d'ethnographie Toba-Pilaga, Gran Chaco (A 32:197–
      219, 320–341).
   1944 Le shamanisme chez les Indiens de l'Amérique du Sud
      Tropicale (Acta Americana 2:197–219, 320–341).
Meyer, Eduard
   1924 Die Sklaverei im Altertum (in Kleine Schriften 1:171–439).
      Halle.
   1925 Geschichte des Altertums. Stuttgart and Berlin.
Michelson, Truman
   1932 The Narrative of a Southern Cheyenne Woman (Smithsonian
      Misc. Collections 87:1–13).
Mommsen, Adelheid
   1937 Theodor Mommsen im Kreise der Seinen. Berlin.
Mooney, James
   1896 The Ghost Dance Religion (BAE–R 14:641–1136).
Morgan, Lewis H.
   1871 Systems of Consanguinity and Affinity. Washington.
   1877 Ancient Society. New York.
Morse, Hosea Ballou
   1909 The Gilds of China. New York.
Murdock, George Peter
   1934 (a) Kinship and Social Behavior among the Haida (AA
      36:355–385).
   1934 (b) Our Primitive Contemporaries. New York.

1937 (editor) *Studies in the Science of Society* presented to Albert
       Galloway Keller. New Haven.

1940 Double Descent (AA 42:555–561).

1947 Bifurcate Merging: a Test of Five Theories (AA 49:56–68).

Myrdal, Gunnar
       1944 An American Dilemma. New York.

Nadel, S. F.
       1935 Witchcraft and Anti-Witchcraft in Nupe Society (Africa 8:423–
       447).

Neue Österreichische Biographie. *See* Bettelheim.

Neuhauss, R.
       1911 Deutsch Neu-Guinea. 3 vols. Berlin.

Niebuhr, M.
       1792 Travels through Arabia and Other Countries in the East.
       Edinburgh.

Nikoloff, Kosta
       1908 Das Handwerk und Zunftwesen in Bulgarien. Borna-Leipzig.

Nimuendajú, Curt
       1914 Die Sagen von der Erschaffung und Vernichtung der Welt (ZE
       46:284–403).

1926 Die Palikur-Indianer und ihre Nachbarn. Göteborg.

1939 The Apinayé (CU 8).

1942 The Šerente. Los Angeles.

1946 (a) The Eastern Timbira (UC 41).

1946 (b) Social Organization and Beliefs of the Botocudo of Eastern
       Brazil (SWJA 2:93–115).

Nopcsa, Fr.
       1925 Albanien: Bauten, Trachten und Geräte Nordalbaniens. Berlin.

Nordenskiöld, Erland
       1912 Indianerleben. Leipzig.

1922 Indianer und Weisse. Stuttgart.

1924 Forschungen und Abenteuer in Südamerika. Stuttgart.

Nydahl, Jens
       1928 Das Berliner Schulwesen. Berlin.

Olson, Ronald L.
       1933 Clan and Moiety in Native America (UC 33:351–422).

1936 The Quinault Indians (UW 6:1–190).

1940 The Social Organization of the Haisla of British Columbia (UC
       Anthropological Records 2:169–200).

O'Malley, L. S. S.
       1927 Indian Caste Customs. Cambridge, England.

O'Neale, Lila M.
   1932 Yurok-Karok Basket Weavers (UC 32:1–184).
Opler, Morris Edward
   1946 Childhood and Youth in Jicarilla Apache Society. Los Angeles.
Osgood, Cornelius
   1936 Contributions to the Ethnology of the Kutchin (Y 14).
Österreichisch-Ungarische Monarchie in Wort und Bild, Die. 24 vols.
   1885–1902. Vienna.
Park, Mungo
   1816 Travels in the Interior Districts of Africa. London.
Parsons, Elsie Clews
   1916 The Zuñi Adoshle and Suuke (AA 18:338–347).
   1922 (editor) American Indian Life. New York.
   1924 Tewa Kin, Clan and Moiety (AA 26:333–339).
   1936 (a) (editor) Hopi Journal of Alexander M. Stephen. New
      York.
   1936 (b) The House-Clan Complex of the Pueblos (ALK, 229–
      231).
   1939 Pueblo Indian Religion. Chicago.
Paulsen, Fr.
   1902 Die deutschen Universitäten und das Universitätsstudium. Berlin.
   1910 Aus meinem Leben; Jugenderinnerungen. Jena.
Petrullo, Vincenzo
   1939 The Yaruros of the Capanaparo River, Venezuela (BAE–B
      123:161–290).
Pettitt, George A.
   1946 Primitive Education in North America (UC 43).
Philbrick, Francis S.
   1938 Changing Conceptions of Property in Law (University of
      Pennsylvania Law Review 86, no. 7).
   1939 Property. New York.
Philipp Fürst zu Eulenberg-Hertefeld
   1934 Erlebnisse aus deutschen und fremden Höfen. Leipzig. 2 vols.
Phillips, Ray E.
   (n.d.) The Bantu in the City. Lovedale.
Pirenne, Henri; Cohen, Gustave; and Focillon, Henri
   1933 La civilisation occidentale au moyen age du XIe au milieu du
      XVe siècle. Paris.
Plekhanov, George
   1940 (a) The Materialistic Conception of History. New York.
   1940 (b) The Rôle of the Individual in History. New York.

Pobiedonostsev, Constantin

    1927 Mémoires politiques, correspondence officielle et documents inédits relatifs à l'histoire du règne de l'empereur Alexandre III de Russie. Paris.

Poupon, M. A.

    1918–1919 Etude éthnographique de la tribu Kouyou (Anthropologie 19:53–88, 397–435).

Powdermaker, Hortense

    1933 Life in Lesu: the Study of a Melanesian Society in New Ireland. New York.

Powell, J. W.

    1884 On Kinship and the Clan (BAE–R 3:xlvi–lv).

Radcliffe-Browne, A. R.

    1924 The Mother's Brother in South Africa (South African Journal of Science 21:542–555).

    1931 The Social Organization of Australian Tribes. Melbourne.

    1940 On Social Structure (JRAI 70:1–12).

    1941 The Study of Kinship Systems (JRAI 71:1–18).

Radin, Paul

    1923 The Winnebago Tribe (BAE–R 37).

    1945 The Road of Life and Death. New York.

Radloff, W.

    1893 Aus Sibirien. Leipzig.

Rasmussen, Knud

    1929 Intellectual Culture of the Iglulik Eskimos. Copenhagen.

    1930 Intellectual Culture of the Caribou Eskimos. Copenhagen.

Rattray, R. S.

    1929 Ashanti Law and Constitution. Oxford.

    1932 The Tribes of the Ashanti Hinterland. Oxford.

Raum, O. F.

    1940 Chaga Childhood. London.

Ray, Verne

    1932 The Sanpoil and Nespelem (UW 5).

Redfield, Robert

    1941 The Folk Culture of Yucatan. Chicago.

Reichard, Gladys

    1928 Social Life of the Navajo Indians. New York.

Reuterskiöld, E.

    1912 De nordiske Lapparnas Religion. Stockholm.

Richards, Audrey I.
    1934 Mother-right among the Central Bantu (Essays presented to
        C. G. Seligman 267–279). London.
    1935 A Modern Movement of Witch Finding (Africa 8:448–461).
    1939 Land, Labour and Diet in Northern Rhodesia. London.
Richardson, Jane
    1940 Law and Status among the Kiowa Indians (AES–M 1). New
        York.
Rivers, W. H. R.
    1906 The Todas. London.
    1914 (a) The History of Melanesian Society. Cambridge, England.
    1914 (b) Kinship and Social Organization. London.
    1924 Social Organization. New York.
Roscoe, John
    1911 The Baganda. London.
    1915 The Northern Bantu. Cambridge, England.
Rosegger, Peter
    1911 Das Volksleben in Steiermark. Leipzig.
Roth, Walter E.
    1906 North Queensland Ethnography, Bulletin 8. Brisbane.
    1924 An Introductory Study of the Arts, Crafts and Customs of the
        Guiana Indians (BAE–R 38).
Routledge, W. S. and K.
    1910 With a Prehistoric People. London.
Roys, Ralph L.
    1940 Personal Names of the Maya of Yucatan (Carnegie Institute of
        Washington, Publication 523:31–48).
Sahagun, B. de
    1880 Histoire générale des choses de la Nouvelle-Espagne. Paris.
Salomon, Alice and Baum, Marie
    1930 Das Familienleben in der Gegenwart; 182 Familienmono-
        graphien. Berlin.
Santa Cruz, Antonio
    1941 Aspects of the Avunculate in the Guajiro Culture (PrM
        14:1–12).
Sapir, Edward
    1910 Yana Texts (UC 9:1–235).
    1915 The Social Organization of the West Coast Tribes (Trans-
        actions of the Royal Society of Canada 9:355–374). Ottawa.
    1916 Terms of Relationship and the Levirate (AA 18:327–337).

Sartorio, Enrico C.
    1918 Social and Religious Life of Italians in America. Boston.
Satow, Sir Ernest
    1921 A diplomat in Japan. London.
Schapera, J.
    1934 (editor) Western Civilization and the Natives of South Africa.
        London.
Schebesta, Paul
    1927 Bei den Urwaldzwergen von Malaya. Leipzig.
Scheffer, J.
    1675 Lappland. Frankfurt am Main and Leipzig.
Schmidt, Wm.
    1935 The Position of Women with Regard to Property in Primitive
        Society (AA 37:244–256).
    1937 (a) Das Eigentum auf den ältesten Stufen der Menschheit.
        Münster in Westfalen.
    1937 (b) Handbuch der Methode der kulturhistorischen Ethnologie.
        Münster.
Schmidt, Wm. and Koppers, Wm.
    1924 Völker und Kulturen. Regensburg.
Schrieke, B.
    1929 (editor) The Effect of Western Influence on Native Civilization
        in the Malay Archipelago. Batavia.
    1936 Alien Americans. New York.
Schünemann-Pott, Friederich
    1871, December and 1872, May. Blätter für freies religiöses Leben.
        Philadelphia and San Francisco.
Schurtz, Heinrich
    1902 Altersklassen und Männerbünde. Berlin.
Schweinfurth, Georg
    (n.d.) The Heart of Africa. London.
Seagle, Wm.
    1937 Primitive Law and Professor Malinowski (AA 39:275–290).
Sée, Henri
    1929 (a) The Economic Interpretation of History. New York.
    1929 (b) Esquisse d'une histoire économique et sociale de la France.
    1929 (c) Histoire économique de la France. Paris.
Seligman, C. G.
    1931 The Religion of the Pagan Tribes of the White Nile (Africa
        14:1–21).

Seligman, C. G. and B. Z.
    1911 The Veddas. Cambridge, England.
    1918 The Kababish, a Sudan Arab Tribe (Harvard African Studies 2:105–185).

Senart, Emile
    1927 Les castes dans l'Inde. Paris.

Shimkin, D. B.
    1939 A Sketch of the Ket or Yenisei "Ostyak" (Ethnos 147–176).

Sieghart, Rudolf
    1932 Die letzten Jahrhunderte einer Grossmacht. Berlin.

Simmons, Leo W.
    1942 Sun Chief. The Autobiography of a Hopi Indian. New Haven.
    1945 The Rôle of the Aged in Primitive Society. New Haven.

Skinner, Alanson B.
    1913 Social Life and Ceremonial Bundles of the Menomini Indians (AMNH–AP 13:1–165).
    1921 Material Culture of the Menomini (Indian Notes and Monographs). New York.

Smith, A. H.
    1906 Village Life in China. Edinburgh.

Soga, John Henderson
    1931 The Ama-Xosa: Life and Customs. Lovedale.

Solem, Erik
    1933 Lappiske Rettstudier. Oslo.

Soustelles, Jacques
    1935 Le Totémisme des Lacandons (Maya Research 2:324–344).

Speck, Frank G.
    1915 The Family Hunting Band as the Basis of Algonkian Social Organization (AA 17:289–305).
    1940 Penobscot Man. Philadelphia.

Speiser, Felix
    1913 Südsee, Urwald, Kannibalen. Leipzig.

Spier, Leslie
    1922 A suggested Origin for Gentile Organization (AA 24:487–489).
    1925 The Distribution of Kinship Systems in North America (UW 1:69–88).
    1928 Havasupai Ethnography (AMNH–AP 29:81–392).
    1933 Yuman Tribes of the Gila River. Chicago.
    1935 The Prophet Dance of the Northwest and Its Derivatives (GSA 1:1–74).

Spinden, H. J.
    1917 Ancient Civilizations of Mexico. New York.
Spott, Robert and Kroeber, A. L.
    1942 Yurok Narratives (UC 35:143-256).
Stair, J. B.
    1897 Old Samoa. Oxford.
Stannus, Hugh Stannus
    1922 The Wayao of Nyasaland (Harvard African Studies 3:229-372).
Steinitz, W.
    1938 Totemismus bei den Ostjaken in Sibirien (Ethnos 125-140).
Steinmann, Friedrich and Hurwicz, Elias
    1933 Konstantin Petrowitsch Pobjedonoszew. Königsberg.
Stephenson, George M.
    1932 The Religious Aspects of Swedish Immigration: A Study of Immigrant Churches. Minneapolis.
Steward, Julian H.
    1936 (a) The Economic and Social Basis of Primitive Bands (ALK 331-347). Berkeley.
    1936 (b) Shoshoni Polyandry (AA 38:561-564).
    1938 Basin-Plateau Aboriginal Sociopolitical Groups (BAE-B 120).
    1946 (editor) Handbook of South American Indians (BAE-B 143), 2 vols.
Strong, William Duncan
    1927 An Analysis of Southwestern Society (AA 29:1-61).
    1929 (a) Aboriginal Society in Southern California (UC 26).
    1929 (b) Cross-Cousin Marriage and the Culture of the North-Eastern Algonkian (AA 31:277-288).
Swanton, John R.
    1905 The Social Organization of American Tribes (AA 7:663-673).
    1906 A Reconstruction of the Theory of Social Organization (Boas Anniversary Volume 166-178). New York.
    1908 Social Conditions, Beliefs and Linguistic Relationship of the Tlingit Indians (BAE-R 26:391-485).
    1911 Indian Tribes of the Lower Mississippi Valley (BAE-B 43).
    1928 Social Organization and Social Usages of the Indians of the Creek Confederacy (BAE-R 42:23-472).
    1930 An Indian Social Experiment and Some of Its Lessons (The Scientific Monthly 31:368-376).
    1946 The Indians of the Southeastern United States (BAE-B 137).

Talbot, D. A.
  1915 Woman's Mysteries of a Primitive People. London.
Talbot, P. Amaury
  1912 In the Shadow of the Bush. London.
  1926 The Peoples of Southern Nigeria. London.
Teit, James H.
  1909 The Shuswap (AMNH–M 4:443–789).
Te Rangi Hiroa. *See* Buck, P. H.
Tessman, Günter
  1913 Die Pangwe. Berlin.
Thalbitzer, W.
  1914 The Ammassalik Eskimo. Copenhagen.
Thomas, W. I.
  1937 Primitive Behavior. New York.
Thomas, W. I. and Znaniecki, Florian
  1927 The Polish Peasant in Europe and America. New York.
Thompson, Laura
  1940 (a) Fijian Frontier. New York.
  1940 (b) Southern Lau, Fiji: an Ethnography (BPBM–B 162).
    Honolulu.
Thomson, Basil
  1908 The Fijians. London.
Thurnwald, Hilde
  1934 Woman's Status in Buin Society (Oceania 5:142–170).
  1935 Die schwarze Frau im Wandel Afrikas. Stuttgart.
  1937 Menschen der Südsee; Charaktere und Schicksale. Stuttgart.
Thurnwald, Richard
  1910 (a) Ermittelungen über Eingeborenenrechte der Südsee (Z vgl.
    R 23:309–364).
  1910 (b) Das Rechtsleben der Eingeborenen der deutschen Südsee-
    inseln. Berlin.
  1921 Die Gemeinde der Bánaro. Stuttgart.
  1931–1935 Die menschliche Gesellschaft. Berlin and Leipzig. 5
    vols.
  1934 Pigs and Currency in Buin (Oceania 5:119–141).
  (n.d.) Ein vorkapitalistisches Wirtschafts-System in Buin (Archiv
    für Rechts-und-Sozialphilosophie 31:1–37).
Timbs, John
  1908 Clubs and Club Life in London. London.

Titiev, Mischa
> 1944 Old Oraibi; a Study of the Hopi Indians of Third Mesa (PM 22:16–201 f.).

Tomašić, Dinko
> 1942 Personality Development in the Zadruga Society (Psychiatry 5:229–261).
> 1945 Personality Development of the Dinaric Warriors (Psychiatry 8:449–493).

Torday, E. and Joyce, T. A.
> 1910 Les Bushongo. Brussels.

Tozzer, A. M.
> 1941 Landa's Relación de las Cosas de Yucatan (PM 18).

Tregear, E.
> 1904 The Maori Race. Wanganui.

Turi, Johan
> 1912 Das Buch des Lappen. Frankfurt am Main.

Turney-High, Henry Holbert
> 1941 Ethnography of the Kutenai (AAA–M 56).

Twain, Mark
> 1900 The Man That Corrupted Hadleyburg, and Other Stories and Essays. New York.

Tylor, E. B.
> 1865 Researches into the Early History of Mankind. London.
> 1889 (a) On a Method of Investigating the Development of Institutions; applied to Laws of Marriage and Descent (JRAI 18:245–272).
> 1889 (b) Primitive Culture. New York.

Vaillant, George C.
> 1941 Aztecs of Mexico. Garden City, New York.

Vinogradoff, Paul
> 1920 Outline of Historical Jurisprudence. 2 vols. London.
> 1928 Collected Papers. Oxford.

Waller, Willard
> 1938 The Family. New York.

Ward, Edward
> 1937 Marriage among the Yoruba (CU, no. 4:1–53).

Ware, Caroline F.
> 1935 Greenwich Village. Boston.

Warner, W. Lloyd
> 1937 A Black Civilization. New York.

Warner, W. Lloyd; Junker, Buford H.; Adams, Walter A.
    1941 Colored Human Nature. Washington.
Warner, W. Lloyd and Lunt, Paul S.
    1941 The Social Life of a Modern Community. New Haven.
Warner, W. Lloyd and Srole, Leo
    1945 The Social Systems of American Ethnic Groups. New Haven.
Waterman, T. T. and Kroeber, A. L.
    1934 Yurok Marriage (UC 35:1–14).
Weber, Max
    1919 Politik als Beruf. München and Leipzig.
Webster, Hutton
    1908 Primitive Secret Societies (second edition 1932). New York.
Weeks, John H.
    1913 Among Congo Cannibals. Philadelphia.
Westermann, Diedrich
    1912 The Shilluk People. Philadelphia.
    1921 Die Kpelle: ein Negerstamm in Liberia. Göttingen and Leipzig.
Westrup, C. W.
    1934 Introduction to Early Roman Law; Comparative Sociological
        Studies. Copenhagen.
White, Leslie A.
    1942 The Pueblo of Santa Ana (AAA–M 60).
Wikman, K. Rob. V.
    1937 Die Einleitung der Ehe. Åbo.
Williams, Mary Wilhelmine
    1920 Social Scandinavia in the Viking Age. New York.
Williams, Phyllis H.
    1938 South Italian Folkways in Europe and America. New Haven.
Williams, S. W.
    1883 The Middle Kingdom. New York.
Wilson, Gilbert L.
    1917 Agriculture of the Hidatsa Indians, an Indian Interpretation
        (University of Minnesota, Studies in Social Sciences 9:1–129).
Wissler, Clark
    1911 The Social Life of the Blackfoot Indians (AMNH–AP 7:1–64).
    1912 Ceremonial Bundles of the Blackfoot Indians (AMNH–AP
        7:65–289).
    1912–1916 (editor) Societies of the Plains Indians (AMNH–AP 11).
    1918 The Sun Dance of the Blackfoot Indians (AMNH–AP 16:223–
        270).

Wissler, Clark and Duvall, D. C.
1908 Mythology of the Blackfoot Indians (AMNH–AP 2:1–163).
Wittfogel, Karl A.
1946 History of a Chinese Society, Liao (Transactions American Philosophical Society 36:1–35).
Yoe, Shway
1896 The Burman: His Life and Notions. London.
Yule, H.
1903 The Book of Ser Marco Polo. London.
Zweig, Stefan
1943 Zeit und Welt; das Wien von Gestern. Stockholm.

# NAME AND TRIBAL INDEX

# SUBJECT INDEX

Abortion, 126

Absolutism. *See* Autocracy

Administration of law, 165–72

Adoption, ceremonial, 356 f.; frequency of, 127; and kinship, 8; reasons for, 57, 126, 354; of siblings, 58; of strangers, 59; and terminology, 64

Adultery, 88, 91; and matrilocal residence, 91; punishment, 91 f., 184

Affinal relatives, 72, 79; *see also* Kinship

Affinity. *See* Kinship, Relationship terms

Agamy, defined, 9, 240; *see also* Exogamy, Kin, Moiety

Age, factor in grouping, 6 ff., 315, 374, 395; and interpersonal relations, 220; *see also* Age-classes

Age-classes, 303–306; number of, 6 f.; relation to grades and sets, 7; ritual entrance, 8; *see also* Age, Sodalities

Agricultural class, 25, 394–97; *see also* Classes

Amitate, 74; and cross-cousin marriage, 75

Ancestor worship, 192

Anti-Semitism, 276, 388, 392

Arbitration, 164

Aristocracy, 269, 280, 374 f., 388 ff.; *see also* Classes, Rank, Titles

Assimilation, 17 ff., 275, 282–88, 386 f.; obstacles to, 282–88

Association, defined, 3, 12 ff.; *see also* Church, Family, Kin, Sodalities, State

Aunt, paternal. *See* Amitate, Kinship

Autocracy, 171, 172, 189, 190, 210 ff., 335 f., 339, 340, 344 f., 374 *et seq.*; *see also* Chiefs, Kings

Avoidance relationships, 68 f.; examples, 72, 81 ff.; hostility lacking, 73, 83; name tabooed, 72, 82, 83, 84; reasons for, 68, 85; types, 69

Avuncular marriage, 42, 105

Avunculate, conflict with paternal ties, 42, 53, 68; defined and described, 73 ff.; and discipline, 73; and education, 75; and inheritance, 73; lack of term and usage, 72; matriliny, 76; matrilocal residence, 76; payment of indemnity, 73, 74

Ayllu, 238

Bachelors' huts, 201, 303, 304; *see also* Sodalities

Barrenness, 100, 126

Barter, 31

Bastards, 100

Behavior patterns, 73 ff.; affected by terminology, 77, 78; *see also* Kinship

Bilateral family, 249; *see also* Family

Bilinear descent, 45, 58, 59, 69, 260 f.

Blacksmiths' caste, 276, 293

Blood brothers, 58

Blood feud. *See* Feud

Brahmans. *See* Caste

Bride price, and dowry, 102; exchanges, 101 f.; lowered by king, 370, 376; return of, 100, 151; and status, 100, 355, 364, 367; used for purchase of bride for brother, 99 f., 373; *see also* Bride wealth, Service

Bride purchase. *See* Bride price

Bride service. *See* Service

Bride wealth, 99–100

Brother and sister taboo, 72; tie, 99 f., 288, 373

Brothers-in-law, 72, 79, 80; and sister-in-law, 80

Bull roarers, 297, 299, 300

Bundles, sacred, 132

Caesaropapism, 190

Calpulli, 238

Campanilismo, defined, 15, 318; examples of, 281, 286, 318 f., 322, 387 *et passim;* *see also* Particularism, Separatism

Capture of bride, 96

Caste, defined, 10; examples, 271–77; influence upon law, 174, 175; *see also* Classes

Cattle, used for fines or fees, 167, 168, 169, 171, 172, 174

Causality, 35–37, 48, 265

Centralization, 52

Ceremonial rights, inherited, 133

Chattels, 143, 153

Chiefs, 25, 118, 120, 154, 157, 159, 162, 166, 167, 168, 170, 171, 328–37, 350, 362 *et seq.;* and shamans, 188 f.; *see also* Kings, Law, State

Children, relation to parents, 216; *see also* Adoption, Family, Kinship

Christianity, in Roman empire, 181; secular associations, 183; *see also* Church, Religion

459